Teaching Struggling READERS

Articles From The Reading Teacher

Richard L. Allington, Editor

National Research Center on English Learning
and Achievement
University at Albany–SUNY
Albany, New York, USA

International Reading Association
800 Barksdale Road, PO Box 8139
Newark, Delaware 19714-8139, USA
www.reading.org

The International Reading Association attempts, through its publications, to provide a forum for a wide spectrum of opinions on reading. This policy permits divergent viewpoints without implying the endorsement of the Association.

Director of Publications   Joan M. Irwin
Assistant Director of Publications   Wendy Lapham Russ
Managing Editor, Books and Electronic Publications   Christian A. Kempers
Associate Editor   Matthew W. Baker
Assistant Editor   Janet S. Parrack
Assistant Editor   Mara P. Gorman
Editorial Coordinator   Beth Doughty
Association Editor   David K. Roberts
Production Department Manager   Iona Sauscermen
Graphic Design Coordinator   Boni Nash
Electronic Publishing Supervisor   Wendy A. Mazur
Electronic Publishing Specialist   Anette Schütz-Ruff
Electronic Publishing Specialist   Cheryl J. Strum
Electronic Publishing Assistant   Peggy Mason

Library of Congress Cataloging in Publication Data
   Teaching struggling readers: Articles from The Reading Teacher/[selected and edited by] Richard L. Allington
     p.   cm.
   Includes bibliographical references and index.
     1. Reading—Remedial teaching.   2. Reading disability.   I. Allington, Richard L.   II. Reading Teacher.
LB 1050.5.T437   1998   97-36583
372.43—dc21
ISBN 0-87207-183-9

Twelfth Printing, August 2006

Contents

SECTION V   Improving Accuracy and Fluency

SECTION VI   Improving Family and Community Collaboration

Introduction

Richard L. Allington

In every nation there are some children who find learning to read difficult regardless of the nature of the writing system, the assessment plan, the national wealth, or the organization of educational system (Elley, 1992). Even when offered good instruction, some children struggle mightily to become literate. Unfortunately, too many children struggle because they do not have access to sufficient instruction. But just how can sufficient instruction be characterized? In other words, what is it that really matters in designing and delivering instruction to children who find learning to read difficult?

After a century of research on reading instruction and on children who find learning to read difficult, there are only a few things of critical instructional importance that have been identified. Unfortunately, professional debates and discussions often ignore each of these important dimensions of effective instructional environments and interventions. The collection of articles in this compilation addresses instructional issues for teachers of children who struggle with learning to read. Before looking at the articles however, it is important to identify and briefly explain what has mattered historically and what matters now in terms of classroom strategies, structures, and environments.

Professional Beliefs Matter

Since the study of reading difficulties began around the turn of the 20th century, three broad factors have been touted regularly as sources of reading difficulties. Each of these factors remains influential in school response to the problem of reading difficulties (Johnston & Allington, 1991).

The Intelligence Factor

First, limited intellectual abilities were viewed as a primary source of the difficulties. But then it was discovered that achievement on purported measures of intelligence and measures of reading achievement did not actually correlate all that well. In fact, terms were invented—hyperlexia and dyslexia—to explain aberrations, those children who read better or less well than was expected. But when educators believed intelligence, or the lack of it, was the source of difficulty, little was offered in the way of instructional interventions because some children were just never going to be readers due to limited intellectual capacity. Some children were just "slow learners" and not much could be expected of them. Thus, the "slow it down and make it concrete" instructional plan was widely implemented—virtually ensuring that some children developed only minimal levels of reading proficiency (Allington, 1991).

The "Disadvantage" Factor

However, after noting the less than perfect correlation between measures of intellect and measures of reading, other explanations emerged. Probably the most popular was targeting "disadvantage"—both economic and educational—as a source of the difficulties (McGill-Franzen, 1987). This explanation got a boost from the research showing that many more poor children had difficulty learning to read. Thus, interventions were developed in the hopes of overcoming the disadvantages of poverty. But few of these programs actually seemed to much enhance the instruction children received and in some cases the older "slow it down" plan was continued with "disadvantaged" children. The result therefore, was that many of the "disadvantaged" children failed to develop into readers and writers even after participating in the compensatory education programs (Puma, Jones, Rock, & Fernandez, 1993). Some educators and researchers argued that schools just could not be expected to overcome the negative effects of growing up poor. But the "disadvantage" conceptualization shaped the sorts of instructional programs that were offered.

The Learning Disabilities Factor

A third, and more recently popularized belief about children who find learning to read difficult is that these children suffer a disability (McGill-Franzen, 1987). Usually this disability is characterized in terms of neurological damage or difference that makes perceptual or verbal learning exceedingly difficult, if not impossible. But evidence of a neurological basis for reading difficulties has been difficult to find. If children with such conditions exist they exist in incredibly small numbers, far too few to account for the range of difficulties now observed (Vellutino et al., 1996). Nonetheless, believing in a neurologically based disability meant some children could not be expected to learn to read and so little effective instruction was offered (Allington & McGill-Franzen, 1989). For instance, few individualized educational plans set annual goals for accelerated literacy development (an annual goal of 1.5 years growth per year, for instance) because the disability conceptualization suggested damaged or limited capacity for learning.

Current Professional Beliefs: Sufficiency of Instruction

Most recently, there has been a growing recognition that reading acquisition is relatively easy for some children and relatively difficult—exceedingly difficult in a few cases—for other children. But only a very few children cannot, seemingly, acquire reading proficiency alongside their peers (Lyons, Pinnell, & DeFord, 1993; Slavin, Madden, Karweit, Dolan, & Wasik, 1993; Vellutino et al., 1996). This might be labeled the sufficiency of instruction conceptualization. Because children vary in the ease with which they acquire literacy and because they arrive at school with varied levels of literacy experience, we should expect that providing a standard instructional program would result in large discrepancies in achievement. Only when the instructional program offers varied levels of instructional intensity can we reasonably expect all children to develop reading proficiency—especially developing that proficiency on a schedule similar to peer development.

However, we must first believe virtually all children can become readers before we even begin to think about how to design instruction to ensure that this happens (Winfield, 1986; Zigmond, 1993). This belief leads us to design programs in which some children have access to larger amounts of higher quality and more intensive instruction.

Beliefs are important because they drive our thinking, our planning, and our actions (Allington, McGill-Franzen, & Schick, 1997). Yet for too long our professional beliefs have literally resulted in educational efforts that produced children who remained largely illiterate. Believing in the inherent educability of all children is a necessary first step in creating schools where all children become readers and writers.

Children Need to Read a Lot to Become Readers

In addition to professional beliefs, it also matters how successful we are at creating instructional environments that foster wide reading by all children, but especially by those children who have found learning to read difficult. Unfortunately, an overwhelmingly consistent finding in the research is that children who find learning to read difficult often participate in educational programs that fail to foster much reading at all—these children do less guided reading with their teachers and less independent, voluntarily reading (Krashen, 1993).

Only occasionally are interventions purposefully designed to alter this situation (Morrow, 1992). More often the instruction for children who find learning to read difficult occupies them with skill games, practice dittos, and drills (Allington, 1983; Allington & McGill-Franzen, 1989). Too often, in some schools children who have difficulty with reading have literally no books in their desks that they can actually read or learn to read from. This occurs even though schools spend substantial additional funds on interventions intended to assist the struggling readers (Guice, Allington, Johnston, Baker, & Michelson, 1996).

The Importance of Instructional Environment

If children are going to engage in substantive amounts of reading, there seem to be at minimum two aspects of the instructional environment that must be attended to. First, children need access to a large supply of books of appropriate difficulty, books that fit the Goldilocks principle (Fountas & Pinnell, 1996); they are not too hard, not too easy, but just right. This means books that they can read fluently while also understanding the story or information. This is not a new idea. For most of this century fitting children to books has been advocated and teachers have been taught to administer informal reading inventories and, more recently, to gather running records, in an attempt to ensure appropriate book placement. In some schools, unfortunately, there is little evidence that this feature of appropriate instruction is of much concern. For instance, we too often still find classrooms where all children are taught from the same book regardless of how well the book matches their level of literacy development. We find remedial and special education programs that offer little support to either children or classroom teachers in this regard (McGill-Franzen, 1994). Many programs exert little effort to ensure that struggling readers have easy access to a large supply of appropriate books. We find state educational policies that support the purchase of more skill and drill workbooks although classrooms have few, if any, books appropriate for the children having difficulty with reading acquisition and although school libraries remain underfunded, understaffed, and understocked.

If we want to foster wider reading there is another feature of instructional environments that is important, but often overlooked. Children need access to books and stories that are interesting and engaging to them and they need the freedom to choose at least some of the books they read, especially if we are attempting to foster independent, voluntary reading. Again, however, too few efforts to help children who find learning to read difficult are focused on ensuring a supply of interesting and appropriately difficult books is readily available.

Often we hear talk of the need to motivate reluctant readers but perhaps we should think more about examining the environments we create more carefully rather than characterizing the lack of voluntary reading as a motivational problem located in children. We need to worry more about putting enticing, just-right books in children's hands and less about schemes that bribe children into taking home an uninteresting book that is too difficult.

Children Need To Be Taught

Although there may be some natural readers, most children need good instruction and some need enormous amounts of personalized instruction if they are to become readers. Research on effective instruction suggests that we have not yet found a way to package good teaching. In study after study, it is the quality of the teacher, not variation in curriculum materials, that is identified as the critical factor in effective instruction (Bond & Dykstra, 1967; Knapp, 1995; Shanklin, 1990). That is not to say that materials are wholly unimportant, but that investing in teacher development has a better result than investing in curriculum materials. Good teachers, expert teachers, produce more readers than other teachers regardless of the curriculum materials used.

Good teachers know their students better and are more precise in targeting instructional needs (Johnston, 1997). Good teachers know more about literacy acquisition and use this expertise in planning instruction. They offer a more comprehensive sort of reading instruction with more attention to individual instructional needs (Pressley et al., 1996). These teachers create literacy-rich classrooms and teach strategies using explicit modeling. In other words, these teachers do not just assign work nor attempt to cover some segment of the curriculum material. Instead, these teachers teach actively and teach the useful strategies students need when they need them as opposed to following some predetermined schedule or pacing (Duffy, 1997). These teachers also push children to become more independent, more thoughtful readers.

Good teachers create classrooms where reading and writing activity fill large blocks of time. They develop effective decoding strategies, spelling strategies, and composing and comprehension activities, and they are constantly monitoring children's reading development and intervening when instruction is needed (Goatley, Brock, & Raphael, 1995).

But some children need more intensive instruction than a classroom teacher can provide. Some children will need additional small-group work and some can be expected to need tutorial assistance. Some children will need such help only for the short term, while others will need assistance for the long term. In other words, some children will need extra instruction this Wednesday after school, some will need a tutorial all next week, and some will need the added time that a summer school experience would provide for the remainder of their school career. Unfortunately, all too often we have designed extra-instructional programs in a one-size-fits-all scheme (Walmsley & Allington, 1995), in which everyone will receive three 30-minute small-group sessions every week all year, regardless of their real needs. Almost no one will participate in tutoring because educators have not devised a plan that makes short term tutoring available (even though such efforts are generally more successful than other efforts [Wasik & Slavin, 1993]).

Until we redesign school programs so that children have access to sufficient instruction—of whatever level of intensity and duration is needed—then we will have children who will struggle with reading acquisition when compared with their peers. The key to success is good teachers working within a flexible school framework that allows them to provide the instruction children need.

Schools Work Better When Families Are Partners

Good schools are more important to literacy development than are families (Snow, Barnes, Chandler, Goodman, & Hemphill, 1991), but the most successful schools have fostered and supported family involvement. It is schools that are charged with responsibility for developing reading proficiency, not families. Inviting family involvement, providing families with support in working with their children, and gaining the confidence of the families of children attending the school are all wonderfully important tasks to be undertaken after the school has ensured the adequacy of the school program.

Creating schools where children are neither rewarded nor penalized for their family status must be the first task of educators (Allington & Cunningham, 1996). Once effective school programs are in place—programs that provide children with access to sufficient high-quality instruction—then work on family support and involvement efforts can proceed. Interestingly, once good school programs are in place, family involvement often seems less a problem.

Developing strategies to support families should be the first order of business. For instance, schools might work to ensure all children have an adequate supply of appropriate books to take home in the evening or over the weekend. Extending this support further might involve opening the school library evenings, on weekends, and over the summer. In some schools this has been accomplished with no added costs by using flexible scheduling of library staff.

Many families simply do not have the discretionary funds to purchase books for a child's bedroom library. A recent study in California reported home supplies of appropriate books varied widely by community with the wealthiest homes reporting nearly 200 age-appropriate books and the least wealthy homes reporting one age-appropriate book available in every other household (Smith, Constantino, & Krashen, 1997). Often the local elementary school has the largest supply of children's books in the near vicinity and yet, that supply often is largely unavailable to the parents of children who own no books of their own. To address this problem, schools might develop sponsorships for book give-away programs so that every child receives a number of personal books each year. Schools also might invite parents of preschool age children to use the library.

Families can support school learning in other ways but many will need substantial guidance and support to help effectively. We need to understand that family literacy experiences differ across families and family ability to support school instruction also varies (Purcell-Gates, 1995). It often seems that schools would do better to make a greater effort to learn from families than to assume that families need to be taught or told what to do.

So What To Do First?

There are only a very few things that really matter in developing avid and proficient readers. A good beginning is a taking stock activity that attempts to evaluate reliably just how those things that really matter are addressed in your school. Do children who find learning to read difficult have easy access to appropriate and engaging books and stories? Has the instructional program been designed to offer children access to reading instruction of sufficient quality and intensity to accelerate their literacy development? Is the instruction exemplary and focused on developing independent, engaged readers?

The challenge of teaching all children to read is large and traditional programs have too often been less successful than we have hoped. This collection of articles is designed to help the reader redefine professional beliefs regarding what can be accomplished and to provide useful, specific examples of programs and practices that foster reading development in all children, both inside and outside the classroom. This collection has its origin in the belief that teachers, by being flexible in the selection of intervention approaches and through the creative use of available resources, can teach any child to read.

The articles included in this collection typically assume that teachers have access only to limited funds and that they only have limited time available for intervention activities. In assembling this collection however, I have worked from the assumption that readers will be interested in taking the time to assess the situation in their classroom and in their school and in working to find the most appropriate approaches and sets of strategies for their particular situation.

Although there are only a few things that really matter, creating schools that work well for all children is not easy. Changing schools is hard work and it takes time, energy, and expertise. It is the latter feature that this book can foster; the other two cannot be packaged in a text. Individuals hold the key in those matters. It is up to you.

The Articles in This Collection

Each of the six sections of this collection offers a set of articles that cluster about a common theme. The articles were selected primarily for their usefulness in providing information and ideas about working with children who find learning to read difficult. While this collection was restricted to articles published in *The Reading Teacher* over the past decade, I am quite happy with the scope of the topics addressed and with both the practicality and the power of the assembled collection. Although the articles were selected in an attempt to avoid unnecessary overlap, a certain amount of information is repeated. But because the contexts and approaches are different in each piece, any redundancy will hopefully reinforce the central theme of early and, when necessary ongoing, intervention. At the beginning of each section I have provided a brief introduction focusing on the broad topic.

I have two goals in mind for this collection. The first is to stimulate thought and conversation about the complexity of helping all children become eager, enthusiastic, and engaged readers. The second is to provide a small but useful compendium of best practice information in literacy instruction for children who have found learning to read and write difficult. If those who read through this collection are challenged, energized, optimistic, and more skillful instructionally, then the collection will have achieved my goals.

REFERENCES

Allington, R.L. (1983). The reading instruction provided readers of differing abilities. *The Elementary School Journal, 83,* 548–559.

Allington, R.L. (1991). The legacy of "slow it down and make it more concrete." In J. Zutell & S. McCormick (Eds.), *Learner factors/teacher factors: Issues in literacy research and in-*

struction (pp. 19–30). Chicago, IL: National Reading Conference.

Allington, R.L., & Cunningham, P.M. (1996). *Schools that work: Where all children read and write*. New York: HarperCollins.

Allington, R.L., & McGill-Franzen, A. (1989). Different programs, indifferent instruction. In A. Gartner & D. Lipsky (Eds.), *Beyond separate education: Quality education for all* (pp. 75–98). Baltimore, MD: Brookes.

Allington, R.L., McGill-Franzen, A., & Schick, R. (1997). How administrators understand learning difficulties: A qualitative analysis. *Remedial and Special Education, 18*, 223–232.

Bond, G.L., & Dykstra, R. (1967). The cooperative research program in first-grade reading instruction. *Reading Research Quarterly, 2*, 5–142.

Duffy, G.G. (1997). Powerful models or powerful teachers? An argument for teacher-as-entrepreneur. In S. Stahl & D. Hayes (Eds.), *Instructional models in reading.* (pp. 351–365). Hillsdale, NJ: Erlbaum.

Elley, W.B. (1992). *How in the world do students read? IEA study of reading literacy*. The Hague, Netherlands: International Association for the Evaluation of Educational Achievement.

Fountas, I.C., & Pinnell, G.S. (1996). *Guided reading: Good first teaching for all children*. Portsmouth, NH: Heinemann.

Goatley, V.J., Brock, C.H., & Raphael, T.E. (1995). Diverse learners participating in regular education "Book Clubs." *Reading Research Quarterly, 30*, 352–380.

Guice, S., Allington, R.L., Johnston, P., Baker, K., & Michelson, N. (1996). Access?: Books, children, and literature-based curriculum in schools. *The New Advocate, 9*, 197–207.

Johnston, P.A. (1997). *Knowing literacy*. York, ME: Stenhouse.

Johnston, P.A., & Allington, R.L. (1991). Remediation. In R. Barr, M. Kamil, P. Mosenthal, & P.D. Pearson (Eds.), *Handbook of reading research: Volume II* (pp. 984–1012). White Plains, NY: Longman.

Knapp, M.S. (1995). *Teaching for meaning in high-poverty classrooms*. New York: Teachers College Press.

Krashen, S. (1993). *The power of reading: Insights from the research*. Englewood, CO: Libraries Unlimited.

Lyons, C.A., Pinnell, G.S., & DeFord. D.E. (1993). *Partners in learning: Teachers and children in Reading Recovery*. New York: Teachers College Press.

McGill-Franzen, A. (1987). Failure to learn to read: Formulating a policy problem. *Reading Research Quarterly, 22*, 475–490.

McGill-Franzen, A.M. (1994). Is there accountability for learning and belief in children's potential? In E.H. Hiebert & B.M. Taylor (Eds.), *Getting reading right from the start: Effective early literacy interventions*. Boston, MA: Allyn & Bacon.

Morrow, L.M. (1992). The impact of a literature-based program on literacy achievement, use of literature, and attitudes of children from minority backgrounds. *Reading Research Quarterly, 27*, 250–275.

Pressley, M., Wharton-McDonald, R., Ranking, J., Mistretta, J., Yokoi, L., & Ettenberger, S. (1996). The nature of outstanding primary grade literacy instruction. In E. McIntyre & M. Pressley (Eds.), *Balanced instruction: Strategies and skills in whole language* (pp. 251–276). Norwood, MA: Christopher-Gordon.

Puma, M.J., Jones, C.C., Rock, D., & Fernandez, R. (1993). Prospects: *The congressionally mandated study of educational growth and opportunity—The interim report* (No. GPO 1993 0-354-886 QL3). Washington, DC: U.S. Department of Education.

Purcell-Gates, V. (1995). *Other people's words: The cycle of low literacy*. Cambridge, MA: Harvard University Press.

Shanklin, N.L. (1990). Improving the comprehension of at-risk readers: An ethnographic study of four Chapter 1 teachers, grades 4–6. *International Journal of Reading, Writing, and Learning Disabilities, 6*, 137–148.

Slavin, R.E., Madden, N.A., Karweit, B.L., Dolan, L.J., & Wasik, B.A. (1993). Success for All: A comprehensive approach to prevention and early intervention. In R.E. Slavin, B.L. Karweit, & B.A. Wasik (Eds.), *Preventing early school failure:*

Research, policy & practice (pp. 175–205). Boston, MA: Allyn & Bacon.

Smith, C., Constantino, R., & Krashen, S. (1997). Differences in print environment: Children in Beverly Hills, Compton and Watts. *Emergency Librarian, 24,* 8–9.

Snow, C., Barnes, W., Chandler, J., Goodman, I.F., & Hemphill, L. (1991). *Unfulfilled expectations: Home and school influences on literacy.* Cambridge, MA: Harvard University Press.

Vellutino, F.R., Sipay, E.R., Small, S.G., Pratt, A., Chen, R., & Denckla, M.B. (1996). Cognitive profiles of difficult-to-remediate and readily remediated poor readers: Early intervention as a vehicle for distinguishing between cognitive and experiential deficits as basic causes of specific reading disability. *Journal of Educational Psychology, 88,* 601–638.

Walmsley, S.A., & Allington, R.L. (1995). Redefining and reforming instructional support programs for at-risk students. In R.L. Allington & S.A. Walmsley (Eds.), *No quick fix: Rethinking literacy programs in America's elementary schools* (pp. 19–41). New York: Teachers College Press; Newark, DE: International Reading Association

Wasik, B.A., & Slavin, R.E. (1993). Preventing early reading failure with one-to-one tutoring: A review of five programs. *Reading Research Quarterly, 28,* 178–200.

Winfield, L.F. (1986). Teachers' beliefs toward academically at-risk students in inner urban schools. *Urban Review, 18,* 253–268.

Zigmond, N. (1993). Learning disabilities from an educational perspective. In G.R. Lyon, D.B. Gray, J.F. Kavanagh, & N.A. Krasgegor (Eds.), *Better understanding learning disabilities: New views from research and their implications for education and public policies* (pp. 229–250). Baltimore, MD: Brookes.

Section I

Rethinking Literacy Interventions

It seems safe to assert that we know more about effective instruction for children having difficulty learning to read than is often reflected in school practices. Older belief systems raise doubts in our minds about the potential of virtually all children to become independent and thoughtful readers. But we have garnered good evidence on the effects and characteristics of effective interventions. The articles in this section raise questions about some typical school programs, provide a quick review of best practice guidelines, and give examples of successful intervention strategies. I hope that the reader is both uncomfortable and energized upon completion of this section.

Diverse Learners and the Tyranny of Time: Don't Fix Blame; Fix the Leaky Roof

Edward J. Kameenui

In this commentary, I argue against a single "right" method or approach to literacy instruction. I assert that such a search for the "right" approach to literacy instruction is misguided and takes its greatest toll on students who have diverse learning and curricular needs. Instead, I suggest that diverse learners face the tyranny of time on a daily basis, in which the educational clock is ticking while they remain at risk of falling further and further behind in their schooling. I maintain that we should not spend any more time and effort determining or assigning fault for why diverse youngsters are failing, or which approach is the "right" approach to literacy instruction. Rather, we ought to move forward by designing, implementing, and validating instructional programs and interventions for children with diverse learning and curricular needs. These programs and interventions should not be wedded to any single, "right" instructional method, but should instead simply work. To achieve this end, I offer six general pedagogical principles that provide a conceptual framework for guiding educators in the development of literacy programs for diverse learners.

The Right Method Myth

As reading professionals, we have imposed upon ourselves an untenable standard of always searching for the single best method, process, or approach to literacy development and instruction, especially for children in the formative years of schooling. The search for "rightness" is not unique to reading, nor is it unique to reading educators. It seems to be a peculiar and persistent artifact of human beings, no matter what craft we profess or practice. According to literary folklore, Mark Twain once observed, "The difference between the almost right word and the right word is really a large matter—'tis the difference between the lightning bug and the lightning." In another attempt to discern the rightness of something, the noted physicist Wolfgang Pauli responded to a highly speculative proposal in physics by stating, "It's not even wrong" (Flanagan, 1988, p. 226).

Discerning what is *right*, what is *almost right*, and what is *not even wrong* is an especially troublesome task for educators, reading researchers, administrators, publishers, and the international reading community in general. The difficulty rests in part in responding to the unique and diverse needs of learners in

10

the classroom. Evidence of this difficulty can be found in the current debates and discussions about definitions of literacy (Calfee, 1991; Goodman, 1990; McGill-Franzen & Allington, 1991; Rush, Moe, & Storlie, 1986; Venezky, 1990, 1992; Venezky, Wagner, & Ciliberti, 1990), literacy instruction (Fisher & Hiebert, 1990; Yatvin, 1991), whole language and direct instruction (Chall, 1992; Goodman, 1992; Kameenui, 1988; Liberman & Liberman, 1990; Mather, 1992), beginning reading (Adams, 1990, 1991; Bower, 1992; Chaney, 1991), and diverse learners (Garcia, Pearson, & Jimenez, 1990; Stein, Leinhardt, & Bickel, 1989). Although such debates are intellectually stimulating, they are often based upon the premise that there is a right approach, philosophy, or method of literacy instruction. This premise is unlikely to be empirically established anytime soon, and even less likely to be accepted by reading professionals who hold multiple perspectives and epistemologies. Further, the identification of children as diverse learners itself suggests that *multiple* perspectives and approaches will be necessary to accommodate the needs of children who possess differences in abilities and learning histories, and who will be schooled in various instructional contexts.

The Realities of Diversity

Although many of these debates and discussions about the right approach to literacy development and instruction take place within the professional community of reading educators, they are often distant from the realities of the world outside the reading community. Some of these realities were made stark in an article by Hodgkinson (1991) entitled "Reform Versus Reality":

• Since 1987, one fourth of all preschool children in the U.S. have been in poverty.

• Every year, 350,000 children are born to mothers who are addicted to cocaine during pregnancy. Those who survive birth become children with strikingly short attention spans, poor coordination, and much worse. Of course, the schools will have to teach these children, and getting such children ready for kindergarten costs around $40,000 each—about the same as for children with fetal alcohol syndrome.

• On any given night, between 50,000 and 200,000 children have no home.

• The "Norman Rockwell" family—a working father, a housewife mother, and two children of school age—constitutes only 6% of U.S. households.

• About one third of preschool children are destined for school failure because of poverty, neglect, sickness, handicapping conditions, and lack of adult protection and nurturance. (Hodgkinson, 1991, p. 10)

These facts, according to Hodgkinson, are indicative of education's "leaky roof," a metaphor he uses "for the spectacular changes that have occurred in the nature of the children who come to school" (p. 10). Hodgkinson's (1991) demographic analysis is reinforced by additional reports in the popular press documenting the plight of diverse learners. For example:

> The child poverty rate rose by more than 11% during the 1980s, reaching 17.9% in 1989. Black children were the most likely to fall into this group. In 1989, a black child had a 39.8% chance of living in poverty, a Native American child a 38.8% chance and a Hispanic child a 32.2% chance. The figure for Asian children was 17.1% and for white children 12.5%. ("Poverty Rates Rise," 1992)

Similarly, an advertisement for the Children's Defense Fund reads:

Approximately 2.5 million American children were reported abused or neglected last year.... Fourteen nations boast smarter 13-years-olds than the United States. (Children's Defense Fund, 1992)

Hodgkinson (1991) concludes his analysis by offering a poignant soliloquy on the current slings and arrows of education's outrageous fortunes:

> There is no point in trying to teach hungry or sick children. From this we can deduce one of the most important points in our attempts to deal with education: *educators can't fix the roof all by themselves.* It will require the efforts of many people and organizations—health and social welfare agencies, parents, business and political leaders—to even begin to repair this leaky roof. There is no time to waste in fixing blame; we need to act to fix the roof. And unless we start, the house will continue to deteriorate, and all Americans will pay the price. (p. 10)

The Tyranny of Time

Hodgkinson's assertion that "*there is no time to waste in fixing blame; we need to act to fix the roof*" is of particular significance to students who reside in the basement of the house with the leaky roof—children identified as poor readers, reading disabled, at-risk, low performers, mildy disabled, language delayed, and culturally disadvantaged, all of whom have diverse learning and curricular needs. Like literacy, the face of diversity is complex, and at this point, it defies a definition comprised of only the right words (Garcia et al., 1990).

Despite the differences that these children bring to school, what is profoundly and unequivocally the same about them is that they are behind in reading and language development. Moreover, they constantly face the tyranny of time in trying to catch up with their peers, who continue to advance in their literacy development. Simply attempting to keep pace with their peers amounts to losing more and more ground for students who are behind. This predicament has been referred to as the "Matthew effect," a concept resurrected and insightfully applied to reading by Stanovich (1986). According to the Matthew effect, the literacy-rich get richer, and the literacy-poor get poorer in reading opportunities, vocabulary development, written language, general knowledge, and so on.

The pedagogical clock for students who are behind in reading and literacy development continues to tick mercilessly, and the opportunities for these students to advance or catch up diminish over time. Benjamin Bloom (1964) concurred with this general phenomenon almost 30 years ago when he observed that "*growth and development are not in equal units per unit of time*" (p. 204, emphasis added). In other words, not all human characteristics (for example, height, intelligence, vocabulary) grow at the same rate over time; there are periods of rapid growth and periods of relatively slow growth. Bloom noted what we have now come to accept as a developmental and pedagogical truism: "Although it is not invariably true, the period of most rapid growth is likely to be in the early years and this is then followed by periods of less and less rapid growth" (p. 204).

Evidence of the critical importance of what Bloom referred to as "the early environment and experience" (p. 214) now appears overwhelming:

• According to a study by Juel (1988), the probability that a child who is a poor reader at the end of Grade 1 will remain a poor reader at the end of Grade 4 is .88. There is a near 90% chance of remaining a poor reader after 3 years of schooling. Juel noted, "Children who did not develop good word recognition skills in first grade began to dislike reading and read considerably less than good readers both in and out of school" (p. 27).

• Allington's program of research (1980, 1983, 1984) on the opportunities children have to read reveals that the average skilled reader reads almost three times more words than the average less-skilled reader (Stanovich, 1986). Similarly, students identified as mildly handicapped appear to "spend significantly less time engaged in writing and silent reading, and more time passively attending, than do their non-handicapped peers" (O'Sullivan, Ysseldyke, Christenson, & Thurlow, 1990, p. 143).

• Prereaders' phonemic awareness and knowledge of letter names upon entering school appear to influence reading acquisition (Adams, 1990; Griffith & Olson, 1992; Stahl, 1992; Williams, 1984). Adams (1990) states the following:

> In the end, the great value of research on prereaders may lie in the clues it gives us toward determining what the less prepared prereaders need most to learn. For these children, we have not a classroom moment to waste. The evidence strongly suggests that we must help them develop their awareness of the phonemic composition of words. (p. 90)

• The amount of reading that children do outside of school appears to strongly influence reading proficiency (Anderson, Wilson, & Fielding, 1988). However, many children come from homes in which there is very little, if any, preschool language and literacy support (Heath, cited in Adams, 1990).

• Children in Grades 2 and 3 who lack decoding skills and a reasonable base of sight words "may be condemned to school careers marred by increasing distance between them and other children unless successful remediation occurs" (Byrne, Freebody, & Gates, 1992, p. 150).

• Matching classroom instruction with reading abilities appears to be difficult for teachers in general education kindergarten classrooms (Durkin, 1990). Durkin notes the following:

> Use of whole class instruction was the practice even when differences in children's abilities were so great as to be obvious to anyone willing to take but a few minutes to observe. Such differences meant that some children kept hearing what they already knew; for others, the observed lesson was too difficult and proceeded too quickly. (p. 24)

Teacher Uncertainty and Experimentation in the Face of Diversity

When this evidence is considered in the context of education's leaky roof, it carries the potential for creating at least two serious problems for reading educators. The first is pedagogical paralysis, which is in part reflected in a teacher's lack of personal teaching efficacy (for example, "What can I possibly do as one teacher to make a difference?") in the face of a "concentration of low-achieving students" in the classroom (Smylie, 1988, p. 23). In a study of teachers' teaching efficacy, Smylie observed, "The lower the achievement level of students in the class, the less likely teachers seem to be to believe that they can affect student learning, despite the level of confidence they may have in their knowledge and skills related to teaching" (p. 23). The characteristics of the classroom (for example, class size) and heterogeneity of learners appear to affect teachers' beliefs about their ability to influence student learning (Chard & Kameenui, 1992).

Equally problematic, however, is the tendency for educators to engage in fashionable experimentation—experimentation that often draws on fad and fashion (Kameenui, 1991; Slavin, 1989)—rather than well-established and documented practice. This kind of experimentation often occurs when teachers are unsure of what to do with children who are behind. As a result, they experiment with practices that leave some children at risk of falling even further behind in their reading and language development. The experimentation reflects teachers' genuine desire to do the best for their children who, they believe, despite their diverse learning and curricular needs, should benefit from the same "literacy events" and reading activities provided more able readers. However, children who are behind because of language, learning, or reading problems do require substantially different kinds of *reading experiences*—ones that go beyond those typically provided more able readers (Mather, 1992).

Some have argued that the current emphasis on "whole language" approaches to beginning reading exacts its harshest consequence on students with learning and language difficulties (Liberman & Liberman, 1990; Mather, 1992). Others have called for striking a reasonable balance between whole language and direct instruction (Chall, 1992; Cunningham, 1991). Still others have argued for whole language only (Edelsky, 1990; Goodman, 1992). Although the debates about how best to teach beginning reading are age-old and reach back more than 100 years to the "beginning of pedagogy" (Bower, 1992, p. 138), the current context requires that we consider the purpose and consequences of these debates.

Although educators alone cannot fix education's leaky roof, the plight of today's children in society (Garcia et al., 1990; Hodgkinson, 1991) places an unusual burden on schools, teachers, and even professional organizations such as the International Reading Association to get their houses in order. The water from the leaky roof is rising in the basement, and its cost is greatest to students with diverse curricular, learning, and literacy needs. There is not time to waste in fixing blame; we need to act *now* to fix the roof.

Principles for Guiding Action

The realities that poor readers remain poor readers, that insufficient opportunities to read seriously deter reading progress, and that particular instructional arrangements (for example, whole-class instruction) fail to promote adequate reading growth set the stage for the reading community to reconsider the needs of students who face pedagogy's ticking clock. The reading experiences required for these students can be derived and constructed from at least six general pedagogical principles (Dixon, Carnine, & Kameenui, 1992). These principles do not prescribe a single method and by no means represent an exhaustive list. Rather, they offer a conceptual framework for informing our decisions about how to develop the early reading and literacy experiences of these students:

1. Instructional time is a precious commodity; do not lose it. If a reading strategy, concept, or problem-solving analysis can be taught two different ways but one is more efficient, use the more efficient way.

2. Intervene and remediate early, strategically, and frequently. The magnitude of growth in the early years for students who are behind is influenced substantially by what we teach and how we teach. As Stanovich (1986) argues, "Educational interventions that represent a *more of the same* approach will probably not be successful....The remedy for the problem must be more of a *surgical strike*" (p. 393). The following applications should be considered:

• Provide children with more frequent opportunities to read.

• Promote instructional arrangements that allow children to actively participate in literacy activities, for example, small-group story reading instead of one-to-one or whole-class instruction (Morrow & Smith, 1990).

• Help children develop phonemic awareness and knowledge of letter names early.

3. Teach less more thoroughly. The conventional wisdom in working with students who have diverse learning and curricular needs is to teach more in less time (Kameenui, 1990; Kameenui & Simmons, 1990). While the logic of this advice seems reasonable (that is, children who are behind in conceptual knowledge and skills must be taught more in a shorter period of time in order to catch up), the actual practice of trying to teach more in less time simply ignores the constraints of teaching. Instead, by selecting and teaching only those objectives that are essential, and by focusing instruction on the most important and most generalizable concepts or strategies (that is, "big ideas," Calfee, Chambliss, & Beretz, 1991; Carnine & Kemeenui, 1992), more can be learned more thoroughly in the limited time available.

4. Communicate reading strategies in a clear and explicit manner, especially during initial phases of instruction. For many students with learning problems, new concepts and strategies should be explained in concise and comprehensible language. Explicit instruction is still most effective for teaching concepts, principles, and strategies to at-risk students.

5. Guide student learning through a strategic sequence of teacher-directed and student-centered activities. Teacher-directed instruction is necessary if students are to catch up and advance with their able-reading peers. Children will not automatically bloom by being immersed in a literacy hothouse rich with literacy events and activities. Although these activities enrich students' literacy development, they are not sufficient for children who are behind. Teacher-directed instruction need not preempt, minimize, or supplant child-directed activities to develop literacy (Yatvin, 1991). Both sets of activities have their place; however, reading instruction guided by an efficacious teacher is essential. The goal of reading and literacy instruction is to move from teacher-directed to student-centered activities.

6. Examine the effectiveness of instruction and educational tools by formatively evaluating student progress. In testimony given on March 18, 1992, to the Select Committee on Education, Kenneth Komoski, Director of the Education Products Information Exchange, noted that educational materials (for example, print materials, computer software) are used during more than 90% of the 30 billion hours in which America's 40 million students are in school. In many cases, the efficacy of these materials is questionable, despite state laws in the United States that require a learner verification and revision process to substantiate their "instructional effectiveness." Teachers must formatively evaluate the effectiveness of their instructional approaches and materials in order to adapt instruction to meet the needs of learners. As a guideline, current research suggests that measuring student performance twice per week provides an adequate basis for instructional decision making (Deno & Fuchs, 1987).

Conclusion

Human beings, like the words they use, are peculiar creatures, idiosyncratically possessive of their thoughts and words (Bryson, 1990). Even under ideal circumstances, finding the *right* words is indeed difficult. Unless you are part of Wolfgang Pauli's professional physics community, selecting the right word in the Twain tradition is risky business. Paradoxically, it seems as though words have gotten in the way of our real goal. The standard of always searching for the single right method for literacy development may be misguided. We should instead search for multiple perspectives of rightness, guided by the diverse needs of learners and sound instructional principles, practices, and craft knowledge.

Hodgkinson (1991) concludes his analysis of the realities in educational reform by posing two "high-priority" questions—"What can educators do to reduce the number of children 'at risk' in America and to get them achieving well in school settings? And how can educators collaborate more closely with other service providers so that we can all work together toward the urgent goal of providing services to the same client?" (p. 16). Before reading educators can begin to collaborate with "other service providers," they must first collaborate with one another. Our charge is clear, and because the rain will not cease, there is no time to waste; we need to act to fix education's leaky roof. These are the right words; anything less is not even wrong.

Author's Note

This article is based in part on a Visiting Minority Scholar lecture at the University of Wisconsin–Madison, March 19, 1992. The preparation of this paper was supported in part by the National Center to Improve the Tools of Educators (NCITE), Grant H180M10006 from the U.S. Department of Education, Office of Special Education Programs.

REFERENCES

Adams, M. (1990). *Beginning to read: Thinking and learning about print.* Cambridge, MA: MIT Press.

Adams, M. (1991). Beginning to read: A critique by literacy professionals. *The Reading Teacher, 44,* 371–372.

Allington, R.L. (1980). Poor readers don't get to read much in reading groups. *Language Arts, 57,* 872–876.

Allington, R.L. (1983). The reading instruction provided readers of differing reading abilities. *The Elementary School Journal, 83,* 548–559.

Allington, R.L. (1984). Content coverage and contextual reading in reading groups. *Journal of Reading Behavior, 16,* 85–96.

Anderson, R.C., Wilson, P.T., & Fielding, L.G. (1988). Growth in reading and how children spend their time outside of school. *Reading Research Quarterly, 23,* 285–303.

Bloom, B.S. (1964). *Stability and change in human characteristics.* New York: Wiley.

Bower, B. (1992). Reading the code, reading the whole: Researchers wrangle over the nature and teaching of reading. *Science News, 141*(9), 138–141.

Bryson, B. (1990). *The mother tongue: English and how it got that way.* New York: Morrow.

Byrne, B., Freebody, P., & Gates, A. (1992). Longitudinal data on the relations of word-reading strategies to comprehension, reading time, and phonemic awareness. *Reading Research Quarterly, 27,* 141–151.

Calfee, R. (1991). What schools can do to improve literacy instruction. In B. Means, C. Chelemer, & M.S. Knapp (Eds.), *Teaching advanced skills to at-risk students* (pp. 176–203). San Francisco, CA: Jossey-Bass.

Calfee, R.C., Chambliss, M.J., & Beretz, M.M. (1991). Organizing for comprehension and composition. In W. Ellis (Ed.), *All language and the creation of literacy.* Baltimore, MD: Orton Dyslexia Society.

Carnine, D., & Kameenui, E.J. (1992). *Higher order thinking: Designing curriculum for mainstreamed students.* Austin, TX: Pro-Ed.

Chall, J. (1992, May). *Whole language and direct instruction models: Implications for teaching reading in the schools.* Paper presented at the 37th Annual Convention of the International Reading Association, Orlando, FL.

Chaney, J.H. (1991). Beginning to read: A critique by literacy professionals. *The Reading Teacher, 44,* 374–375.

Chard, D.J., & Kameenui, E.J. (1992). *Instructional efficacy: Toward a specification of efficacy research.* Monograph Number 3, Project PREPARE. Eugene, OR: University of Oregon.

Children's Defense Fund. (1992, July). *SV Entertainment,* p. 13.

Cunningham, P. (1991). *What kind of phonics instruction will we have?* Paper presented at the annual meeting of the National Reading Conference, Palm Springs, CA.

Deno, S., & Fuchs, L. (1987). Developing curriculum-based measurement systems for data-based special education problem solving. *Focus on Exceptional Children, 19*(8), 1–16.

Dixon, R., Carnine, D.W., & Kameenui, E.J. (1992). *Curriculum guidelines for diverse learners.* Monograph for National Center to Improve the Tools of Educators. Eugene, OR: University of Oregon.

Durkin, D. (1990). Matching classroom instruction with reading abilities: An unmet need. *Remedial and Special Education, 11*(3), 23–28.

Edelsky, C. (1990). Whose agenda is this anyway? A response to McKenna, Robinson, and Miller. *Educational Researcher, 19*(8), 7–11.

Fisher, C.W., & Hiebert, E.H. (1990). Characteristics of tasks in two approaches to literacy instruction. *The Elementary School Journal, 91,* 3–18.

Flanagan, D. (1988). *Flanagan's version: A spectator's guide to science on the eve of the 21st century.* New York: Vintage.

Garcia, G.E., Pearson, P.D., & Jimenez, R.T. (1990). *The at risk dilemma: A synthesis of reading research.* Champaign, IL: University of Illinois, Reading Research and Education Center.

Goodman, K. (May, 1992). *Whole language and direct instruction models: Implications for teaching reading in the schools.* Paper presented at the 37th Annual Convention of the International Reading Association, Orlando, FL.

Goodman, Y.M. (Ed.). (1990). *How children construct literacy.* Newark, DE: International Reading Association.

Griffith, P.L., & Olson, M.W. (1992). Phonemic awareness helps beginning readers break the code. *The Reading Teacher, 45,* 516–523.

Hodgkinson, H. (1991). Reform versus reality. *Phi Delta Kappan, 73,* 9–16.

Juel, C. (1988, April). *Learning to read and write: A longitudinal study of fifty-four children from first through fourth grade.* Paper presented at the annual meeting of the American Educational Research Association, New Orleans, LA.

Kameenui, E.J. (1988). Direct instruction and the Great Twitch: Why DI or di is not the issue. In J.R. Readence & S. Baldwin (Eds.), *Dialogues in literacy research: Thirty-seventh Yearbook of the National Reading Conference* (pp. 39–45). Chicago, IL: National Reading Conference.

Kameenui, E.J. (1990). The language of the REI—Why it's hard to put into words: A response to Durkin and Miller. *Remedial and Special Education, 11*(3), 57–59.

Kameenui, E.J. (1991). Guarding against the false and fashionable. In J.F. Baumann & D.D. Johnson (Eds.), *Writing for publication in reading and language arts* (pp. 17–28). Newark, DE: International Reading Association.

Kameenui, E.J., & Simmons, D.C. (1990). *Designing instructional strategies: The prevention of academic learning problems.* Columbus, OH: Merrill.

Liberman, A., & Liberman, I. (1990). Whole language vs. code emphasis: Underlying assumptions and their implications for reading instruction. *Annals of Dyslexia, 40,* 52–76.

Mather, N. (1992). Whole language reading instruction for students with learning disabilities: Caught in the cross fire. *Learning Disabilities Research and Practice, 7,* 87–95.

McGill-Franzen, A., & Allington, R.L. (1991). Every child's right: Literacy. *The Reading Teacher, 45,* 86–90.

Morrow, L.M., & Smith, J.K. (1990). The effect of group size on interactive storybook reading. *Reading Research Quarterly, 25,* 213–231.

O'Sullivan, P.J., Ysseldyke, J.E., Christenson, S.L., & Thurlow, M.L. (1990). Mildly handicapped elementary students' opportunity to learn during reading instruction in mainstream and special education settings. *Reading Research Quarterly, 25,* 131–146.

Poverty rates rise. (1992, July). *Time,* p. 15.

Rush, R.T., Moe, A.J., & Storlie, R.L. (1986). *Occupational literacy education.* Newark, DE: International Reading Association.

Slavin, R. (1989). PET and the pendulum: Faddism in education and how to stop it. *Phi Delta Kappan, 90,* 750–758.

Smylie, M.A. (1988). The enhancement function of staff development: Organizational and psychological antecedents to individual teacher change. *American Educational Research Journal, 25,* 1–30.

Stahl, S.A. (1992). Saying the "p" word: Nine guidelines for exemplary phonics instruction. *The Reading Teacher, 45*, 618–625.

Stanovich, K.E. (1986). Matthew effects in reading: Some consequences of individual differences in the acquisition of literacy. *Reading Research Quarterly, 21*, 360–407.

Stein, M.K., Leinhardt, G., & Bickel, W. (1989). Instructional issues for teaching students at risk. In R.E. Slavin, N.L. Kesweit, & N.A. Madden (Eds.), *Effective programs for students at risk* (pp. 145–194). Boston, MA: Allyn & Bacon.

Venezky, R.L. (1990). Definitions of literacy. In R.L. Venezky, D.A. Wagner, & B.S. Ciliberti (Eds.), *Toward defining literacy* (pp. 2–16). Newark, DE: International Reading Association.

Venezky, R.L. (1992, Summer). Matching literacy testing with social policy: What are the alternatives? *Connections.* Philadelphia, PA: National Center on Adult Literacy, University of Pennsylvania.

Venezky, R.L., Wagner, D.A., & Ciliberti, B.S. (Eds.). (1990). *Toward defining literacy.* Newark, DE: International Reading Association.

Williams, J.P. (1984). Phonemic analysis and how it relates to reading. *Journal of Learning Disabilities, 17*, 240–245.

Yatvin, J. (1991). *Developing a whole language program for a whole school.* Richmond, VA: Virginia State Reading Association.

A Case Study of Middle School Reading Disability

Darrell Morris, Criss Ervin, Kim Conrad

As director of a university reading clinic, each year I (Morris) see scores of children who struggle with reading. Our clinical program is straightforward and short on frills; it consists of a parent interview (1 hour), informal testing to determine each student's reading level (1 hour), and intensive one-to-one tutoring (two times per week during the school year), all designed to help the student improve his or her reading ability. Some of the students we tutor improve rapidly in reading, others make slow but steady progress, and a few show little gain despite our best efforts.

Sometimes a specific clinic case captures my attention. Usually it is a child who is having an undue amount of difficulty processing written language. But on occasion, a case stands out less for its exceptionality than for its apparent generality. That is, in getting to know a particular disabled reader and his or her family, and reflecting on the educational havoc caused by the reading problem, I recognize that this student represents many others in the public schools.

This article describes such a case. Brett (a pseudonym), a sixth-grade boy of average intelligence, came to us reading at the second-grade level. His school diagnosis was learning disabled, and his chances for becoming fully literate appeared slim. This case study report includes a summary of the initial parent interview, a detailed description of the student's tutoring program (including assessment), and a commentary on the public school's responsibility to provide effective remedial reading instruction.

Parent Interview

Brett's mother, Mrs. Stacey (also a pseudonym), took off from work early on a Friday afternoon and drove 60 miles to have Brett evaluated at our reading clinic. I interviewed her as Brett was being tested. Mrs. Stacey lived with her husband and three children in a small town in western North Carolina, USA. Although neither she nor her husband had attended college, her oldest daughter was now a freshman at a state university and her other daughter was doing well academically in junior high school. Brett, her youngest, was her concern because he had scored at the second-grade level (2.8) on a recent, school-administered standardized reading test.

According to Mrs. Stacey, Brett had repeated kindergarten and experienced difficulty learning to read in first grade. "He would memorize the basal stories," she said, "but he couldn't read them." In December of second grade, Brett was tested for a possible learning disability and was diagnosed as dyslexic. He spent his third- and fourth-grade years in a self-contained special education class but advanced little in reading despite the help of an after-school tutor. In the fifth and sixth grades Brett was mainstreamed into the regular classroom, receiving resource help 90 minutes per day. Mrs. Stacey approved of her son's placement in the regular academic classes; however, the special education assistance program in Brett's middle school was changing, and Mrs. Stacey did not like the changes. In the sixth grade, Mrs. Stacey explained, the special education resource teacher no longer provided Brett with direct instruction in reading but instead concentrated on helping him understand and complete assignments in all his academic subjects. Mrs. Stacey recognized the need for such assistance, but she stated adamantly:

> Brett is finishing the sixth grade and he can't read his textbooks. If the resource teacher isn't helping him improve his reading skills, then who is going to do it? I think the school is giving up on reading, and I'm not going to have it. I've come up here [to the university] to get some help.

I must admit that I had nothing but admiration for this forceful, straight-talking mother. Not only had Mrs. Stacey diligently supported her child through 6 trying years in school, but now she was interpreting and rightly confronting a change in school policy that could adversely affect her son's chances of achieving literacy. If the learning disabilities resource teacher was no longer going to provide direct reading instruction for Brett (a rising seventh grader reading on a second-grade level), who then was going to teach him to read—his middle-school English teacher, science teacher, or math teacher? This seemed highly unlikely.

At this point in my interview with Mrs. Stacey, I was handed some early and tentative results from Brett's reading evaluation. His word recognition, passage reading, and spelling scores all indicated a second-grade instructional level. I explained to Mrs. Stacey that Brett was 5 years below grade level in reading; however, I also told her that I could not be sure about the severity or intractability of his reading problem without working with him over a few weeks in a clinical teaching situation. I mentioned that we ran a 4-week reading clinic each summer and was about to say that the distance might be prohibitive. Mrs. Stacey interrupted me in mid-sentence: "Brett will be here this summer."

Reading Instruction

Summer 1992

During the summer of 1992, I assigned Mrs. Ervin, an experienced first-grade teacher taking a reading practicum course, to work with Brett. We began by looking back at Brett's performance on the spring reading evaluation (see Table 1).

On the initial informal reading inventory (IRI), Brett's oral reading was slow, labored, and barely audible. He consistently waited for the examiner's help on difficult words, not wanting to risk a mistake. Brett's silent reading was little better. His silent comprehension of the second- and third-grade passages was poor, and his silent reading rates approximated those of a first grader. Notice in Table 1 that Brett's oral reading accuracy and oral reading rate dropped significantly at second grade. However, he did show some strength in word recognition at the second-grade level (flash 70%; untimed 85%).

Mrs. Ervin tutored Brett 1 hour per day, Monday through Thursday, during the 14-day summer practicum (2 days in week 1; 4 days per week in weeks 2–4). The principles that guided her instruction were traditional but timeless in their importance:

Table 1
Brett's initial test results in word recognition, passage reading, and spelling (May 1992)

| Grade level | Word recognition | | Passage reading | | | | | Spelling |
| | | | Oral | | | Silent | | |
	Flash (%)	Untimed (%)	Accuracy (%)	Comp. (%)	Rate (wpm)	Comp. (%)	Rate (wpm)	(%)
First	70	90	94	80	69	80	72	65
Second	70	85	90	80	55	60	63	44
Third	30	60	84	60	51	50	65	20

Note: Instructional level criteria (%) varied by assessment task: word recognition (flash) 70%, oral reading accuracy 92%, oral and silent reading comprehension 75%, and spelling 40%.

• Determine the student's reading instructional level—the level where he is challenged but not frustrated—and present instruction accordingly.

• Use reading material that is of personal interest and significance to the student.

• Build comprehension through informal discussions of stories or articles as they are being read.

• Assess the student's word recognition along a continuum of written word knowledge (for example, beginning consonants, word families, vowel patterns, multisyllable words) and then, over time, provide systematic, developmentally appropriate word study.

• Explore ways of getting the student to practice reading when he is away from the tutorial setting.

Mrs. Ervin's lesson plans, which did not vary across the 14-day summer session, reflected the four principles shown in Figure 1 and described in detail in the following section.

1. *Guided reading.* After previewing a second-grade story (or book chapter), Brett and his tutor would alternate reading pages orally, stopping occasionally to check comprehension. After four or five pages of this partner reading, Mrs. Ervin would elicit a plot prediction from Brett and then have him silently read the remaining three or four pages of the story. He was encouraged to ask for help on difficult words. Again, comprehension was checked.

Brett began the summer by reading four stories in an old second-grade basal reader titled *Tricky Troll* (Eller & Hester, 1976). He then read two chapter books [books long enough to be divided into chapters but not long enough to be considered novels], *The Stories Julian Tells* (Cameron, 1981) and *Shoeshine Girl* (Bulla, 1975), both written at a second-grade reading level. Mrs. Ervin developed an interesting and effective plan for supporting Brett's reading in the chapter books:

• Brett read a chapter with Mrs. Ervin in the tutoring session.

Figure 1
Sample lesson plan

1. *Guided reading*

   Begin by having Brett orally read a 200-word sample from Chapter 2 of *Shoeshine Girl* (graph accuracy and rate).

   Review content of Chapter 2, and then begin Chapter 3 (partner read first three pages; Brett reads last three pages silently).

   Send Chapter 4 home on tape.

2. *Word sort*

   Sort *a* patterns (*a, a-e, ar, all*).

   Play Concentration game with 12 of the words.

   Do spelling check on 6 words.

3. *Writing*

   Have Brett add to, and possibly finish, his story on Atlanta trip.

4. *Easy reading*

   Introduce new Starpol book *Testing Hunter 4* (partner read first four pages, then let Brett proceed independently).

• Brett then took the next chapter home on an audiotape. His task was not just to listen to the taped chapter (six to eight pages), but to practice reading it in preparation for an oral reading check the next day.

• Brett began the next tutoring session by reading a 200-word sample from the practiced chapter. Mrs. Ervin recorded his oral reading accuracy and rate, and shared this information with Brett.

• The content of the practiced chapter then was discussed. A third chapter was part-

ner read in the tutoring session, and a tape of the fourth chapter sent home.

By reading the same book in the tutoring sessions and at home (with audiotapes to support him), Brett was able to finish both chapter books in the short 4-week session. Not only did his reading ability improve, but his self-concept as a reader changed. He was completing meaningful reading assignments, possibly for the first time in his life.

2. *Word study*. At each tutoring session Brett spent a few minutes sorting one-syllable words into vowel patterns (see Figure 2).

Brett enjoyed these brief lessons where he and his tutor categorized words by pattern. He also benefited from the short spelling checks (five or six words) that followed each sorting activity. Over 3 weeks, he worked across the common *a*, *e*, and *i* vowel patterns (see Invernizzi, Abouzeid, & Gill, 1994; Morris, 1982; or Schlagal & Schlagal, 1992, for more information on word sorting).

3. *Writing*. At first Brett was reluctant to write, and writing did prove to be a slow, arduous process for him. Mrs. Ervin was firm but encouraging. She allowed Brett to select his own writing topics and emphasized the expression of ideas, not mechanical correctness, in first drafts. Choosing to write about sports and later a family trip to Atlanta, Brett progressed from short three-sentence accounts at the beginning of the summer to two-paragraph stories several weeks later. Mrs. Ervin helped him revise and edit two of his favorite pieces, which then were typed and illustrated.

4. *Easy reading*. Brett quickly became hooked on the Starpol books (Tully, 1987), a series of space adventures written at a late-first-grade to late-second-grade difficulty level. (Each Starpol book is 24 pages with engaging, colorful illustrations on each page.) Brett and his tutor would begin a Starpol story in the tutoring session and on most days

he would finish the story at home. This easy but meaningful reading in a single series helped to improve Brett's word recognition, fluency, and confidence.

At the end of the summer session it was apparent to everyone involved that Brett had made gains in reading and self-confidence. Mrs. Stacey was very pleased, but at the same time concerned about the summer clinic coming to an end. I suggested that she ask Mrs. Ervin to continue tutoring Brett during the upcoming school year (the Staceys lived approximately 45 minutes from Mrs. Ervin's school). To my delight, Mrs. Ervin agreed to tutor Brett after school if I would provide professional assistance now and then, a request to which I readily agreed.

School Year 1992–1993

Brett was tutored once per week during the 1992–1993 school year; the busy work schedules of his mother and tutor precluded more frequent sessions. Mrs. Ervin, for the most part, followed her tutoring plan from the summer reading clinic. This included guided reading of chapter books, word study, repeated readings of familiar passages, writing, and taped readings for homework. Brett read third- and fourth-grade chapter books during the year. In order, these were *Mustard* (Graeber, 1983), *Stone Fox* (Gardiner, 1983), *How to Eat Fried Worms* (Rockwell, 1973), *Owls in the Family* (Mowat, 1981), and *Skinnybones* (Park, 1982). He again alternated reading a chapter in the tutoring session and the following chapter at home (with the support of an audiotape). Brett's comprehension of these books was excellent, his oral reading accuracy and rate adequate, and his interest high.

To improve Brett's reading fluency, Mrs. Ervin employed the method of repeated readings (Samuels, 1979). In this activity Brett read a familiar passage for 3 minutes. The

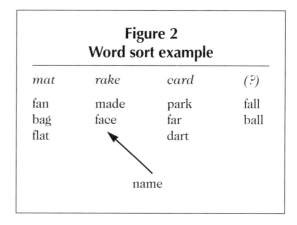

Figure 2
Word sort example

mat	*rake*	*card*	*(?)*
fan	made	park	fall
bag	face	far	ball
flat		dart	

name

number of words read was graphed. He then read the same passage again, and then a third time in the following tutoring session. Each time the number of words read in 3 minutes was graphed (see Figure 3).

Brett benefited from the repeated readings in several ways: the timed trials heightened his concentration, rereadings of the same passage consistently increased his fluency or rate, and the immediate graphing of results provided Brett with much-needed performance feedback.

After a few weeks of tutoring, Mrs. Ervin shared with me the difficulty Brett was having with spelling instruction. He was being asked to learn 10 seventh-grade words per week (for example, horrible, elegant, brilliant, companion, doubtful); however, Brett was unsure of even third-grade spellings (that is, whether boil was spelled "boil," "bole," or "boyl"). His frustration over weekly spelling assignments was building rapidly.

At this point Mrs. Ervin and I devised a plan for helping Brett with spelling. First, we assessed his spelling ability by administering the first three levels of a diagnostic spelling inventory (Schlagal, 1989). Results showed that Brett was functioning at a second-grade level in spelling. With these results in hand, Mrs. Ervin

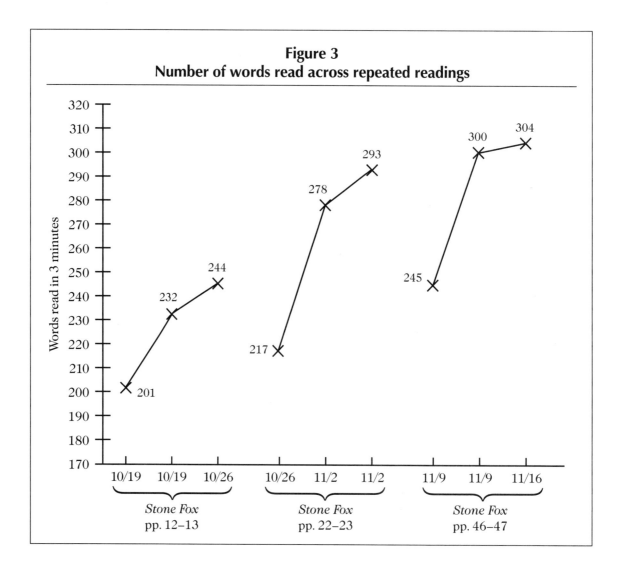

Figure 3
Number of words read across repeated readings

approached the school about providing Brett's spelling instruction during his tutoring sessions. The classroom teacher and learning disabilities resource teacher consented readily, with the stipulation that some type of weekly assessment be turned in to the school.

In late October, Mrs. Ervin located a third-grade spelling book and used this as a resource to provide Brett with both spelling and word-study instruction for the remainder of the school year. Each Monday, in the tutoring session, Brett took a pretest on a unit of 15 words from the spelling book. (Note: The first six units in the book reviewed second-grade spelling patterns.) Brett, on average, misspelled four to six words on the weekly pretest. He immediately self-corrected the pretest, writing each misspelled word correctly three times, and then sorted the 15 spelling words into patterns (see Figure 4).

Brett's homework assignment was to use each misspelled pretest word in a meaningful sentence and to review the entire spelling unit for a Friday posttest to be administered at school by his resource teacher. The following Monday, a new spelling unit was introduced in the tutoring lesson. From November through May, Brett worked through 20 of the 36 units in the third-grade book. He consistently scored 93% or better on the Friday posttests.

School Year 1993–1994

Mrs. Ervin and a colleague, Mrs. Conrad, continued to tutor Brett once per week during the school year. Brett was now a stronger reader and, consequently, his tutors increased the challenge level of his assignments. In year two, Brett read narrative and content material written at a fourth- or fifth-grade level; he studied spelling patterns selected from a fourth-grade spelling book. Basic tutoring procedures did not change significantly from year one to year two.

Posttesting

Mrs. Ervin used posttesting to evaluate Brett's reading progress once per year. Each time, she administered the same word recognition and spelling lists, along with different but equivalent sets of reading passages.

Table 2 summarizes Brett's posttutoring (May 1994) performance. Comparing this performance against his initial assessment (Table 1) shows that Brett made considerable improvement in all areas of contextual reading: word reading accuracy, rate, and comprehension. A second-grade-level reader in 1992, 2 years later he was reading fluently at the fourth-grade level. Brett also improved in spelling. Using 40% accuracy as an instructional level criterion (Morris, Blanton, Blanton, & Perney, 1995), Table 2 shows that Brett progressed 2 years in spelling, from a second-grade to a fourth-grade level. Interestingly,

---

Figure 4
Example of third-grade spelling unit and accompanying word sort activity

Spelling pretest		Word sort activity			
1. tray	+				
2. feel	+				
3. paint	PANT				
4. sneak	SNEK				
5. seem	+	*fail*	*lay*	*sweet*	*real*
6. real	+				
7. hay	+	paint	hay	seem	treat
8. chain	CHANE	chain	tray	feel	wheat
9. free	+				
10. lay	+		train		
11. fail	+				
12. treat	TREET				
13. train	TRANE				
14. sweet	+				
15. wheat	WHET				

Table 2
Test results after 2 years of tutoring (May 1994)

| Grade level | Word recognition | | Passage reading | | | | | Spelling |
| | | | Oral | | | Silent | | |
	Flash (%)	Untimed (%)	Accuracy (%)	Comp. (%)	Rate (wpm)	Comp. (%)	Rate (wpm)	(%)
First								95
Second								76
Third	55	100	98	100	110	93	116	70
Fourth	30	70	99	93	104	100	112	48
Fifth	—	—	94	100	55	100	89	—

Note: Instructional level criteria (%) varied by assessment task: word recognition (flash) 70%, oral reading accuracy 92%, oral and silent reading comprehension 75%, and spelling 40%.

Brett's smallest gain was in decontextualized word recognition (flashed and untimed). Here, he advanced from a second- to a third-grade level, with most of this gain coming in the first year of tutoring.

Summary of Reading Instruction and Test Results

Summary of reading instruction and test results shows that Brett received 78 hours of tutorial instruction over the 2-year period. His reading lessons were characterized by balance, support, and adherence to instructional level. Balance was reflected in the consistent lesson routine of reading for meaning, word study, fluency drill, and writing. Although reading for meaning in narrative and content materials dominated, the systematic study of word patterns also was emphasized. In fact, a unique feature of the after-school lessons was the tutor's skillful integration of spelling and word-study instruction.

When tutoring began in the summer of 1992, Brett was a struggling reader, severely lacking in confidence. He required tutorial support to read in context, and this support was provided in several ways: partner reading in which tutor and child alternated reading aloud pages at the beginning of a story; taped reading in which Brett read along with a tape-recorded version of a story or chapter at home; repeated readings in which he read aloud one short passage three successive times, working on fluency; and guided reading in which the tutor's questions and probes facilitated Brett's silent reading of a story. Significantly, much of this contextual reading support was phased out as Brett became a stronger reader over the 2-year period. For example, in year one Brett often read an assigned chapter at home with the assistance of a tape recorder; in year two he was able to read a chapter at home without the tape recorder.

Balanced instruction and appropriate tutor support were important, but the essential element in Brett's successful reading program was the tutor's diligent, unrelenting attention to instructional level. Initial testing showed Brett to have, at best, a second-grade reading level. Mrs. Ervin, putting aside age and grade expectations, began working with Brett at the second-grade level. Over a 2-year period, Brett progressed steadily—from a second- to a fourth-grade instructional level in both reading and spelling. Progress was slow but foundational, and, importantly, it was understood and appreciated by the tutor and student alike.

Brett's 2-year gain in reading and spelling was encouraging, particularly in light of the minimal reading and spelling progress he had made during his first 6 years in school. One less positive test finding, however, warrants mention. It was noted earlier that Brett's ability to recognize isolated words lagged behind his contextual word recognition ability, particularly in the second year of tutoring. It can be argued that the second-year gain in reading skill was contextual in nature and that the underlying word recognition competence stalled (Chall, Jacobs, & Baldwin, 1990). Such an interpretation is certainly consistent with Brett's longstanding word-recognition problem. It also highlights the necessity of a continuing word study program—systematic study of developmentally appropriate word patterns—if Brett is to make further advances in reading and spelling.

Commentary

I believe that there are many thousands of Bretts sitting in middle-school classrooms. These students struggle mightily with grade-level reading assignments and, because they are forced to read at frustration level most of the school day, their reading skills may improve little from year to year, causing them to fall further behind their peers. Some of these students are labeled learning disabled or slow

learners, but the inescapable fact remains that they have the potential to learn if they receive appropriate instruction.

Appropriate instruction in Brett's case rested, in large part, on his tutor's knowledge of how to teach reading. Mrs. Ervin understood the fundamental importance of instructional level, she exercised good judgment in selecting interesting material, she was skillful in getting Brett to search for meaning in text, and she possessed knowledge of the English orthographic system and of appropriate strategies for teaching that system. Moreover, Mrs. Ervin's summer practicum experience, although short in duration, allowed her to practice her teaching—to refine her understanding of the process—in a one-to-one context under the watchful eye of an experienced clinician.

Obviously we need more Mrs. Ervins in our schools to meet the needs of students like Brett. I have no formula for producing such teachers, but I do think it must be done at the graduate level and at least two conditions must be satisfied. First, graduate methods courses in reading instruction must be rigorous and provide teachers with a balanced, comprehensive view of the reading process. Reading teachers must understand both word recognition and comprehension development and be able to facilitate growth in both areas through thoughtful, carefully planned instruction. Second, reading teachers-in-training must be provided with carefully supervised clinical teaching experiences. Henderson (1981) addressed this issue eloquently:

> I am convinced that a year-long practicum should be required for all reading specialists. The work should be carried on under the direct supervision of an experienced clinician who can show by example both the techniques and the exercise of judgment that are needed. No formula will suffice nor will practice by a teacher alone convey what must be mastered.... It is only by experiencing the effects of refined teaching that students learning to be teachers are gradually able to free them-

selves from the false belief that it is the method rather than they themselves that must control the set for learning.... Such teaching skill is learned only gradually, by example and practice. (pp. 129–130)

There are no shortcuts. One learns to teach reading by teaching—and reflecting on the teaching act—under the supervision of an experienced guide. For those who believe that clinical training is a relic from reading education's past, keep in mind that today such training receives impressive theoretical support from the "reflective practitioner" work of Schon (1987) and the "assisted learning" work of Tharp and Gallimore (1988). Also note that Reading Recovery (Clay, 1985), the most successful early reading intervention program to come along in years, is a pure example of clinical teacher training.

Are we providing prospective reading and learning disabilities teachers with rigorous, balanced reading methods courses and carefully supervised clinical teaching experiences? This question must be answered by individual graduate programs. I do know that there has been a general lessening of interest and vitality in clinical training as part of U.S. reading education over the last two decades. I also know that in the three states in which I have worked (Virginia, Illinois, and North Carolina), only one graduate course in reading has been required for a master's degree in learning disabilities (a course that was not a teaching practicum). This is an unfortunate situation, because expertise is needed to help disabled readers. Until reading and special education faculty members in colleges of education commit themselves to developing teaching expertise in their graduate students, I do not foresee significant improvements in the quality of school-based remedial reading instruction (see Kauffman, 1994).

Given adequate training in teaching reading (a crucial assumption), a Title I [U.S. fed-erally funded education program for at-risk children; formerly Chapter 1] or learning disabilities teacher can make a positive difference with students like Brett. The same general principles apply to tutoring and to small-group instruction: identifying students' instructional levels, giving them interesting books that they can read, and pacing them efficiently in accordance with their advancing reading skill. Several of the specific tutoring activities mentioned in this case study can be adapted easily to small-group contexts (for example, guided reading, taped reading, writing, word study).

Unfortunately, many Title I and most learning disabilities teachers have difficulty assembling workable instructional groups during the day (that is, a small group of students working at a similar reading level). Disabled readers come to the resource room when their academic schedule allows, not necessarily when there is an optimal time or context for teaching them to read. Conducting an effective 40-minute reading lesson with four students from two different grades who read at three different reading levels is next to impossible, and a year's worth of ineffective lessons adds up to minimal reading growth. Note, however, that prioritizing instructional time for students is a school scheduling problem, not a student learning problem. If reading improvement were the priority for students like Brett, then scheduling conflicts could be resolved at the beginning of the year through discussion among teachers and principals.

A current trend in special education, called inclusion, is to deemphasize "pull-out" programs, where direct reading instruction has traditionally been provided, and instead to have the resource teacher assist the student with academic assignments in the regular classroom. But, as Brett's mother observed in the parent interview, "That's fine, but who is going to teach Brett how to read?" It may be possible to provide appropriate instruction to remedial readers within the inclusion model, but it is difficult. At a minimum, there needs to be coordinated planning of lessons by the classroom and resource teachers, textbook materials written at several difficulty levels, and opportunities for small-group teaching within the regular classroom (Walsmley & Walp, 1990). Anyone who spent time in schools recognizes that this is a tall order. If the inclusion model leads to resource teachers abandoning direct instruction in reading to become teacher consultants or academic subject facilitators, then students like Brett will pay a huge price in terms of their reading development.

An alternative to total inclusion models, and one that I favor, is a specialist position that combines small-group pull-out teaching with some classroom consultation. If we can assume expertise on the part of the specialist, there are several advantages to this role. By continuing to provide direct reading instruction to small groups on a daily basis, the specialist teacher continually refines his or her teaching skills. By sharing expertise with classroom teachers through conferences and model teaching, the specialist can influence a larger number of students in the school. My own experience points to a third advantage to this reading teacher/consultant role. Regular classroom teachers listen most attentively to those consultants who work directly with at-risk students on a regular basis and make a difference in their learning.

Allington (1994) points out that, historically, U.S. public schools have not been successful in meeting the needs of students like Brett. He suggests that we disband the current remediation system (Title I and learning disabilities) and start over. My concern with this radical analysis is that I am not sure we have given the current system a fair chance. In my opinion, much blame should be assigned to graduate teacher-training programs. If all Title I and learning disabilities teachers were well trained in teaching reading, and if all these teachers had adequate freedom in scheduling workable instructional groups during the school day, then I see no reason why they could not make a significant difference in their students' learning. The present case study illustrates that even a child who has fallen 4 years behind in reading can make substantial progress if he or she receives effective instruction. As Mrs. Ervin stated:

> In many ways I have changed after working with Brett.... Certainly I have learned things from the tutoring experience, but more important I have come to believe even more strongly that it is never too late to help a child learn to read.

REFERENCES

Allington, R. (1994). Critical issues: What's special about special programs for children who find learning to read difficult? *Journal of Reading Behavior, 26*, 95–115.

Chall, J., Jacobs, V., & Baldwin, L. (1990). *Reading crisis: Why poor children fall behind.* Cambridge, MA: Harvard University Press.

Clay, M. (1985). *The early detection of reading difficulties* (3rd ed.). Auckland, NZ: Heinemann.

Henderson, E.H. (1981). *Learning to read and spell: The child's knowledge of words.* DeKalb, IL: Northern Illinois University Press.

Invernizzi, M., Abouzeid, M., & Gill, J.T. (1994). Using students' invented spellings as a guide for spelling instruction that emphasizes word study. *The Elementary School Journal, 95*, 155–167.

Kauffman, J.M. (1994). Places of change: Special education's power and identity in an era of educational reform. *Journal of Learning Disabilities, 27*, 610–618.

Morris, D. (1982). Word sort: A categorization strategy for improving word recognition ability. *Reading Psychology, 3*, 247–259.

Morris, D., Blanton, L., Blanton, W., & Perney, J. (1995). Spelling instruction and achievement in six elementary classrooms. *The Elementary School Journal, 96*, 145–162.

Samuels, S.J. (1979). The method of repeated readings. *The Reading Teacher, 32,* 403–408.

Schlagal, R. (1989). Constancy and change in spelling development. *Reading Psychology, 10,* 207–232.

Schlagal, R., & Schlagal, J. (1992). The integrated character of spelling: Teaching strategies for multiple purposes. *Language Arts, 69,* 418–424.

Schon, D. (1987). *Educating the reflective practitioner.* San Francisco, CA: Jossey-Bass.

Tharp, R., & Gallimore, R. (1988). *Rousing minds to life: Teaching, learning, and schooling in social context.* New York: Cambridge University Press.

Walmsley, S., & Walp, T. (1990). Integrating literature and composing into the language arts curriculum: Philosophy and practice. *The Elementary School Journal, 90,* 251–274.

READING MATERIALS USED WITH BRETT

Bulla, C.R. (1975). *Shoeshine girl.* New York: Harper Trophy.

Cameron, A. (1981). *The stories Julian tells.* New York: Knopf.

Eller, W., & Hester, K. (1976). *Tricky troll.* River Forest, IL: Laidlaw.

Gardiner, J.R. (1983). *Stone fox.* New York: Harper Trophy.

Graeber, C. (1983). *Mustard.* New York: Bantam Skylark.

Mowat, F. (1981). *Owls in the family.* New York: Bantam Skylark.

Park, B. (1982). *Skinnybones.* New York: Knopf.

Rockwell, T. (1973). *How to eat fried worms.* New York: Dell Yearling.

Tully, J. (1987). *The Starpol series.* San Diego, CA: Wright Group.

Early Literacy: What Does "Developmentally Appropriate" Mean?

Anne McGill-Franzen

In 1991 I attended a reunion of women who, like me, had been legislative fellows sponsored by the Center for Women in Government at the State University of New York at Albany. All of these women are deeply committed to supporting policies that will improve the lives of women and children. I was engaged in a lively debate about the benefits of U.S. Federal legislation to increase the participation of "at-risk" 3- to 5-year-old children in early intervention programs for the handicapped. Such children are said to be developmentally "behind" their peers because of social, emotional, language, or cognitive factors, although their "handicap" may not be precisely identified at this early age. When I said that I did not believe in identifying children as disabled before they had even experienced whatever it was they were supposed to learn, I was asked: "Aren't you a developmentalist?" The question gave me pause.

Would a developmentalist isolate children who already know a lot about written language and literacy from those who do not? Does a developmentalist believe that early school programs can be powerful equalizers of children's literacy experiences so that all children achieve with their peers? Or does a developmentalist believe that there has to be a "bottom" group and children who fail because they are "not ready"?

As it turns out, *developmental learning* or *developmentally appropriate instruction* are buzz words for educating young (and not so young) children. Like all buzz words, "developmentally appropriate instruction" can have multiple interpretations.

There are few who would quibble with the argument that children differ from one another in important ways. As research studies have demonstrated again and again, children differ in language use and social competence, in their memory for what we as teachers view as important, and in the attention they are willing to invest in the tasks we present as our literacy curriculum. Most important, I would argue that children differ in the personal literacy histories they bring to school, and families differ in the resources they have to promote the educational well-being of their children.

In her book, *Beginning to Read: Thinking and Learning about Print*, psychologist Marilyn Adams (1990) tells us that middle-class children typically come to school with

31

thousands of hours of guidance about print—storybook reading, message writing, letter identification, and so on—from parents, preschool teachers, educational toys, and television, whereas less advantaged children may have no such experiences. Nonetheless, all parents—regardless of social class—value education for their children. The sociologist Annette Lareau (1989), for example, suggests in her book that the "home advantage" enjoyed by children of the middle and upper classes is not money per se, but rather parents' knowledge of how schools work. Like middle-class parents, working-class parents expect their young children to learn to read in first grade. However, working-class parents usually are not able to compensate at home when the first-grade curriculum turns out to be weak or their children have trouble keeping up.

In short, there are real differences in the development and histories of children. If we want to personalize our instruction, engage children, and make them feel valued, these differences *must* inform what we do and say in our interactions with children. Yet these differences should not become the rationale for not teaching all children whatever it is they need to know to participate fully in the literate culture of our schools.

A Trap for Poor Children?

I believe there is a trap in the concept of developmental appropriateness. Not long ago, the National Association for the Education of Young Children broadly defined developmental appropriateness as a concept related to both "predictable sequences of growth and change that occur in [most] children during the first 9 years of life" and to the "individual pattern and timing of growth, as well as individual personality, learning style, and family background" (1986, p. 5). In practice, however, developmental appropriateness has been interpreted to mean that reading and writing are "academic skills" that do not belong in child-centered early childhood programs and that there is no role for adult modeling or teaching in so-called "active" learning environments. Artificial dichotomies that pit academic learning against social learning, direct-instruction against activity-based models, and academics against child development have been set up. As the early childhood researcher Susan Robinson (1990) found, preschool teachers are reluctant to display print, read extended stories, or allow children to write because they are not sure these trappings of our literate culture are appropriate for 3-, 4-, and 5-year-olds.

Unfortunately for poor children, the restrictions of such developmentally appropriate practices are most burdensome for them. Private nursery schools and other early childhood programs can and do teach whatever they please, often providing instruction in not only written English but also some Spanish or French, and perhaps the Hebrew alphabet or a few Chinese words as well. By contrast, in many publicly funded early childhood programs for poor children it is considered developmentally inappropriate to display the letters of the English alphabet or even to sing the alphabet song. One African American teacher told me that Head Start does not believe in teaching kids to write:

> The goal is self-esteem. Maybe 25 years ago when they started the program children were so delayed they needed a whole year of social skills. That's not the case now. The program assumes the children are stupid.... There's no money for books and paper...circle time is not supposed to last longer than 10 minutes...and they are not supposed to do whole group activities.

Yet this same teacher noted that children were screened both in preschool and in kindergarten for developmental benchmarks such as being able to retell stories and print some letters of the alphabet. When children perform poorly, it is attributed to their delayed development or disability, rather than to the paucity of experiences and opportunities to explore written language and literary understandings.

Developmental Metaphors: Flowers or Scaffolds?

For some Piagetian psychologists or Gesell developmentalists, children's development is biologically fixed and the timetable cannot be influenced by instruction. Teachers may be admonished not to tamper with the unfolding maturation of the child. For those who hold this view, to say that development may be accelerated is to propose the unthinkable. In fact, the contemporary "hothouse" metaphors of the late 1980s and early 1990s not only espouse this position, but they are indeed reminiscent of much earlier times. Amariah Brigham, an influential 19th-century physician, and many of his peers believed that "cultivating intellectual faculties of children before they are six or seven" would harm body and soul:

> Early mental excitement will serve only to bring forth beautiful but premature flowers, which are destined soon to wither away, without producing fruit. (cited in Kaestle & Vinovskis, 1980, p. 59)

According to these doctors, more than an hour of school for children under 8 years old would induce the "morbid condition of precocity," which could lead to "imbecility or premature old age." Arnold Gesell, an influential physician of the next century, related human development to "neural ripening," and a prominent progressive educator of the same time period, Carleton Washburne, identified the mental age of $6\frac{1}{2}$ years as the optimal time to begin to teach reading. Over the years, these theories have persisted within certain school commu-

nities even though no credible evidence supports them. As late as 1988, David Elkind, early childhood educator and author of several books on the "hurried child" and "miseducation" of children, cited Washburne's 1930s work as testimony to the wisdom of teaching children to read at 7 or 8 years old, rather than at younger ages. Unfortunately, in our culture, a child who is 8 years old and not a reader is a child in deep trouble at school. Yet the irony of it all is that no child needs to be in that kind of trouble. We are so much smarter now than we were in the 1800s and the early 1900s about how children come to literacy. We know now that reading instruction does not start in preschool, or kindergarten, or first grade. We learn to read, as Frank Smith says, from "the company we keep," and children are in the company of adults from the moment they are born.

Vygotskian psychologists and developmentalists would agree with Smith. They believe that instruction should move ahead of development and pull it along. By talking with grown-ups and capable peers as they go about doing the kinds of things literate people do, children are able to construct meanings for tasks that they could not understand on their own. This modeling or scaffolding enables children to perform tasks that they could not otherwise do. But such instruction actually *transforms* the child's development so that tomorrow the child is able to independently do what he or she could do *only with assistance* today.

Believing in Ourselves as Teachers

The interaction between *instruction* and *development* is complex, and an uncontested definition of the relation does not exist. Nonetheless, our own beliefs about the relation are extremely important. As researchers Mary Lee Smith and Lorrie Shepard (1988) discovered, teachers who hold a nativist view (the flower metaphor) do not believe that they can accelerate development of children who arrive unready for kindergarten. Such teachers urge parents to give children the "gift of time" by holding them out of school for an extra year or by placing them in developmental kindergartens or other transitional-grade classrooms. These teachers retain children deemed unready to go on and classify them as developmentally delayed and in need of special education services. The nativist perspective might preclude reading to children who prefer to spend all of their time at the sandbox. Children who claim that they cannot write a story or their names might not be invited to explore with paper and pens if we believe that children's thinking passes through invariant stages regardless of how we support their learning.

On the other hand, teachers who hold remedial or interactionist views of development (the scaffold metaphor) revise their instruction, not their expectations for learning, when children are not progressing. These teachers believe in themselves as able to "bring children along." The noted New Zealand educator, Marie Clay, spoke recently in Columbus, Ohio, about the results of early intervention in reading instruction in her country. Clay expressed amazement that between 98% and 99% of all children were able to achieve at the expected level for first grade, and in New Zealand children with learning disabilities and other mild handicaps were not separated from their peers. Trained as a developmental psychologist in the Piagetian tradition, Clay said that

she was unprepared for the dramatic way that *appropriate instruction* in reading *accelerated development*.

We should not look at development as something that *limits* what children can accomplish as learners and what we can accomplish as teachers. Rather, the individual and variable development of children is an opportunity to personalize our instruction. As teachers we must celebrate and affirm, but also *extend and elaborate* each child's developing knowledge of written language.

REFERENCES

Adams, M.J. (1990). *Beginning to read: Thinking and learning about print.* Cambridge, MA: MIT Press.

Elkind, D. (1988). Educating the very young: A call for clear thinking. *National Education Association Today, 6,* 22–27.

Kaestle, C.F., & Vinovskis, M. (1980). *Education and social change in nineteenth century Massachusetts.* New York: Cambridge University Press.

Lareau, A. (1989). *Home advantage: Social class and parental intervention in elementary education.* Philadelphia, PA: Falmer.

National Association for the Education of Young Children. (1986, September). Position paper on developmentally appropriate practice in early childhood programs. *Young Children,* 3–29.

Robinson, S.S. (1990). *A survey of literacy programs among preschools.* Paper presented at the annual meeting of the American Educational Research Association, Boston, MA.

Smith, M.L., & Shepard, L. (1988). Kindergarten readiness and retention: A qualitative study of teacher's beliefs and practices. *American Educational Research Journal, 25,* 307–333.

Preventing Reading Failure: A Review of Five Effective Programs

John J. Pikulski

lavin, Madden, Karweit, Dolan, and Wasik (1991) write of a mythical town where 30% of the children were falling ill from contaminated drinking water. Many became permanently disabled and many died. The town spent millions for the medical care of these victims. At one point, a town engineer proposed building a water treatment plant that could virtually eliminate the illnesses. The town council rejected the proposal as being too expensive, because funds would not then be sufficiently available to treat current victims and because some 70% of the children never fell ill.

Slavin et al. (1991) compare the situation in the mythical town to our efforts to remediate reading problems. Enormous amounts of money are spent annually in efforts to remediate reading problems, or so-called "learning disabilities," but only a fraction of that funding is used to prevent these problems. This focus on correction rather than prevention continues in spite of an impressive and growing body of authoritative opinion and research evidence that suggests that reading failure is preventable for all but a very small percentage of children (for example, Clay, 1985; Hall, Prevatte, & Cunningham, 1993; Hiebert, Colt, Catto, & Gury, 1992; Hiebert & Taylor, 1994; Ohio State University, 1990; Pinnell, 1989; Reynolds, 1991; Slavin,

Madden, Karweit, Livermon, & Dolan, 1990; Slavin, Madden, Karweit, Dolan, & Wasik, 1992; Taylor, Frye, Short, & Shearer, 1992; Taylor, Strait, & Medo, 1994). These positive findings are particularly important because I could locate very little evidence that suggested that programs designed to correct reading problems beyond second grade were successful. Indeed, one study (Kennedy, Birman, & Demaline, 1986) suggested that efforts to correct reading problems beyond third grade are largely unsuccessful.

On the surface, successful programs for the prevention of reading problems may seem expensive, but they actually are very cost effective when compared with the costs involved in remedial efforts; in retaining students for 1 or more years of schooling; and in placement in expensive, yet minimally effective, special education programs (Dyer, 1992; Slavin, 1989; Slavin et al., 1992; Smith & Strain, 1988). In addition, there is no way to calculate the savings in human suffering, humiliation, and frustration that would occur if children did not experience the painful failure that all too often follows them through school and life.

The term *early intervention*, used in a variety of ways in professional literature, often refers to programs designed for preschool children. Research reviews suggest strongly that these programs will play a critical role in efforts to eradicate reading and school failure (Slavin, Karweit, & Wasik, in press). This article focuses on five school-based intervention programs designed for implementation early in a child's school career, primarily in first grade: Success for All (Madden, Slavin, Karweit, Dolan, & Wasik, 1991); the Winston-Salem Project (Hall et al., 1993); the Boulder Project (Hiebert et al., 1992); the Early Intervention in Reading (EIR) Project (Taylor et al., 1992); and Reading Recovery (Pinnell, 1989; Pinnell, Fried, & Estice, 1990). These programs were chosen for review on the basis of three criteria: (1) they were described in reasonable detail in a nationally distributed U.S. education journal that subjected its articles to review by an editorial board; (2) their primary focus was working with first-grade, at-risk students, those identified as likely to make limited progress in learning to read; and (3) data were presented that suggested that they were "effective," that is, student participation in the programs led to substantially better reading achievement than that of similar students who had not participated in the programs.

The primary purpose of this article is to compare these five programs using a number of criteria and to identify common features that seem related to preventing reading problems. The identification of features common to successful early intervention programs may be useful for those working with students who require early intervention or for those planning such programs. No attempt will be made to "prove" the effectiveness of these five programs. The articles cited earlier should be consulted for evidence of their effectiveness. The position taken here reflects Archambault's (1989) suggestion that there comes a time when we should stop focusing on justifying program effects and focus instead on recommendations for program improvement. Likewise, no attempt will be made to determine which of the five programs is best. While all of them have proven effectiveness, some might be better than others depending on the circumstances of individual schools or school districts. For example, schools that have a high percentage of at-risk students might consider total school intervention programs like Success for All or the Winston-Salem Project. EIR and the Boulder Chapter 1 program [U.S. federally funded education program for at-risk children now called Title I] are designed for use with small groups of students and so can serve a larger number of students than Reading Recovery, which requires one-to-one tutoring. However, some children may need the intense one-to-one support of Reading Recovery. It therefore might be more effective to provide some children with one form of early intervention and other children with a different form even within the same school.

Five Programs of Early Intervention for the Prevention of Reading Problems

Success for All

This project has been implemented primarily in schools in Baltimore, Maryland, USA and Philadelphia, Pennsylvania, USA that serve students from very low socioeconomic, inner-city communities. Success for All is a total school program for Kindergarten through Grade 3 that focuses both on regular classroom instruction and supplementary support. Students in Grades 1 through 3 are heterogeneously grouped in classrooms of about 25 students, except for a 90-minute daily reading period in which they are regrouped by reading level across all three grades, in groups of 15 to 20 students. This allows whole group, direct instruction and eliminates seatwork using worksheets and workbooks.

Individual tutoring sessions of 20 minutes supplement group instruction for those students who are falling behind. Tutoring sessions emphasize the same strategies and skills as classroom reading activities. Where possible, the classroom teacher also is the child's tutor. Most children attend a half-day preschool and a full-day kindergarten the following year.

The Winston-Salem Project

This project has operated in the first-grade classroom of two schools in Winston-Salem, North Carolina, USA. One school serves students from middle-class backgrounds; the other serves students from low socioeconomic backgrounds. In both schools classroom instruction is reorganized into four 30-minute blocks in which students are instructed in heterogeneous groups.

The Basal block consists primarily of selective use of instructional suggestions from a recently published basal reading program that includes an anthology of children's literature and accompanying paperback books. The Writing block consists of 5- to 10-minute minilessons and student independent writing activities. The Working with Words block consists of "word wall" activities in which students learn to read and spell words that are posted by the teacher each week, and a "making words" activity in which students manipulate groups of letters to form as many words as possible. During the Self-Selected Reading block, students read self-selected books, including informational books related to science and social studies topics.

First-grade teachers who initially implemented the program were encouraged by the reading progress of their students, but believed many of the students needed continued support. Therefore, they continued to teach the same class of students, using the same intervention procedures, through the second grade.

Students in the project spend a sizable amount of time in reading-related activities—a total of 3 hours and 15 minutes. At the school with a high proportion of at-risk students an additional 45 minutes of small-group instruction is added to the schedule. Small-group size is achieved by having Chapter 1 and special education teachers teach reading during these 45 minutes.

Early Intervention in Reading (EIR)

This first-grade intervention program has been implemented in several schools in the state of Minnesota, USA, representing both middle and lower socioeconomic levels. It is conducted almost completely by the regular classroom teacher. In addition to their regular reading instruction, these teachers work daily with the 5–7 lowest achieving students in each of their classes for an additional 20 minutes of reading instruction.

The small-group instruction focuses on the repeated reading of picture books or summaries of these books and on developing students' phonemic segmentation, blending abilities, and other word recognition skills. Students also work individually or in pairs for 5 minutes with an aide, a parent volunteer, or the teacher rereading materials from their small-group instruction sessions.

The Boulder Project

This program involves Chapter 1 teachers and students from two schools. The project involves reorganizing and modifying Chapter 1 instruction.

In order to create small groups, a Chapter 1 teacher works with three children for 30 minutes each day while a teacher's aide instructs another group of three children at the same time. Midway through the school year the teacher and the aide exchange groups. It appears that the teacher plans and coordinates students' instructional programs. The program focuses on the repeated reading of predictable tradebooks, teaching word identification skills through the use of analogy or word patterns, writing words from the word pattern instruction, and writing about topics of choice in notebooks.

Reading Recovery

Reading Recovery is an individual tutoring program in which a tutor meets with a child for 30 minutes each day outside the child's regular classroom. Although the tutor determines instructional strategies, Reading Recovery lessons operate within a clearly defined framework. Each day teachers and students are involved in five major activities.

The first activity is the reading of familiar stories. Students read at least two stories from books they have read previously. Second, the teacher takes a running record of a book that was introduced to the student the previous day. A running record is a set of notations that records the child's oral reading. Next is working with letters, though letter activities can occur at several points in the lesson. Fourth, the child dictates a sentence or short story that the teacher records and then rereads to the child, guiding her or him to write it accurately. The teacher then rewrites the message on a strip of paper, cuts it into individual words, and asks the child to reconstruct the message. This material is taken home daily for further practice. The final activity is the reading of a new book. Before reading, the teacher and child thoroughly explore the book and the teacher introduces concepts, language of the story, or specific vocabulary items as needed.

Comparing the Five Programs

Relation of Early Intervention to Regular Classroom Instruction

The five programs vary greatly in their coordination with or connection to the reading instruction in the students' regular classrooms. Reading Recovery and the Boulder Project appear to be exclusively supplemental programs that assume no responsibility for the students' regular classroom reading instruction; both are conducted outside the classrooms. This is not to suggest that either program fails to recognize the importance of the ongoing classroom instruction that children receive. Clay (1985), who developed Reading Recovery procedures, states:

> The first essential of a satisfactory early intervention program is to have a good reading instruction program in the schools.... Against the background of a sound general program it is possible to develop a strategy for reducing the number of children with reading difficulties. (p. 48)

However, the descriptions of the Reading Recovery and Boulder Project do not address the complex issue of how to improve poor classroom reading instruction.

Although EIR instruction is implemented primarily by the students' regular classroom teacher and takes place within the classroom, no mention is made of attempts to alter the classroom reading instruction or to coordinate classroom activities with the EIR instruction, which is simply added to the classroom schedule.

Success for All and the Winston-Salem Project, on the other hand, involve classroom instructional changes at several grade levels. Success for All provides preschool and full-day kindergarten experiences for all students and implements a clearly defined approach to teaching reading. Chapter 1 teachers, schoolwide special education teachers, and Success for All tutors provide classroom reading instruction in order to reduce reading group size. Students in Grades 1 to 3 are grouped across all classes according to their reading achievement.

The Winston-Salem Project also seems focused on schoolwide change. Classroom reading instruction is organized into four instructional blocks for all students, whether at risk or not. An additional 45 minutes of instruction is provided for all students at the school serving a high percentage of at-risk students.

Quality instruction for at-risk students in the regular classroom is desirable. Allington and McGill-Franzen (1989) document the need for improving classroom instruction for at-risk students and for coordinating regular and compensatory instruction. Although the positive effects of all five programs are well documented, the impact of some might be even greater if classroom instruction were improved. School districts or schools that are adding early intervention programs also should carefully review their regular instruction. Efforts should be made to ensure that students receive quality classroom reading instruction that is carefully coordinated with the compensatory instruction.

Organization for Early Intervention

Success for All and EIR use some individual tutoring, and Reading Recovery employs it exclusively. Most EIR instruction takes place in small groups, and Success for All provides moderate-sized group instruction with individual tutoring for students needing extra help. Small-group instruction is used by the Boulder (three students) and Winston-Salem (five to six students) projects.

Wasik and Slavin (1993) reviewed evidence that one-to-one tutoring is the most powerful form of instruction. The positive results of the EIR and the Boulder Project, however, suggest that at least some at-risk students can make progress with very small group instruction. In a comprehensive program of early intervention it might be efficient to begin with small-group instruction, but to move to one-to-one tutoring for students who are not making sufficient progress.

Amount of Instructional Time

In all five programs students spend more time in reading and writing activities than do students not at risk but none of the early-intervention programs was a substitute for regular classroom instruction. In the three add-on programs, students receive about 30 extra minutes of individual or small-group reading instruction. Of the two classroom intervention programs, the Winston-Salem Project seems more ambitious in terms of time allotment—over 2 hours of instruction in the four blocks, with an additional 45 minutes of small-group instruction in some schools. Success for All involves 90 minutes of reduced-sized group classroom instruction and 20 minutes of tutoring.

Devoting extra time to reading instruction appears a necessary but not sufficient factor for at-risk student success. For example, Hiebert et al. (1992) compared the progress of the students in their Boulder Project against a comparison group of students who received an equal amount of special help in a traditional program. The comparison group made essentially no demonstrable progress in reading during first grade in spite of extra instructional time. Lyons, Place, and Rinehart (1990) report similar results in a study comparing Reading Recovery and Chapter 1 programs. Indeed, there is little evidence to suggest that added time for reading instruction in many compensatory or special education programs yields positive effects (Rowan & Guthrie,

1989). Indeed, one study (Glass & Smith, 1977) suggests that the more time at-risk students spent in some pull-out, compensatory programs, the poorer their progress. Although additional time for reading seems essential, what is done instructionally during that time is what makes the difference.

Length of Intervention

Reading Recovery has a clearly specified time frame. It is exclusively a first-grade program, and intervention lasts until a student is achieving at an average level for his or her class, or for up to a maximum of 100 sessions. EIR also is exclusively a first-grade program that lasts most of the school year. The Boulder Project is a first-grade program, but Hiebert et al. (1992) note that some children need, and should receive, help beyond first grade. The Winston-Salem Project echoes this sentiment and has extended the project into second grade. The philosophy of Success for All seems to have been laid down from its inception—the amount and intensity of intervention must vary with students' needs; some will require preschool intervention, home support, and help during and beyond primary grades.

At-risk students' needs will be met most fully and efficiently only if intervention programs of various durations are available. A growing case can be made that treatment is most effective if it comes early in a child's school career—in first grade or perhaps even before; however, some students will need additional, intense support beyond first grade.

Types of Texts and Materials Used

A great variety of texts is used in these programs. Predictable, easy-to-read texts and authentic tradebooks are extremely popular for first-grade classroom use. Such texts also figure prominently in these programs and seem, with the possible exception of Success for All, to be the major type of texts used. Each project uses texts that students can read successfully; initial texts are easy, and those introduced thereafter present increasing levels of challenge.

There is a very clear absence of traditional workbook and isolated skill practice materials in all of the programs. The Winston-Salem Project mentions the use of workbooks, but these are part of a recently published reading program, which emphasizes open-ended responses rather than isolated skill-drill or multiple-choice items.

Success for All and the Winston-Salem Project include the use of basal materials. In addition, Success for All uses kindergarten and first-grade texts specifically written to include vocabulary that exercises phonic skills. The Boulder Project includes the use of "little books" that appear to be written with vocabulary that focuses on word patterns taught to students.

All these successful projects rely on texts that use natural, noncontrolled vocabulary, but only Reading Recovery uses them exclusively. The others use some specially written texts in order to reduce reading demands or exercise word recognition skills. An example of the latter is EIR's use of written summaries of trade books in the beginning phases of intervention. Later, complete trade books are used.

Some combination of this variety of text types seems ideal. For example, predictable texts are particularly advantageous at the beginning stages of intervention, because students can use extratextual clues such as recurring phrases or strong picture clues, but students sometimes become overly focused on such clues and pay insufficient attention to word-level information. The Boulder Project's use of pictureless versions of some books is a reasonable approach to this potential problem.

There is great value in using interesting, motivating, quality literature, but it also seems possible to develop texts, as in the Success for All and Boulder Projects, that specifically attempt to exercise word identification skills. These books also can be interesting and motivating. Dr. Seuss creations such as *The Cat in the Hat* were written with vocabulary restrictions but have become favorites of children.

Text-Level Strategies

The instructional strategies of all five programs show that classifying beginning reading programs as either code emphasis or meaning emphasis is a myth that has far too long been argued by extremists. Each program is clearly oriented toward ensuring that students conceptualize reading as a meaning-construction process, but each also emphasizes teaching word identification strategies to help students become independent readers. There is a firm research base for the position that a balance between the reading of meaningful, connected texts and systematic word identification instruction results in superior achievement (Adams, 1990).

In all five programs repeated reading is the most common instructional activity with books and other texts. The impact of repeated reading on young readers' developing fluency is well documented (for example, Dowhower, 1987; Herman, 1985; Samuels, 1979). The procedures used vary. In Reading Recovery, the teacher familiarizes the student with the content and vocabulary of a new book, the student does a first reading and then reads the same book the next day. Finally, the book becomes part of a library from which the student can choose books for later rereadings. Other programs have students do repeated readings in pairs or small groups. The number of times the texts are reread varies from program to program, and the number of times

a particular book is read varies even within a program. Although instruction in comprehension strategies is provided, most of the instructional time is spent with text-level activities designed to develop word recognition fluency, because poor word identification skills are a major stumbling block for these students.

Word-Level Strategies

All of the programs include instruction that focuses students' attention on letters and words. EIR, Reading Recovery, and Success for All include very deliberate instruction in phonemic awareness—ensuring that children develop a conscious understanding that spoken words are composed of identifiable sounds. Success for All and EIR also provide instruction in blending sounds into words. Both the Winston-Salem and Boulder Projects focus on working with word patterns (such as, *in*, *pin*, *tin*), based on the work of Cunningham (1991). The specific approaches to word recognition vary among the programs, but systematic instruction in word recognition is a major focus for all programs.

Writing Component

All five programs prominently include writing activities, most of which seem geared to reinforce word recognition. As Clay (1985) writes, "A case can be made for the theory that learning to write letters, words and sentences actually helps the child to make the visual discriminations of detailed print that he will use in his reading" (p. 54). Clarke (1988) also suggests a positive effect of writing on reading progress, particularly for at-risk students. In some of the programs (Reading Recovery, EIR, and the Boulder Project) the writing activities are brief: Students write a few words, a sentence, or a few sentences related to the vocabulary in stories they are reading or word patterns that have been taught. More extended writing is included in the Winston-Salem and Success for All programs, both of which operate as classroom instruction models as well as supplementary programs.

Assessment Procedures

All five projects include regular, ongoing assessment. In Reading Recovery running records are taken daily as a check of reading fluency. In EIR, running records are taken every 3 days. The Boulder Project checks oral reading weekly and includes more extensive assessments quarterly. Oral reading is monitored in all three supplementary programs. This seems appropriate, because word recognition is a prominent difficulty for their students. In Success for All students are formally evaluated every 8 weeks. Writing portfolios are kept for students in the Winston-Salem Project, and teacher observations are also considered important. Successful early intervention programs include systematic, regular assessment in order to monitor progress and provide a basis for instructional planning.

Home Connections

Only the Winston-Salem Project fails to mention efforts to extend instructional time by having students take materials home for reading to parents or others. However, this may be an oversight, because the project description notes dramatically greater parent participation in school activities since the initiation of the project. Success for All has the most substantial parent component, including establishing a parent support team at every school. Students in Success for All schools are expected to read books from classroom libraries at home for 20 minutes every day. Boulder Project students are expected to take

books home nightly and are rewarded with gift books for regular at-home reading. In EIR, students are expected to read a story summary at home every third day. In Reading Recovery students take a sentence or two home for reading each day and also are encouraged to take home books and read them. Although the amount of home reading expected of students varies, at-home reading appears as a consistent element in all projects.

Teacher Training

All five programs use experienced, certified teachers, and two use teacher aides. In the EIR program, an aide may meet briefly with one or two children to listen to them read a story; however, the instruction is conducted by the regular classroom teacher who has been trained in EIR procedures. In the Boulder Project a teacher aide conducts the same activities as a certified teacher, who is responsible for planning and decision making.

All five programs have built-in consultation available at least throughout the first year of implementation. Teachers who are using the intervention for the first year can meet with others who are familiar with the program. This is an important point for anyone who is planning to initiate an early intervention program.

Reading Recovery provides the most defined and intense consultation. First-year teachers meet weekly with teacher leaders. These meetings include observations of the first-year teachers working with students and follow-up discussions of instructional strategies. The Boulder and EIR projects seem to include more flexibly scheduled, less intense consultation.

The length of initial teacher training varies. Again, Reading Recovery is most specific. Teachers attend a 30-hour workshop before the beginning of the school year and also meet $2^{1}/_{2}$ hours weekly thereafter for the first year. Teachers in the Winston-Salem Project meet for a week before the school year and spend an unspecified amount of time in consultation with the curriculum coordinator through the year. The Success for All program and the EIR program provide only 1 or 2 days of training before the beginning of the school year. The written information about the Boulder Project does not describe training prior to the beginning of the school year.

General Conclusions

Those planning early intervention programs in reading should consider the multiple dimensions of these five programs. It seems reasonable to conclude that attention to the following issues will increase the probability of program success.

• Students' total program of reading instruction should be considered when planning for early intervention. Tutoring and extra time pull-out programs certainly can be effective; however, for maximum impact, early intervention programs should try to ensure that students are receiving excellent and coordinated instruction both in their classrooms and in the special intervention programs.

• Children who are experiencing difficulty with reading should spend more time receiving reading instruction than children who are not experiencing difficulty. Quality instruction must be provided during this extra time.

• For at-risk children to be successful readers, individual or very small group (no more than four or five students) instruction is essential. Some children definitely will require one-to-one tutoring.

• Special reading instruction for at-risk students is most profitably focused on first grade. Where school resources are limited, they should be spent on first-grade intervention that leads to the prevention of reading difficulties. Some students will need support beyond first grade.

• Texts for early intervention programs should be very simple so that students will be successful in reading them. Predictable texts have merit, particularly at the beginning stages of the program. Interesting literature that uses natural language patterns seems important although texts constructed to encourage application of word identification skills also may be beneficial.

• Reading the same text several times is a very effective approach to helping at-risk children develop reading fluency. Instructional procedures should ensure that students see reading as an act of constructing meaning.

• In early intervention programs, at-risk children need instruction that focuses their attention on words and letters. Phonemic awareness and phonics instruction should be included. Focusing on word patterns also appears to have merit.

• Writing is important in early intervention programs. When children write words they attend to the details of those words, which supports development of word identification skills. Students should write daily, the writing activities should be relatively brief, and the instruction should ensure that students focus attention on features and details of letters and words.

• Ongoing assessment that monitors student progress is necessary. The assessment of oral reading fluency is an informative, effective assessment procedure.

• Effective early intervention programs encourage communication between home and school. Students should be provided with materials for daily reading at home.

• Professionally prepared, accomplished teachers are the mainstay of successful early intervention programs. Initial training should be provided so that teachers learn to deliver consistently effective instruction. Continuous professional support also should be available, at least through a teacher's first year of implementation.

The devastating effects of reading failure are widely acknowledged. Stanovich (1986) offers cogent arguments and good evidence that children who encounter problems in the beginning stages of learning to read fall further and further behind their peers—the poor do get poorer. A substantial portion of the enormous amount of money spent annually on marginally, if at all, effective compensatory and special education programs needs to be redirected toward preventing initial reading failure. It is time we built the water treatment plant!

REFERENCES

Adams, M.J. (1990). *Beginning to read: Thinking and learning about print.* Cambridge, MA: MIT Press.

Allington, R., & McGill-Franzen, A. (1989). School response to reading failure: Instruction for Chapter 1 and special education students in grades two, four, and eight. *The Elementary School Journal, 89,* 529–542.

Archambault, F.X. (1989). Instructional setting and other design features of compensatory education programs. In R.E. Slavin, N.L. Karweit, & N.A. Madden (Eds.), *Effective programs for students at risk* (pp. 220–261). Boston, MA: Allyn & Bacon.

Clarke, L.K. (1988). Invented versus traditional spelling in first graders' writings: Effects on learning to spell and read. *Research in the Teaching of English, 22,* 281–309.

Clay, M.M. (1985). *The early detection of reading difficulties.* Portsmouth, NH: Heinemann.

Cunningham, P.M. (1991). *Phonics they use: Words for reading and writing.* New York: HarperCollins.

Dowhower, S.L. (1987). Effects of repeated reading on second-grade transitional readers' fluency and comprehension. *Reading Research Quarterly, 22,* 389–406.

Dyer, P. (1992). Reading Recovery: A cost-effectiveness and educational-outcomes analysis. *ERS Spectrum, 10,* 10–19.

Glass, G.V., & Smith, M.L. (1977). *Pull-out in compensatory education.* Washington, DC: U.S. Department of Health, Education, and Welfare.

Hall, D.P., Prevatte, C., & Cunningham, P.M. (1993). *Elementary ability grouping and failure in the primary grades.* Unpublished manuscript.

Herman, P.A. (1985). The effects of repeated readings on reading rate, speech, pauses, and word recognition accuracy. *Reading Research Quarterly, 29,* 553–564.

Hiebert, E.H., Colt, J.M., Catto, S.L., & Gury, E.C. (1992). Reading and writing of first-grade students in a restructured Chapter 1 program. *American Educational Research Journal, 29,* 545–572.

Hiebert, E., & Taylor, B. (Eds.). (1994). *Getting reading right from the start: Effective early literacy interventions.* Needham, MA: Allyn & Bacon.

Kennedy, M.M., Birman, B.F., Demaline, R.E. (1986). *The effectiveness of Chapter 1 services.* Washington, DC: U.S. Department of Education Office of Educational Research and Improvement.

Lyons, C.A., Place, W., & Rinehart, J. (1990). *Factors related to teaching success in the literacy education of young at-risk children* (Tech. Rep. No. 10). Columbus, OH: The Ohio State University.

Madden, N.A., Slavin, R.E., Karweit, N.L., Dolan, L.J., & Wasik, B.A. (1991). Success for All: Ending reading failure from the beginning. *Language Arts, 68,* 47–52.

Ohio State University. (1990). *Reading Recovery 1984–1990.* Columbus, OH: Author.

Pinnell, G.S. (1989). Reading Recovery: Helping at-risk children learn to read. *The Elementary School Journal, 90,* 161–183.

Pinnell, G.S., Fried, M.D., & Estice, R.M. (1990). Reading Recovery: Learning how to make a difference. *The Reading Teacher, 43,* 282–295.

Reynolds, A.J. (1991). Early schooling of children at risk. *American Educational Research Journal, 28,* 392–422.

Rowan, B., & Guthrie, L.F. (1989). The quality of Chapter 1 instruction: Results from a study of twenty four schools. In R.E. Slavin, N.L. Karweit, & N.A. Madden (Eds.), *Effective programs for students at risk* (pp. 195–219). Boston, MA: Allyn & Bacon.

Samuels, S.J. (1979). The method of repeated readings. *The Reading Teacher, 32,* 403–408.

Slavin, R.E. (1989). Students at-risk of school failure: The problem and its dimensions. In R.E. Slavin, N.L. Karweit, & N.A. Madden (Eds.), *Effective programs for students at risk* (pp. 3–23). Boston, MA: Allyn & Bacon.

Slavin, R.E., Madden, N.A., Karweit, N.L., Livermon, B.J., & Dolan, L. (1990). Success for All: First year outcomes of a comprehensive plan for reforming urban education. *American Educational Research Journal, 27,* 255–278.

Slavin, R., Madden, N., Karweit, N., Dolan, L., & Wasik, B. (1991). Research directions; Success for All: Ending reading failure from the beginning. *Language Arts, 68,* 404–409.

Slavin, R.E., Madden, N.L., Karweit, N.L., Dolan, L., & Wasik, B.A. (1992). *Success for All: A relentless approach to prevention and early intervention in elementary schools.* Arlington, VA: Educational Research Service.

Slavin, R.E., Karweit, N.L., & Wasik, B.A. (Eds.). (1993). *Preventing early school failure: Research on effective strategies.* Boston, MA: Allyn & Bacon.

Smith, B.J., & Strain, P.S. (1988). *Does early intervention help?* Reston, VA: Council for Exceptional Children.

Stanovich, K.E. (1986). Matthew effects in reading: Some consequences of individual differences in the acquisition of literacy. *Reading Research Quarterly, 21,* 360–407.

Taylor, B.M., Frye, B.J., Short, R., & Shearer, B. (1992). Classroom teachers prevent reading failure among low-achieving first-grade students. *The Reading Teacher, 45,* 592–597.

Taylor, B.M., Strait, J., & Medo, M.A. (1994). Early intervention in reading: Supplementary instruction for groups of low achieving students provided by first grade teachers. In E.H. Hiebert & B.M. Taylor (Eds.), *Getting reading right from the start: Effective early literacy interventions* (pp. 107–121). Needham Heights, MA: Allyn & Bacon.

Wasik, B.A., & Slavin, R.E. (1993). Preventing early reading failure with one-to-one tutoring: A review of five programs. *Reading Research Quarterly, 28,* 178–200.

Teachers as Evaluation Experts

Peter Johnston

The process through which we examine and keep track of children's literacy development is currently dominated by multiple-choice, product-oriented, group-administered, norm-referenced reading tests. These tests have been developed in the names of science and efficiency by "experts" so that the teacher need only be a technician who administers a test and later receives scores.

The goal is to collect efficiently objective data which can be used for a variety of purposes such as classification, accountability, and progress monitoring. However, these so-called goals are properly subgoals. The most fundamental goal of all educational evaluation is optimal instruction for all children and evaluation practices are only legitimate to the extent that they serve this goal.

In this context, current evaluation practices are extraordinarily inefficient and we have been valuing the wrong sort of evaluation expertise. Rather than refining tests and testing, we should be dealing with the fact that the bulk of instructional decision making takes place in the classroom on a moment to moment basis. Teachers must evaluate individual students' needs and respond to them. Informal observations and hunches about how and why children behave in particular ways form the basis of instructional decisions far more than do test scores (Shavelson & Stern, 1981).

Thus we must ensure that teachers' hunches and informal observations are as accurate, insightful, and valid as possible. In other words we must help teachers become experts at evaluating the process of literacy development.

Detecting Patterns

What are characteristics of an expert in classroom literacy evaluation? A very important characteristic of experts in general is their ability to recognize patterns. A good analogy for classroom evaluation expertise is provided by chess masters who recognize approximately 50,000 board patterns (Chase & Simon, 1973). If we think of students engaging in recognizable patterns of behavior that are motivated, organized, and goal directed, the analogy to the chess master is accurate. Indeed, Peterson and Comeaux (1985) found that expert teachers could recall many more incidents from videotapes of teaching than could novice teachers.

The analogy is most appropriate in exhibition matches in which a master chess player plays 20 or 30 club players simultaneously. The analogy is not perfect, however. The chess player faces a less complex problem, because the context beyond the board is of little concern. Teachers, on the other hand, must not only know what patterns to look for but also know the conditions under which the patterns are likely to occur. In a sense, unless teachers understand the patterns *and* how and where to look for them, they simply will not see them.

A novice at classroom evaluation will pick up the sample of beginning writing in this article and see scribble. The expert will look at the same piece and see signs of the child's development of hypotheses about the nature of written language, an understanding of the format of a letter, the development of some concepts about print, skill at phonemic segmentation, and a strong "literacy set." In addition, the expert will have spent some time watching the writing being done, and possibly discussing it with the author, enabling an even more insightful analysis.

Similarly, the novice listens to oral reading, including disfluency and self-correction, and simply hears many errors. The expert hears in the same rendition the development of voice-print matching, prediction, self-monitoring, self-correction, and independent learning. The expert has knowledge of reading and writing processes and of the process of development.

Knowing Classroom Procedures

Aside from the ability to see and hear patterns in the development of reading and writing processes, experts have procedural knowledge. In the case of the classroom evaluation expert, this involves, for example, how to set a context so that certain behaviors are most likely to occur, how to record those behaviors, file and update the records, and prevent some children from being missed.

The expert would know, for example, how to keep (and interpret) regular running records (Clay, 1985) of children's oral reading behaviors and use them to describe reading growth. An expert also will know how to keep

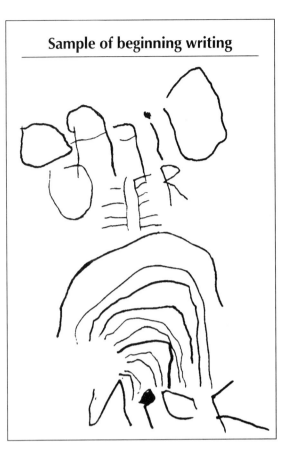

Sample of beginning writing

writing files, schedule interviews with individual children, and plan and carry out daily observations of the children's independent literacy behaviors.

Even simple classroom management skills are part of evaluation expertise. Without a well-managed classroom in which the children have learned to work independently, a teacher cannot step back from instruction and watch the class as a whole, or work uninterrupted with particular individuals.

Listening

Teachers who are evaluation experts have even more complex skills. They know how important it is to listen and they know how to listen with appropriate attention, patience, and thoughtful questioning.

Listening is at the heart of the writing conference portrayed by Graves (1983) and others and the interview described by Nicholson (1984). Listening, the expert evaluator strives to understand the child's understanding of the reading or writing process and helps the child come to grips with what he or she is doing and how to extend it.

Conferences, which last about 5 minutes, are focused and concern manageably sized pieces of information. Both teacher and student are likely to respond to such exchanges actively and accurately.

Evaluation That Serves Instruction

To suggest that individualized evaluation is efficient may seem counterintuitive. But consider this. Efficiency is the ability to produce the desired effect with a minimum of effort, expense, or waste. Evaluation procedures have been designed to produce efficiently the sort of objective data that can be compared across individuals and groups, but they are singularly inefficient at helping attain the goal of optimal instruction for all children. Indeed, in many ways they afford obstructions to this end and are expensive and wasteful (see Frederiksen, 1984; Johnston, 1987).

Test-centered evaluation procedures cast teacher and learner in fundamentally adversarial roles that preclude effective teaching, but classroom evaluation is process oriented and requires the teacher to adopt the role of an advocate (Graves, 1983). An advocate sits beside the child at a comparable height, engaging in eye contact, and waits to be offered the child's work. This role conveys respect, recognizable control by both parties, and a recognition that the learner's concerns deserve serious consid-

eration. Holdaway (1979) refers to this as a professional-client relationship. It is a relationship based on trust that involves the alignment of the goals and task definitions of teacher and student and the development of collaboration. The concept is reflected clearly in the early reading evaluation work of Clay (1985). Her informal "running records" and more formal Concepts About Print test both involve the teacher and student sitting side by side sharing the same text and working toward the same end.

This view of evaluation implies the need to liberate teachers and students from the disempowering and isolating burden of centralized accountability testing. The cost of this liberty is increased responsibility on the part of the classroom teacher, some of which is passed on to the student. A learning process or teaching process (or any other process for that matter) cannot be controlled without feedback.

Empowering the Learner

Process-oriented evaluation strongly emphasizes the development of continual self-evaluation so that learners may be responsible for and direct their own learning. Not only are self-assessed difficulties caught at the most teachable point, but the development of self-evaluation is critical if learners are to become independent.

Indeed, probably the clearest indicator of reading difficulties is failure to self-correct. Similarly, self-evaluation is at the center of the revision and editing processes in writing. Process-oriented evaluation is thus continually directed toward causing "intelligent unrest." Teachers ask reflective questions, questions that teach (Graves, 1983). These questions provide the teacher with information, but also give responsibility back to the student and simultaneously model the self-evaluation process.

Teachers often are encouraged to model reading processes, but rarely to model self-evaluation. Similarly, they do not seem to be encouraged to model listening. The type of questioning to which I have referred is part of listening. Indeed, Easley and Zwoyer (1975) refer to this general notion as "teaching by listening."

By making process evaluation an integral part of teaching and learning, we get multiple returns on our time investment, and at the same time, in good management style, we delegate responsibility for evaluation to those closest to the teaching-learning process, making that process more efficient.

Timely Assessment

Individualized, process-oriented evaluation by the teacher can boast even more efficiency. The roles of teacher and evaluator allow teaching and evaluation to occur at the same time, while encouraging and modeling independence. The information gathered is instructionally more relevant and timely, and teachers are more likely to use it. When teachers observe a child actually performing a task, the knowledge they gain will influence their instructional interactions because the teacher "owns" it. If the information is secondhand, no matter how detailed, it is much less likely to influence the automatic instructional interactions.

Some may respond "Of course we need such evaluation but we need *real* evaluation too." I want it clearly understood that this *is* the real evaluation. There is a place for the more intrusive norm-referenced, product-oriented approach but it is a small one, certainly much smaller than the pretentious position it currently occupies.

Showing Our Skill

One cannot be an expert teacher without being an expert evaluator, and I hope that it is apparent that this expertise is complex and does not simply come with years of classroom experience. Indeed, as Marie Clay points out, such experience can easily produce a "naive theory that prevents accurate observation." Teachers should not expect this expertise to be gained without effort. There is much to know.

If teachers are ever to gain public trust and win professional status we must show that we are responsible. Athough children are our primary clients, parents, among others, have rights too.

When parents wish to know about their child's development, there should be no hesitation. A teacher should be able to say "Let me show you how Jane has developed since last month. This is what she was doing at the beginning of the year. Last month she had developed to this point. Now she has begun to...." As The Scottish Council for Educational Research put it:

> We stopped short of asking the parents bluntly: "Do you trust the teachers?" If they do not, then it is time we took steps to remedy our public relations. If we are not to be trusted, then the whole edifice of the school falls down, whatever the external supports. We have to show that we can be trusted.... *Perhaps if we prove that we know our pupils, this will challenge the community to value our work more highly.* (Broadfoot, 1979, p. 23, italics added.)

I have a simple test of teacher evaluation expertise that can be used as a self-test. Look at the extent and quality of an impromptu description of a particular child's literacy development. Two features that will be most evident in an expert's description will be an emphasis on processes and an emphasis on what the child can do.

Unless we know our children it is not possible to tailor our instruction to their needs, particularly in the language arts, which require a supportive, communicative context.

We must observe and listen, and if they will not talk, we cannot listen.

This principle holds at levels of evaluation outside the classroom. Indeed, without the foundation of trusting relationships at all levels, development of the educational enterprise will be beyond our grasp.

REFERENCES

Broadfoot, P. (1979). *Assessment, schools and society*. New York: Methuen.

Chase, W., & Simon, H. (1973). Perception in chess. *Cognitive Psychology, 4*, 55–81.

Clay, M. (1985). *The early detection of reading difficulties* (3rd ed.). Portsmouth, NH: Heinemann.

Easley, J., & Zwoyer, R. (1975). Teaching by listening—toward a new day in math classes. *Contemporary Education, 47*, 19–25.

Frederiksen, N. (1984). The real test bias: Influences of testing on teaching and learning. *American Psychologist, 39*, 193–202.

Graves, D. (1983). *Writing: Teachers and children at work*. Exeter, NH: Heinemann.

Holdaway, D. (1979). *The foundations of literacy*. Gosford, Australia: Ashton-Scholastic.

Johnston, P. (1987). Assessing the process, and the process of assessment, in the language arts. In J. Squire (Ed.), *The dynamics of language learning: Research in reading & English arts*. Urbana, IL: National Council of Teachers of English.

Nicholson, T. (1984). You get lost when you gotta blimmin watch the damn words: The low progress reader in the junior high school. *Topics in Learning and Learning Disabilities, 3*, 16–23.

Peterson, P., & Comeaux, M. (1985, April). *Teachers' schemata for learners and classrooms: The mental scaffolding of teachers' thoughts during classroom instruction*. Paper presented at the annual meeting of the American Educational Research Association, Chicago, IL.

Shavelson, R., & Stern, P. (1981). Research on teachers' pedagogical thoughts, judgments, decisions, and behavior. *Review of Educational Research, 41*, 455–498.

SECTION II

Organizing Instruction to Meet Diverse Student Needs

Mobilizing expertise is one of the challenges faced in most schools. Many schools have available knowledge and resources but do not know how to structure these resources to meet diverse student needs. The articles in this section were selected because they focus on approaches for mobilizing the expertise available in many schools, looking primarily at the practical dilemmas that student diversity creates and different school responses to adjusting instructional planning and delivery. It may seem odd that the section begins with an article on anecdotal records but I selected it and placed it at the beginning because responding to student diversity requires us to have in place a system for gathering useful information about that instructional diversity. There is no more appropriate basis for planning than individual student needs. Thus each article in this section offers ideas for effective instructional planning to adjust classroom instruction—both for reading and content learning—and to adjust specialized instructional support services such as reading teachers and learning disability consultants. But meeting individual needs does not mean that instruction is limited to tutorials. Individual needs can and should be met through a variety of student grouping arrangements— a critical, but often overlooked, aspect of instructional planning.

Anecdotal Records: A Powerful Tool for Ongoing Literacy Assessment

Lynn K. Rhodes, Sally Nathenson-Mejia

A great deal of attention is being paid to the assessment of process in addition to product in reading and writing. Observing a student's process provides the teacher with a window or view on how students arrive at products (that is, a piece of writing or an answer to a comprehension question). This allows the teacher to make good decisions about how he or she might assist during the process or restructure the process in order to best support more effective use of strategies and students' development as readers and writers. Anecdotal records can be written about products or can include information about both process and product. As process assessment, resulting from observation, anecdotal records can be particularly telling.

Observations of students in the process of everyday reading and writing allow teachers to see for themselves the reading, writing, and problem-solving strategies students use and their responses to reading and writing. Genishi and Dyson (1984), Jaggar (1985), Pinnell (1985), Y. Goodman (1985), Galindo (1989), and others discuss the need to observe children while they are involved in language use. Goodman notes:

> Evaluation provides the most significant information if it occurs continuously and simultaneously with the experiences in which the learning is taking place....Teachers who observe the development of language and knowledge in children in different settings become aware of important milestones in children's development that tests cannot reveal. (p. 10)

When teachers have developed a firm knowledge base that they can rely on in observations of students' reading and writing, they usually prefer recording their observations in anecdotal form. This is because the open-ended nature of anecdotal records allows teachers to record the rich detail available in most observations of literacy processes and products. The open-ended nature of anecdotal record taking also allows teachers to determine what details are important to record given the situation in which the student is reading and writing, previous assessment data, and the instructional goals the teacher and student have established. In other words, what is focused on and recorded depends on the teacher, the student, and the context, not on the predetermined items on a checklist.

Taken regularly, anecdotal notes become not only a vehicle for planning instruction and documenting progress, but also a story about an individual. The definition of an anecdote is "a short narrative (or story) concerning a particular incident or event of an interesting or amusing nature" (*The Random House Dictionary of the English Language*, 1966). A story is "a way of knowing and remembering information—a shape or pattern into which information can be arranged....[A story] restructures experiences for the purpose of 'saving' them" (Livo, 1986, p. 5). Anecdotes about events in the reading and writing life of a student tell an ongoing story about how that child responds to the classroom's literacy environment and instruction. Because stories are how we make sense of much of our world, anecdotal records can be a vehicle for helping us make sense of what students do as readers and writers. In addition, teachers find that telling the story accumulated in anecdotal records is a natural and easy way to impart information about students' literacy progress to parents and other caregivers.

In short, anecdotal records are widely acknowledged as being a powerful classroom tool for ongoing literacy assessment (Bird, 1989; Cartwright & Cartwright, 1974; Morrissey, 1989; Thorndike & Hagen, 1977). In this article we will provide information about techniques for collecting and analyzing anecdotal records. In addition, we will review uses of anecdotal records including planning for instruction, informing parents and students, and generating new assessment questions.

Techniques for Writing Anecdotal Records

Reflecting about techniques for writing anecdotal records can positively affect both the content of the records as well as the ease with which they are recorded. Thorndike and Hagen (1977) suggest guidelines for the content of anecdotal records that teachers may find helpful:

1. Describe a specific event or product.

2. Report rather than evaluate or interpret.

3. Relate the material to other facts that are known about the child.

We have found these points particularly helpful if teachers feel that the content of their previous anecdotal records has not been useful to them. Below we have included an example of an anecdotal record for a first grader, Eleanor. Note how Eleanor's teacher uses detailed description to record how Eleanor is starting to understand sound-letter relations, but is still confused about word boundaries and sentences.

> Eleanor
> STRDAIPADENBSNO
> (Yesterday I played in the snow)
> STRDA = yesterday
> I = I
> PAD = played
> EN = in
> B = the (said "du" and thought she was writing "D")
> SNO = snow
>
> Showed her how to stretch her words out like a rubberband—doing it almost on her own by SNO. E does have a fairly good grasp of sound/letter relations. However, has a hard time isolating words and tracking words in sentences in her mind. That may hold up progress for awhile. Asked her—at end—what she did in writing today that she hadn't done in previous writing. She said, "I listened to sounds." Told her to do it in her writing again tomorrow.

Instead of recording the descriptive detail found in Eleanor's anecdotal note, the teacher might have written, "Eleanor sounded out words in writing for the first time today and will continue to need lots of help to do so." A general conclusion such as this is not as useful to instructional planning or to documenting progress as the detailed description in the note written by Eleanor's teacher. However, we believe that Thorndike and Hagen's points should be treated as guidelines, not as strict rules. We find that it is sometimes helpful to evaluate or interpret what has been observed. For example, read the sample anecdotal record that follows written about Katie, a fourth grader.

> Katie
>
> I asked if I could read more of the poetry book she had written at home over the last two years. (She had read selected poems to her classmates earlier.) She showed me a poem she didn't want to read to the class "because they wouldn't understand." (It's quite serious and deep.) Poetry doesn't look like poetry though she reads it as poetry—could use a formatting lesson.

The teacher's comment, "could use a formatting lesson," in Katie's note provides useful evaluation and interpretation as long as it is supported by a description of the event or product itself. The comment "Poetry doesn't look like poetry though she reads it as poetry," is the description that supports the interpretive comment.

Observational guides can be valuable complements to anecdotal recording because they serve to remind teachers what might be observed. If teachers find an observation guide helpful, they may want to post for themselves a list of the kinds of observations that might be recorded anecdotally. The Table illustrates such a guide resulting from teachers' brainstorming. The list is displayed in a place in the classroom where the teachers can easily consult it, especially when they feel they need to improve the content of their notes.

In addition to increasing the content value of anecdotal notes, teachers also are concerned about increasing the ease with which anecdotal notes can be recorded. In part, ease of recording emanates from the classroom environment the teacher has established. Classroom routines that encourage students to be increasingly independent and responsible as readers and writers enable teachers to more easily record anecdotal records than classrooms in which literacy tasks are more teacher directed. Once students are familiar with and secure about the structure and behaviors demanded in routines such as Sustained Silent Reading, Author's Circle, Literature Circles, Writers' Workshop, and Readers' Workshop, teachers can find the time to work with and record observations of individuals or groups.

In addition to encouraging student independence and responsibility in literacy situations, it is easier for teachers to write anecdotal notes as they discover recording techniques that fit their styles and busy classroom lives. Carrying a clipboard to a variety of classroom settings is useful, as is using such complementary recording tools as sticky notes to transfer information to a notebook sectioned off by students' names. Teachers can take notes on a prearranged list of children each day, labeling sticky notes with the date and the names of students to be observed. This technique makes it possible to take notes on every child a minimum of once a week in each curricular area in which notes are taken.

Students can keep records too. Following a conference, the teacher might ask the student to record a summary statement of what they worked on together, what the student learned, or what the student still had questions about or wanted help with. Students can use sticky notes too so that their notes may be placed in the notebook along with the teacher's notes.

Teachers can take notes on groups as well as on individuals. For example, in working with a group of Chapter 1 [U.S. federally funded education program for at-risk children now called Title I] students, one teacher noted that all five students were having difficulty putting the information they were gathering from books into their own words as they took notes. Instead of writing the same information five times, she wrote it once and put the note in a spot in her notebook reserved for notes about the group. When a note is taken in a group, but applies only to selected students in the group, the note can be photocopied for the file of each student to whom it applies.

Analyzing Anecdotal Records

Good techniques for recording anecdotal notes must be matched with good techniques for analyzing those notes if the potential for anecdotal records is to be realized. Effective analysis techniques include making inferences from the notes, looking for developmental trends or patterns within individuals and across children, identifying both strengths and weaknesses in learning and teaching, and making time for analysis.

Making Inferences

Teachers continually make inferences about students' reading and writing on the basis of observations. Looking back at the sample anecdotal record on Eleanor, you can see that

Eleanor's teacher made one of her inferences explicit: "E does have a fairly good grasp of sound/letter relations." Because the teacher observed that Eleanor was able to consistently produce letters that matched the sounds she heard, she was able to infer that Eleanor had developed knowledge of sound-letter relations.

Katie's teacher does not explicitly infer anything in the first anecdotal record but it is possible for us to hypothesize that Katie may think she is different from many of her classmates with regard to what she thinks and writes. An analysis of other anecdotal records on Katie may lead the teacher to uncover a pattern in Katie's responses that confirms her hypothesis.

Identifying Patterns

Patterns of behavior can be uncovered for individuals and groups by reading and rereading anecdotal records looking for similarities and differences. For example, the following two notes were taken during a reading period in a second-grade classroom in which the majority of the students elect to read in pairs or small groups. What pattern of behavior do you see?

> Brooke & Larry reading a Nate the Great story together—switching off at each paragraph. Brooke jumps in to correct Larry or give him a word at the slightest hesitation. Aaron & Shawn reading—switching off after every 2 pgs. Shawn loves the story—keeps telling Aaron the next part will be funny & chuckling as he reads aloud. Shawn is the leader in this situation. He interrupts with immediate help when Aaron hesitates with a word.

In recording and reviewing these notes, the teacher noticed that she had observed the same problem in both pairs of readers; one reader would take over the responsibility for working out words from the other reader. Because she had notes on only two pairs of students, however, the teacher interviewed the class the next day, focusing on what they did to help classmates who encountered difficult words to find out whether the pattern she had uncovered in these two situations was a more general problem. Differing patterns in language use, both oral and written, can be seen through regular anecdotal record keeping.

To illustrate with another example, a second-grade teacher, one of our practicum students, was concerned about Raul, who was new to the United States. She felt he was gaining more control over written and oral English, but she had nothing to document his progress. Moreover, she did not want to push him too hard if he was not ready, or cause him to lag behind. The following are excerpts from anecdotal records Sally took as the practicum supervisor while observing Raul working with his peers, none of whom spoke his native Spanish. These notes demonstrate not only his interaction with print, but also his use of oral language.

> The boys begin reading through the questions. Raul looks at the book and says, "Que es esto?" (What is this?) No one answers him. They are sitting next to a chart that has all their names on it. They proceed to copy one anothers' names from the chart. Raul says to the group, "You can get my name from the chart." T [the teacher] comes over to see what they are doing. She asks which question they are on. Raul replies, "Where do they live? Water." T reminds them to write the answer in the appropriate square.

Using these and other notes, the teacher was able to see patterns in Raul's use of language on two levels, interacting with print, and interacting with peers. Getting no response when he initiated interaction in Spanish, Raul proceeded to use English to read from the chart, read from the book, speak to his classmates, and respond to his teacher. Together the teacher and Sally were able to plan for how his use of English could continue to be encouraged in context-laden situations without worrying about pushing him too fast.

Identifying Strengths and Weaknesses

Anecdotal records can be analyzed for both strengths and weaknesses in students' reading and writing. Katie's anecdotal record, which we discussed already, reveals that she writes poetry for herself outside of school and that she has a sense of audience. These are strengths. The record also reveals an area in which Katie can grow—formatting the poetry she writes. A look back at Eleanor's note also reveals strengths and weaknesses. For example, the teacher discovered that Eleanor has graphophonic knowledge not previously revealed in their writing and that she could verbalize what she learned during the conference with the teacher. The teacher also discovered that Eleanor previously had been using random strings of letters in her writing because she had such difficulty tracking words in sentences in her mind.

Finding Time for Analysis

Finally, just as it is important to find time to *record* anecdotal records, it is important to find time to *analyze* anecdotal records. Some analysis occurs concurrently with recording anecdotal notes and is recorded along with a description of the event that was observed. However, other analysis follows the recording of notes. We recommend that teachers try two things to make time for such analysis. First, use the start of each instructional planning period for an analysis of anecdotal records for individuals and groups. This will serve to focus planning time so that it may be used more efficiently. Second, if teachers meet on a regular basis with other teachers, analyzing anecdotal records can be a fruitful part of the meeting. For example, if a classroom teacher and Chapter 1 teacher both take anecdotal records on the same child, they can analyze both sets of notes together by comparing in-

dividual notes and looking for shared patterns and trends. If a group of teachers from the same grade level meets regularly, an analysis of one another's notes may uncover a great deal to talk about, including how best to adapt teaching to students' needs.

Uses of Anecdotal Records

Analysis of anecdotal records allows teachers to find patterns of success and difficulty for both individuals and groups of students. Students who have a need for particular information or for particular kinds of reading and writing opportunities can be grouped together and provided with the information or opportunities meeting their needs. In addition to instructional planning, the records also can be used to inform students and parents about progress and the value of various instruction and learning contexts. Finally, anecdotal records can help teachers generate new assessment questions.

Instructional Planning

To extend what Genishi and Dyson (1984) say about oral language to written language, anecdotal records on children's social behaviors and responses to written language can help teachers plan stimulating situations for the reluctant as well as the enthusiastic reader and writer. Using the set of anecdotal notes taken in the second-grade classroom during buddy reading discussed previously, we will show how the earlier analysis we provided can lead naturally to an instructional plan.

To review, the teacher noted that students in the buddy reading activity were taking reading responsibility away from the classmates when they hesitated or showed any sign of difficulty with reading words. When she interviewed the class the next day to glean more information about why this happened, she found that few students knew any options for helping partners with difficult words except to tell them the words. These assessment data helped the teacher plan lessons to demonstrate how to help readers retain responsibility for figuring out difficult words. For example, she talked to the children about the strategies she used with them—providing plenty of wait time, suggesting that they read on, suggesting that they reread, and so on. Then she demonstrated each of these strategies with a child and made a list of the strategies for the children to refer to. Finally, she ended the next several reading sessions early so that the children could share with her and one another the strategies they used to successfully figure out their own words and to assist peers in figuring out words they did not know. The children also shared problems they encountered and talked about how to solve them.

During the week, as the class focused on improving their strategies, the teacher observed pairs as they read, provided individual coaching for some, recorded more anecdotal notes, and used the notes to couch her lessons in detailed examples. In short, though the original anecdotal records and class interview were the basis of her first lesson, the anecdotal notes taken *after* the lessons became equally important in planning ongoing instruction to further develop the students' strategies and understanding.

Informing

In addition to using anecdotal records for planning ongoing instruction, teachers also may use them to periodically inform others, including the students themselves, about students' strengths, weaknesses, and progress. Reviewing anecdotal records with students helps them see the growth they have made as readers and writers, and helps them gain a sense of progress over time and learn to pin-

point where improvements need to be made. To illustrate, one Chapter 1 teacher who involved students in generating instructional goals claimed that the process of writing anecdotal records affected the students' attention to the goals they had set: "The children seem to get more focused faster since I started carrying a clipboard and taking notes. It seems to remind them about the goals they decided to work on."

Anecdotal records also can help teachers create support systems for students outside the classroom. Report cards, parent conferences, and staffings are all situations in which instructional planning can take place on the basis of the teacher's analysis of anecdotal records. Specific examples pulled from anecdotal records help parents or other school personnel see the child in the same way as the teacher who has collected the anecdotal records. They can augment the home or test information provided by others and provide clues about what contexts are and are not supportive of the child's learning in school.

Generating New Questions

Analyzing anecdotal records and using them to plan instruction encourages teachers to generate new questions that lead full circle to further assessment of students and of teaching itself. One teacher commented, "As I review kids' notes, sometimes even as I write them, I realize what else I need to find out." Bird (1989) commented that anecdotal records "not only guide [a teacher] in her instructional decision making but also provide her with a frequent opportunity for self-evaluation, enabling her to assess her role as a teacher" (p. 21). We agree, and find that the use of anecdotal records to inform instruction helps teachers become more aware of how their instruction is interpreted by students. Teachers are able to see how they can influence students' interactions with one another as well as with books and other materials through specific instructional practices. To illustrate, the following are some assessment questions generated by the teacher who recorded the anecdotal notes on pairs of students who were reading together in her classroom:

- What effect will the planned lessons have on students' interactions over words during reading?

- What other interactions do students have with one another over *ideas* in the story when they read together? (Her notes about Shawn led her to wonder this.)

- Do different pairings during reading make a difference in how readers interact with one another? What kinds of pairings are optimal?

- In what other situations is Shawn a leader? What can be done to further encourage that side of him?

The teacher has come full circle. Her original anecdotal notes were analyzed and used to plan instruction. But the notes also led to more focused assessment of individuals as well as assessment of a wider range of students and incidents. Her analysis and instructional planning led her to consider new assessment questions, questions not only about the students' reading but also about the effect of her teaching on their reading. For this teacher and for others who have realized the potential of anecdotal records, these "stories" are the basis from which they assess both their students' learning and their own teaching.

Conclusion

Anecdotal records are a powerful tool for collecting information on an ongoing basis during reading and writing and for evaluating the products of instruction. Keeping anecdotal records on a regular basis can enhance a teacher's classroom observation skills. Teachers report that they see and hear with more clarity when using anecdotal records, by focusing more intensively on how children say things and how they interact with one another. Anecdotal records are advantageous not only for planning instruction but for keeping others informed of children's progress in reading and writing and for focusing future assessment. When teachers discover the value of anecdotal records and figure out techniques to embed them in classroom literacy events and planning, anecdotal record keeping becomes a natural and important part of teaching and learning.

REFERENCES

Bird, L.B. (1989). The art of teaching: Evaluation and revision. In K. Goodman, Y. Goodman, & W. Hood (Eds.), *The whole language evaluation book* (pp. 15–24). Portsmouth, NH: Heinemann.

Cartwright, C.A., & Cartwright, G.P. (1974). *Developing observational skills*. New York: McGraw-Hill.

Galindo, R. (1989). "Así no se pone, Sí'" (That's not how you write, "sí"). In K. Goodman, Y. Goodman, & W. Hood (Eds.), *The whole language evaluation book* (pp. 55–67). Portsmouth, NH: Heinemann.

Genishi, C., & Dyson, A.H. (1984). *Language assessment in the early years*. Norwood, NJ: Ablex.

Goodman, Y. (1985). Kidwatching. In A. Jaggar & M.T. Smith-Burke (Eds.), *Observing the language learner* (pp. 9–18). Newark, DE: International Reading Association; Urbana, IL: National Council of Teachers of English.

Jaggar, A. (1985). On observing the language learner: Introduction and overview. In A. Jaggar & M.T. Smith-Burke (Eds.), *Observing the language learner* (pp. 1–7). Newark, DE: International Reading Association.

Livo, N. (1986). *Storytelling: Process and practice*. Littleton, CO: Libraries Unlimited.

Morrissey, M. (1989). When "shut up" is a sign of growth. In K. Goodman, Y. Goodman, & W. Hood (Eds.), *The whole language evaluation book* (pp. 85–97). Portsmouth, NH: Heinemann.

Pinnell, G.S. (1985). Ways to look at the functions of children's language. In A. Jaggar & M.T. Smith-Burke (Eds.), *Observing the language learner* (pp. 57–72). Newark, DE: International Reading Association.

The Random House Dictionary of the English Language. (1966). New York: Random House.

Thorndike, R.L., & Hagen, E.P. (1977). *Measurement and evaluation in psychology and education* (4th ed.). New York: Wiley.

No More "Rocks": Grouping to Give Students Control of Their Learning

Beth Berghoff, Kathryn Egawa

When we taught the "low" reading group it never felt right. The sixth graders with the third-grade reading books were never eager to read. The first graders who could not break the code wiggled and squirmed as they sounded their way through the preprimer stories. We were as relieved as the children when the "low" reading group was finished. Although they named themselves the Super Heroes or the Cardinals, everyone knew all classes had three groups: the Eagles, the Bluebirds, and the Rocks (a low-group nickname actually used in the teachers' lounge). And everyone knew who belonged to each group.

To us the disadvantage of being in the low group was painfully obvious. Yet many educational systems adhere to the philosophical stance that students are more efficiently and effectively educated when they are ability grouped. The prevalence of ability grouping as a teaching strategy might seem to suggest that its merits outweigh its negative consequences. Recently, however, a growing body of research indicates that ability grouping does not increase student achievement, and may, in fact, have detrimental effects on the self-concept and potential achievement of students in lower groups (Morgan, 1989). This research, combined with what we were experiencing, provoked us to rethink literacy instruction.

A New Understanding of Literacy

As elementary school teachers, we have come to understand our task to be something much more complex than teaching reading, writing, and arithmetic. Our students need more than knowledge. They need an understanding of how to organize and connect knowledge. They need to experience making their knowledge part of the class conversations. Every child needs to be an active participant, negotiating within the class culture:

> It is not just that the child must make knowledge his own, but that he must make it his own in a community of those who share his sense of belonging to a culture. It is this that leads me to emphasize not only discovery and invention but the importance of negotiating and sharing—in a word, of joint culture creating as an object of schooling and as an appropriate step en route to becoming a member of the adult society in which one lives out one's life (Bruner, 1986, p. 127).

We see learning as a social endeavor. Reading and writing are social things to do and can be learned easily when they enable the child to participate in the creation of a learning community. This happens naturally outside school:

> Children who can do things help children who can't. Younger children expect to get assistance from older children and to assist even younger ones in their turn. Some of the most successful instruction occurs in school when children help each other....When children of different ages—and more mature students of differing degrees of ability—work together, everybody learns (Smith, 1986, p. 184).

It can happen just as naturally inside school, but only if there are opportunities for children to work together. School can be a place where children learn to control knowledge rather than be controlled by it.

The grouping practices described in this article have worked for us in our elementary classrooms. We offer them with assurance of their value, but we caution that they work because they are connected with our understanding of literacy, learning, and community. They are not simply logistical mechanisms that can be plugged into any classroom. They are thoughtful choices of organizational patterns that support learning and the creating of meaning in the way we theorize it can best be accomplished. The importance of what we share here is not the grouping possibilities alone, but the underlying beliefs and assumptions that led us to their use.

Having three reading groups makes sense only if a teacher believes in the assumptions underlying ability grouping: that all learning should progress in a linear manner, that a teacher has the sole responsibility for supporting each student in the class, and that the stigma attached to being grouped is negligible. The grouping practices that follow grow out of a different set of assumptions. We believe that learners need to have choices that allow them to make connections and develop their own courses for learning, that learners in a community should support one another, and that every student brings a unique and equally valuable contribution to the dynamics of the learning community.

Alternative Grouping Practices

The Table gives an overview of the grouping patterns we use and the considerations we make in deciding what organization to offer. We see it as the teacher's role to illuminate the strengths and knowledge, the cultural perspectives and expectations each child brings to the learning community. We attempt to design curriculum that coaxes these individual understandings into the forum of the classroom. The richness of each classroom's culture originates from this diversity.

Whole-Group Learning

In third grade, we studied "communities." Each of the children was asked to interview a member of the community to find out about his or her job and how that job supported the community. Greg told the whole class about his interview, showing his neighbor's firefighter's badge. The children seated around Greg took turns telling about their own trips to fire stations. Then Chris told about a visit she had made to the Stay-Alive House. She told about smoke filling the pretend bedroom and her practice escape down the stairs. The children began to ask Chris where the house was and who could go. She had sparked their interest.

"Could we go?"

As is so often the case in whole-group sharing, new questions and problems are generated. It was a natural place to involve the

Grouping in the elementary classroom

	Whole group	Small group	Pairs	Independent
Why?	Develops the learning community; time to share culture and literacy.	Common interests; strategy instructions; opportunities to plan, think, and work toward a goal.	More intimate group requires less negotiation about agenda; more opportunity to construct.	Allows sustained reading and writing; allows personal choice; time for personal reflection.
How?	Possibilities include sitting in a circle, having a special chair for authors or report givers, musical signals to call the group together.	Groups of three or four self-chosen for interest; teacher planned considering social relationships, expertise, or needed language support.	Self-chosen partner; teacher assigned partner to assure success—stronger/weaker, expert/novice; to encourage new friendships.	Teacher specifies time for independent work; children separate themselves to work alone.
When?	Decision making—class rules, plans; problem solving—playground issues; listening to stories; choral reading; teacher or "expert" demonstrations; shared experiences—cooking, science experiments, art activities; celebrating—completion of a major project, individual accomplishments; sharing individual scholarship.	Discussion groups; literature study; content-area explorations; writing support groups; teacher instruction groups; any inquiry project.	Shared reading; study partners; cross-age tutors; letter exchanges; skill pairings—author/illustrator, reader/actor.	Sustained reading and writing; personal investigation; journal writing; alternative sign system response; gathering personally inviting resources; time for personal reflection.
How does it foster literacy?	Provides a meaning-rich context in which language is used to share meaning and students' individuality is explored and supported.	Opportunity to use oral language in social context to construct meaning; functional reasons to read and write; allows students to shape their own development of personal literacy.	Opportunities to practice making personal meanings public in face-to-face interaction with a peer; "two heads are better than one"—learning can go farther with two.	Allows the child to set a personal pace for thinking; allows the child to make personal connections to the class learning; time to savor language; time to use written language.

Grouping in the elementary classroom (continued)

	Whole group	Small group	Pairs	Independent
How does it support students with diverse language, cultural, ability, or experience back grounds?	Shared experiences give the class a shared vocabulary and practice in social meaning making. Exposes differences and similarities of all students so that they are expected and accepted.	Develop awareness of multiple perspectives; peers provide support and language opportunities.	Opportunities to make connections with all class members; reasons to relate in spite of differences.	Allows time for the child to do what he or she enjoys without pressure to negotiate with the larger community; time to practice, to own new learning; time to work in the child's first language.
What does the teacher learn from the students?	What the children value. What energizes the group. Which children need more help in making their meaning public.	Can see the children try out different perspectives and roles; can see how the children's personal sense of power is evolving; can see what knowledge is constructed.	What the child can do with support; what kind of support the child needs; how the child accepts or rejects different perspectives.	What the child's interests are; what the child thinks about; what aspects of reading and writing make sense to the child and can be used for his or her own purposes.

whole group in the inquiry process. How could we find out more about the Stay-Alive House? We could write to the fire department or Chris's parents. Children volunteered to start the information gathering. Letters were written and sent. Soon, the fire department responded with an invitation to the Stay-Alive House which we accepted. It was a marvelous experience that led naturally into more reading, writing, and thinking.

As teachers, we believe that children come to school knowing how to think, how to be a part of a social group, and how to use language to express personal meanings. Their knowledge, however, is specific to contexts and communities outside the school (Taylor, 1989). A classroom of students needs to share experiences that provide common language and an opportunity to construct meaning together. Each learner also needs opportunities to connect his or her outside life to life in the school.

During whole-group sessions, we concentrate on these shared experiences and connecting activities. We use whole-group sessions as a forum for demonstrating possible ways of relating in smaller work groups. We support the students in learning to appreciate the differences among themselves by working toward shared understandings and language. The students learn to question one another, to discuss the merits of one another's thoughts and ideas, and to generate new questions and problems.

Some reading instruction can take place during whole-group sessions: read-aloud stories, choral reading, strategy instruction, group story writing, poems, newspapers, and sharing literature extensions or children's writings. As noted in the Table, we also use whole-group sessions to work out our rules and consequences. We make decisions about field trips and visitors. Each of these conversations gives us opportunities to put our ideas into language and to hear the ideas of others.

Often our discussions serve as springboards into more personal or small-group inquiry.

Small Groups

Small groups have taught us the power of student-controlled learning. Rather than showing a lack of initiative, our students are deeply involved in learning. As Wells (1986) points out, most learners are accustomed to participating in teacher-dominated activities. When a teacher maintains the majority of control in a learning community, the students get the message:

1. that the only valid learning is that which takes place when they are engaged in teacher-prescribed tasks;

2. that personal experience, particularly that gained outside the classroom, is unlikely to be relevant for learning at school; and

3. that taking the initiative is unwise... thinking things out for oneself frequently leads to unacceptable answers—it is better... to follow only the steps laid down by the teacher (Wells, 1986, pp. 93–94).

Putting students in control of their learning in small groups challenges all these constructed understandings children have of school. It requires the teacher to trust the process of collaborative learning. It means watching and listening more than ever before, and reflecting on what happens.

As part of our community study, students were invited to build a clay model of our school and the buildings nearby. Scott, Dylan, and Maurice volunteered to be a group. In an ability-grouped classroom this threesome would have been in a low reading group. They avoided reading and writing whenever possible and were easily frustrated by written language.

Not surprisingly, none of the three could spell the name of the school, the nearby grocery store, or the street. What was surprising was how they decided to meet after school and copy words from the buildings and signs. In the morning, they had sheets of words to label their model buildings and plans for a map with street signs. Their flurry of energy for the project caused their classmates to ask what they were working on and what the words were for. The boys asked if they could write a response to the questions on the blackboard, which turned out to be the perfect medium for their learning. Over the next several days, they composed messages about their project to the class. One of the boys would write while the other two formulated the words, reread the script, and pointed out needed conventions and corrections. Other students would stop by occasionally and make suggestions as well.

This episode illustrates the potential for involvement when students own the learning process. Working in small groups increases each learner's experience in language and negotiation. Individuals think and share their ideas. Groups have to decide on a plan that satisfies all the members and then actualize it. Members make lists and plans, give one another assignments, and decide on timelines. They begin to recognize when they need the teacher's intervention and when they are making good progress. Most importantly, they learn to use one another to deepen their understanding of who they are, what they know, and what they are capable of doing.

The Table in this article addresses the issues of why, how, and when small groups might be used. Some groups work together for months, others for an afternoon. The inquiry undertaken by the group really determines what works best.

Pairs

Lyle, Lyle, Crocodile (Waber, 1965) was one of the stories read to the children during the community study. It is a humorous story about a crocodile participating in a human community. Tina was intrigued by the story. She talked Jared, a weaker reader, into reading it with her by promising to help him with the hard words. Her teaming up with Jared was not just a goodwill gesture, though. She knew he was artistic, and she was planning to ask for his help with illustrations for a book. The story of Lyle had sparked an idea and she wanted Jared to help her develop it.

Like Tina and Jared, many learners choose a partner because they have a common interest or one has a valuable expertise. Pairs usually work more quietly than small groups, but pairing still allows the language exchange that learners need. Especially during sustained reading and writing times, pairs can use strategies for organizing knowledge with language to construct understandings and responses (Harste, Short, & Burke, 1988).

Independent

Keisha wrote in her journal: "We went to First Source Bank and we got to ride up and down the elevator. And we each got a ruler and a pencil and a balloon. We got to see where they had their meetings. It was so fun!"

She was recording what seemed important to her. Individuals need time to record and reflect on events along with opportunities to choose and immerse themselves in the experiences books can provide. Learning to focus one's energies takes practice. As teachers, we can encourage each child to spend some time each day doing independent learning by offering diverse invitations. There may be possibilities generated by small groups: research questions, reports, script writing, data collection, or science observations. There may be invitations related to the whole-group sessions: rereading the poems shared that day, hearing a suggested book at a listening center, working with mathematics manipulatives, or creating a response project.

Many of our students have been intensely focused on personal investigations. They have read for weeks on a single topic like birds, knights and weapons, or outer space. These children need more individual time. Flexible grouping provides a space for their personal interests. It sends a message that the student's choice is important and that the child's initiative for learning will be supported.

Conclusion

Ability grouping is currently being criticized for "buying the achievement of a few at the expense of many" (Oakes, 1986, p. 17). We concur, with the caution that there are no simple solutions. The inequities created by ability grouping have led us to rethink the schooling process. It is time to reconceptualize literacy as "the ability to outgrow ourselves" (Harste, 1989). Literacy is a life-learning process in which children are engaged regardless of their differing abilities or backgrounds. School must be a forum where children can express and negotiate meanings, where each child is engaged and supported in growing toward an understanding of his or her power to participate in the community. Then the knowledge gained can be functional and meaningful.

The organization of the classroom is a teaching tool. It works to optimize children's opportunities to be in control of their learning and to be participants in culture creation. We have offered four possible alternatives to ability grouping that have worked for us in balancing the opportunities for all children. The organization we have described works be-cause we collaborate with our students in its operation. Their interests and needs shape group memberships, size, and purpose. Like everything in our classrooms, grouping is a negotiated matter. Although we teachers are older and more experienced members of the classroom culture and are certainly charged with creating a supportive and rich learning environment, we see ourselves as participants in the negotiation and construction of a literate community.

REFERENCES

Bruner, J. (1986). *Actual minds, possible worlds.* Cambridge, MA: Harvard University Press.

Harste, J. (1989, November). *A vision of curriculum for a democracy.* Paper presented at the Annual Meeting of the National Council of Teachers of English, Baltimore, MD.

Harste, J., Short, K., & Burke, C. (1988). *Creating classrooms for authors: The reading/writing connection.* Portsmouth, NH: Heinemann.

Morgan, M. (1989). *Ability grouping in reading instruction: Research alternatives.* (Fast Bib No. 21 RCS). Bloomington, IN: ERIC Clearinghouse on Reading and Communication Skills.

Oakes, J. (1986). Keeping track, part 1: The policy and practice of curriculum inequality. *Phi Delta Kappan, 68,* 12–17.

Smith, F. (1986). *Insult to intelligence.* Portsmouth, NH: Heinemann.

Taylor, D. (1989, November). Toward a unified theory of literacy learning and instructional practices. *Phi Delta Kappan, 71,* 184–193.

Wells, G. (1986). *The meaning makers: Children learning language and using language to learn.* Portsmouth, NH: Heinemann.

CHILDREN'S LITERATURE REFERENCE

Waber, B. (1965). *Lyle, Lyle, crocodile.* Boston, MA: Houghton Mifflin.

Using Whole Language With Students Who Have Language and Learning Disabilities

Carol Zucker

Enhancing literacy learning by employing instructional techniques based on a whole language philosophy has well documented effects in a regular classroom (Butler & Turbill, 1984; Cambourne, 1988; Goodman, 1986; Holdaway, 1979; Weaver, 1990). Support is mounting for the value of this philosophy for students who have special needs as well (Hollingsworth & Reutzel, 1988; Poplin, 1988b; Rhodes & Dudley-Marling, 1988).

Instruction for students with learning disabilities often focuses on remediating underlying ability deficits through drill and practice before academic learning can proceed (Rhodes & Dudley-Marling, 1988). In contrast, advocates of the whole language philosophy shift the emphasis from a deficit approach to one capitalizing on students' strengths and abilities. In such a climate "students are treated as competent rather than as deficient, as readers and writers rather than as children who have not yet learned prerequisite skills" (Weaver, 1990).

According to whole language philosophy, the fundamental basis for literacy learning emphasizes, among other things, the integration of content curriculum areas and the four related language processes of reading, writing, listening, and speaking in authentic settings. Whole language literacy learning is based on the premise that students can gain competence in these areas if they are immersed in a literate environment, given opportunities to communicate through print, and provided with supportive feedback (Sawyer, 1991).

Benefits of Applying the Whole Language Philosophy With Special Needs Students

Employing whole language methods with special needs students facilitates the learning process by addressing their weaknesses more effectively than traditional models. First, whole language focuses on language processes and thus directly targets many of these students' learning difficulties. Because whole language recognizes the integrity of all learners, no student is viewed as disabled or deficient (Smith-Burke, Deegan, & Jagger, 1991).

Second, the whole language philosophy emphasizes a developmental approach that enables a more individualized format and increases the likelihood that the students will meet with success. This individualization is particularly well suited to students with learning disabilities who have difficulty keeping up with the typical scope and sequence of lessons.

Third, a whole language teaching philosophy moves away from the reductionist principles that emphasize fragmented skills toward a more meaningful, integrated approach to learning subject material. Hence, the development of skills takes place within the broader context of literacy development (Weaver, 1990). This is especially helpful to students who have sequencing and organization weaknesses.

Fourth, a day in a classroom built around the whole language philosophy permits multisensory language learning experiences that are meaningful, varied, and enjoyable. Learning is greatly enhanced for children with processing difficulties when it involves more than one modality.

Finally, adherence to a whole language philosophy enables coordination of various remedial support services in a way that replaces the fragmentation of different delivery systems of the past. Thus, instruction by the special- and regular-education teachers, as well as the related support personnel such as the speech and language teachers, is all organized under one thematic umbrella with each professional complementing the others' skills.

The PASS Program

The following is a description of a special education class that incorporated the whole language philosophy into specially designed teaching techniques to enhance the literacy development of children with language-learning disabilities. This class was the youngest age group at the Concord Road Elementary School in the Ardsley School District's Program of Assisted Studies and Support (PASS), in suburban Westchester County, New York, USA.

The PASS children were referred by the district Committee on Special Education following evaluations and recommendations by professional staff. They were identified as being language impaired, having learning disabilities, or both; all were in need of special class placement and additional speech and language services. Three kindergartners and two first graders started at the beginning of the year, and three more first graders entered as the year progressed. Some of the children had been in special preschool language enrichment programs, and others came directly from a regular public school setting.

The distinguishing feature of the PASS program, which followed the integrative-collaborative model, was that it did not have self-contained special education classes. The children instead were assigned to a mainstream homeroom class and began each day there. During the remainder of the day, they divided their time about equally between their regular and special education programs. The children therefore received daily instruction in many academic and nonacademic subjects in their mainstream class with the assistance of a special education teacher. Consequently, the children were pulled out of the mainstream class only when they required direct instruction by a special education teacher who employed novel teaching methods in a separate environment. Because of the students' language disabilities, this setting typically focused on the language arts curriculum, which was compatible with the use of whole language techniques that could be modified to creatively teach the subject material.

My class was this type of setting; my main goal for these children was that they attain higher levels of literacy and improve their communication skills. I wanted to ensure that my students developed a perception of themselves as competent language learners who would become successful readers and writers

(Smith-Burke et al., 1991). To accomplish this goal, I tried to provide them with daily multiple exposures to various kinds of oral and written language and to have them engage in interesting activities that allowed for practice and the development of fluency.

Philosophical Framework

I designed my whole language classroom around Cambourne's (1988) seven conditions for successful literary acquisition. Following are some ways in which I created a learning environment compatible with Cambourne's conditions.

Immersion. The classroom environment was print-rich and filled with meaningful literary experiences that were adapted to accommodate the children's special needs. The walls were covered with environmental print (labels, signs, posters) and the children's work (including writing samples, annotated drawings, projects, charts, and small, self-made books). Author studies, both completed and in progress, were mounted for the children to track what they were reading. All display material was appropriate and usually coincided with the theme currently being followed.

Demonstration. My students learned through modeling, both by their fellow classmates and me. We took turns leading the class in shared readings from a Big Book or large-print poem written on a chart. Sing-along books were especially popular, and the rhythm and beat in many of them were helpful in sustaining the students' short attention spans and in enabling them to learn new or difficult literary concepts.

Expectation. The high standards I established for the children were the key to the success of the program. I instilled in them the conviction that they would learn to read and write, although it was difficult for them. Focusing on what the children could do, rather than on what they could not, motivated them to build on that base.

Responsibility. I trusted the students to act responsibly to complete the tasks that they often chose. They were active rather than passive learners primarily because they directed what they were to learn. I took my cues from their interests and needs and planned a menu of activities from which they could decide what they wanted to do. This self-selection gave them a sense of ownership of their learning.

Employment. The classroom was an exciting, supportive place where children were engaged in meaningful literary processes. They had many opportunities to practice and use the skills they had acquired within this setting. Everyone had a sense of purpose and persistently pursued it, whether in a large group, a small collaborative group, in partnership with another child, or independently at one of the learning stations.

Approximation. From the very beginning, the children knew that my classroom was a safe, risk-free place to learn. Their successes were continuously rewarded, no matter how small. Because they were all at different stages of linguistic competence in their reading and writing, together we contracted individual acceptable standards of performance that were constantly modified as the students got closer to achieving their goals.

Response. Reading and writing conferences, both with classmates and with me, provided the children with opportunities to exchange ideas and receive reactions from others. We practiced how to respond to another's shared work in the author's chair by giving thoughtful comments or constructive critiques. For many of the children, being asked to express their opinions was a novel experience, and they gradually learned to trust their own judgments.

Activities Based on the Four Integrated Language Processes

The classroom activities were designed to immerse the children in reading, writing, listening, and speaking around a central theme on a daily basis. Through this immersion I hoped they would become more comfortable with and engage more willingly and competently in these processes.

The Daily Schedule. A typical day in the PASS class consisted of a whole group time, known as "combo" time, first thing in the morning. Combo time lasted for about an hour, with all the PASS students from both kindergarten and first grade together. The focus of combo time was usually on listening and speaking activities related to a shared reading.

During the next hour and again in the afternoon, the children were divided into two smaller groups by grade level. In this "breakdown" time, the emphasis was on teaching specific reading and writing skills within a literary context appropriate to the developmental level of the children. Kindergarten children remained in the PASS class, while the first-grade children returned to their mainstream class. Then the two groups would switch; the first grade would return to the PASS class, while kindergarten rejoined the mainstream. At the end of the day, everyone would reconvene for another combo time in the PASS room. Figure 1 visually represents the daily schedule, the process it focuses on, and the related activities.

Listening and Speaking Activities. Morning combo time provided a forum for discussion when the children could talk freely about anything that was on their minds. It enabled a camaraderie to grow among the children and fostered mutual respect and the ability to listen and respond to one another easily.

Following this open forum, the children formed a semicircle on the rug in front of the easel and began the morning's background building discussion for the current theme. Tapping prior knowledge was an integral part of helping children who had difficulty with temporal concepts to feel an initial connectedness to the theme; it also helped them make sense of what they would subsequently be reading by being able to relate it to their personal experiences.

Reading Activities. I included several types of reading activities in both large and small group and individualized configurations. These activities, which are described in the following list, were designed to enhance the children's facility with print, promote their use of effective comprehension strategies, and boost their confidence.

• *Large group shared reading activities.* Combo time flowed naturally into the shared reading, using either a Big Book or an enlarged print poem copied on a chart. Before the first read-through the children would discuss what they thought would happen in the story and why. On the second reading, I would demonstrate relevant phrasing and expression and emphasize the pronunciation of new vocabulary. I used shared reading time for teaching language skills, reading strategies, story structure, and print conventions through think-alouds. I also would target certain unique features of the story, such as dialogue, rhyming words, or repetition. The children responded eagerly, and I was able to keep their attention for relatively long periods of time.

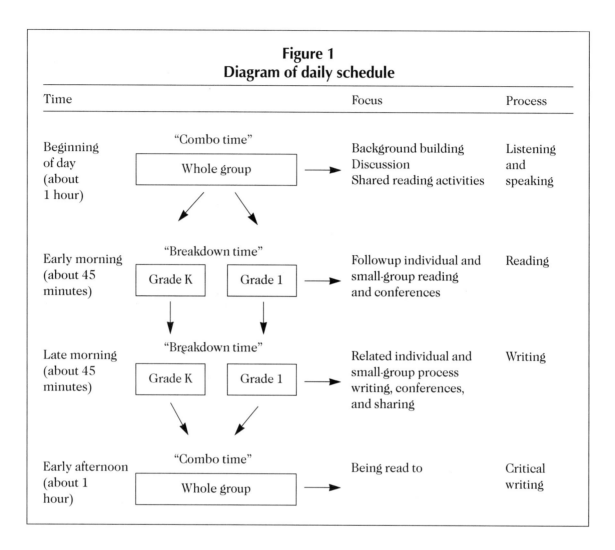

Figure 1
Diagram of daily schedule

Time			Focus	Process
Beginning of day (about 1 hour)	"Combo time" Whole group →		Background building Discussion Shared reading activities	Listening and speaking
Early morning (about 45 minutes)	"Breakdown time" Grade K	Grade 1 →	Followup individual and small-group reading and conferences	Reading
Late morning (about 45 minutes)	"Breakdown time" Grade K	Grade 1 →	Related individual and small-group process writing, conferences, and sharing	Writing
Early afternoon (about 1 hour)	"Combo time" Whole group →		Being read to	Critical writing

They loved hearing selections repeatedly, so I would allow extra time to give each child a turn reciting the selection in front of the class using a pointer. This made him or her feel important and served to reinforce the vocabulary and strengthen their fluency. Now that they were all partners in the teaching process, they became more attentive and involved!

A poignant example of the self-assurance they came to feel was when John came up to me one day brandishing a miniature copy of *The Very Hungry Caterpillar* (Carle, 1979). "I want to read this to the class," he an-nounced, "the way you do. I know how. I prac-ticed at home with my Mom!" "OK," I replied, delighted, "but perhaps it would be easier for the class to see the pictures if you use this larg-er copy," I said as I withdrew the regular size version from our class library and showed it to him. "No," he stated emphatically. "I want to use my copy. While I read, you can point to the pictures in that book." And that was how we did it. John had gained enough confidence in his ability to read that he was prepared to do so in front of everyone, as he had seen me do every day.

• *Small group follow-up reading activities.* I tried to incorporate additional types of daily follow-up reading experiences that were related to the previous shared reading. Three or four children would engage in a guided reading activity if small books were available to accompany the Big Book we had read that day. During this time the children would discuss the story in more detail, sometimes retelling it to the group with each child picking up the story line from where the last person left off. Other times we would record this new version on tape, or we would invent new characters or make up a new ending for the story.

Several children also might listen independently to the book on a tape while following along with the text and then try to read sections that they were able to. They particularly enjoyed reading with a partner or a student from another class who often would help them over the tough spots.

Frequently, I would be just an outside observer as the children gathered around in a circle and had their own informal book talk.

• *Individualized reading activities.* The children took home a little book from the Wright Group's Sunshine or Story Box reading collection daily. These little books were placed in manila envelopes that were signed on the front by a parent when the reading was completed. This home reading was preceded by an individual conference in class with me. During the conference we would predict the book's content by its cover and title page and read through it together; we then would discuss the text briefly, giving particular attention to any unique literary features of the book, like unusual pictures or rhyming words. I also would use this opportunity to address whatever specific strategy instruction students required. The following day when students brought the little book back to class, each of them would team with a partner as I listened from nearby. When they were through, either

I or the partner would initial the sheet on the front of their envelope. In this way, a record was maintained of what the children had read, which served as a visual reinforcement of their progress. Because the children had read a new book almost every night, they accumulated an impressive list of books, which did wonders for improving their self-esteem and motivation.

Students reread each little book several times at home and at school in order to develop their reading fluency. Repetition and practice were necessary for achieving fluency; the ability to read fluently was pivotal to changing the children's perception of themselves as able readers.

Because we focused on meaning, the emphasis during the reading process was shifted away from reading with perfect pronunciation or phrasing, to developing strategies that used contextual, semantic, and graphophonic clues to improve comprehension.

The children also kept a reading-response log in which they made entries after they completed their books. They could write or draw anything about the book that they wished, as long as they varied the format from day to day. One day Frank wrote the following about the book *Ratty-Tatty* (Cowley, 1987):

> Ratty-tatty is to clever. He stol the wumen egg. The man and the wumen and the cat put the snape trap. I like the part of the book when the cat stol the catfish.

They now saw themselves as capable readers who could read independently for a variety of purposes; they were willing to read to others, able to think and write about what they read, and comfortable picking up a book to read for their own enjoyment during independent reading time. The real evidence of their empowerment was seeing the children so excited about doing something that had always been very hard for them in light of their language difficulties.

Writing Activities.   As with reading, I tried to include different types of writing experiences with each thematic lesson. I included both group and individual activities that were either teacher-directed and skills-based or student-generated and creative. These activities were designed to develop strategies that fostered written communication for various purposes. We used a process approach, and all children's writing was always shared and celebrated. Following, I explain four types of writing included in the program.

• *Individual writing.* Almost daily, the children wrote in their learning logs about anything that they wanted to, as long as it was related in some general way to the theme. This writing encouraged the children to think about the theme and to express it in written form. For example, when we were working on an author study about Eric Carle, Julie decided to react to the book *The Very Hungry Caterpillar*, which John and I had read together the previous day. We had followed the reading with a discussion and science mini-lesson about the process the caterpillar goes through before it turns into a butterfly. She drew several diagrams depicting her interpretation of the changes and wrote:

> The hug caterpilar is a butterfly because he eat a late. I likke the part wen he get fat and he ture to a cunne. Thn he put a hol in the cuut and cum ot.

When we were studying about seeds and how plants grew, Emily was thinking about planting tomatoes in her garden when she wrote:

> I gow tlmdos becus I like tlmdos. It giv me enjnne. The tlmdos R Ymme.

She accompanied that with very elaborate pictures to illustrate what she meant.

• *Group writing.* Frequently the writing activity involved a group effort. Following a discussion related to the theme we were studying, I organized the children's comments by generating a prewriting web. They then practiced "writing" the story orally by using the words and phrases from the web as cues, expanding the story as they went. After several repetitions I took down exactly what they dictated onto a language experience chart. This dictation was cut up into sentence strips and placed on the bottom of a large oaktag page, so that the children had their own pages in their own words, which they then illustrated. When the Big Book was complete, the children took turns reading it to the class.

Sometimes a wordless book provided the basis for the writing of a sequential story to which the children added their own words. First, I wrote what they said on sentence strips and put the strips under the pictures to be read as a shared reading. Then these sentences were copied by the children into little books of their own, illustrated, and added to the class library.

• *Individual directed writing.* Directed writing activities were those that emphasized proper sentence form and dictionary spelling and were intended to serve as models of conventional writing or to teach a skill appropriate to the children's developmental level.

In one of their more formal practice writing activities, the children were seated in front of a pocket chart in which there were cards with their current vocabulary words. After selecting the words they wanted to use, they took the cards out of the pocket chart and arranged them on their desks in proper sentence order. Then they copied them into their writing books, adding whatever punctuation was necessary. This allowed them to use their own ideas while practicing writing conventions.

• *Individual creative writing.* As a balance to the directed approach, unstructured time was devoted to spontaneous, creative writing. This time was usually tied to the shared reading experience. At these times, in contrast to during the directed writing, the children were encouraged to use invented spelling and any format they were comfortable with, as long as they could make their ideas understood.

When we were studying about spring, for example, we brainstormed ideas related to the season by classifying its attributes under different categories (for example, weather, clothing, foods, likes, dislikes). The children chose to write about those qualities of spring that they especially liked and generated a list of descriptive phrases that we displayed on a wall chart. Next, the children picked out those attributes that pertained to them and made up their own complete expanded sentences. Then they wrote them in little accordion books, illustrated the books, and brought them home; each book was a unique reflection of themselves. One of the pages of Steven's book read as follows:

> I lik wen the rains stps bekz the rainbo cms ot.

Paul wrote,

> It is wrm and You can pla awtsod.

Keith wrote,

> Levs trn green and flawrs gro.

Following a writing process approach helped these students overcome their fears of completing a task with which they had multiple difficulties. Despite perceptual-motor, language, organization, or sequencing problems, the children knew that they had ample time and successive stages of rewrites to go through before the final product was complete. They became less inhibited about writing and very proud to become authors. It was especially rewarding when their work was published.

• *Culminating activity.* As a final activity at the end of each day, the whole group would come together again for another shared discussion time and a chance to hear their teacher read to them from a book related to the current theme or author study. The primary emphasis at this time was on strengthening listening and critical thinking skills through higher level questioning techniques. Final discussion time also served to reinforce the pleasure of reading so that the children would develop an appreciation for books and become lifelong readers.

Integrated Speech and Language Through Storytelling

IEP-designated speech and language services were incorporated during language arts instruction while the children were in the PASS room. The speech and language teacher and I team-taught and planned our lessons around a mutually derived theme. Thus, the speech and language work was integrated into what the children learned in the related language areas. Furthermore, our collaboration eliminated additional fragmentation of the children's day because they did not have to be pulled out separately to receive this service. Also, as teachers we maximized our instructional potential by complementing each other's areas of expertise and learning from each other.

We decided to involve our students in a storytelling activity because it afforded the children an opportunity to use the language processes of listening, speaking, reading, and writing in an integrated, purposeful way. In addition to language growth, it provided a setting where the children could develop more poise and vocal clarity, strengthen memory, and stimulate imagery (Hamilton & Weiss, 1990).

It was springtime, and we were in the middle of a thematic unit on seeds and plants. Because it tied into our theme, we decided to use *Jack and the Beanstalk* as the basis for our storytelling vehicle. We planned activities that required the children to use all their modalities to facilitate their remembering the story.

First, we read the children various versions of the story and had them choose which one they wanted to use. Next, we reread the one they picked several times and reviewed the sequence and the story structure. Third, we had the children retell the story and used flannelboard pictures of different parts of the story to cue their recall. In addition, using special stenciled copies of these pictures, children colored and cut out their own set of storyboard pictures and took them home each night to practice again in front of their families. Fourth, we had them practice retelling the story into a tape recorder so that they could hear the tempo and clarity of their presentation and improve their performance. Fifth, we showed them a filmstrip of the story to help them visualize it through another medium. They then made their own copies of the book and illustrated them. We thought that experiencing the story also might help the children to remember it better, so we had them act it out, with each child bringing in props from home, making a playbill, and taking turns playing different roles. Finally, after they had rehearsed many times using the flannelboard pieces to trigger their memory, children who wanted to became storytellers in their mainstream classes. Scotty, a child who had been reticent and unsure of himself throughout the year, exclaimed, "Wow! I never thought I could do this. I didn't think I'd ever be able to remember all the parts of the story when I saw everyone looking at me!" It was gratifying for us to see how far he had come.

Author Studies

Team teaching was integral to coordinating whole language themes between the students' regular and special education classrooms. To ensure greater consonance between the two settings, the students' mainstream teacher, Mrs. Leo, and I collaborated a great deal. One way in which we did this was when we were conducting an in-depth study of an author.

We would use two basic approaches. The first was for each of us to conduct the same author study but at different times. If the children already had heard one of the author's books in one class (for example, the PASS class), then we appointed those students the resident experts in their other class (for example, their mainstream class). Each expert was given the responsibility of leading the discussion about the author and the book and even asking the class some questions. The children often announced how privileged they felt to be able to do this.

In the second approach, both of us conducted the same author study simultaneously. In this case, Mrs. Leo and I had our students read a similar core of books by a selected author, and then extended our readings to include additional books by that author, which we chose separately. This permitted both some overlap and some differentiation. We divided our follow-up activities similarly, doing one project that was the same and several that were different from one another. These activities included dramatizing a story or writing in the same genre, style, or format as the author. We usually allowed the children to choose which project they wanted to do, and whether they wanted to do it in the mainstream or PASS class. This choice afforded them the opportunity to decide where they were most comfortable, thus increasing their likelihood of success. Often they chose to do both sets of activities.

One positive outgrowth of these author studies was the children's increased familiarity with authors and their works. After a visit to the school book fair one morning Peter excitedly exclaimed, "Look, Mrs. Zucker, look what I bought at the book fair." When I looked down, there was a copy of one of the Eric Carle books that we had read recently during our author study of Carle. "Now I will have a copy of my very own to read," he said proudly. He then marched over to the Eric Carle display poster we had mounted on the wall and emphatically pointed to the name of the book that he had just bought, which was on the list. "See, here's *Swimmy*," he said, and then went on to read all the other titles on the list. "The next time I go, I'm going to get *The Mixed-Up Chameleon* too!" I could not have wished for a better carry-over from our lesson. Peter had become knowledgeable about an author and his books and was excited about literature. He had the makings of a lifelong reader.

The Value of Whole Language Techniques

Providing an educational environment that is influenced by a whole language teaching and learning philosophy is very beneficial to children who are language impaired and learning disabled. Instruction based on whole language tenets creates a climate for improvement because it compensates for those factors that often cause students with language and learning disabilities the most trouble.

Learning was facilitated through the use of a multimodality approach in which reading, writing, listening, and speaking were presented frequently throughout the day using the visual, auditory, and kinesthetic channels. Further, varying interrelated methods of presentation and use reinforced each of these language areas. Thus, reading was taught through shared reading, guided reading, independent reading, choral reading, sustained silent reading, paired partner reading with a classmate or parent, or listening to an audio book. Writing was similarly strengthened through observation and modeling from language experience

charts, dictation, response journals, creative stories, expository writing, wordless books with provided captions, learning logs, and published students' work from both group and individual efforts.

Speaking and listening skills were developed collaboratively by both the speech and language teacher and me through strategy building activities that correlated with the theme and supported the literature-based reading and writing lessons. These activities focused on improving the children's communication ability and social skills by teaching them to better attend and respond to oral information from both adults and peers. This was accomplished through role-playing, drama, storytelling, sing-alongs, audiotapes, games, flannelboard stories, and formal and informal discussion groups.

The strong social orientation was another benefit of a whole language classroom. Interaction, fostered through the collaborative environment, was especially valuable in helping the children learn how to work cooperatively with peers. Partner and small-group work helped the students sustain their attention and become more actively involved in what they were doing.

Another positive consequence of a whole language learning environment was that its similarity to the mainstream enabled students to move easily between and feel connected to both settings. Additionally, team teaching prompted greater curriculum alignment between the regular and special education classrooms and furthered the homeroom teachers' feeling of ownership for their special needs students. Moreover, the students were more frequently included in important aspects of the mainstream experience. Where there was overlap between the programs, the children were often able to take on leadership roles.

The improvement in the students' self-esteem was typified by a comment made by Mrs.

Golden as two of them returned to her mainstream kindergarten class. "Mrs. Zucker," she remarked with a grin, "you'd better do something about your children's behavior. They are feeling too full of themselves today!" For students who had started the year with a defeatist attitude, these words were like music to my ears.

When they entered the PASS program, all except one child were achieving at a basic readiness level in both reading and writing according to informal preassessment measures. They had literacy skills that were only sporadically applied in the reading-writing process and were linguistically weak in both the receptive and expressive language areas.

Positive gains were made by the children in all the language areas according to several assessment measures. Portfolios of the children's progress, including quarterly samples of the children's multipurpose writing products, running records, skills checklists, anecdotal records, journals, tape recordings of their reading and speaking, and informal evaluations, displayed growth in linguistic competence across the four language areas of reading, writing, listening, and speaking. Posttesting in June, via the Peabody Individual Achievement Test-R, revealed that almost all of the children gained at least a year or more from the program and were now achieving at beginning- to mid-first-grade level. Children who began the program earlier in the school year evidenced more growth than those who entered later in the year. Some of the children, though still experiencing language difficulties at the end of the year, were outperforming many of their grade-level peers in the mainstream population in both reading and writing ability. In their final reports, some of the mainstream teachers described the children's growth: "Peter has gained self-confidence and is proud of his performance." "Julie has shown improvement in her ability to think critically." "Emily has started to use some original thoughts in her work."

The lasting impact of incorporating a literature-based whole language teaching and learning philosophy in the education of students with language and learning disabilities was that it changed their attitudes and literacy enactments so that they came to see themselves as readers and writers, rather than as failures. They evolved into successful students who were able to employ alternative strategies for achieving independent learning. They were more sociable and communicative because of their experiences in a supportive environment that fostered their development.

REFERENCES

Butler, A., & Turbill, J. (1984). *Towards a reading-writing classroom*. Rosebery, NSW, Australia: Bridge Printery.

Cambourne, B. (1988). *The whole story: Natural learning and the acquisition of literacy in the classroom*. Auckland, NZ: Scholastic.

Goodman, K. (1986). *What's whole in whole language?* New York: Heinemann.

Hamilton, M., & Weiss, M. (1990). *Children tell stories*. Katonah, NY: Richard C. Owen.

Holdaway, D. (1979). *The foundations of literacy*. Sydney, Australia: Ashton Scholastic.

Hollingsworth, P., & Reutzel, D. (1988). Whole language with LD children. *Academic Therapy, 23*, 477–481.

Poplin, M.S. (1988a). The reductionist fallacy in learning disabilities: Replicating the past by reducing the present. *Journal of Learning Disabilities, 21*, 389–400.

Poplin, M.S. (1988b). Holistic/constructionist principles of the teaching/learning process: Implications for the field of learning disabilities. *Journal of Learning Disabilities, 21*, 401–416.

Rhodes, L., & Dudley-Marling, C. (1988). *Readers and writers with a difference: A holistic approach to teaching learning disabled and remedial students*. Portsmouth, NH: Heinemann.

Sawyer, D.J. (1991). Whole language in context: Insights into the current debate. *Topics in Language Disorders, 11*, 1–13.

Smith-Burke, T., Deegan, D., & Jagger, A. (1991). Whole language: A viable alternative for special and remedial education? *Topics in Language Disorders, 11,* 58–68.

Weaver, C. (1990). *Understanding whole language: From principles to practice.* Portsmouth, NH: Heinemann.

TRADE BOOKS CITED

Carle, E. (1979). *The very hungry caterpillar.* New York: Putnam.

Carle, E. (1991). *The mixed-up chameleon.* New York: HarperCollins.

Cowley, J. (1987). *Ratty-tatty.* Bothell, WA: The Wright Group Sunshine Series.

Classroom Organization for Instruction in Content Areas

Laura S. Pardo, Taffy E. Raphael

Chad, Megan, Anna, David, and Dennis, a group of children at varying ability levels in Laura Pardo's urban third-grade classroom, have been studying newspapers for approximately 5 weeks as part of a social studies unit on communication. To write their report about newspapers, they have gathered information from their textbook, taken a field trip to the city newspaper, interviewed an expert on newspapers, and read trade and reference books.

Laura organized instruction in three different ways to give the students optimal opportunities to learn new concepts and strategies, and to apply and practice these strategies in a variety of situations. The three forms of classroom instruction allowed students to (1) participate in teacher-led whole class lessons, (2) work in a cooperative small group, and (3) work independently.

By emphasizing the social nature of learning, Laura sought to create a classroom environment to meet the overall goal of content-area instruction which is to help students become skillful at learning and organizing content-area information. Students should be able to meet this goal both when working independently and when working in a group.

In this article we examine three ways to organize classrooms to meet the goals of content-area instruction. We begin by examining research on grouping practices that support students in their learning and organizing of content-area information. We then follow Anna and her peers as they use selected strategies while participating in different forms of grouping during the class unit on communication. We use the experiences of these students to illustrate how different grouping arrangements foster particular kinds of learning.

The Research Base: Grouping Practices

Using groups within classrooms has a long history, dating back over 80 years to when ability was first used as a basis for forming small groups (Barr, 1989). Ability grouping has continued to dominate reading instruction in spite of research suggesting that the instruction received in the lower achieving groups differs substantially from, and is inferior to, that received by higher achieving children (Allington, 1983). Furthermore, research suggests that there is no justification for separating students into ability groups (Yates, 1966), and that instruction in heterogeneous groups leads to higher achievement for all students (Dishon & O'Leary, 1984).

Issues of grouping are often ignored in content-area instruction, in which a single textbook typically is used for students of all reading abilities, and instruction centers on whole-class lessons. Yet research indicates that students earn higher grades, develop more skill in critical thinking, and become better decision makers when they study in smaller cooperative learning groups (Johnson & Johnson, 1984; Slavin, 1985). Cooperative learning groups may produce academic benefits, including higher individual achievement, as well as social benefits. Also, learning within collaborative groups more closely parallels activities found in the workplace.

The research indicates that participating in heterogeneous groups can help students acquire and share content-area knowledge, especially when the purposes of the groups fit the goals of the lesson or unit and the students have the necessary academic and social strategies to succeed in the group activities. Thus, determining the organization for a particular lesson depends on the purposes of the lesson, the content to be learned, and the strategies needed.

Selected Comprehension Strategies

Merely using a variety of grouping arrangements in classrooms will not automatically create independent and successful learners. Fundamental to students' success is learning a common vocabulary about strategies and learning the strategies themselves. Dennis, Megan, and their peers were able to take responsibility for planning, organizing, and writing their report on newspapers because of their familiarity with specific reading comprehension strategies. These strategies, described in Table 1, included: K-W-L (Ogle, 1986), journals (Fulwiler, 1982), Author's Chair (Graves & Hansen, 1983), concept maps (Johnson,

Pittelman, & Heimlich, 1986; Schwartz, 1988), QARs (Raphael, 1986), and Cognitive Strategy Instruction in Writing (Raphael & Englert, 1990). These strategies were the tools that provided students with the means to acquire and remember the content knowledge in the communication unit and other units.

Organizing for Content-Area Instruction

Studying subject matter in Laura's classroom involved four broad phases. First, students needed to develop a general concept of the topic (in this case, communication). This would give them a shared understanding and vocabulary to use in discourse about the general topic and related subtopics. Second, students gathered information both about general concepts and their specific subtopics, using a variety of information sources and comprehension strategies. Third, students organized and synthesized the information through charts and summaries. Fourth, students drafted and shared their final reports. Students' success in each of these phases was enhanced by their participation in reading and writing activities within appropriate grouping arrangements (see Table 2).

Teacher-Led Whole-Class Discussions

There are several purposes for teacher-led whole-class discussion, including: (1) introducing new strategies and concepts, (2) sharing related background knowledge, (3) building common experiences and reviewing previously presented ideas, (4) learning from difficult text, and (5) enrichment activities. The communication unit provided ample opportunities for students to participate as a whole class for

Table 1
Selected comprehension strategies

K-W-L	This framework helps students build background knowledge and share common experiences. K stands for "What do I already know?" W stands for "What do I want to learn?" and L stands for "What have I learned?" It prompts students' thinking about: (1) their relevant background knowledge, (2) questions that reflect their purposes for reading, and (3) the information they learned from reading the text. Using K-W-L encourages students to attack informational text with a purpose, and recognize the information they have gleaned from it.
Focus journals	This type of journal encourages students to review their background knowledge, reflect on their previous learning, and predict their future learning. The journal focus is written on the board by the teacher each day before the students arrive. Students read the focus, reflect on their responses, and write in their journals. Frequently, the focus of the journal is on content-area studies, though some days students choose their own topics. The focus journal helps students focus on their own learning and serves as a basis for discussion.
Concept maps	These visual organizers help students literally "map" their knowledge base. The maps can be used to help students understand a vocabulary term by having students identify the concept to be defined (for example, communication); a superordinate category or phrase that helps them understand what it is (for example, sending and receiving messages); traits (for example, ideas from one person are shared with someone else; can be done out loud); and examples (for example, newspapers, letters, telephone calls). Maps can also be used to organize information from different sources.
The author's chair	The author's chair provides students with a real audience as they share their journals, text, trade books, reports, and so forth. It is a special chair in the front of the room in which a child sits to read aloud to the rest of the class. During the time the child reads, he or she is speaking for the author. During content-area study children may: (1) sit in the author's chair to read from their textbook to the rest of the class, (2) share their journal reflections and predictions with their peers, and (3) share their rough drafts for help in revisions and final drafts for general comments.
QAR	QAR teaches children about sources of information, helping students discover and use the many sources of information from which questions can be answered. It provides direction to those students who are overreliant on their background knowledge at the expense of information from texts, or those who are overreliant on the text as sole source of information and do not consider their own background knowledge and experience.
CSIW	CSIW is a framework for guiding students as they plan, organize, write, edit, and revise expository texts. A set of "thinksheets" serves as a basis for the teacher to model strategies. The thinksheets act as prompts for students to take notes and keep records about the information for their reports, to sustain their thinking about topics, and as a basis for discussion. Thinksheets may be adapted to serve the specific needs students have as they gather and organize their information.

each of these purposes. Lessons focused on the content to be learned and on processes or strategies that supported content learning (Roehler, Duffy, & Meloth, 1986).

Introducing New Strategies and Concepts

These introductions occurred on three occasions: when the communication unit began and the concept itself was defined using a concept map, when the students used K-W-L to develop new concepts about newspapers, and when students learned to create an organizational chart as they reviewed information they had gathered during the unit. The K-W-L lesson, used as students prepared to read the section of the text on newspapers, illustrates how process and content instruction were merged. During the *W* phase of the lesson, Laura asked

---

Table 2
Patterns and purposes of classroom organization

Group size	Purposes	Strategies used	Examples
Whole class	Introduce new strategies and concepts Review previously presented ideas Build common experiences Share related background knowledge Learn from difficult text Enrichment activities	K-W-L QAR Author's chair	Concept map to begin unit K-W-L on newspapers Preparing for and taking field trip Modeling organizing information Reading and sharing textbook information (for example, partner read; oral reading to group) Journal share
Small group	Apply and practice newly learned strategies and concepts with new texts Work collaboratively to create text (for example, generate questions, gather information, organize and write drafts, revise) Encourage discourse about ideas in text	CSIW and adaptations Concept maps	Generating questions/setting purpose Gathering information from trade books Preparing interview questions Conducting interview of expert Organizing field trip information Drafting reports Peer conferences on reports Sharing among groups
Individual	Reflect on ideas, text, and interactions Set individual goals/purposes Apply and practice strategies, concepts Evaluate students' progress	Repeated readings Journals	Journal focus Generating questions Teacher/student conferences

students to think about their individual questions about newspapers.

Nina: Why does that black stuff get all over you?

Jenny: Newsprint.

Laura: Newsprint, Jenny said, but why does it get all over us?

Dennis: [interrupting] Ink!

Laura: Yes, why does that *ink* get on our hands?

Figure 1
K-W-L thinksheet

What do I Know?	What do I Want to know	What did I Learn?
I know that newspapers Are printed in black and white	What kind of papers do they use?	I learned that over 60 million people read newspaper a year.
Newspapers tell you what is going around your state or world	Who invented Newspapers?	Some Newspapers are printed evry day some are printed on weekends
On Sundays they have comics	What's so important about Newspaper?	there are about 1,800 daily papers in the U.S.
	Why do you get Newsprint on your fingers?	Many Large Communitys have more than one daily paper
	What kind of ink do you use? Is it special	Newspaper is stamped instead of printed.

Chad's thinksheet (see Figure 1) illustrates how the children individually wrote questions about newspapers to guide their reading. Because many students were not able to read the text comfortably, they read the section on newspapers with a partner. They completed the last column of their thinksheets individually, then participated in a teacher-led whole class discussion of the new concepts they had learned. The following segment illustrates how students made connections among earlier discussions, the questions on their thinksheets, and what they had learned from reading:

Laura: Jenny, do you want to share with the class what you and I were just talking about, about what you learned?

Jenny: [reading from text] "Print means words in ink stamped on paper."

Laura: What does that tell you about one of your questions?

Jenny: It means that the newsprint comes off because it's *stamped.*

Laura: What question did you find the answer to?

Mike: The one about why does that black stuff come off on your fingers.

The connections that students made among the discussions, questions, and textbook were reflected in their reports. In a paragraph of their report, the students in the newspaper group discussed the importance of newspapers. This section was directly related to Dennis's and Chad's question, "What's so important about newspapers?" on their K-W-L thinksheets. They had also raised this question in class and on their field trip.

Sharing Related Background Knowledge

The students' journal entries served as a basis for a teacher-led whole-group lesson in which students shared their knowledge about communication. This provided an introduction to students' initial reading of the textbook section in which communication was introduced. Students also shared background knowledge during the unit's culminating activity, in which each group presented its report to the whole class. What had been new concepts for each group gradually became their background knowledge, knowledge they were able to share with their peers and eventually the whole class.

Building Common Experiences

Teacher-led whole-class discussions aimed at creating shared experiences occurred throughout the communication unit. Students' participation in field trips to such places as a newspaper office and television and radio stations contributed to this process. Each trip was framed by discussions about what they might see and learn, questions they might ask, and discussion about how information learned on each of the trips was related (for example, people had a variety of jobs at the post office and at the newspaper).

Learning From Difficult Text

It was important for students with reading difficulties to receive support and guidance during the teacher-led whole-group discussions. Laura combined two purposes, helping students learn from difficult text and modeling strategies (for example, notetaking and summarizing). For example, in one lesson, three students took turns reading aloud to the class from their social studies textbook. The students had rehearsed the one or two paragraphs they had been assigned, until they could read aloud fluently.

After each student finished reading his or her section to the class, Laura provided instruction. She thought aloud, stating that one way she remembers ideas later is by writing down notes that will help jog her memory. She modeled stopping after each set of paragraphs to think about the main topics and the most important idea. She elicited ideas from students, provided her own thinking as a model, and modeled notetaking using a concept map.

Enrichment Activities

During the communication unit students enriched their understanding by listening to a modern form of communication: rapping. Two students from a local high school were invited to perform for the third graders. In an earlier unit, the enrichment activity involved students creating a videotape for their California penpals. The video was based on reports about their community.

Cooperative Small Groups

Cooperative small groups provide opportunities for students to: (1) practice newly learned strategies and apply newly learned concepts to further study in their chosen area; (2) work collaboratively to create texts, whether the texts be full reports, questions, or information synthesized from such sources as interviews of experts in a particular field; and (3) engage in discourse about the content and processes they are learning. Cooperative groups in the communication unit were formed to study subtopics such as newspapers, television and radio, and computers.

Application and Practice of Newly Learned Strategies

Students had worked with question generation and question answering as part of large group lessons with QARs, K-W-L, and concept mapping. They also had been asked to generate and respond to questions in their individual journals. The use of questions to guide

learning was further emphasized in several small-group activities.

To underscore that field trips were serious opportunities to learn more information, Laura had the students meet in their small groups to identify the questions that they planned to pursue during the field trip. Megan's question "Where do the colors come from?" helped focus students' attention on the printing press. Chad's question "How do you make a newspaper?" led them to notice the steps followed to create the daily paper. Their interest was reflected in a paragraph in their final report (note that all student writing samples are included without corrections for spelling or punctuation):

> This is how newspapers are made. First the reporter finds a story then he/she writes the story. next an illustrator draws a picture for the story. Another person takes the drawing and draws it on a computer. Then the story is typed and edited. Last it is waxed and put on the page. Finally the newspaper is printed.

Working Collaboratively to Create Text

In addition to the drafts of their reports, students created many other texts. These included interview questions and summaries of information gathered during the interview. One of the sources of information available to students in each group was an expert from the community (for example, a supervisor from the local post office or a computer software engineer). Megan and the other students in the newspaper group identified what they already knew, what they wanted to learn, and the questions they wished to ask their expert. They then met with Sarah, whose family operates a city newspaper, and asked their questions. The answers were recorded on a second thinksheet (see Figure 2), which provided students with the opportunity to practice the strategy of summarizing, in addition to working collaboratively to generate the text.

Figure 2
"Expert interview" organization thinksheet

Organizing thinksheet

Question: What Kind of things you have a newspaper?

Art	Traviling
Sports	Local
T.V.	adds
Bissness	comics

Question: What's so impoment about newspapers?

So you'll know what's going on all around you.

Question: How is your newspaper made?

It is written then ededitied, and printed and waxed then it is made.

Another opportunity to work collaboratively to generate text occurred in the writing of the drafts for their final reports. To create the first draft, each student volunteered to draft a paragraph on one of the areas they had collectively decided to include: names of newspapers, jobs in the newspaper office, sections contained in newspapers, how newspapers are made, and why they are important. Students then shared their paragraphs and discussed issues such as the order of the paragraphs, the accuracy of each other's information, and the content of the introduction and conclusion.

Sections of their report reflected these discussions. Their sensitivity to different sources of information was seen in the introduction: "This report is about newspapers. We talked about them, we read books about them, and we visited the Lansing State Journal." Their individual questions, such as Chad's and Dennis's questions about the importance of newspapers, were reflected in their second paragraph:

> This is what's so important about newspapers. You can see what's going on around the world. We read newspapers to see if theres danger and to see what the wether is. Adults read newspapers because they think it is very very important. And that's what so important.

The group's consensus about important categories of information (for example, on the field trip and during the interview, asking how newspapers are made and focusing again on their importance) was seen in their inclusion of paragraphs containing such information. They agreed that an ending should reflect their goal that "we hope you learned from our report about newspapers."

Encourage Discourse About Ideas in or Related to Text

The many examples listed earlier illustrate the value of small groups. Small groups provided unique opportunities for students to engage in discourse about their topics and to use strategies for conveying their information. These opportunities helped students value one another as members of the community of scholars with knowledge of social studies topics. Students helped one another use strategies, such as question generation and summarizing, and learned about content by means similar to those of mature learners in the workplace and nonschool sites.

Individual

As Table 2 suggests, the reasons for students to work individually include the opportunities to (1) reflect on their ideas, the texts they are reading, and their interactions with the teacher and peers; (2) set individual goals and purposes; (3) apply and practice strategies learned; and (4) provide information regarding individual progress.

Reflection on Ideas, Text, and Interactions

At the beginning of the communication unit, students were asked to reflect on what they already knew about communication by writing in the dialogue journals. Two focus questions guided their thinking and writing: What do you think of when you hear the word *communication*? What are some ways that you communicate? Different levels of knowledge were apparent, as seen in Chad's and Anna's journal entries.

Chad wrote a single paragraph in which he identified "taking, calling, and singh [sign] language" as ways people communicate. He then wrote: "I can communicate by calling or talking on the phone."

Anna used two text structures to convey her ideas. First she listed six ways people communicate: phone, talking, newspapers, letter writing, computer, and movies. Beneath that she wrote four paragraphs, each consisting of a single sentence identifying ways she communicates and expanding on ideas in her list:

> I communicate by letter writing, phone & Talking that was I communicate. Like if I was calling my uncle I would be communicating by phone. Or if I was writing a letter to my grandma. or if I was talking to my friend thats communiting.

Setting Individual Goals and Purposes

A second reason for working individually is to set goals or purposes for one's reading. In the communication unit Laura used K-W-L as such an opportunity. The students individually completed the first column, identifying what they knew, and then participated in a whole-class discussion in which they could learn from one another. Then Laura asked them each to consider what they would like to learn about newspapers. As mentioned earlier, Figure 1 shows the five questions Chad identified to direct his reading.

Apply and Practice Learned Strategies

Laura had taught students question generation as a strategy for identifying both what they already knew and what they wished to learn. The K-W-L lesson allowed Chad to set his own goals, and it also provided him and his peers with the opportunity to practice generating questions that might be answered through reading the textbook. Students also received practice in generating questions prior to using the trade and reference books.

Individual Assessment

Assessment should occur within the context of instruction (Au, Scheu, Kawakami, & Herman, 1990). Thus, individual writing and reading activities provided natural opportunities to judge students' success in a variety of ways. For example, Chad wrote a journal entry about communication, a list of questions on the K-W-L thinksheet, and a related list of what he had learned. All of these gave Laura information about his growing ability to identify important information, to generate relevant questions about the topic to be studied, to comprehend content-area text, and to write to express ideas. Laura also could see the content Chad had learned from the text, and she could assess his knowledge of conventions of print and his penmanship.

Concluding Remarks

In this article we explored the use of various grouping arrangements in content-area instruction. Anna and her peers experienced several rewards from the practices we described. First, over time they succeeded in working cooperatively with their peers on learning tasks, something that is often difficult even for adults. Second, they became risk takers. They were not afraid to try new forms of writing or different ways of conducting conversations to meet their goals, because they believed in their own abilities. Third, they made noticeable improvements in their writing habits. They enjoyed writing and many chose to write in their free time. Not surprisingly, their writing skills improved. We saw these students progress from writing one or two word responses to sustained thinking and writing about content-area topics.

Whether or not we should group children for instruction has been debated historically and continues to be debated today. The debate focuses on a wide range of issues, such as equity across groups, the validity of ability grouping, and the value of cooperative learning. This debate is nowhere more critical than in the content areas, in which often a single textbook is mandated for use within a classroom and in which whole-class instruction provides a helpful contrast to the ability groups often used in the reading program.

Yet we should be cautious about maintaining only whole-class instruction in the content areas, just as we are now cautious about only using ability grouping in the reading program. Perhaps we have been asking the wrong question about grouping practices. We suggest that the question is not "Should we have groups?" but instead "What groups should we have for what purposes?"

REFERENCES

Au, K.H., Scheu, J.A., Kawakami, A.J., & Herman, P.A. (1990). Assessment and accountability in a Whole Literacy curriculum. *The Reading Teacher, 43,* 574–578.

Allington, R. (1983). The reading instruction provided readers of different reading ability. *The Elementary School Journal, 83,* 548–559.

Barr, R. (1989). The social organization of literacy instruction. *National Reading Conference Yearbook,* 19–33.

Dishon, D., & O'Leary, P.W. (1984). *A guidebook for cooperative learning: A technique for creating more effective schools.* Holmes Beach, FL: Learning Publications.

Fulwiler, T. (1982). The personal connection: Journal writing across the curriculum. In T. Fulwiler & A. Young (Eds.), *Language connections: Writing and reading across the curriculum* (pp. 15–32). Urbana, IL: National Council of Teachers of English.

Graves, D.H., & Hansen, J. (1983). The author's chair. *Language Arts, 60,* 176–183.

Johnson, D.D., Pittelman, S.D., & Heimlich, J.E. (1986). Semantic mapping. *The Reading Teacher, 39,* 778–783.

Johnson, D.W., & Johnson, R.T. (1984). Cooperative small-group learning. *Curriculum Report, 14* (1).

Ogle, D.M. (1986). K-W-L: A teaching model that develops active reading of expository text. *The Reading Teacher, 39,* 564–570.

Raphael, T.E. (1986). Teaching question answer relationships, revisited. *The Reading Teacher, 39,* 516–522.

Raphael, T.E., & Englert, C.S. (1990). Writing and reading: Partners in constructing meaning. *The Reading Teacher, 43,* 388–400.

Roehler, L.R., Duffy, G.G., & Meloth, M.B. (1986). What to be direct about in direct instruction in reading: Content-only versus process-into-content. In T.E. Raphael (Ed.), *The contexts of school-based literacy* (pp. 79–95). New York: Random House.

Schwartz, R.M. (1988). Learning to learn vocabulary in content area textbooks. *Journal of Reading, 32,* 108–118.

Slavin, R.E. (1985). Cooperative learning: Applying contact theory in desegregated schools. *Journal of Social Issues, 41*(3), 43–62.

Yates, A. (1966). *Grouping in education.* New York: Wiley.

The Reading Specialist as Collaborative Consultant

Elizabeth L. Jaeger

For a long time, reading specialists have been viewed as glorified mechanics, called in to fix problem readers. As site-based professionals responsible for helping students who struggle with reading, they have worked primarily with small groups of like-aged children in pull-out programs or, more recently, they have served as in-class models to teach the skills needed for children to catch up with classmates. Because many U.S. reading specialists work under the auspices of Title I funding, they often have been constrained to operate in this fashion by a fundamental misunderstanding of federal regulations (Allington & Johnston, 1989). It is clear, however, that this paradigm for reading assistance is no longer viable, if in fact it ever was. This is true for three essential reasons.

First, there continues to be disagreement about whether such "fix-it" programs are truly effective. Some research highlights the successes of Chapter 1 programs [U.S. federally funded education program for at-risk children now called Title I] in raising standardized test scores (Jennings, 1991). Other research points out the many shortcomings of such remedial programs. There are statistical concerns such as an inability to raise test scores to the level of peers (LeTendre, 1991) and a tendency for the neediest children to make the least pro-gress (Carter, 1984). Other problems not specifically related to statistical data include a lack of coordination between remedial and classroom services and negative effects on the self esteem of students who are separated from their peers (Allington & Johnston, 1989; Bean & Wilson, 1981).

Second, we live in a society that demands more of our students than ever before. Basic literacy skills, emphasized by skill-oriented pull-out programs and measured by standardized tests, are not sufficient to function adequately in today's world.

Third, in a time of great fiscal distress within school systems, we do not have the resources to offer programs of ongoing, small-group instruction to all who need assistance. More and more, reading assistance programs that have proved effective are using federal funds in more creative ways (Clayton, 1991).

In light of these concerns, I feel we need to rethink completely the role of the reading specialist at the school-site level. The purpose of this article is to describe how reading specialists could function as collaborative consultants, spending the preponderance of their time working with other adults to meet the needs of students. First I will examine some of the literature on educational consultation as it relates to reading specialists. Next I will explain four dimensions that flesh out the reading specialist's collaborative role: curriculum development, instructional problem solving, assessment, and parent liaison. I will conclude the article with some implications for the future.

Educational Consultation

The concept of consultation within schools is defined clearly by Friend and Cook (1990) as "interaction between at least two co-equal parties voluntarily engaged in shared decision making as they work towards a common goal" (p. 72). To understand this concept, we need to take a look at the reasons why educational consultation has become popular (especially within special education), what attributes are characteristic of effective consultants, and what institutional changes would enhance the effectiveness of this model.

Since the 1970s, a significant trend has developed toward educational consulting for students with special educational needs (McKenzie et al., 1970). The movement toward adaptation of curriculum and instruction to meet the needs of these students within the regular classroom, rather than in full- or part-time pull-out programs, has its roots primarily in two areas. First, increases in special education staff often are overtaken quickly by the increase in referrals for placement in such programs. Second, there is movement, both philosophical and legal, away from segregation of special needs students (Friend, 1988). Studies have shown consultation to have positive effects for both teaching and learning (Medway & Updike, 1985).

Teachers who operate effectively as consultants tend to share several basic characteristics and strategies. They attend to the internal motivation of colleagues and students, the environmental conditions present, and the process of consultation itself (Conoley & Conoley, 1988). They have a basic plan in mind prior to

consultation but begin from the needs of teachers (Idol-Maestas & Ritter, 1985). Good interpersonal skills are evident in their interactions with others. They show a sincere interest in the needs of the classroom teacher, listen carefully, avoid the role of "expert," and focus on each situation as it exists (Heron & Kimball, 1988). Conoley and Conoley (1988) note that "the key task of the consultant is to use theory to inform practice, that is, to be sophisticated about what helps people change their skills, behaviors, attitudes, and expectations" (p. 19).

There is general agreement in the research literature that several issues must be addressed before the power of the consulting process can be fully realized. First, consultation needs to take its place on a continuum of services that includes instruction of students and inservice to teachers and parents. Likewise, it must be adapted to fit the context of the particular situation and meet the needs of the people involved. Second, those professionals who will be involved in consultation, classroom teachers as well as consultants, need to be trained to operate effectively in these roles (Friend, 1988). Third, there must be a concerted effort to remove barriers to productive consultation, both pragmatic (such as lack of time) and conceptual (such as mistrust or conflict of mismatched knowledge bases) (Johnson, Pugach, & Hammitte, 1988).

Literacy Learning and Collaborative Consultation

Johnson et al. (1988) suggest that, due to the frequent disparity among instructional methods chosen by classroom teachers versus those utilized by resource specialists, the special education teacher may not be "the most appropriate professional to be responsible for introducing changes into the general education classroom" (p. 45). However, the reading specialist is well suited to operate in this role, at least in part because, as Vacca and Padak (1990) note, there are clear parallels between what we know about literacy learning and what we know about professional adult interaction; both are, at best, collaborative processes. Reading specialists can use their knowledge of literacy learning to inform their role as collaborative consultants.

Collaboration works best when the adults involved bring their own unique strengths to the process. Classroom teachers have the advantage of consistent, long-term experience with their students in all areas of the curriculum. Reading specialists bring a different perspective. They usually do not have the classroom teacher's breadth of knowledge about a given child; however, they are in a position to make in-depth observations of the student in tutorial, small-group, and large-group settings. They can focus substantial knowledge of the reading process, as well as significant amounts of time and energy, toward understanding a child's literacy development.

As a reading specialist works intensively with a child who is learning to read, this careful observation of the student's reading behaviors is crucial. The specialist notes which strategies the child uses effectively, which he or she struggles with, and which ones are new and unknown. The specialist then develops a tentative plan that reinforces the child's strengths and expands his or her repertoire of strategies. As the specialist continues to teach, this initial plan is refined or even substantially revised to fit the student's needs.

The same type of interaction is at the heart of the collaborative consultation process as well. As in the game of Mirrors, in which two people face each other and begin to move simultaneously with no real leader and no real follower, this collaboration occurs as a sometimes tentative exchange of ideas. It is a complex process.

Not all reading specialists are naturally comfortable in this role. Many years ago, Veatch (1968) lamented that "most reading specialists are genuinely frightened, insecure, and ignorant when it comes to working with teachers themselves. They are safe, secure, and satisfied when they work alone with children" (p. 23). Veatch insisted, even then, that such a model could not be allowed to continue indefinitely and that a different kind of person would have to emerge—a person with particular skills.

Reading specialists need certain qualities in order to function effectively as collaborative consultants. They must have a wealth of knowledge about all aspects of literacy and always must be in search of new knowledge and experience that can be shared with students and teachers. They must have in mind an effective road map for the consultation process itself—where to begin, how to employ theory to inform practice, and when and how to move from talk to action.

Of equal or greater importance is keeping the needs of teachers and students paramount. This includes beginning from and accepting the perspective of those with whom one consults, demonstrating a sensitivity to and genuine interest in the problem-solving process, using time well—in short, communicating effectively. Inevitably, the process of change will engender conflict. It is important that the reading specialist be able to work through such conflict in productive ways.

In the remainder of this article I explore examples of four significant dimensions of the reading specialist's role as collaborative consultant:

- curriculum development
- instructional problem solving
- assessment
- parent liaison

For each area, I will describe a conversation between a reading specialist (referred to as "me") and a classroom teacher, followed by a description of the actions taken by those professionals. I have made an effort to incorporate into these descriptions the qualities of effective collaborative consultation noted above.

Curriculum Development

Carolyn, a second-grade teacher new to the district, makes an appointment to discuss her concerns about a lack of continuity within the literature curriculum with me. She is somewhat daunted by the number of literature selections at her grade level, none of which have lesson plans available. She worries that her teaching has become fragmented and that she is out of touch with what is really important for her students.

I tell Carolyn about an activity called "Gifts and Expectations" (H. Maniates, personal communication, February 11, 1993). Based on the work of Katz (1988), this activity asks teachers to focus very specifically on the knowledge, skills, and dispositions they wish children to have upon entering their classrooms and take with them when they move on at the end of the year. These standards then become the basis for any curriculum development in that area.

Carolyn takes this suggestion to her colleagues, and we all meet again after they have generated their lists of knowledge, skills, and dispositions. Most of the teachers are familiar with the minilesson format as it is used in writing workshop. The group agrees that we will work together to prepare a series of minilessons aimed at addressing the reading-related knowledge, skills, and strategies the teachers have designated and that can be taught in the context of the students' self-selected reading materials. These minilessons might include preparing to read, dealing with unknown words, and finding information. The classroom teachers also will focus on cultivating essential literacy dispositions such as curiosity, love of story, and interest in print.

The movement toward whole language instruction has placed our classroom teachers in an unparalleled state of flux. Although this instruction can be exciting and stimulating, for many teachers it also can be somewhat overwhelming. Gone are the basal reader teachers' manuals. Ideally, classroom teachers would have time to develop, in conjunction with colleagues, a literacy curriculum well-suited to their children, chosen materials, and teaching style. Unfortunately, this rarely occurs. So, what frequently happens is an overreliance on teachers' guides for literature that are developed en masse by textbook companies or by firms set up specifically to fill this need. As might be expected, the plans developed by basal companies look much like basal plans, and even those developed by other groups tend to be formulaic. Curriculum codeveloped by teachers and reading specialists offers a good compromise. Because this curriculum begins from a foundation developed by school staff, it can be much better suited to the needs of the children of the district, without requiring each teacher to begin from scratch.

Instructional Problem Solving

Evan, a veteran intermediate teacher, recently has added writing workshop to his curriculum. He is excited about the progress of his students, but he still feels uncomfortable with the day-to-day management of process writing. He explains that he meets with a few children each day, but seems to get caught up with those students and is then unsure about what the others are doing. I agree to observe in his classroom and, although his students seem to be more productive in their independent work time than he had thought, his perception that he touched base with only a few children is confirmed.

As we talk further, it becomes clear that the real issue is grouping—if, how, and when to group, and what to do with the other students not meeting directly with him. I offer several selections from my professional library that focus primarily on establishing procedures for writing workshop—*Write On: A Conference Approach to Writing* by Parry and Hornsby (1985), and *Classroom Experiences: The Writing Process in Action* by Gordon (1984) —and we agree to meet again in a week or so. At this meeting, we talk at length about options— his own prior experiences with grouping, the pros and cons of forming groups, how kids can be grouped and for what purposes, and how students might spend their time both in and out of groups.

Evan is interested in the idea of student-run writing response groups. He and I decide that, as a starting point, we need to prepare some lessons that will teach the students to work in independently functioning groups. We do so and observe each other teaching the lessons. Sharing responsibility for planning and instruction in this way increases the likelihood that these lessons will be incorporated into Evan's teaching repertoire. We meet regularly during the course of several weeks to refine what has occurred and plan for future work.

In the earlier example, I offered resources, personal suggestions, demonstration teaching, and team teaching as aids to problem solving. Often, however, depending on the nature of the situation, the teacher may be able to solve the problem almost independently; the specialist's role in such an interaction is to listen attentively, ask appropriate questions, and tease out possible solutions from the teacher's own mind. This relationship often results in the most effective, respectful, and long-lasting change (Idol, Paolucci-Whitcomb, & Nevin, 1986). The following is an example of such an exchange.

Barry is a third-grade teacher, well known on the staff as a person who can handle the needs of virtually any child. So I am a little surprised when he comes to me just before fall conference time. He is really puzzled by Belinda, a student in his class. Belinda seems to understand what she reads and once in a while contributes some wonderful ideas in discussion. But she has yet to read a single book cover to cover.

This discrepancy in Belinda's reading is puzzling to Barry. He has considered the possibility that the materials Belinda chooses are too difficult, but when he asks her to read a bit and talk about what she has read, Belinda can do both. Then Barry remembers Belinda's intense interest in science, an interest which may not be well-served by Barry's classroom collection of predominantly fiction books.

Barry has generated a hypothesis about this student's reading: Belinda never finishes books because she does not enjoy the kind of reading material that is available to her (fiction). The next step in the process involves collecting some nonfiction science books, including Joanna Cole's (1987) *The Magic School Bus Inside the Earth* (and others in the series), a unique combination of fact and story. Then he will test his hypothesis by offering the books to Belinda, and carefully observing her independent reading over the next few days. These procedures may confirm Barry's hypothesis, or he may need to reject or revise it.

How do classroom teachers make the transition to a stronger, more student-centered curriculum? For some, it is very much a personal odyssey, based on independent reading and attendance at workshops. But for many teachers, the support of knowledgeable colleagues is essential. Although connections with other classroom teachers undergoing similar change are extremely useful, there are very real constraints on the amount of cooperative teaching and consultation that occur in the typical school setting. Ideally, the reading specialist can fill this role more effectively, allowing staff development to be an ongoing process, especially when regularly scheduled conference time is a part of the specialist's schedule.

Assessment

Because our staff has found the first few weeks of school to be crucial to a new student's academic and social adjustment, we do all we can to make that transition a pleasant and productive one. I make it a point to check on the literacy progress of students new to our school—have they internalized the concept that reading is a meaning-based activity? Do they seem to enjoy reading? Do they have the skills needed to keep up with classroom work?

Frank has been a member of Maureen's fifth-grade class for about a week now. Maureen notes that he can read fluently and that, when asked direct questions about what he has read, he usually can answer them. But when called upon to review a chapter read the previous day, Frank offers just one or two unrelated facts. He cannot seem to sort out what is really important.

I suggest that, because we do not know much about Frank, it might be a good idea to assess his skills using an Informal Reading Inventory (IRI); this would give us a good idea of his strengths and weaknesses as a reader. Maureen reminds me that her instructional aide, Anna, has been trained to give an IRI. Frank seems to be somewhat uncomfortable with adults he does not know; so Anna, who works with him each day, will do the assessment. Maureen also agrees to keep anecdotal records on Frank's behavior in any situation that requires him to tell a story.

The results of the IRI serve to reinforce what Frank's teacher has noticed: He cannot structure a retelling of what he has read, but when asked direct questions about plot, he responds accurately most of the time. In contrast, Maureen observes that Frank seems to have little trouble offering summaries of events in which he has actually participated.

At this point, it seems profitable to talk with Frank about his reading. I ask Maureen which of us should conduct the interview and, expecting her to say that she should (due to Frank's discomfort with strangers), I plan to suggest that she and I might rehearse the interaction. But it turns out that Frank has noticed me helping out in the classroom and has asked who I am and what I do. Maureen mentions our idea to Frank, and he agrees to talk with me informally.

When asked to tell something about reading that is easy for him, Frank says that he cannot, that it is all hard. I remind him that he does not have much trouble figuring out words. Frank agrees, but adds that when his teacher asks him to tell what has happened in a story he does not know what to say. He also notes that his friend, Roberto, is good at summarizing.

This interview, though short, offers three salient bits of information. Frank has a reading strength, fluency, to which he reluctantly admits. He is aware of the trouble he has with retelling, and he has noticed someone in his class whose strength corresponds to his weakness.

Given this information, Maureen and I are able to do several things to help Frank. First, we give him the chance to do something in front of his peers that he does well—reading aloud. We encourage him to choose a selection he thinks other students will enjoy hearing. Second, Maureen and I develop a series of lessons, beginning with very simple stories, which will assist Frank in learning to recap what he has read. I train Frank's classmate Roberto to work through these lessons with Frank, gradually giving Frank more of the responsibility for the retelling. Roberto reads less fluently than Frank, so the potential exists for a balanced relationship between them as teacher and learner. Third, we alert Frank's parents to the focus of our work with him, and they agree to reinforce this work at home by listening to him retell chapters of a novel, preparing him to do the same in class the following day.

Obviously, if the reading specialist spends the majority of time engaged in activities other than direct instruction of needy students, it is even more important that the classroom teacher has substantial knowledge of students' literacy strengths and weaknesses. It is crucial for the reading specialist to find and develop assessment tools that provide accurate data about students' performance. These would include tests, such as an Informal Reading Inventory, and observational tools, like the keeping of anecdotal records. Both involve the ability to be acutely aware of clues exhibited by the child of his or her needs as a reader and writer.

Of equal importance is the ability to interpret the results of such assessments with the classroom teacher and together develop an instructional plan. If the specialist is no longer to be viewed as the fix-it person, then care must be taken to assist teachers in translating an awareness of the child's needs into effective classroom practice. A diagnostic scheme that connects data obtained by "kid watching/listening" to a theoretical description and recommendations for instruction, like that developed by Phinney (1988), may be helpful. For example, a child who relies too heavily on print, rarely self-corrects, and has difficulty taking risks would be considered an underpredictive reader. Instruction that helped expand the child's repertoire of meaning-based, predictive strategies would be appropriate.

Parent Liaison

Last year, several teachers from our school participated in a workshop that dealt with portfolio assessment. Jean, a first-grade teacher, was particularly taken with the process and began using portfolios with her students. After a parent education session, Jean tells me that parents from her classroom are enthusiastic about the portfolios. One father has asked how he and his child might keep a similar portfolio at home.

Jean likes this idea, but feels that having two separate portfolios for each child implies an artificial distinction between home and school literacy. She is considering the possibility that there could be one portfolio, including artifacts from both environments, but she is unsure how to guide this process. I suggest that, in much the same way that she and I have worked together informally, we might simply begin with a meeting for interested parents and see what evolves.

The meeting is well attended, and the families bring in all kinds of amazing things, from menus the children have read to notes written among family members to art projects. These artifacts relate quite clearly to the elements that are already present in the children's school portfolios—the usefulness of print, the connection between reading and writing, the importance of audience, the integration of curriculum. We talk at length about similarities and differences exhibited by children in various settings, decide on an organizational scheme for the home and school portfolios, and set up a schedule for portfolios to "travel."

As this example illustrates, the reading specialist can serve as literacy liaison between home and school. Traditionally, this has meant little more than notifying parents that their child was enrolled in a special class and providing some suggestions for helping the child, but this limited role is not adequate.

Young readers benefit from quality literacy experiences at home as well as at school. In order for this to occur, parents need an understanding of the kind of instruction their children are receiving at school and how they can best complement that instruction at home. Home literacy experiences should be validated; parents should see the many interactions they have with their child each day as a potential literacy gold mine. Parents need the chance to work with their children at school, allowing children to expand the scope of their literacy activities. All these activities can be facilitated by the reading specialist.

Implications for the Future

At the core of the reading specialist's role as collaborative consultant is a commitment to the process of instructional change. Although the need for such change is not unique to school systems, the process suitable to schools differs from that in other environments. Because the nature of their day-to-day lives is so firmly rooted in the unique situation of their particular classrooms, teachers need to exercise ultimate control of the change to which they commit. Such a process of change can best succeed when classroom teachers work in close consort with another professional, such as a reading specialist.

Expanding the scope of the reading specialist's work to include the roles described in this article is not easy. The sooner site-based reading specialists confront the fact that they are no longer classroom teachers and have none of the administrative authority of a principal or district supervisor, the easier this transition will be.

But there needs to be a substantial change in the training offered to reading specialists, as well. Although the International Reading Association's *Guidelines for the Specialized Preparation of Reading Professionals* lists organizational tasks and staff/curriculum development responsibilities as falling within the scope of the reading resource teacher, it requires no course work in these areas (IRA's Professional

Standards and Ethics Committee, 1986). As I informally surveyed reading specialist programs in California, there was little evidence that training programs currently emphasize the role of the specialist as resource person.

If we want reading specialists to become actively involved in the evolution of classroom teaching, we must carefully prepare them to take on this role. Such training would require coursework that emphasizes problem-solving and communication strategies as well as literacy education content. It would need to go further to include a practicum based in a school setting. The role of a collaborative consultant is a difficult one, primarily because of the complexities involved in maintaining a working relationship with dozens of adults as well as with children. To a certain extent only guided practice can allow the potential reading specialist to gain the experience needed to work with real teachers (both veterans and novices) dealing with real literacy issues. A reading specialist attempting to work in collaboration without such training and practice will face interpersonal issues that may be overwhelming.

Of equal importance is a concerted effort to diminish the pragmatic and conceptual barriers to collaboration that have plagued the reading specialist setting. This can best be accomplished by allowing significant flexibility in the specialist's schedule, thereby promoting communication with classroom staff. Without substantial blocks of time to plan together and a willingness on the part of all concerned to consider new ways of approaching problems, the collaborative consultation model is doomed to fail. It is only through such regular, ongoing communication that reading specialists and teachers can reach the mutual understanding necessary to best provide for the students they serve.

The move toward greater collaboration among educators surely will prove to be complex and challenging. Any number of factors addressed in this article have the potential to short-circuit this transition. Ultimately, however, children and adults alike will benefit from an educational process that makes the best possible use of teachers' time, energy, and expertise.

REFERENCES

Allington, R.L., & Johnston, P. (1989). Coordination, collaboration, and consistency: The redesign of compensatory and special education interventions. In R.E. Slavin, N.L. Karweit, & N.A. Madden (Eds.), *Effective programs for students at risk* (pp. 320–354). Boston, MA: Allyn & Bacon.

Bean, R.M., & Wilson, R.M. (1981). *Effecting change in school reading programs: The resource role.* Newark, DE: International Reading Association.

Carter, L. (1984). The sustaining effects study of compensatory and elementary education. *Educational Researcher, 13*(7), 4–13.

Clayton, C. (1991). Chapter I evaluation: Progress, problems and possibilities. *Educational Evaluation and Policy Analysis, 13,* 325–327.

Conoley, J., & Conoley, C. (1988). Useful theories in school-based consultation. *Remedial and Special Education, 9*(6), 14–20.

Friend, M. (1988). Putting consultation into context: Historical and contemporary perspectives. *Remedial and Special Education, 9*(6), 7–13.

Friend, M., & Cook, L. (1990). Collaboration as a predictor of success in school reform. *Journal of Educational and Psychological Consultation, 1*(1), 69–86.

Gordon, N. (Ed.). (1984). *Classroom experiences: The writing process in action.* Exeter, NH: Heinemann.

Heron, T.E., & Kimball, W.H. (1988). Gaining perspective with the educational consultation research base: Ecological considerations and further recommendations. *Remedial and Special Education, 9*(6), 21–28, 47.

Idol, L., Paolucci-Whitcomb, P., & Nevin, A. (1986). *Collaborative consultation.* Austin, TX: PRO-ED.

Idol-Maestas, L., & Ritter, S. (1985). A follow-up study of resource-consulting teachers: Factors that facilitate and inhibit teacher consultation. *Teacher Education and Special Education, 8,* 121–131.

International Reading Association's Professional Standards and Ethics Committee. (1986). *Guidelines for the specialized preparation of reading professionals.* Newark, DE: Author.

Jennings, J. (1991). Chapter I: A view from Congress. *Educational Evaluation and Policy Analysis, 13,* 335–338.

Johnson, L.J., Pugach, M.C., & Hammitte, D.J. (1988). Barriers to effective special education consultation. *Remedial and Special Education, 9*(6), 41–47.

Katz, L. (1988). What should young children be doing? *American Educator: The Professional Journal of the American Federation of Teachers, 12*(2), 28–33, 44–45.

LeTendre, M.J. (1991). The continuing evolution of a federal role in compensatory education. *Educational Evaluation and Policy Analysis, 13,* 328–334.

McKenzie, H.S., Egner, A.N., Knight, M.F., Perelman, P.F., Schneider, B.M., & Garvin, J.S. (1970). Training consulting teachers to assist elementary teachers in the management and education of handicapped children. *Exceptional Children, 37,* 137–143.

Medway, F.J., & Updike, J.F. (1985). Meta-analysis of consultation outcome studies. *American Journal of Community Psychology, 13,* 489–505.

Parry, J., & Hornsby, D. (1985) *Write on: A conference approach to writing.* Portsmouth, NH: Heinemann.

Phinney, M.Y. (1988). *Reading with the troubled reader.* Portsmouth, NH: Heinemann.

Vacca, J.L., & Padak, N.D. (1990). Reading consultants as classroom collaborators: An emerging role. *Journal of Educational and Psychological Consultation, 1*(1), 99–107.

Veatch, J. (1968). The clientele of the reading specialist. *Journal of the Reading Specialist, 8,* 22–25.

CHILDREN'S LITERATURE REFERENCE

Cole, J. (1987). *The magic school bus inside the earth.* New York: Scholastic.

Coordinating a Literacy Support Program With Classroom Instruction

Margaret Ann Richek, Linda Conviser Glick

Researchers have noted a disturbing lack of congruence between regular, core classroom instruction and remedial services (Allington & Broikou, 1988; Allington & Shake, 1986). They cite examples of instructional practices in which children who are unable to master regular classroom material are given a competing load of material to master in their remedial resource classes. For example, children might use one basal reader in their regular classroom and another in their resource program. Such situations confuse children; *curriculum congruence* or coordination of all the instruction provided is needed. Learning in support programs should build on the core curriculum that children must master.

Other authorities deplore the banality of what, in many schools, forms the core curriculum. For a substantial number of children in the United States, instruction is based almost entirely on a basal reader and accompanying worksheets (Aaron, 1987; Allington & McGill-Franzen, 1989a; Anderson, 1984). These materials provide limited reading experiences presented in an artificial context of excerpts (Anderson, Hiebert, Scott, & Wilkinson, 1985; Goodman, Shannon, Freeman, & Murphy,

1988). This practice is particularly lamentable for children in many remedial programs who often read less and do more worksheets than normally achieving peers (Allington & McGill-Franzen, 1989b).

If resource teachers, in an attempt to deliver instruction that is congruent with the material of the regular classroom, simply end up reinforcing the "same old, unmotivating thing," they unintentionally may be providing more frustration and dullness.

Curriculum Congruence in a Total Literacy Environment

In this article we describe a resource room program that met a dual challenge. To ensure curriculum consistency, this program used the same basal reading material that the children read in their regular classroom. However, it was used in a different and interesting way. To assure involvement and enhance interest in literacy experiences, the basal reader selections were enlivened with material from informational sources, trade book reading, and personal writing. All these experiences supported and extended the basal material. Thus, this program enriched, augmented, and complemented the children's classroom instruction and their overall literacy development.

Note that curriculum congruence refers to the coordination of the topics covered in the classroom, rather than to the coordination of specific skills (for example, short vowels, main idea). For example, if students were reading about how animals sleep, resource-room instruction focused on reading, writing, and information-seeking experiences concerning animals, sleep, and related topics. In this way entirely new yet relevant worlds of information and expression were opened to the children. Schema theorists (for example, Anderson & Pearson, 1984) consider topic coordination to be a powerful way of increasing mastery of literacy and world knowledge. Because topic coordination connects to children and their world, it enables them to interweave and deepen their knowledge, creative power, and ability to interact with schoolwork and texts. Finally, children can apply the discrete skills they may have learned in the context of meaningful reading.

The program we describe should be contrasted to the instruction it replaced. In the previous program, one basal reader was used in the core classroom and another in the resource room.

The children involved in this project were first graders who attended a Chicago public school. They were chosen for Mrs. Glick's resource room based on kindergarten teachers' recommendations. Eighty percent of these children were ESL students whose first languages included Romanian, Assyrian, Arabic, and Spanish. Many came from homes with economic problems. For example, more than 70% of them participated in a free or reduced-fee lunch program.

Four classes of 10 students each met with Mrs. Glick for resource assistance each day for 40 minutes. In this overcrowded school, instruction took place in a basement room shared by other resource teachers.

Mrs. Glick planned her program around the basal selections that the children were currently reading in their regular classrooms. The program started in January as the children moved into a primer, *Sun and Shadow* (Early, Cooper, & Santeusanio, 1979, 1983). The resource program consisted of three parts: building background, providing active involvement in reading, and extending reading and writing. Each part served a function in the children's literacy development. Increased background knowledge gave them experience with information relevant to the basal selection and with different literary genres. Providing active involvement made the children's interaction with text more meaningful and provided the repetition that they needed to fully master the material. In activities designed to extend reading and writing, children's exposure to and the use of language was increased.

In the following section, Mrs. Glick describes the three parts of this program using the basal story, "Jack's Star," in which children capture a lightning bug and then set it free.

Building Background

Before the children began the basal story, I introduced expository material to enrich their background knowledge. Because this material was too difficult for the children to read for themselves, I read it to them. For "Jack's Star," I chose an article about fireflies from *Compton's Preencyclopedia*. Next, I read *The Berenstain Bears' Nature Guide* section about collecting bugs. After I read, the children composed a group language-experience story based on facts they had heard. As the children dictated, I wrote each contribution. One group's story reflects the depth of the children's newly acquired knowledge.

The Lightning Bug

They do not burn or pinch you.

They light up.

They get dark.

Their light is cold and will not burn you.

People put them in jars in the jungle to see at night on a dark jungle path.

It is also called a firefly and glowworm.

Providing Active Involvement in Reading

Their curiosity whetted, the children were now ready to read the basal story. To help them master this story, which they also read in their regular classroom, I followed a three-part procedure adapted from Hoffman (1985) and Nelson and Morris (1986) that consisted of a Directed Listening-Thinking Activity (DL-TA), (Stauffer, 1980), paired reading, and dramatization.

First I read the story to the children, stopping frequently to ask them to predict the events that would happen next. The DL-TA procedure provided a model of fluent reading. It also enabled the children to concentrate on the storyline without interference from nonfluent word recognition abilities. DL-TA proved to be a motivating, nonthreatening activity. (If children had already been introduced to the story in their regular classrooms, they were asked to simply listen to me as I read the story.)

The next day, the children each chose a partner and read the story aloud, alternating pages. For example, if Nadine read page 23, then Cynthia, her partner, read page 24; Nadine read page 25, Cynthia, page 26. After the children completed the story they then exchanged parts and listened to their partners read the pages they had read previously. As the children listened to their partners, they acted as monitors. Instead of passive involvement, the listeners concentrated intently and

helped their partners read fluently. These co-operative paired reading ventures demonstrated that the text was meaningful and that repeated readings of a story could be fun. I tried to change partners for each new story, but some teams insisted on staying together.

In the third step, children dramatized the story. Each part was assigned to one child, and an additional child was chosen as narrator. This dramatic reading included gestures. For example, children reached high in the air to capture fireflies. Children who were not assigned a part served as the audience, watching, listening politely, and, of course, applauding when the dramatization was completed. To ensure that all children had an opportunity to participate, we often dramatized the story twice. Dramatization helped my children to improve their ability to understand punctuation (including quotation marks) and to read expressively.

Extending Reading and Writing

After the children completed the basal story, I brought in trade books on related topics. As an introduction, I showed each book and gave a short, enthusiastic book talk. The books were displayed in the room, and children were given time to explore them with a partner and to exchange the books with other teams. One full class period was spent perusing the books, and they remained available to the children for several weeks. Titles that accompanied "Jack's Star" included *I Know an Old Lady Who Swallowed a Fly*, *The Very Hungry Caterpillar*, *The Big Honey Hunt*, *Over in the Meadow*, *We Like Bugs*, and *Where Does the Butterfly Go When It Rains?*

Personal writing, an activity that these children had never experienced, was an important component of my program. To encourage writing, I posted a large sheet containing a list of "insect words" that became longer with each new activity. Next, each child was given a sheet of paper containing a picture of a lightning bug and was asked to compose a story using his or her own spelling. Children then revised their stories and read them to their classmates. To further encourage writing, a "graffiti board" was posted each day. Children were asked to write anything they wished. Each child recorded thoughts in a different colored magic marker.

After only 1 week of instruction, the atmosphere of my room had changed completely. The neat, precise bulletin boards I had used before the program began were replaced with children's word lists and written pieces. Multiplying each display by the four groups that came in throughout the day resulted in an impressive array of colorful child-centered materials. As each group entered the room, they excitedly read the works composed by others as well as their own productions. Worksheets gave way to a variety of trade books and children's writings, all relevant to the current basal selection.

The activities in my room looked as different as the environment. Instead of responding to teacher questioning, the children were predicting, sharing reading with their peers, recording their thoughts in writing, and dramatizing reading selections. Children who reached an exciting part in a book would race up to a peer, saying "Look what the caterpillar ate!" or "Here's a funny bug!"

Most important, for the first time children started to approach books independently, exploring the ones I brought in and others that they found for themselves. They also demonstrated an appreciation of authors by reading sequels of favorite books. After two children shared *Miss Nelson Is Missing*, they were delighted with *Miss Nelson Is Back*, secure in the fact that they knew where Miss Nelson had been. Children started to request more books from me and often provided me with a shopping list of authors. My cooperating first-grade teachers began to report that the children were reading their basal text with greater fluency and comprehension.

Literacy Experiences on Many Topics

As I guided the children through more basal selections I consistently added to their fund of information. We studied facts about vision in preparation for reading "Eyes at Night," a story about nocturnal animals. Using a plastic model of an eye, children were able to locate the iris, pupil, and cornea. They compared human beings with owls and cats, the animals in the story. *Animals at Night*, a more difficult informational book I read to them, helped students discover that mice, weasels, and spiders are also nocturnal animals. Such knowledge developed rich schema for the selection.

For the story "They Sleep Out," children learned facts about sleep from *A New True Book: Sleeping and Dreaming*. They were amazed to discover that our eyelids flutter when we sleep, that children grow when they sleep, and that if they do not sleep, they will not grow properly. The trade books that I used for this unit developed children's natural love of fantasy and included *Ira Sleeps Over*, *Where the Wild Things Are*, and *Pierre*. One child's writing shows his version of a sleepover:

> If I slept at my friend's, I will tell a ghost story. I would put on my dirty clothes. My bed is clean. My closet is dirty. We would have pizza. We would play with my babies. We will go to sleep. We will go to my room to go to sleep. We will go to my friend's house.

Dramatizations of the spooky story "They" actively involved my students in reading and helped them internalize plot structure. Children spontaneously supplied sound effects ("Woooh") and gestures (creeping, slow arm swaying) that delighted their audience. This story also illustrated their growing awareness of story structure. One child commented that the ending of this story had been surprising, and the group started to talk about other stories with unexpected endings. Because the story dealt with shadows, I read from the *Mammoth Book of Trivia* and *Let's Find Out About the Sun*, both of which explained how shadows are formed. The children practiced making shadows in different lights. To further extend experiences, they read mystery trade books, such as *The Snoring Mystery* and *The Case of the Cat's Meow*.

The basal selection "They Work at Night" was one of the children's favorites. One group wrote their career choices on a "loveable words" poster: policeman, nurse, doctor, cook, chef, firefighter, rock and roll singer, newspaper reporter, waiter, movie star, and telephone operator. When the reading coordinator visited, these children, straining to get out of their seats, insisted on reading him the words on the poster. One child who spoke Tagalog as a native language explained, "Everybody knows a cook is a chef!" Throughout this story children reacted with surprise and delight as they learned all of the things that women could do. Their experiences had been limited to women working as waitresses, child caregivers, and factory workers.

The children and I continued in this fashion throughout all the remaining basal selections for the year. The structure of the lessons provided the security as well as the excitement that the students needed. We seldom needed to vary from the basic instructional format.

Effects Within Our School

In order to assure that I was working on the same material as the classroom teachers, I asked my cooperating teachers to tell me their schedule for covering basal stories. I carefully followed each classroom teacher's schedule. Soon all three teachers reported that because of the topic consistency in the resource room, they were able to increase the pace of their basal reading instruction.

Furthermore, I was delighted to find that within a few weeks this program started to open the lines of communication among our staff. Intrigued by the changes they saw in their students, two of my cooperating teachers asked me to meet with them before the school day began. As a result of these talks Mrs. Jones started to give children more time to read and began to supply more trade books in her classroom. Mrs. Manion began to use an independent silent reading program and writing activities. In addition, Mrs. Gilfillian and Mrs. Solovy started using a story-mapping strategy (Beck & McKeown, 1981). At my suggestion the school reading coordinator, Mr. Coletta, ordered Big Books (Holdaway, 1979), which are now being used by all first-grade teachers. My colleagues asked me to share additional strategies in primary-level inservice meetings.

The intermediate resource teacher, Mrs. Schuman, also asked me to talk with her about what I was doing and then started using the "Curious George" strategy which involves students learning to read by reading books with natural lanuage patterns and appealing situations that often are rated above the students' instructional level (Richek & McTague, 1988). She also encouraged students to read trade books independently. Effects multiplied as other teachers began using Mrs. Schuman as a resource. Teaching in my school has become an exciting, cooperative venture.

Effects on Children and the Community

My students' reactions left no doubt about the effectiveness of this program. Before the program began, Michael had never asked for a book. Within 2 weeks he started begging for books to read by himself. Michael and his classmates used the trade books they had read for leisure reading activities. Betsy became so excited about the facts she was learning that she literally dragged her mother to the library. She and others helped supply the class with supplementary books about such subjects as parts of the body, animals at night, careers, and ghost stories. The next summer, Betsy enrolled in a library program in which she read 78 books.

Having learned interesting facts about their world, children started to manipulate them and assume ownership through writing. In successive units, as the children became more comfortable with the writing process, they started to ask if they could have paper to write stories about topics that interested them. There were soon stories about first-grade adventures such as playing tag and "Duck, Duck, Goose" at recess and eating desserts in the lunchroom. Children started to voice their feelings about playmates who had ignored them, tattletales, and eating tacos with a friend. Children spontaneously practiced decoding strategies to try to decipher a friend's story.

Excited by what their children were doing, parents responded strongly to the program. Several began to purchase books and take their children to the library. Four different parents requested that their children be placed in this program.

Because my program provided extra practice in the basal reader and enriched the concepts it presented, every student who participated in it completed the entire set of first-grade reading books.

Perhaps the most rewarding change I observed was in the children's attitudes toward reading. Instead of passively following along in a basal reader, children started to actively enjoy and comprehend the stories. The classroom became a full-fledged literacy environment planned around the core of the assigned reader. The core expanded until children found themselves writing and reading as an essential part of their daily experience.

REFERENCES

Aaron, I.E. (1987). Enriching the basal reading program with literature. In B.E. Cullinan (Ed.), *Children's literature in the reading program* (pp. 126–138). Newark, DE: International Reading Association.

Allington, R., & Broikou, K.A. (1988). Development of shared knowledge: A new role for classroom and specialist teachers. *The Reading Teacher, 41,* 806–812.

Allington, R.L., & McGill-Franzen, A. (1989a). Different programs, indifferent instruction. In D.K. Lipsky & A. Gartner (Eds.), *Beyond separate education: Quality education for all.* Baltimore, MD: Brookes.

Allington, R.L., & McGill-Franzen, A. (1989b). School response to reading failure: Instruction for Chapter 1 and special education students in grades two, four, and eight. *The Elementary School Journal, 89,* 529–542.

Allington, R.L., & Shake, M.C. (1986). Remedial reading: Achieving curricular congruence in classroom and clinic. *The Reading Teacher, 39,* 648–654.

Anderson, L. (1984). The environment of instruction: The function of seatwork in commercially developed curriculum. In G.G. Duffy, L.R. Roehler, & J. Mason (Eds.), *Comprehension instruction: Perspectives and suggestions* (pp. 93–103). New York: Longman.

Anderson, R.C., Hiebert, E.H., Scott, J.A., & Wilkinson, I.A. (1985). *Becoming a nation of readers: The report of the commission on reading.* Washington, DC: National Institute of Education.

Anderson, R.C., & Pearson, P.D. (1984). *A schema-theoretic view of basic processes in reading comprehension.* (Tech. Rep. No. 306). Champaign, IL: University of Illinois, Center for the Study of Reading.

Beck, I.L., & McKeown, M.G. (1981). Developing questions that promote comprehension: The story map. *Language Arts, 58*, 913–918.

Early, M., Cooper, E.K., & Santeusanio, N. (1979, 1983). *Sun and shadow.* New York: Harcourt Brace Jovanovich.

Goodman, K.S., Shannon, P., Freeman, Y.S., & Murphy, S. (1988). *Report card on basal readers.* Katonah, NY: Richard C. Owen.

Hoffman, J.V. (1985). *The oral recitation lesson: A teacher's guide.* Austin, TX: Academic Resource Consultants.

Holdaway, D. (1979). *The foundations of literacy.* New York: Scholastic.

Nelson, L., & Morris, D. (1986). *Supported oral reading: A year-long intervention in two inner-city primary grade classrooms.* Paper presented at the annual meeting of the National Reading Conference, Austin, TX.

Richek, M.A., & McTague, B.K. (1988). The "Curious George" strategy for children with reading problems. *The Reading Teacher, 42*, 220–225.

Stauffer, R.G. (1980). *The language experience approach to the teaching of reading* (2nd ed.). New York: Harper & Row.

CHILDREN'S LITERATURE REFERENCES

Allard, H. (1977). *Miss Nelson is missing.* Boston, MA: Houghton Mifflin.

Allard, H. (1985). *Miss Nelson is back.* Boston, MA: Houghton Mifflin.

Berenstain, S., & Berenstain, J. (1982). *The big honey hunt.* New York: Random House.

Berenstain, S., & Berenstain, J. (1984). *The Berenstain bears' nature guide.* New York: Random House.

Bonnie, R. (1961). *I know an old lady who swallowed a fly.* New York: Scholastic.

Bonsall, C. (1965). *The case of the cat's meow.* New York: Harper.

Carle, E. (1974). *The very hungry caterpillar.* New York: Scholastic.

Compton, F.E. (1973). *Compton's preencyclopedia.* Chicago, IL: Compton's.

Conklin, G. (1962). *We like bugs.* New York: Scholastic.

Garelick, M. (1967). *Where does the butterfly go when it rains?* New York: Scholastic.

Keats, E.J. (1971). *Over in the meadow.* New York: Scholastic.

Meyers, J. (1979). *Mammoth book of trivia.* New York: Harcourt.

Milios, R. (1987). *A new true book: Sleeping and dreaming.* Chicago: Children's Press.

Pape, D.L. (1988). *The snoring mystery.* Champaign, IL: Garrard.

Sendak, M. (1962). *Pierre.* New York: Harper.

Sendak, M. (1963). *Where the wild things are.* New York: Harper.

Shapp, M.C. (1975). *Let's find out about the sun.* New York: Franklin Watts.

Waber, B. (1972). *Ira sleeps over.* Boston, MA: Houghton Mifflin.

Whitcombe, B. (1988). *Animals at night.* New Mark, England: Bramix Books.

Section III

Fostering Motivation and Ownership in Reluctant Readers

When we are successful at creating school environments where children experiencing difficulty read voluntarily and avidly, we are well on the way to creating a school where all children develop high levels of reading proficiency. If children read only when we are watching—when we coerce their involvement in the reading—then children will not read enough to become proficient. In this section the articles focus on creating school environments where children read and then read some more. Three themes stand out in these selections:

- Improving access to appropriate texts and providing opportunities to read them,
- Enhancing ownership of reading activity with a focus on self-selection of texts to be read, and
- Fostering conversation about texts before, during, and after reading as a way to stimulate deeper understandings.

When schools organize instruction and instructional support programs around these themes, even children who find learning to read difficult become readers and writers. These are schools where children having difficulty still request books to take home for the weekend. Such schools are characterized not by awards and prizes for reading, but by children's easy access to interesting, appropriate books and by their access to adults who help them see the range of opportunities available and the power of personal reading.

Creating Classroom Cultures That Foster Reading Motivation

Linda B. Gambrell

What can teachers do to motivate students to read? Here are some responses from elementary-age children who were asked what teachers should do to get their students more interested and excited about reading:

- "Teachers should let us read more."

- "When we have 'Read and Respond Time' the teacher should let us read our own books and tell about them in a group."

- "Let us read more...about 10 more minutes every day."

- "Please make sure you do not interrupt us while we're reading."

- "Read to the class. I always get excited when I hear my favorite book...and my favorite book is *Frog and Toad*."

- "Do not let DEAR (Drop Everything and Read) time end so soon."

- "Make sure there are lots of books. There are not a lot of books in our classroom."

- "My teacher gets me interested in reading. She lets me read to her! She gave me a hug because I did so well...and she said, 'Good job!'"

I have long been convinced that the central and most important goal of reading instruction is to foster the love of reading. The children's responses listed earlier highlight the critical role of the teacher in creating a classroom culture that fosters reading motivation. My interest in the role of motivation in literacy development is grounded in this belief about the importance of teachers in helping children develop into readers who read for both pleasure and information.

How can we create classroom cultures that support and nurture children in becoming highly motivated readers? The results of a national survey conducted by the National Reading Research Center reveal that this is a question of great interest to teachers (O'Flahavan, Gambrell, Guthrie, Stahl, & Alvermann, 1992). Out of 84 reading topics, teachers identified "creating interest in reading" as the top priority for reading research. Three other topics related to motivation appeared in the top 10: increasing the amount and breadth of children's reading; developing intrinsic desire for reading; and exploring the roles teachers, peers, and parents play in increasing children's motivation to read.

It is generally acknowledged that motivation plays a critical role in learning. It often makes the difference between learning that is shallow and superficial and learning that is deep and internalized. Because of the influential role that motivation plays in literacy learning, teachers are more interested than ever before in understanding the relations that exist between motivation and achievement and in learning how to help all students achieve the goal of becoming effective, life-long readers.

In this article I discuss what research and theory suggest about the role of motivation in literacy development. First, I briefly review some of the research that has led to the current interest in motivation. I then describe some of the work my colleagues and I have been involved in for the past 4 years in the Literacy Motivation Project at the National Reading Research Center. This work has focused on identifying classroom factors associated with literacy motivation. Finally, I discuss six research-based factors that appear to be related to increased motivation to read and suggest some implications for practice.

A Resurgence of Interest in Motivation

The current interest in reading motivation is an outgrowth of the research of the 1980s that emphasized cognitive aspects of reading such as prior knowledge and strategic behaviors (Anderson & Pearson, 1984; Garner, 1987; Pressley, Borkowski, & Schneider, 1987). A number of these scholars have cautioned, however, that in order for students to develop into mature, effective readers they must possess both the skill and the will to read (Anderson, Hiebert, Scott, & Wilkinson, 1985; Borkowski, Carr, Rellinger, & Pressley, 1990; Paris & Oka, 1986; Winograd & Greelee, 1986). These researchers and theorists have emphasized the importance of balancing both affective and cognitive aspects of reading development. With this background, the reading research of the 1990s has begun to focus on a more comprehensive and balanced view of

reading that includes an emphasis on motivation and social interaction, as well as cognition and knowledge acquisition (Brandt, 1990; Csikszentmihalyi, 1991; McCombs, 1989; Turner & Paris, 1995).

The elementary school years are of considerable consequence for shaping subsequent reading motivation and achievement (Allington, 1994; Purcell-Gates, McIntyre, & Freppon, 1995; Turner, 1992). During this critical period, children must be supported and nurtured in both affective and cognitive aspects of literacy development (Alexander & Entwisle, 1988; Lau & Cheung, 1988; Oldfather, 1993; Snow, Barnes, Chandler, Goodman, & Hemphill, 1991). Our Literacy Motivation Project has focused on the role of motivation in literacy development and on identifying classroom and home practices that encourage children to spend time reading.

We have focused on these aspects of motivation for several reasons. First, we know that children who are motivated and who spend more time reading are better readers (Anderson, Wilson, & Fielding, 1988; Morrow, 1992; Taylor, Frye, & Maruyama, 1990). Second, some children arrive at school having far more experience with print, books, and book language and home support for reading than others (Allington, 1991). Third, supporting and nurturing reading motivation and achievement is crucial to improving educational prospects for children who find learning to read difficult (Allington, 1986, 1991; Smith-Burke, 1989).

Much of the recent work conducted by the National Reading Research Center has been guided by the engagement perspective (Alvermann & Guthrie, 1993; Guthrie, 1996), which builds on theories of motivation, knowledge acquisition, cognition, and social development. This perspective suggests that an engaged reader is motivated, knowledgeable, strategic, and socially interactive. In the following section I describe the engaged reader and the role that motivation plays in this conceptualization of the idealized reader.

The Engaged Reader

Teachers are guided in their decision making about the literacy curriculum by the view they hold of the idealized reader. One such conceptualization is that of the engaged reader who is motivated, knowledgeable, strategic, and socially interactive (see Figure). The engaged reader chooses to read for a variety of purposes, such as gaining new knowledge, escaping into the literary world of the text, and learning how to perform a task. The engaged reader is knowledgeable, able to use information gained from previous experiences to construct new understandings from text; to acquire knowledge from

text; and to apply knowledge gained from text reading in a variety of personal, intellectual, and social contexts. The engaged reader is also strategic, employing cognitive strategies to decode, interpret, comprehend, monitor, and regulate the reading process so that goals and purposes of reading are satisfied. Finally, the engaged reader is socially interactive, able to share and communicate with others in the process of constructing and extending the meaning of text.

Portrait of an Engaged Reader

In one of the interviews we conducted as a part of a study of fifth-grade students' motivation to read (Gambrell, Codling, & Palmer, 1996; Palmer, Codling, & Gambrell, 1994), a student described reading about World War II

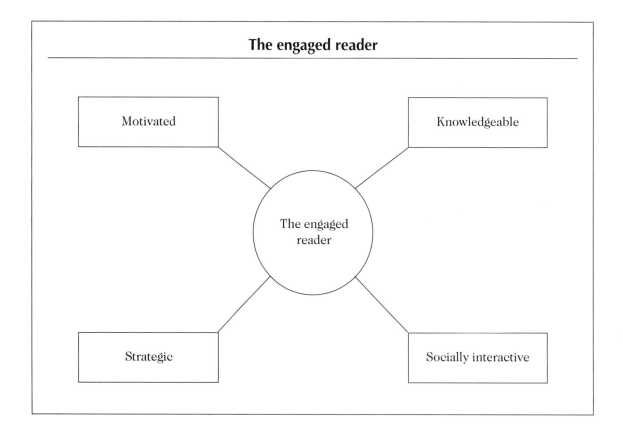

The engaged reader

Motivated

Knowledgeable

The engaged reader

Strategic

Socially interactive

in the encyclopedia and in the award-winning book *Number the Stars* (Lowry, 1990). Her response reveals a compelling picture of an engaged reader.

> Well, I became interested in the Jewish people and World War II and Hitler and all that...so I went and I took the "H" book and I started reading some stuff...and I found out all kinds of different things. Then, I went and I read a book from my teacher called *Number the Stars*. And when I read that, I found out...more from a child's point of view...her best friend is Jewish and they're trying to get her away from all the soldiers...it was just tragic, you know. I like reading about characters, and how the authors take real-life things and make it into their own fiction.

This girl's comments reveal the depth of her emotional involvement in the book *Number the Stars* and her compassion for the young Jewish girl who tries to escape the Nazi soldiers. She also describes how reading informational text has contributed to her understanding of World War II. The power of intertextuality is revealed as she describes how her reading of information in the encyclopedia (the "H" book) about Hitler and World War II provided background information for her interpretation of *Number the Stars*. In addition, she describes how reading *Number the Stars* helped her understand, in a more personal way, the impact of the war on children. Her comment, "it was just tragic, you know," suggests that this is a reader who has also come to better understand her own feelings about war and discrimination through reading. The personal, intellectual, and social nature of engaged reading is revealed in this student's reflections. Her words paint a portrait of a reader who is motivated, knowledgeable, strategic, and socially interactive.

It is not by accident that motivation is mentioned first in the description of the engaged reader. Teachers have long recognized that motivation is at the heart of many of the pervasive problems we face in educating today's children. A question that teachers often ask regarding the children they are most concerned about is, "How can I motivate this student to read?" The research we have conducted in the Literacy Motivation Project, as well as research conducted by noted motivational theorists such as Deci and Ryan (1985) and Lepper (1988), suggests that a more appropriate question for us to ask is, "How do we create an environment in which this student will be motivated to read?"

For several years my colleagues and I have worked with classroom teachers on a series of studies designed to explore the literacy motivation of first-, third-, and fifth-grade students, with particular emphasis on classroom contexts that promote reading engagement. In the following section, several of the studies that focus on reading are described briefly.

The First-Grade Motivation Studies

The first-grade studies involved the implementation of a classroom-based motivation program designed to increase reading motivation. The Running Start (RS) program, developed by Reading Is Fundamental, is grounded in Cambourne's (1988) model of literacy learning. It proposes that motivation and reading development are fostered when children are immersed in a book-rich environment; exposed to many demonstrations of how books are used; engaged in interactions with others about books; given the responsibility for making decisions about what, when, and how they read; provided with opportunities to approximate literacy activities; and supported by interactions with adults who have high expectations for their success.

The RS program was designed to support the literacy development of first graders by providing them with high-quality children's literature and increasing opportunities for reading both at school and at home. The motivational program brings school, home, and community together in a 10-week celebration that is designed to help children develop a love of reading. The RS program recognizes that the availability of books is a key factor in reading development; therefore, funds are provided for teachers to select and purchase high-quality fiction and informational children's books for their classroom libraries. This results in an infusion of approximately 50–60 new books for the typical first-grade classroom. Teacher book selection is an important aspect of the program because teachers know which books will be appropriate and appealing to their particular students.

The theme of the RS program is "Creating Readers for the 21st Century" and, in keeping with the theme, children are challenged to read, or have someone read to them, 21 books during the 10-week program. The program values equally both independent reading and being read to. Teachers support children in their efforts to meet the challenge of reading 21 books by creating classroom opportunities for reading and book sharing. For example, in some classrooms first graders are paired with older students who either read to them or listen to them read. In other classrooms guest readers read to individual students and small groups. In addition, parents and other family members are encouraged to read to the first graders to assure that every child is successful.

Children are provided with a number of reading-related incentives during the program. Each child receives a personal Challenge chart and stickers for keeping track of individual progress toward the 21-book goal. In addition, bookmarks are given to the children as reminders and incentives to read. Finally, when children meet the challenge of reading 21 books they get to choose books for their home libraries. The goal of the RS program is to increase the reading motivation and behaviors of first-grade children by increasing the number of books in the classroom library, allowing children to choose what they read, encouraging children to take books home to share with family members, supporting children in reaching the 21-book goal, and rewarding children for achieving the goal (for a more complete description of the RS program, see Gambrell, Almasi, Xie, & Heland, 1995).

We were interested in a number of questions about how an intervention program like Running Start might affect young children's motivation to read and how such a program might affect family literacy practices. We conducted four studies that provided some interesting insights about the value of programs designed to increase the reading motivation of young children.

Can a Motivational Reading Program Make a Difference in Young Children's Motivation to Read?

In our first RS study, more than 7,000 children, 4,000 parents and 320 teachers from 49 schools in 9 U.S. states participated in the program and responded to pre- and posttest survey instruments designed to assess program effects (Gambrell et al., 1995). Schools included urban, suburban, and rural settings, as well as diverse populations and economic levels. The results revealed statistically significant increases in the reading motivation and behaviors of the first graders and parents who participated in RS. Although findings must be interpreted with caution, the results suggest that a classroom-based, 10-week motivational program can enhance the reading motivation and behaviors of children as well as the number and quality of literacy experiences in the home.

Can a Reading Motivation Program Make a Difference With Children From Low-Literacy-Achieving Schools?

We were especially interested in whether this motivational reading program would benefit children from schools with depressed reading achievement scores. Therefore, study two explored the effectiveness of the RS program with first-grade children from an economically depressed urban area who attended low-literacy-achieving schools (Gambrell et al., 1995; Gambrell & Morrow, 1995). The study also included similar matched schools. The control schools completed all assessments but did not participate in the motivational program. Approximately 550 first graders and their parents participated in the study. Both children and their parents responded to survey instruments designed to assess reading motivation and behaviors, as well as the number and quality of family literacy practices. In addition, approximately 200 students were selected randomly from RS and matched schools to participate in individual interviews. The results of this study revealed that the children who participated in the RS program were more motivated to read, spent more time reading independently, engaged more frequently in discussions about books and stories with family and friends, took more books home to read, and spent more time reading with family members. The results of the family literacy practices survey revealed that parents who had children in RS spent more time reading to their children, discussed books and stories more often, and purchased more books for their children. In comparison to the matched-school parents, parents of RS children reported that their children enjoyed reading to a greater extent and spent more time reading independently.

The results of this study provided compelling evidence that a motivational reading program can enhance the reading motivation and behavior of children from low-literacy-achieving schools and can increase both the quantity and quality of family literacy practices. There was consistent and converging evidence from children and their parents, across all assessments, that participation in the program promoted engagement in reading in the classroom and in the home.

Is a Motivational Reading Program Worth the Time and Effort?

One concern about motivational programs is that any positive effects that accrue may be limited to the duration of the program; therefore, we conducted study three to determine possible long-term effects of the RS program. This follow-up study was conducted with the children and parents who participated in study two. In the fall of the following year, when the children were in the second grade, children and parents in both RS and matched schools responded to the survey instruments used in study two. Statistically significant differences again were found in favor of the children and parents who had participated in the 10-week RS program during first grade. Six months after the conclusion of the program, children who had participated in RS reported spending more time talking about books with friends, reading out loud to family members, and perhaps of most significance, perceiving themselves as more competent readers than students in the control group. Perhaps the RS emphasis on sharing books with family members resulted in home literacy practices that nurtured and supported children's literacy development or that helped children and their parents establish the habit of reading on a consistent basis. Clearly, the results suggest that a book-rich classroom environment and parental support appear to be linked to the long-term positive effects of this program.

How Did the Motivational Reading Program Affect the Classroom Culture?

In study four, observations were conducted in RS classrooms and in matched classrooms to determine whether the increase in the number of books available to children and the emphasis on increasing reading opportunities at school and at home made a difference in the classroom culture. Classrooms were observed for one full day on the first visit, and the reading and language arts period was observed during a second visit. These observations revealed interesting differences across classrooms. The RS classrooms had specific areas designated as reading corners or reading centers. We were not surprised that the RS classrooms had more books than the control classrooms, but they also had more elaborate reading corners (pillows, rocking chairs, puppets, etc.) and more visual displays (posters, bulletin boards, etc.) that related to the celebration and value of reading than did the control classrooms. Of particular interest was the finding that more time was devoted to sustained silent reading in the RS classrooms. In addition, more verbal interactions about books and reading were observed between teachers and children and between children and their peers in the RS classrooms. In the matched classrooms no verbal interactions about books or reading were observed between individual children and the teachers other than those that occurred during reading instruction. The results of this observational study suggest that a motivational reading program can foster a physical environment and social interactions that encourage and support children in their reading development.

The Third- and Fifth-Grade Motivational Studies

In our work with third- and fifth-grade students we developed and used the Motivation to Read Profile (MRP) to explore elementary students' motivation to read. The MRP consists of a survey instrument and a conversational interview. The survey instrument assesses self-concept as a reader and the value placed on reading; the semistructured conversational interview is designed to assess personal, social, and text factors related to reading motivation (Gambrell, Palmer, Codling, & Mazzoni, 1996). The results of the Self-Concept as a Reader subscale revealed that although many elementary students reported that they were "very good readers" (47%), significant numbers of students do not view themselves as competent readers. For example, 45% of the students reported that they worry about what other classmates think about their reading, and 17% reported that when they read out loud they feel embarrassed or sad. We also found, as have other researchers (Henk & Melnick, 1995; McKenna & Kear, 1990) that students' self-concepts as readers are linked to reading achievement, with less proficient readers having significantly lower self-concepts than their more proficient counterparts (Gambrell et al., 1996).

The Value of Reading subscale revealed that, in general, elementary students value reading, but many children do not view reading as a positive activity or as an activity of high priority. For example, 17% of the students reported that they would rather clean their room than read a book, 14% predicted that they would spend very little or no time reading when they grow up, and 10% reported that people who read are boring. These are the types of responses about literacy motivation that most concern teachers. One finding of particular interest in our study was that the younger third-grade students reported that they valued reading more highly than did the older fifth-grade students. This was somewhat surprising in that we had hypothesized that older students would be more aware of the value of reading than would younger students.

In addition to the information we collected on the survey, conversational interviews were conducted to gain insights about what motivated third- and fifth-grade children to read (Palmer et al., 1994). The interviews were conducted with children from across three levels of reading achievement (above grade level, on grade level, and below grade level) and across levels of reading motivation (highly motivated, less motivated). The results of the analysis of the interviews revealed four key features that appear to be associated with motivation to read: access to books in the classroom, opportunities to self-select books, familiarity with books, and social interactions with others about books.

Fostering Reading Motivation

The insights revealed by the first-, third-, and fifth-grade students who participated in our studies have heightened our awareness of the importance of supporting students in their reading development by creating classroom cultures that foster reading motivation. The research conducted in our Literacy Motivation Project and the work of other researchers (Oldfather, 1993; Ruddell, 1995; Turner, 1995; Turner & Paris, 1995) suggest that classroom cultures that encourage reading motivation are characterized by a teacher who is a reading model, a book-rich classroom environment, opportunities for choice, familiarity with books, social interactions about books, and literacy-related incentives that reflect the value of reading.

The Teacher as an Explicit Reading Model

One of the key factors in motivating students to read is a teacher who values reading and is enthusiastic about sharing a love of reading with students. I believe that it is within the power of every teacher to inspire children to find a lifetime of pleasure and information in the reading of good books. Throughout our interviews with children we were constantly reminded of the important role of the teacher because children made so many spontaneous comments about teachers being a motivating influence. At the conclusion of one interview we asked third- and fifth-grade students, "Who gets you really excited and interested in reading things?" Not surprisingly, teachers, parents, and peers were frequently mentioned. In some classrooms the teacher was brought up by almost every student, while in other classrooms the teacher was rarely mentioned.

One very important way in which teachers motivate students to read is by being an explicit reading model. Research suggests that teachers who love reading and are avid readers themselves have students who have higher reading achievement than do students of teachers who rarely read (Lundberg & Linnakyla, 1993). One possible explanation for this is that teachers who read are more likely to be explicit models for their students.

Many teachers "model" reading during sustained silent reading in their classrooms, and although this is an admirable practice, I believe it presents a passive, rather than an explicit, model of what it means to be a reader. Teachers become explicit reading models when they share their own reading experiences with students and emphasize how reading enhances and enriches their lives. There is usually something worth sharing in most of the books and materials we read—an exciting or informative paragraph, a description of a character, or an interesting turn of a phrase.

For several years we have encouraged teachers in our Summer Reading Program at the University of Maryland to share their personal reading with students and to be more explicit in illustrating to children the value of reading in their own lives. For example, one teacher told her class that the book she was reading, *The Prince of Tides* by Pat Conroy, was extremely well written. She read aloud an interesting description of the main character's family and the class then discussed what the character meant by that description. Another teacher read *The Right Stuff* by Thomas Wolfe, a book about the U.S. space program. Across a 2-week period she shared sections of this book with her students, particularly parts of the book that dealt with historical facts.

When we, as teachers, share our own reading with students, we show how reading enhances our lives. In this way, we demonstrate to our students that reading helps us learn more about the world in which we live, gives us pleasure and enjoyment, develops our vocabulary, and helps us become better speakers and more effective writers. Most importantly, when we share appropriate selections from our own personal reading, students begin to see us as real readers. If we serve as explicit reading models for our students and specifically associate reading with enjoyment, pleasure, and learning, our students will be encouraged to become voluntary lifelong readers.

A Book-Rich Classroom Environment

A number of studies during the past decade have provided support for the notion that when children have environments that are book-rich, the motivation to read is high (Allington & McGill-Franzen, 1993; Elley, 1992; Gambrell, 1993; Lundberg & Linnakyla,

1993; Morrow, 1992; Purcell-Gates et al., 1995). When asked to tell about the most interesting book they had read recently, the overwhelming majority of children in our studies reported that they had selected the book from the classroom library rather than from school, community, or home libraries (Gambrell et al., 1996). The first-grade motivational studies clearly suggest that increasing the number of books available to children in the classroom can have a positive effect on the amount and quality of the literacy experiences in the classroom as well as the home environment. The first-grade studies also suggest that there are positive benefits to encouraging children to take books home from the classroom to share with family members. These findings suggest that book access is a significant factor in literacy development and that greater attention should be devoted to assuring that high-quality classroom libraries are a priority in schools.

A book-rich classroom environment is essential to nurturing and supporting young readers, but it is not sufficient for the development of highly motivated readers. The Bradford Book-Flood experiment (Ingham, 1981), a large-scale study conducted in England, investigated the effects of increased book access on students' reading motivation and achievement. No significant increase was found for either, despite the substantial increase in books available to children. One of the major findings of this study was that it is what is done with books that makes a difference. Just as having a piano in the home will not necessarily make a child a pianist, simply having books available is not sufficient for the development of highly motivated readers. On the other hand, a pianist must have a piano to perform, and children must have high-quality books and other reading materials available to support them in becoming motivated, engaged readers.

Opportunities for Choice

The role of choice, in motivation in general and reading motivation in particular, is well recognized (Spaulding, 1992). One of the most consistent findings across our studies with first-, third-, and fifth-grade children was the power of choice. When children told us about both narrative and information books they "most enjoyed" reading, over 80% responded that they had self-selected the books from the classroom libraries. The research related to self-selection of reading material supports the notion that the books and stories that children find "most interesting" are those they have selected for their own reasons and purposes. In a study conducted by Schiefele (1991), students who were allowed and encouraged to choose their own reading material expended more effort in learning and understanding the material. It appears that opportunities for choice promote students' independence and versatility as readers (Turner, 1995).

Only 10% of the children in our study talked about books or stories that had been "assigned" by the teacher. Other researchers (Deci & Ryan, 1985; Turner, 1995) have documented that task engagement increases when students are provided with opportunities to make choices about their learning. In addition, findings from a number of studies suggest a strong correlation between choice and the development of intrinsic motivation (Paris & Oka, 1986; Rodin, Rennert, & Solomon, 1980; Turner, 1992).

Opportunities to Interact Socially With Others

Across all three grade levels, children talked enthusiastically about interacting with others about the books and stories they were reading. Children frequently commented that they chose a book because someone had told them about it. Children reported that friends had most often told them about the book, but teachers and parents also were mentioned frequently. For example, one student said, "My friend Kristin was reading it and told me about it and I said, 'Hmmm, that sounds pretty interesting...,' so I read it." Another child reported that "I hear about good books from my teachers...they read good books to us...." Our findings support the current emphasis on student book-sharing opportunities, book clubs, and discussion groups, as well as the importance of teacher read-aloud sessions. The more books that children are exposed to, and know about, the more books they are likely to read.

Current theories of motivation recognize that learning is facilitated by social interactions with others (McCombs, 1989; Oldfather, 1993). A number of recent reading studies have indicated that social collaboration promotes achievement, higher level cognition, and intrinsic desire to read (Almasi, 1995; Slavin, 1990; Wood, 1990). A recent study by Guthrie, Schafer, Wang, and Afflerbach (1993) revealed the important role of social interactions in reading development. In addition, the results of the 1992 National Assessment of Educational Progress (NAEP) (Mullis, Campbell, & Farstrup, 1993) indicated that students who engaged in frequent discussions about their reading with friends and family were more motivated and had higher reading achievement scores than did students who did not have such interactions. Both the Guthrie et al. study and the NAEP results suggest that social interactions with others about books and stories foster wide, frequent reading. Taken together, this body of research suggests that opportunities for sharing and talking with others about books is an important factor in developing engaged, motivated readers and supports the contention that social interactions have a positive influence on reading achievement.

Opportunities to Become Familiar With Lots of Books

Two underlying assumptions in our studies were that interest is a key factor in reading motivation, and consequently, that children's interests would be reflected in the books and stories they chose to discuss. Numerous recent studies have documented that interest fosters depth of processing and enhances learning (Alexander, Kulikowich, & Hetton, 1994; Hidi, 1990). A related factor that has not been as extensively researched is curiosity. In our conversations with children we found an interesting link between book familiarity and curiosity. It appears that young children want to read and are curious about books that are somewhat familiar. When children in our study talked about books they "most enjoyed" reading, they frequently mentioned that they got interested in the book because they had "heard about it from a friend," "read other books about the character," "knew the author," or had "read other books in the series." This same pattern of responses occurred when we asked children to tell us about books they wanted to read. Curiosity is acknowledged to be a driving force in motivation, and the children in our study were curious about and more motivated to read books that were familiar.

Appropriate Reading-Related Incentives

In a recent analysis of the research on rewards and incentives Cameron and Pierce (1994) found that rewards do not negatively impact intrinsic motivation with respect to attitude, time on task, and performance. This finding runs counter to views expressed by many educators and psychologists and points to the complex nature of the relation between incentives and motivation. Clearly, we need to know more about the role of incentives in promoting literacy development, particularly with respect to the development of intrinsic motivation.

Our research in first-grade classrooms taught us that children tend to view the "reward" as desirable. Our findings suggest that when a book is the reward for reading, as was the case in the first-grade Running Start program, children learn to value books and reading. In our exit interviews with children who participated in the RS program we asked what they liked best about the program. We fully expected that children would mention the incentives such as the stickers, bookmarks, or book. But only a few children mentioned the incentives. The most frequently occurring comments focused on social interactions related to books and reading. For example, children mentioned "reading to my partner," "reading with my parents," and "reading lots of good books."

The findings of our study suggest that if we are interested in developing an intrinsic desire to read, books are indeed the best reward. We believe that extrinsic rewards that are strongly related to reading and reading behaviors (such as books, bookmarks, or teacher praise) can be used effectively to increase intrinsic motivation, particularly for children who do not have a literacy-rich background (Cameron & Pierce, 1994). Our studies with first-grade children provide some evidence that reading-related rewards increase children's motivation to read and the frequency of reading activities. As a result of these studies we have put forth the reward proximity hypothesis: the closer the reward to the desired behavior (for example, books to reading), the greater the likelihood that intrinsic motivation will increase. Rewards that are strongly linked to the desired behaviors may help to shape and direct the development of intrinsic motivation.

One teacher in a school where we have worked created a classroom climate where books and reading were viewed as valuable and rewarding. She collected old books at flea markets, garage sales, and library sales. (She often received free books by offering to pick up any books that were not sold.) Her goal was to collect enough books to be able to present every child in her classroom with a book on his or her birthday. She decorated a large box and attached a poster that read, "Mrs. Brown's Beloved Birthday Books." She also duplicated a fancy bookplate that read: "Happy Birthday and Happy Reading! This special book was given to *(child's name)* by Mrs. Brown on *(date)*" Parent volunteers pasted the blank bookplates in the front of each book before they were placed in the book box. On a child's birthday, he or she got to choose a book from the box, and the teacher signed the book plate. This is a wonderful example of how a teacher can show that books and reading are valued.

Conclusion

The motivational research of the last decade supports what good classroom teachers have known for a long time. Supporting children in their literacy learning is not an exact science, nor is it a simple matter. We can, however, make a real difference in the literacy lives of young children when we serve as reading models and motivators and create classroom cultures that are book-rich, provide opportunities for choice, encourage social interactions about books, build on the familiar, and reflect the view that books are the best reward.

Author Notes

The work reported herein is a National Reading Research Center Project of the University of Georgia and the University of Maryland. It was supported under the educational Research and Development Centers Program (PR/AWARD NO. 117A20007) as administered by the Office of Educational Research and Improvement, U.S. Department of Education. The findings and opinions expressed in this report do not reflect the position or policies of the National Reading Research Center, the Office of Educational Research and Improvement, or the U.S. Department of Education.

REFERENCES

Alexander, K.L., & Entwisle, D.R. (1988). Achievement in the first 2 years of school: Patterns and processes. *Monographs of the Society of Research in Child Development, 53,* 1–157.

Alexander, P.A., Kulikowich, J.M., & Hetton, T.L. (1994). The role of subject matter knowledge and interest in the processing of linear and nonlinear texts. *Review of Educational Research, 64,* 210–253.

Allington, R.L. (1986). Policy constraints and effective compensatory reading instruction: A review. In J. Hoffman (Ed.), *Effective teaching of reading: Research and practice* (pp. 261–289). Newark, DE: International Reading Association.

Allington, R.L. (1991). The legacy of "slow it down and make it more concrete." In J. Zutell & S. McCormick (Eds.), *Learner factors/teacher factors: Issues in literacy research and instruction* (pp. 19–30). Chicago, IL: National Reading Conference.

Allington, R.L. (1994). The schools we have. The schools we need. *The Reading Teacher, 48,* 14–29.

Allington, R.L., & McGill-Franzen, A. (1993, October 13). What are they to read? Not all children, Mr. Riley, have easy access to books. *Education Week,* p. 26.

Almasi, J. (1995). The nature of fourth graders' sociocognitive conflicts in peer-led and teacher-led discussions of literature. *Reading Research Quarterly, 30,* 314– 351.

Alvermann, D.E., & Guthrie, J.T. (1993, January). Themes and directions of the National Reading Research Center. *Perspectives in Reading Research,* No. 1.

Anderson, R.C., Hiebert, E.H., Scott, A., & Wilkinson, I.A.G. (1985). *Becoming a nation of readers: The report of the Commission on Reading.* Washington, DC: National Institute of Education.

Anderson, R.C., & Pearson, P.D. (1984). A schema-theoretic view of reading. In P.D. Pearson, M. Kamil, P. Mosenthal, & R. Barr (Eds.), *Handbook of reading research*: Volume 1 (pp. 255–291). New York: Longman.

Anderson, R.C., Wilson, P.T., & Fielding, L.G. (1988). Growth in reading and how children spend their time outside of school. *Reading Research Quarterly, 23*, 285–303.

Borkowski, J.G., Carr, M., Rellinger, E., & Pressley, M. (1990). Self-regulated strategy use: Interdependence of metacognition, attributions, and self-esteem. In B.F. Jones & L. Idol (Eds.), *Dimensions of thinking: Review of research* (pp. 2–60). Hillsdale, NJ: Erlbaum.

Brandt, D. (1990). *Literacy as involvement: The acts of writers, readers, and texts*. Carbondale, IL: Southern Illinois University Press.

Cambourne, B. (1988). *The whole story: Natural learning and the acquisition of literacy in the classroom*. Auckland, NZ: Ashton Scholastic.

Cameron, J., & Pierce, W.D. (1994). Reinforcement, reward, and intrinsic motivation: A meta-analysis. *Review of Educational Research, 64*, 363–423.

Csikszentmihalyi, M. (1991). Literacy and intrinsic motivation. In S.R. Graubard (Ed.), *Literacy: An overview by fourteen experts* (pp. 115–140). New York: Farrar, Straus, Giroux.

Deci, E.L., & Ryan, R.M. (1985). *Intrinsic motivation and self-determination in human behavior*. San Diego, CA: Academic Press.

Elley, W.B. (1992). *How in the world do students read?* Hamburg, Germany: International Association for the Evaluation of Educational Achievement.

Gambrell, L.B. (1993). *The impact of RUNNING START on the reading motivation and behavior of first-grade children* (Research Rep.). College Park, MD: University of Maryland.

Gambrell, L.B., Almasi, J.F., Xie, Q., & Heland, V. (1995). Helping first graders get a running start in reading. In L. Morrow (Ed.), *Family literacy: Connections in schools and communities* (pp. 143–154). Newark, DE: International Reading Association.

Gambrell, L.B., Codling, R.M., & Palmer, B. (1996). *Elementary students' motivation to read* (Research Rep.). Athens, GA: Universities of Georgia and Maryland, National Reading Research Center.

Gambrell, L.B., & Morrow, L.M. (1995). Creating motivating contexts for literacy learning. In L. Baker, P. Afflerbach, & D. Reinking (Eds.), *Developing engaged readers in home and school communities* (pp. 115–136). Mahwah, NJ: Erlbaum.

Gambrell, L.B., Palmer, B.M., Codling, R.M., & Mazzoni, S. (1996). Assessing motivation to read. *The Reading Teacher, 49*, 518–533.

Garner, R. (1987). *Metacognition and reading comprehension*. Norwood, NJ: Ablex.

Guthrie, J.T. (1996). Educational contexts for engagement in literacy. *The Reading Teacher, 49*, 432–445.

Guthrie, J.T., Schafer, W., Wang, Y., & Afflerbach, P. (1993). *Influences of instruction on reading engagement: An empirical exploration of a social-cognitive framework of reading activity* (Research Rep. No. 3). Athens, GA: National Reading Research Center.

Henk, W.A., & Melnick, S.A. (1995). The reader self-perception scale (RSPS): A new tool for measuring how children feel about themselves as readers. *The Reading Teacher, 48*, 470–483.

Hidi, S. (1990). Interest and its contribution as a mental resource for learning. *Review of Educational Research, 60*, 549–571.

Ingham, J. (1981). *Books and reading development*. London: Heinemann.

Lau, K.S., & Cheung, S.M. (1988). Reading interests of Chinese adolescents: Effects of personal and social factors. *International Journal of Psychology, 23*, 695–705.

Lepper, M.R. (1988). Motivational considerations in the study of instruction. *Cognition and Instruction, 5*, 289–309.

Lundberg, I., & Linnakyla, P. (1993). *Teaching reading around the world*. Hamburg, Germany: International Association for the Evaluation of Educational Achievement.

McCombs, B.L. (1989). Self-regulated learning and academic achievement: A phenomenological view. In B.J. Zimmerman & D.H. Schunk (Eds.), *Self-regulated learning and achievement:*

Theory, research, and practice (pp. 51–82). New York: Springer-Verlag.

McKenna, M.C., & Kear, D.J. (1990). Measuring attitude toward reading: A new tool for teachers. *The Reading Teacher, 43,* 626–639.

Morrow, L.M. (1992). The impact of a literature-based program on literacy achievement, use of literature, and attitudes of children from minority backgrounds. *Reading Research Quarterly, 27,* 250–275.

Mullis, I.V.S., Campbell, J.R., & Farstrup, A.E. (1993). *NAEP 1992 reading report card for the nation and the states.* Washington, DC: Office of Educational Research and Improvement.

O'Flahavan, J., Gambrell, L.B., Guthrie, J., Stahl, S., & Alvermann, D. (1992, August-September). Poll results guide activities of research center. *Reading Today,* p. 12.

Oldfather, P. (1993). What students say about motivating experiences in a whole language classroom. *The Reading Teacher, 46,* 672–681.

Palmer, B.M., Codling, R.M., & Gambrell, L. (1994). In their own words: What elementary students have to say about motivation to read. *The Reading Teacher, 48,* 176–178.

Paris, S.G., & Oka, E.R. (1986). Self-regulated learning among exceptional children. *Exceptional Children, 53,* 103–108.

Pressley, M., Borkowski, J.G., & Schneider, W. (1987). Cognitive strategies: Good strategy users coordinate metacognition and knowledge. In R. Vasta & G. Whitehurst (Eds.), *Annals of child development, 4* (pp. 89–129). Greenwich, CT: JAI Press.

Purcell-Gates, V., McIntyre, E., & Freppon, P. (1995). Learning written storybook language in school: A comparison of low-SES children in skills-based and whole language classrooms. *American Educational Research Journal, 32,* 659–685.

Rodin, J., Rennert, K., & Solomon, S. (1980). Intrinsic motivation for control: Fact or fiction. In A. Baum, J.E. Singer, & S. Valios (Eds.), *Advances in environmental psychology II* (pp. 177–186). Hillsdale, NJ: Erlbaum.

Ruddell, R.B. (1995). Those influential literacy teachers: Meaning negotiators and motivation builders. *The Reading Teacher, 48,* 454–463.

Schiefele, U. (1991). Interest, learning, and motivation. *Educational Psychologist, 26,* 299–323.

Slavin, R.E. (1990). *Cooperative learning: Theory, research and practice.* Englewood Cliffs, NJ: Prentice-Hall.

Smith-Burke, T.M. (1989). Political and economic dimensions of literacy: Challenges for the 1990's. In S. McCormick & J. Zutell (Eds.), *Cognitive and social perspectives for literacy research and instruction* (pp. 1–18). Chicago: National Reading Conference.

Snow, C.E., Barnes, W.S., Chandler, J., Goodman, I.F., & Hemphill, L. (1991). *Unfulfilled expectations: Home and school influences on literacy.* Cambridge, MA: Harvard University Press.

Spaulding, C.L. (1992). The motivation to read and write. In J.W. Irwin & M.A. Doyle (Eds.), *Reading/writing connections: Learning from research* (pp. 177–201). Newark, DE: International Reading Association.

Taylor, B.M., Frye, B.J., & Maruyama, G.M. (1990). Time spent reading and reading growth. *American Educational Research Journal, 27,* 351–362.

Turner, J.C. (1992, April). *Identifying motivation for literacy in first grade: An observational study.* Paper presented at the annual meeting of the American Educational Research Association, San Francisco, CA.

Turner, J.C. (1995). The influence of classroom contexts on young children's motivation for literacy. *Reading Research Quarterly, 30,* 410–441.

Turner, J.C., & Paris, S.G. (1995). How literacy tasks influence children's motivation for literacy. *The Reading Teacher, 48,* 662–675.

Winograd, P., & Greelee, M. (1986). Students need a balanced reading program. *Educational Leadership, 43*(7), 16–21.

Wood, K. (1990). Collaborative learning. *The Reading Teacher, 43,* 346–347.

CHILDREN'S LITERATURE REFERENCE

Lowry, L. (1990). *Number the stars.* Boston, MA: Houghton Mifflin

A Matter of Interest: Literature That Hooks Reluctant Readers and Keeps Them Reading

Jo Worthy

In the mid 1970s I graduated from college and accepted a job as a third-grade teacher in a rural, high-poverty area in the southern United States. I was naive and idealistic and figured I could make a real difference with my third graders, most of whom were very poor and few of whom had even a single book in their homes. The third-grade classes were homogeneously grouped, and I was given a challenging assignment: the sixth-lowest group of seven. In the inservice days before school started, the teacher with the seventh-lowest group approached me with the idea of team teaching for reading. I had heard about team teaching in my education classes, and I knew that it was the state of the art, so I eagerly agreed. She suggested that we break our two classes into four groups and that I take the "high group," whose students were all in my class, and the "low group," whose students were all in her class, and she would take the "middle groups" of students from both classes. The idea was that, since the "low group" was the smallest, I would be able to give the students a lot of individual attention. I could not wait to tackle the challenge.

Having heard the warnings about self-fulfilling prophecies (Rosenthal & Jacobson, 1968), I chose not to look at the low group's cumulative folders, so I did not know their histories of failure and frustration that included repeating at least two grades each. Incredibly, they had been using the same preprimers for instruction each year since "the first" first grade but had repeatedly failed the accompanying tests. Reality assaulted my ideals when four angry young men, Sammy, Michael, David, and James, entered my classroom on the first day of school. The books I was expected to use with them—the third preprimer, which contained about eight words per page —were placed around the reading group table. Those "third graders," ranging in age from 10 to 12, stood around the table and glared at me and the hated books.

Every day these students waged an angry war with the books and with me until the thought of going to school made me want to cry. I knew this struggle could not be right and, if I had been allowed to do so, I would have taken the boys outside and helped them burn the basals. Beyond respecting their well-founded hatred of reading, however, I had very few ideas. One of the tools I had learned about in education classes was the Language Experience Approach (LEA) (Stauffer, 1970), so I had the boys dictate stories about their lives and then read their own and one another's tales. This worked well at first, but it was not long before the same experiences were being rehashed to the point of boredom. I was at a dead end. I was frustrated every day and, to survive as a first year teacher, I copped out and returned the boys to their regular teacher, who returned them to the basal reader.

I vowed that if I did survive that first year, I would try to find ways of helping struggling readers. After that year, I taught for 6 additional years while pursuing a master's degree in reading education. I found some answers to my questions about struggling readers, but with every new class of students there came more questions, so I returned to school full time to pursue a doctoral degree in reading education.

Now, almost 20 years later, I still feel guilty about abandoning Sammy, Michael, David, and James. If I had known then what I know now, they might have had a different experience—one that centered on making reading meaningful and successful through the use of interesting literature.

It Is Not Just a Matter of Reading

Like Sammy and friends, most struggling readers begin with word learning difficulty, although the initial problem is usually complicated by failure to succeed and its accompanying self-concept issues (McCormick, 1994). Students who have continually met with failure see reading as the enemy. For struggling readers, then, the first focus of instruction should be to rebuild their damaged self-concepts through motivation that is "fueled by successful experiences" (Mealey, 1990, p. 598). Struggling readers should not be segregated from their age and grade peers, though. The negative effects of such practices far outweigh the positive effects (Allington, 1994). To continue to make progress in thinking and learning, as well as to fuel self-concept and motivation, readers should participate in regular classroom experiences appropriate to their cognitive and maturational levels, including interesting, cognitively challenging books presented orally or on tape. To make progress in reading, however, struggling readers need opportunities to read appropriately challenging material independently. It is not enough, however, to provide books that speak only to their reading difficulty. When only reading level is considered, below-grade-level basal readers and "baby books" often become the standard fare. Nothing could be more defeating for students whose self-concept is already low, and such a focus rarely leads students to lifelong reading. Far more important than readability is interest; in fact, when students have strong interest in what they read, they can frequently transcend their so-called reading level (Hunt, 1971). Indeed, many educators and researchers consider interest to be a paramount factor in all learning (Dewey, 1913; Hidi, 1990; Schiefele, 1991).

A similar point can be made about students who are capable readers but who choose not to read. Although most children begin their school careers with a positive attitude toward reading, many show a steady decline in voluntary reading as they progress through school (Heathington, 1979; McKenna, Ellsworth, & Kear, 1995; Shapiro & White, 1991). Students who do not enjoy typical school texts and novels often never engage with reading at all, and many develop an aversion to reading that may be lifelong. Even if they are not initially struggling readers, reluctant readers tend to gradually lose some academic ground, because wide reading is related to increases in general knowledge and reading comprehension (Anderson,

Hiebert, Scott, & Wilkinson, 1985; Williamson & Williamson, 1988).

Despite the wealth of children's literature now available, it is difficult to find material that is interesting and fosters success for students who have grown to dislike reading. During the past 10 years, however, through working in a university-based remedial reading clinic, teaching and working with preservice and inservice teachers, talking to students, and staying current with children's literature, I have been compiling such materials. Keeping Sammy, Michael, David, and James in mind, I look for materials from many cultures with interesting content and attractive illustrations. The list is always growing and contains a wide variety of texts in a range of reading levels, so that students can choose based on their interests.

In this article, I describe categories of reading materials that are interesting and supportive for struggling readers and reluctant readers and offer examples for each category. I begin with repetitive texts, followed by texts that can be performed, and finally popular texts that have particular appeal for reluctant readers. The booklist at the end contains additional selected texts from each category.

Repetitive Texts

To progress in reading, emerging and early readers benefit from the support of shared reading experiences with teachers and peers (Holdaway, 1979) in materials that provide both repetition (McCormick, 1994) and a low rate of reading errors (Gambrell, Wilson, & Gantt, 1981). Struggling readers benefit from the same kinds of meaning-centered, literature-based instruction that achieving readers do (Worthy & Invernizzi, 1992; Zucker, 1993), including the use of language experience dictations, pattern and predictable texts, familiar song lyrics, poetry, and rhymes.

Pattern Books

With young emerging readers, pattern books or books with predictable language are a mainstay of instruction, and while there are hundreds of pattern books suitable for young emerging readers, many of them can be insulting to older learners. Not all pattern books are too simplistic however; some that appeal to older readers are Aardema's *Bringing the Rain to Kapiti Plain* (1981) and Komaiko's *Earl's Too Cool for Me* (1987). In addition, Harve Zemach's *The Judge* (1969) is an enduring favorite; its title character unwisely ignores a warning of impending doom repeated by different characters throughout the book.

Poetry and Verse

Many poetry collections include sophisticated poems that appeal to older readers while providing the support of predictable text. *A Caribbean Dozen* (Agard & Nichols, 1994), a collection of poems by Caribbean authors, is accompanied by bright, colorful illustrations. In *Soul Looks Back in Wonder* (1993), Tom Feelings's art is accompanied by previously unpublished poems written by African American authors including Maya Angelou, Walter Dean Myers, and Langston Hughes. Collections by Arnold Adoff (1995), Lori Carlsen (1994), Judith Viorst (1981), and Nikki Giovanni (1993) are also appropriately sophisticated and appealing to older students but not difficult to read. An exquisite volume, entitled *Something Permanent* (Rylant, 1994), combines Walker Evans's photographs depicting ordinary people living during the U.S. Depression with the poetry of Cynthia Rylant. Among the most popular authors of humorous verse are Shel Silverstein (1974, 1981), Wallace Tripp (1973), and Jack Prelutsky (1980, 1984). Many students can identify with Prelutsky's ode to a universally detested task,

"Homework, Oh Homework," from *The New Kid on the Block* (1984).

Jump Rope and Street Rhymes

Recently, a seventh-grade language arts teacher, Donna Lynd, whose classes include students who cover a wide range of reading achievement, told me about a literature unit of jump rope and clapping rhymes that she and her students compiled together. Students recorded rhymes from their neighborhoods and interviewed older relatives about their childhood rhymes, and, in the process, discovered many variations among the same verses. As Donna found, the rhymes provide the support of easily memorized text and are inherently interesting to many students. Jane Yolen's *Street Rhymes Around the World* (1992) includes verses from 17 different countries, all illustrated by artists from the corresponding country. Other compilations are *Anna Banana: 101 Jump-Rope Rhymes* (Cole, 1989) and *Miss Mary Mack, and Other Children's Street Rhymes* (Cole & Calmenson, 1990).

Performance Texts

Many literature-based activities provide both support for reading and opportunities for social interaction. Setting up multiage partnerships, in which an older struggling reader reads to a younger child, makes repeated reading an authentic task and improves self-concept and attitude toward reading (Leland & Fitzpatrick, 1994). In addition, such partnerships open up more possibilities for choice in literature, allowing older learners to read books designed for young children without losing face. Other opportunities for performing texts are afforded through speeches and Readers Theatre, described in the following two paragraphs.

Speeches

Inspirational speeches by historical heroes also provide an incentive for repeated readings, and many are available in books or on videocassette. These include Sojourner Truth's "Ain't I a Woman?" and speeches by other African American women (McKissack & McKissack, 1992; Walker, 1992), Martin Luther King's "I Have a Dream" (Berry, 1995), and a play about Cesar Chavez (Stevens, 1978). These experiences can lead to or follow historical study.

Books and Poems for Readers Theatre

Another vehicle for performance is Readers Theatre with stories that are scripted and performed as plays. The teacher can write the scripts initially, and later, students can benefit greatly from the experience of writing scripts themselves. Fairy tales with dialogue and strong story lines are particularly suitable for Readers Theatre. For older emerging readers, fractured fairy tales or fairy tale transformations (Sipe, 1993) are engaging. Examples are William Hooks's *The Three Little Pigs and the Fox* (1989), Babette Cole's *Prince Cinders* (1987), and John Scieska's *The Frog Prince, Continued* (1991). Paul Fleischman's poems about insects in *Joyful Noise: Poems for Two Voices* (1988) are meant to be read aloud by two readers or groups of readers speaking in synchrony. Other appropriate books are *Knots on a Counting Rope* (Martin & Archambault, 1987), *The Ghost-eye Tree* (Martin & Archambault, 1985), *Yo! Yes?* (Raschka, 1993), and *That's Good! That's Bad!* (Cuyler, 1991).

Popular Texts

Recently, a colleague and I surveyed middle school students about their attitudes toward reading. We then selected those students with the most negative attitudes and interviewed them about their general free-time activities, reading habits, and preferences in reading materials. Although none of the students reported reading regularly for pleasure and all were negative about most school reading, they expressed interest in materials that are considered "light reading" including comics, series books, and magazines (Krashen, 1992), and most said they would read these materials if they were readily available.

The popularity of such materials is widespread (Kulleseid, 1994–1995; McKenna, Kear, & Ellsworth, 1991). Many of the avid adult readers interviewed by Carlsen and Sherrill (1988) reported being hooked on comics (such as superheroes, Archie, and even classic comics) or series books at one time; Carlsen and Sherrill concluded, "These materials seem to be as much a part of one's literary maturation as are the children's classics" (p. 16). Other materials that topped the list of favorites for the reluctant readers were scary books and stories (such as Alvin Schwartz's Scary Stories series and R.L. Stine's Goosebumps series), sophisticated picture books, and specific kinds of nonfiction books (books about drawing, animals, and sports). Several students expressed an interest in specific authors, including Coville, Dahl, and Pinkwater. Adult novels also were popular among the reluctant readers.

Comics and Cartoon Collections

Comics and cartoon collections are a popular genre among all ages. Well over half of the elementary students surveyed by McKenna, Kear, and Ellsworth (1991) reported reading comic books and newspaper comics. My seventh-grade son says that the most popular book in his language arts teacher's classroom library is a book of Calvin and Hobbes cartoons (Watterson). Other humorous comics include Davis's *Garfield*, Larson's *The Far Side*, and Marvel Comics's *Archie*. Adventurous comics include *The Adventures of Tin Tin* (Herge), *Asterix* (Goscinny & Uderzo), and Marvel's superheroes (*X-Men*, *Spiderman*, and *Superman*, for example). The presence of illustrations and less-dense text makes these materials nonthreatening for struggling readers, and their plots, vocabulary, and characterization can be quite sophisticated (Cramer, 1994; Dorrell & Carroll, 1981).

Series Books

Series books have long been a solid reading staple for both adults and children. Mackey (1990) speculates that the popularity of series books may be due partly to the fact that they provide readers with a sense of mastery over the conventions of reading. With characters, language, and content that grow more familiar with every book read, "even a reader inexperienced in an absolute sense has the opportunity to behave like an experienced reader in this one regard at least" (p. 484). The continued popularity of such series as The Hardy Boys (Dixon), Nancy Drew (Keene), and The Boxcar Children (Warner), and the bestseller status of new children's series (for example, Martin's The Baby Sitters Club and Stine's Goosebumps) and adult romance and horror series speaks to the hardiness of the genre. Fortunately for today's young readers, there are dozens of different series on a variety of subjects including mysteries, science fiction and adventure, books about animals, and scary stories.

Popular Magazines

Magazines are so specialized that they can provide something to interest everyone. Publications that are particularly popular among adolescents and preadolescents include *Seventeen, Gamepro, Hot Rod, Cracked, Sports Illustrated, Ebony, Jet, People,* and *Road and Track.*

Sophisticated Picture Books

Several authors write picture books that are particularly appealing to many older readers, including John Scieska's fractured fairy tales (*The True Story of the Three Little Pigs* [1989]). Other examples are William Steig's more recent picture books, such as *Shrek* (1990); Harry Allard's amazingly dim-witted family, the Stupids (e.g., *The Stupids Step Out* [1974]; and Dav Pilkey's campy books illustrated with photographs of his own pets playing the parts of townspeople (mice) and monsters. In *Dogzilla* (Pilkey, 1993), the town of Mousopolis is terrorized by an enormous prehistoric doggie monster with bad breath who wreaks havoc by "doing those things that come naturally to dogs": chasing cars off the highway, chewing furniture and furniture stores, and digging up bones at the natural history museum. Superbly illustrated picture books about more serious topics include *The Lotus Seed* (Garland, 1993), *Rose Blanche* (Innocenti, 1985), *Hiroshima No Pika* (Maruki, 1980), *The Ballad of Belle Dorcas* (Hooks, 1990), and *The Boy Who Held Back the Sea* (Locker, 1987). Chris Van Allsburg writes and illustrates enigmatic but compelling stories, for example, *Jumanji,* (1981) and *The Wretched Stone,* (1991).

Nonfiction Books

An often neglected genre, nonfiction books were popular with the reluctant readers described earlier and with students of all ages (Hubbell, 1990; Stoelfen-Fisher, 1990). In particular, books about drawing, animals, cars, and sports are "always checked out," according to middle school librarians (Worthy, in press). Doubleday publishes books about sports heroes, including Larry Bird (Bird, 1989) and Bo Jackson (Jackson & Schaap, 1990). Lovett's Extremely Weird animal series (Lovett, 1992) and the Eyewitness Juniors animal series (Parsons, 1990) are also highly popular.

Authors Who Appeal to Reluctant Readers

Some authors write about subject matter that is appealing to reluctant readers. Roald Dahl, for example, is very popular with preadolescent reluctant readers, perhaps because some of his books are quite irreverent. *The BFG* (1982) and *The Twits* (1980) are two of his less controversial but still popular books. Humorous books about implausible situations are also popular; examples include *Fat Men From Space* (Pinkwater, 1977), *Make Four Million Dollars by Next Thursday* (Manes, 1991), and *How to Eat Fried Worms* (Rockwell, 1973). Coville's series about schoolteachers who turn out to be extraterrestrials (for example, *My Teacher Is an Alien* [1990]) combines humor with science fiction. Christopher writes sports novels that are popular with preadolescents (for example, *Return of the Home Run Kid* [1992]).

Adult Books That Appeal to Adolescent Reluctant Readers

Many adolescents are insulted by "children's literature," preferring instead to read adult books that explore sophisticated and compelling issues but are still both appealing and appropriate for young readers. Mystery and horror authors, including Michael Crichton, John Grisham, and Stephen King, are popular with older middle school and high school students. The science fiction books of

Piers Anthony and Robert Asprin are also popular. Many students identify with multicultural selections, including some that focus on coming-of-age issues, by authors such as Sandra Cisneros and Maya Angelou.

Respecting Students' Choices

My 13-year-old son, who struggled with reading in his early elementary years, discovered comic books as a third grader. When he began spending all of his allowance on them and neglecting all other reading material, I became concerned. After all, I owned more than 1,000 critically acclaimed children's books. I worried that he was not reading the "right kinds" of books. I wrestled with this issue for several years until I realized that he was becoming an avid and fluent reader, and it seemed like the comics were at least partly responsible (Carlsen & Sherrill, 1988). He still reads comics but has now widened his reading to include some sports books and magazines and adult horror and mystery including King, Crichton, and Grisham.

Although these kinds of materials—popular magazines, comics, and adult books—are among the most read and requested by preadolescents and adolescents, many school libraries either do not carry such materials at all or do not carry enough to keep up with student demand (Pettit, 1992; Worthy, in press). Many teachers may prefer that their students read more conventionally accepted literature, such as that typically found in school libraries. I see this as a serious problem because, in my opinion, it is of paramount importance that students read, regardless of the perceived quality of the literature. From talking with the reluctant readers described earlier and from observing my son's reading development, I conclude that interest must be a primary factor in book selection. If it is not, many students will choose not to read outside of school.

Making interesting materials available for free reading may encourage otherwise reluctant readers to read.

The booklist provided here includes reading materials chosen for their demonstrated appeal to students who have struggled either with learning to read or with motivation to read. My intent is for these to be offered to students as suggestions. I think it is very important to introduce a wide variety of materials to students and let them select the ones that interest them. Students also need opportunities to talk with their peers about what they are reading and to exchange recommendations with one another. These experiences should provide a foundation for students to begin finding books on their own. Like adults who read for pleasure, students should know that personal interest is the most important factor in choosing a book to be read for pleasure—not readability, and certainly not someone else's view of what is worth reading.

This article and the booklist are dedicated to Sammy, Michael, James, and David. I wish I could take back the years.

REFERENCES

Allington, R.L. (1994). What's special about special programs for children who find learning to read difficult? *Journal of Reading Behavior, 26,* 1–21.

Anderson, R.C., Hiebert, E.H., Scott, J.A., & Wilkinson, I.A.G. (1985). *Becoming a nation of readers: The report of the commission on reading.* Washington, DC: U.S. Department of Education.

Carlsen, G.R., & Sherrill, A. (1988). *Voices of readers: How we come to love books.* Urbana, IL: National Council of Teachers of English.

Cramer, E.H. (1994). Connecting in the classroom: Ideas from teachers. In E.H. Cramer & M. Castle (Eds.), *Fostering the love of reading: The affective domain in reading education* (pp. 125–141). Newark, DE: International Reading Association.

Literature to hook reluctant readers and keep them reading

Repetitive texts
Pattern books
Aardema, V. (1981). *Bringing the rain to Kapiti Plain.* Jefferson City, MO: Scholastic.
Komaiko, L. (1988). *Earl's too cool for me.* New York: Harper & Row.
Zemach, H. (1969). *The judge.* Toronto, ON: Collins.

Poetry and verse
Adoff, A. (1982). *All the colors of the race.* New York: Beech Tree Books.
Adoff, A. (1995). *Street music: City poems.* New York: HarperCollins.
Agard, J., & Nichols, G. (Eds.). (1994). *A Caribbean dozen: Poems from Caribbean poets.* Cambridge, MA: Candlewick.
Bruchac, J., & London, J. (1992). *Thirteen moons on turtle's back: A Native American year of moons.* New York: Philomel.
Carlsen, L.M. (Ed.). (1994). *Cool salsa: Bilingual poems on growing up Latino in the United States.* New York: Holt.
Cole, W. (Ed.). (1981). *Poem stew.* New York: Harper Trophy.
Feelings, T. (Ed.). (1993). *Soul looks back in wonder.* New York: Dial.
Giovanni, N. (1993). *Ego tripping and other poems for young people.* New York: Lawrence Hill.
Linthwaite, I. (Ed.). (1990). *Ain't I a woman? A book of women's poetry from around the world.* New York: Wings.
Prelutsky, J. (1980). *Rolling Harvey down the hill.* New York: Mulberry.
Prelutsky, J. (1984). *The new kid on the block.* New York: Greenwillow.
Rylant, C. (1994). *Something permanent.* New York: Harcourt Brace.
Silverstein, S. (1974). *Where the sidewalk ends.* New York: Harper & Row.
Silverstein, S. (1981). *A light in the attic.* New York: Harper & Row.
Tripp, W. (Ed.). (1973). *A great big ugly man came up and tied his horse to me: A book of nonsense verse.* Boston: Little, Brown.
Viorst, J. (1981). *If I were in charge of the world.* New York: Aladdin.

Jump rope and street rhymes
Cole, J. (Ed.). (1989). *Anna Banana: 101 jump-rope rhymes.* New York: Scholastic.
Cole, J., & Calmenson, S. (Eds.). (1990). *Miss Mary Mack, and other children's street rhymes.* New York: Beech Tree Books.
Yolen, J. (Ed.). (1992). *Street rhymes around the world.* Honesdale, PA: Boyds Mills Press.

Performance texts
Speeches
Berry, J. (Ed.). (1995). *Classic poems to read aloud.* New York: Kingfisher.
McKissack, P.C., & McKissack, F. (1992). *Sojourner Truth: Ain't I a woman?* New York: Scholastic.
Stevens, L. (1978). *Cesar Chavez: A miniplay.* Stockton, CA: Relevant Instructional Materials.
Walker, R.J. (Ed.). (1992). *The rhetoric of struggle: Public address by African American women.* New York: Garland.

(continued)

Literature to hook reluctant readers and keep them reading (continued)

Books and poems for Readers Theatre

Cole, B. (1987). *Prince Cinders.* New York: G.P. Putnam's Sons.

Cuyler, M. (1991). *That's good! That's bad!* New York: Holt.

Fleischman, P. (1988). *Joyful noise: Poems for two voices.* New York: Harper & Row.

Hooks, W.H. (1989). *The three little pigs and the fox.* New York: Macmillan.

Martin, B., & Archambault, J. (1985). *The ghost-eye tree.* New York: Holt.

Martin, B., & Archambault, J. (1987). *Knots on a counting rope.* New York: Holt.

Raschka, C. (1993). *Yo! Yes?* New York: Scholastic.

Scieska, J. (1991). *The frog prince, continued.* New York: Viking.

Trivizas, E. (1993). *The three little wolves and the big bad pig.* New York: Margaret K. McElderry.

Popular texts

Cartoon collections and comics

The adventures of Tin Tin by Herge. Boston: Little, Brown.

Archie. Mamaroneck, NY: Archie Comics.

Asterix by R. Goscinny & A. Uderzo. Paris: Dargaud.

Batman. New York: D.C. Comics.

Calvin and Hobbes by B. Watterson. Kansas City, MO: Andrews & McMeel.

The far side by G. Larson. Kansas City, MO: Andrews & McMeel.

Garfield by J. Davis. New York: Ballantine Books.

Spiderman. New York: Marvel Comics.

Superman. New York: D.C. Comics.

X-men. New York: Marvel Comics.

Series books

The Baby Sitters Club by A.M. Martin. New York: Scholastic.

The Baily School Kids by D. Dadey & M.T. Jones. New York: Scholastic.

The Boxcar Children by G.C. Warner. New York: Scholastic.

Cam Jansen by D. Adler. New York: Puffin.

Choose your own adventure by S. Saunders. New York: Bantam Skylark.

The Culpepper Adventures ("Dunc") by G. Paulsen. New York: Dell.

The Goosebumps by R.L. Stine. New York: Scholastic.

The Hardy Boys by F.W. Dixon. New York: Grosset.

Nancy Drew by C. Keene. New York: Grosset.

Nate the Great by M.W. Sharmat. New York: Dell Yearling.

The time warp trio by J. Scieska. New York: Puffin.

Magazines

Cracked, Ebony, Gamepro, Hot Rod, Jet, People, Road and Track, Seventeen, Sports Illustrated, Zoobooks.

Sophisticated picture books

Allard, H. (1974). *The Stupids step out.* New York: Trumpet.

(continued)

Literature to hook reluctant readers and keep them reading (continued)

Emberley, M. (1990). *Ruby.* Boston: Little, Brown.
Garland, S. (1993). *The lotus seed.* San Diego, CA: Harcourt Brace Jovanovich.
Hooks, W.H. (1990). *The ballad of Belle Dorcas.* New York: Knopf.
Innocenti, R. (1985). *Rose Blanche.* New York: Stewart, Tabori, & Chang.
Locker, T. (1987). *The boy who held back the sea.* New York: Dial.
Maruki, T. (1980). *Hiroshima no pika.* New York: Lothrop, Lee, & Shepard.
Pilkey, D. (1993). *Dogzilla.* New York: Harcourt Brace.
Scieska, J. (1989). *The true story of the three little pigs, by A. Wolf.* New York: Viking.
Scieska, J. (1992). *The stinky cheese man and other fairly stupid tales.* New York: Viking.
Steig, W. (1988). *Spinky sulks.* New York: Trumpet.
Steig, W. (1990). *Shrek.* New York: Trumpet.
Van Allsburg, C. (1981). *Jumanji.* New York: Scholastic.
Van Allsburg, C. (1991). *The wretched stone.* Boston: Houghton Mifflin.
Wegman, W. (1993). *Cinderella.* New York: Hyperion.
Yorinks, A. (1990). *Ugh.* New York: Michael di Capula.

Nonfiction books
Bird, L. (1989). *Drive: The story of my life.* With Bob Ryan. New York: Doubleday.
Boyd, B., & Garrett, R. (1989). *Hoops: Behind the scenes with the Boston Celtics.* Waltham, MA: Little, Brown.
Hollander, P., & Hollander, Z. (1990). *More amazing but true sports stories.* New York: Scholastic.
Jackson, B., & Schaap, D. (1990). *Bo knows Bo: The autobiography of a ballplayer.* New York: Doubleday.
Lake, E.D. (1995). *Low rider.* Minneapolis, MN: Capstone.
Lee, S., & Buscema, J. (1978). *How to draw comics the Marvel way.* New York: Simon &Schuster.
Lovett, S. (1992). *Extremely weird animals series.* Santa Fe, NM: John Muir.
Parker, S. (1992). *Inside the whale and other animals.* New York: Doubleday.
Parsons, A. (1990). *Eyewitness Juniors animals series.* New York: Knopf.
Sabin, L. (1992). *Roberto Clemente: Young baseball hero.* New York: Troll.

Authors who appeal to reluctant readers
Christopher, M. (1992). *Return of the home run kid.* Waltham, MA: Little, Brown.
Coville, B. (1990). *My teacher is an alien.* New York: Minstrel.
Dahl, R. (1980). *The Twits.* New York: Puffin.
Dahl, R. (1982). *The BFG.* New York: Trumpet.
Jacques, B. (1991). *Seven strange and ghostly tales.* New York: Avon.
Manes, S. (1991). *Make four million dollars by next Thursday.* New York: Bantam Skylark.
Pinkwater, D.M. (1977). *Fat men from space.* New York: Dell.
Rockwell, T. (1973). *How to eat fried worms.* New York: Dial.
Schwartz, A. (1991). *Scary stories 3: More tales to chill your bones.* New York: HarperCollins.

(continued)

Literature to hook reluctant readers and keep them reading (continued)

Adult books and authors that appeal to adolescent reluctant readers

Angelou, M. (1969). *I know why the caged bird sings.* New York: Random House.

Anthony, P., & Kornwise, R. (1989). *Through the ice.* New York: Simon & Schuster.

Asprin, R. (1983). *Hit or myth.* Norfolk, VA: Donning.

Cisneros, S. (1994). *The house on Mango Street.* New York: Knopf.

Crichton, M. (1980). *Congo.* New York: Knopf.

Grisham, J. (1993). *The client.* New York: Dell.

King, S. (1981). *Cujo.* New York: Viking Press.

Rivera, T. (1992). *This migrant earth.* (R. Hinojosa, Trans.). Houston: Arte Publico. (Original work published 1970)

Dewey, J. (1913). *Interest and effort in education.* Boston, MA: Riverside.

Dorrell, L., & Carroll, E. (1981). Spiderman at the library. *School Library Journal, 27,* 17–19.

Gambrell, L.B., Wilson, R.M., & Gantt, W.N. (1981). Classroom observations of task-attending behaviors of good and poor readers. *Journal of Educational Research, 24,* 400–404.

Heathington, B.S. (1979). What to do about reading motivation in the middle school. *Journal of Reading, 22,* 709–713.

Hidi, S. (1990). Interest and its contribution as a mental resource for learning. *Review of Educational Research, 60,* 549–571.

Holdaway, D. (1979). *The foundations of literacy.* Portsmouth, NH: Heinemann.

Hubbell, V. (1990, January). *Using informational material to spark reading interests in adolescents.* Paper presented at the International Conference on Adult and Adolescent literacy, Washington, DC.

Hunt, L.C. (1971). The effect of self-selection, interest, and motivation upon independent, instructional, and frustration levels. *The Reading Teacher, 24,* 146–151.

Krashen, S.D. (1992). *The power of reading.* Englewood, CO: Libraries, Unlimited.

Kulleseid, E.R. (Compiler). (1994–1995). EL K–12 bestsellers. *Emergency Librarian,* January/February 1994 through May/June 1995.

Leland, C., & Fitzpatrick, R. (1994). Cross-age interaction builds enthusiasm for reading and writing. *The Reading Teacher, 47,* 292–301.

Mackey, M. (1990). Filling the gaps: The Baby Sitters Club, the series book, and the learning reader. *Language Arts, 67,* 484–489.

McCormick, S. (1994). A nonreader becomes a reader: A case study of literacy acquisition by a severely disabled reader. *Reading Research Quarterly, 29,* 156–177.

McKenna, M., Ellsworth, R.A., & Kear, D. (1995). Children's attitudes toward reading: A national survey. *Reading Research Quarterly, 30,* 934–957.

McKenna, M., Kear, D., & Ellsworth, R.A. (1991). Developmental trends in children's use of print media: A national study. In J. Zutell & S. McCormick (Eds.), *Issues in literacy research and instruction* (pp. 319–324). Chicago, IL: National Reading Conference.

Mealey, D. (1990). Understanding the motivational problems of at-risk college students. *Journal of Reading, 33,* 598–601.

Pettit, D. (1992). *A study to determine how public libraries serve reluctant readers in Ohio.* Unpublished master's thesis, Kent State University, Kent, OH.

Rosenthal, R., & Jacobson, L. (1968). *Pygmalion in the classroom: Teacher expectation and* pupils' intellectual development. New York: Holt, Rinehart & Winston.

Schiefele, U. (1991). Interest, learning, and motivation. *Educational Psychologist, 26*, 299–323.

Shapiro, J., & White, W. (1991). Reading attitudes and perceptions in traditional and nontraditional reading programs. *Reading Research and Instruction, 30*, 52–66.

Sipe, L.R. (1993). Using transformations of traditional stories: Making the reading-writing connection. *The Reading Teacher, 47*, 18–26.

Stauffer, R.G. (1970). *The language experience approach to reading instruction.* New York: Harper & Row.

Stoelfen-Fisher, J.M. (1990). Teacher judgments of student reading interests: How accurate are they? *American Annals of the Deaf, 135*, 252–256.

Williamson, M.M., & Williamson, S.H. (1988). Reluctant readers: The librarian's greatest challenge. *The Book Report, 6*, 18–21.

Worthy, J. (in press). Removing barriers to voluntary reading for reluctant readers: The role of school and classroom libraries. *Language Arts.*

Worthy, J., & Invernizzi, M.A. (1992, December). *Hyperlexia and dyslexia in siblings: Approaching instruction from a developmental model.* Paper presented at the annual meeting of the National Reading Conference, San Antonio, TX.

Zucker, C. (1993). Using whole language with students who have language and learning disabilities. *The Reading Teacher, 46*, 660–671.

"I'm Really Worried About Joseph": Reducing the Risks of Literacy Learning

JoBeth Allen, Barbara Michalove, Betty Shockley, Marsha West

Reading workshop has ended and Betty Shockley calls her first graders to the rug to share. Joseph asks if he can read *King of the Mountain* (Martin, 1970). Delia cries, "Presenting the Great Joseph!" as he moves to the author's chair. His buddy Cory moves beside the chair. Joseph smiles as he reaches the end of each page, then carefully shows the pictures to everyone. Cory reads softly under his breath most of the time, louder at points where Joseph seems to need more support. Darnell and Caleb crowd closer, but Joseph reminds Caleb that he's already seen the pictures (when Joseph read it to him earlier in the workshop). When Joseph realizes he has forgotten to show one of the pictures, he backtracks, saying, "I gotta show the kids the picture—I'm the grown up—me and Cory the grownup." Later, he forgets again and Missy reminds him. "Oh, thank you, Missy," he replies, showing the picture. He reads the final line of the book triumphantly, "I am the king of the universe!" He grins at his audience and declares, "That's me!" [Field notes, March 17, 1989]

Few people who had known Joseph in his first two years of kindergarten, or in the first grade from which he was removed in September of 1988, would have recognized this diligent, engaged reader. Few people who knew his older siblings, both placed in self-contained settings for children with behavior disorders, would have recognized this polite, considerate brother. Some had ascribed terms like "retarded," "disturbed," and "hoodlum" to this "King of the Universe." Yet Joseph was, against all predictions, an active and contributing member of his community of readers and writers.

The expectation for a growing number of children like Joseph is that they will not succeed, will not become readers and writers, will not graduate from high school or attend college, and certainly are not likely to become truly literate members of our society (Heath, 1985). They rarely engage in extended literacy events, and often find themselves outside the successful community of learners. More often than not, these students are poor and belong to caste-like minorities (Ogbu & Matute-Bianchi, 1986). They are often placed in special remedial programs or have been retained (some two or three times). In spite of these well-intentioned interventions, here in the United States we have an increasing number of students who are not succeeding, according to major reports by such groups as the Children's Defense Fund (1987) and the

Committee for Economic Development (1987).

Joseph's school, Fowler Drive Elementary, has a large population of students who risk being failed if the school system does not provide flexible educational opportunities. Three years ago through their school-based staff-development process (Gibney, 1989), the faculty identified increased success for all students as their number-one priority. They began exploring alternatives to retention, ways to build self-esteem, and changes in the curriculum. In the spring of 1988, they invited JoBeth Allen to work with the school to explore how the reading curriculum might be changed to reduce the risks many children incur during literacy learning. They felt that following the basal curriculum rigidly was contributing directly to school failure, in part because grade promotion was based largely on progress in the basal. Further, they felt that too many students were not becoming truly literate, that is, real readers and writers.

Fowler Drive teachers were echoing concerns raised throughout the United States. Educators are questioning the efficacy of present approaches to helping such children succeed. Few remedial programs provide students with enough time, individual attention, or appropriate instruction to overcome the gap between their performance and that of their classmates (Allington, Boxer, Broikou, Gaskins, King, McGill-Franzen, & Stuetzel, 1987). Retention has not proven effective for students academically or socially (Holmes & Matthews, 1984; Shepard & Smith, 1988). "Learning the basics" often has led to an emphasis on teaching componential reading and writing skills in isolation; such practices are contrary to a growing body of research on how children become literate in classrooms where language learning is whole and meaningful. Graves (1983) documented how children grow as writers when they have daily time to write, choose their top-

ics, and learn to be critical readers of their own writing. Hansen (1987) documented how children grow as readers when they have these same opportunities of time, choice, and responsibility. Children in such classrooms do experience success as members of a literate community, a community of readers and writers (Atwell, 1987).

To date, most of the literate communities that have been studied in detail are populated by children who do not have histories of school failure. There are some studies that do focus on how rich language learning environments aid in reducing risks, such as a study by university and teacher researchers (Martinez, Cheyney, McBroom, Hemmeter, & Teale, 1989) of kindergartners in San Antonio, Texas, USA. There are excellent reports on individual classrooms (for example, Edelsky, Draper, & Smith, 1983) and individual learners (for example, Avery, 1987). However, there is a need for more research on how teachers reduce risks through their literacy curricula (Mitchell, 1989).

We are in the process of studying how whole language instruction affects the students teachers worry about the most, those students labeled in current educational jargon as "at risk." In this paper we will share the first year and a half of the study as we address three questions:

1. Why did we think that whole language instruction would increase successful literacy learning (our conceptual framework)?

2. How did we learn about the effects of our instruction (a brief methods section)?

3. What are teachers doing that seems to be increasing successful literacy learning (our findings to date)?

We will close with a brief profile of Joseph, King of the Universe.

Why Did We Think Whole Language Instruction Would Increase Successful Literacy Learning?

We came to our beliefs about the appropriateness of whole language instruction through both shared and divergent paths. All of us had previously been kindergarten teachers; we each believed that our most effective teaching had taken place during those years when we had more freedom to develop curriculum based on the needs of the children. Creating classrooms rich in experiences, with no workbooks or academic promotion pressures, we had taken students on field trips, cooked, recorded class and individual stories, acted out our stories, hiked in the woods, built and labeled buildings in the block corner, painted, and read hundreds of books to the children. We believed that all children want to learn, and that the teacher's job is to create a stimulating environment and observe and respond to the students' interests and needs. In these rooms every child felt valued and successful—and they were.

Now, we all were teaching at a different grade level: Betty Shockley was applying her kindergarten beliefs to first grade for the first time and was worrying about the basal; Barbara Michalove had not been happy with her first year's textbook attempt at second grade; and Marsha West was going to teach fifth grade for the first time.

JoBeth began her work with the school by listening to the history and concerns raised by these teachers and others who wanted to increase successful literacy learning. She had worked in whole language classrooms, studying how children learn to read and write (Allen, 1989; Allen & Carr, 1989; Allen, Combs, Hendricks, Nash, & Wilson, 1988). We began reading books and articles on literacy development (for example, Bissex, 1980; Calkins, 1983; Paley, 1981) and on designing classrooms where literacy learners thrive (for example, Atwell, 1987; Butler & Turbill, 1984). We began the 1988–1989 school year committed to creating whole language classrooms: interactive language and literacy environments where all children could succeed. Our initial focus was on writing workshop (Graves, 1983) and reading workshop (Hansen, 1987).

However, we often struggled; we saw the individuality of our emergence as whole language teachers as clearly as we saw the individuality of our students as literacy learners. There were some systemic constraints regarding basal and curriculum sequence requirements. We felt the pressure of competency tests, both those the children took and the one Marsha took.

Barbara initially tried alternating days of reading workshop with days of basal instruction. Her husband was able to predict with great accuracy, "This must have been a basal day." She then began integrating basal skills and tests within her now daily reading workshop (Michalove, 1990). Marsha also worked on balancing textbook and whole language instruction, concentrating on one or the other entirely for critical periods during the year. She speculates that these shifts may have limited her students' literacy development (West, 1990). We all got varying degrees of what our teacher researcher colleague Emily Carr called "skills attacks," such as the day Betty tried word cards with Joseph. He soon set her straight (Shockley, 1990). During this time, we learned with the children and with one another, based on some implicit assumptions about how we believe children learn.

During the 1989 summer data-analysis sessions, we made our assumptions explicit. We asked, "Why did we think whole language instruction would increase literacy learning success? Why did we believe it might be particularly important for the students we worry about the most?"

Our Beliefs About Language Learning

The following assumptions, based both on reading the research literature and on professional experiences, serve as our working definition of whole language as well as the analytic frame for this article.

1. Whole Texts   During the critical period of emergent literacy, most children learn best by going from whole to part. Children who come to Fowler Drive School have extensive verbal and experiential interactions, but many have not participated in such literacy events as bedtime stories, repeated storybook readings, or interactive writing times. Providing the "whole" of these experiences before digging into the "parts" of sound, letter, and word analysis seemed essential.

2. Adult Models   Children who observe literate others develop a desire to be members of this "literacy club" (Smith, 1988), just as children who observe language users want to learn to talk. Children who have had limited supported associations with literacy need to be around adults who "model joyous literacy" (Holdaway, 1979).

3. Real Reasons   All real learning must make sense and must be purposeful. The literacy activities at the core of our curriculum were designed to engage students in real reasons for reading and writing: reading self-selected books, reading to learn about a research topic, corresponding with university pen pals, writing to share information, writing to express personal experiences and feelings, and reading and writing just for fun.

4. Time   We had studied developmental stages and "the gift of time." We also had studied the statistics on retention and drop-out rates: about half of the students who have been retained once do not graduate from high school; nearly 90% of the students who have been retained more than once drop out of school. We felt that the gift of time should be given every day, not with an extra year in school. Every child should have time to read, to write, to interact with peers, and to extend a learning activity to its natural, rather than preordained, conclusion.

5. Responsibility   Developing responsibility for one's own learning is especially important for children who view themselves as failures (Hansen, 1989). We emphasized real choices—what books will you read, how will you figure out unfamiliar words, what part of a book will you share, what will you write about today, who will help you, which words might be spelled incorrectly, which story will you publish, what will you do when you get frustrated? We felt making choices would lead to responsibility for an individual's own learning.

6. Supported Risk Taking   Children who "fail" in school often have been failed by the school. We wanted to create literate environments where students could take risks without risking failure. In such classrooms, all children would be equal, not in what they already knew, but in what they could learn. We suspected that some of our children would have to relearn risk taking because of the failure they already had experienced as learners. Seven of the nine children we studied had been retained at least once.

7. Belonging   Students who do not view school as a positive, successful experience often do not feel they really "belong" in a particular class or even in the school as a whole.

We thought that through our development of communities of readers and writers, everyone would experience that sense of belonging. Everyone would know he or she had something important to contribute; everyone would be both a teacher and a learner.

These were our beliefs about why whole language instruction was particularly important for the students we were most worried about, but were they true? Did "whole" learning, literate models, real purposes for reading and writing, supported risk taking, responsibility, time, and belonging really increase successful literacy learning?

How Did We Learn About the Effects of Our Instruction?

We spent the first month observing and discussing which children we would study. We did not approve of the popular new label "at risk" (see Allen, 1989). We thought that labeling children was a detrimental and ineffective way to meet their needs. Yet we were acutely aware that there were multiple factors in the lives of some of our children that mitigated against school success. We decided to use a term from the practical knowledge of teachers and study the children we were *particularly* "worried about," based on observations of both academic and social behaviors, interactions with other students, and knowledge of other factors (such as retention).

Data Collection, Analysis, and Interpretation

JoBeth *observed* one day a week in each collaborative research classroom, writing field notes wherein she recorded her observations. Teacher researchers kept teaching journals in which they *reflected* on the focal children. To gain the children's perspectives, we *inter-*

viewed the focal children four times each year about what they were learning as readers and writers, how they were learning, what they planned to learn next, and how they planned to learn (for example, who might help them); questions were adapted from Hansen and Graves's evaluation study. Teachers saved as much as possible of the *written work* children produced. *Reading records* included notes on books the children read, response journals in Marsha's room, and tapes of each child reading a basal selection or a passage from a trade book and telling about the passage. *Informal interviews* were also conducted with other members of the child's world, including parents, siblings, the director of the Boy's Club, teachers in art, music, physical education, library, Chapter 1 [U.S. federally funded education program for at-risk children now called Title I], and special education classes. A serendipitous data source was the weekly pen pal letters students wrote to and received from undergraduates in JoBeth's classes.

Through several phases of data analysis (weekly, monthly, and end-of-year), we identified major issues in each child's development. These issues led to the positing of two overarching themes that seem critical to increased success: engagement with literacy and membership in the literate community. We began to see the importance of key instructional decisions we had made; these decisions are the heart of the next section.

What Are Teachers Doing That Seems To Be Increasing Successful Literacy Learning?

We have learned a great deal from the children who became our teachers: Joseph, Shannon, and Jeremiah in first grade; Ricky, Reggie, and Lee in second grade; and Dr. L,

Santana, and Kabona in fifth grade (most of the students chose their own pseudonyms).

The major themes that became evident in our analyses were *engagement* and *community*. The children who worried us at the beginning of the year were often those who were not engaging with literacy events or children who had nonproductive roles within the literate community. Many of the decisions Betty, Marsha, and Barbara made increased students' engagement with literacy activity: interacting with characters, authors, language, and ideas as they read and wrote. Engagement overlapped with community, for in many cases engagement with literacy came about through membership in the classroom community. But community was also broader than a road to literacy. We illustrate these themes with several specific decisions we made, decisions based on our beliefs about language learning and on our specific attention to increasing success for the children we were worried about the most.

Engagement

Engagement emerged as a serious issue with fifth-grader Santana. Initially, she appeared to be an enthusiastic reader. She always seemed to have a book in her hands, talked enthusiastically with both Marsha and JoBeth about what she was reading, and became very excited when JoBeth brought in several books about her passion, horses. However, through several weeks of careful observation, it became obvious that Santana rarely ever actually read. She seemed to have learned "literate behavior" and knew that it was valued both at home and at school. She was successfully engaging in literate behaviors but not in reading or writing. We began to look at engagement—actual time spent reading and writing, time spent in talking and thinking that seemed literacy related—as a theme for many of the children.

For our analysis, decisions we made that seemed to increase genuine engagement with literacy were based on our beliefs that children need whole texts initially, children need adult models of literacy, children need real reasons for reading and writing, children need time to read and write, and children need support for their risk taking. Some of these decisions had to do with the overall structure of our classrooms and instruction; others were based on the observed needs of the focal children.

Whole Texts

All of us tried from day one to involve children in a whole language and literacy curriculum. We read to the children frequently and provided regular reading and writing workshop times. During these workshops students interacted with and created self-selected books and topics. From these "wholes," we discussed language "parts" that we hoped would help children become skilled analyzers as well as users of language. This emphasis on whole texts seemed important to all the emergent readers, but it may have been most crucial to Lee.

Lee came to second grade with several labels: repeater, MIMH (mildly mentally handicapped), and nonreader (in fact his previous year's teacher noted in an interview that it was doubtful he would ever learn to read or write). However, he enjoyed books from the first day, mostly as a listener. He joined groups of children reading and sat close to Barbara during her many read-aloud times. But his favorite activity was to listen to read-along tapes at the listening center, playing favorite stories over and over and eventually following along in the texts. He became very involved with the stories, often commenting aloud, warning a character that something was about to happen, joining in a song, or talking about the good-tasting soup in *Stone Soup*. Because this repeated storybook reading seemed so important, perhaps something there had been little time for in Lee's foster home, Barbara encouraged this intense engagement, even at times other than during reading workshop.

Lee began to seek out these familiar stories to read with friends. He discovered that by reading a book numerous times, he became competent. He branched out and began "practicing" other books, working on one book for weeks at a time, until he could read it fluently. One day in early spring, he asked if he could read one of his favorite books to his former first-grade teacher's class. He wrote a note making his request to Ms. Williams, chose a part of the book he thought the younger kids would enjoy, and practiced with Barbara for several days. Sandra Williams reported, tears still in her eyes, that Lee, a child who had not spoken in front of the class one time last year, had read the book confidently to her whole class. Reading whole books makes whole readers.

Adult Models

One of the rewarding aspects of exploring the whole language philosophy was rediscovering our own literacy (Graves, 1990). All of us loved to read. Now, however, we began seeing our "pleasure" reading as an integral part of our roles as teachers of reading. We told our kids about the books we were reading. We occasionally used our own books in minilessons. Betty read "When Augustus came out on the porch the blue pigs were eating a rattlesnake—not a very big one," the opening lines of *Lonesome Dove* (McMurtry, 1985), as she began a discussion with her class about how to start a new story. We also developed a strong sense of how our enjoyment of both "adult" and "kid" books, our models of "joyous literacy," affected our students as readers. In each grade, the books we chose to read aloud were ones we ourselves enjoyed. And without fail, these were the books the kids clamored to

read next. When *The Pinballs* (Byars, 1977) was shared in fifth grade, a dozen students quickly checked out the multiple copies.

But we were modeling more than the joy of reading; we were modeling many processes of reading. We self-corrected, phrased for meaning, talked about unfamiliar words, reread old favorites, sought other books by favorite authors, and occasionally abandoned a book we did not like. For first-grader Joseph and second-graders Lee and Reggie, children who were at the earliest stages of emergent reading (Sulzby, 1985), these models seemed especially important. We recorded regularly that the books we read to the class were ones they chose to read. Because there was always a clamor for the read-alouds, Betty and Barbara often gave these books to the children who needed that kind of supported reading experience most, with the suggestion to others to "read with Joseph" or "ask Lee if you can read it after he finishes." We not only were inviting children into the "literacy club" (Smith, 1988), we were providing successful initiation experiences. These invitations and initiations led to extended, successful engagement with books.

Real Reasons

There were many opportunities for real reasons for reading and writing, reasons that were important to the children that we had not anticipated. We saw our students writing about their lives, working out problems, and exploring their identities. First-grader Shannon wrote about "The Girl with the Black and White Face," who eventually falls into a volcano. The piece could be a parable of her life and fears. The first personal writing Ricky produced, 10 weeks into the school year, was "Me and my mom wet to see my dad. He sed woh [who] are you, I am (Ricky)" (see Figure). Kabona wrote about the death of her mother the previous year, and her guilt over telling her she hated her. The students included these struggles not only in their workshop writing but in transactional writing to peers and teachers. One day when she had been asked to leave the room until she could collect her thoughts and calm down, Kabona sent a note to Marsha: "Mrs. West, the reason I got snappy is because my mom birthday is sunday and no one has said any thin about it. I have been snappy ever since I got up."

Fifth-grader Dr. L seemed to make a conscious effort to change his role at school from a two-time repeater, whose previous teacher had thought he might have a behavior disorder, to a model student. When he chose his seat at the beginning of the year, he explained that he was closer to the books ("and to the air-conduction"), and away from friends he had gotten in trouble with in the past. He ignored direct invitations from peers to get off task and in trouble. Much of his writing indicated a strong sense of goal directedness. He wrote about going to college, playing college and professional basketball, and becoming a doctor, "delivering babies and having a good life." In a reflection on what his life might have been like if he had lived during slavery times, he wrote about "working hard, ignoring people calling me names and just staying in the house"; Marsha noted in her journal that this summarized his school-success strategy. He seemed to be reminding himself, through his writing, that he was a responsible young man with plans for "having a good life."

Correspondence with university pen pals provided an important reason for reading and for writing with more precision than classroom sharing demanded. The authors of difficult-to-decipher texts were readily available in the classroom, but not so for the college pen pals. On October 14, 1988, Reggie wrote briefly to university student Carol regarding his upcoming birthday: "Dear Carol/I want a rmkberncar/I want to have to u/lnepb!" Carol wrote back, ex-

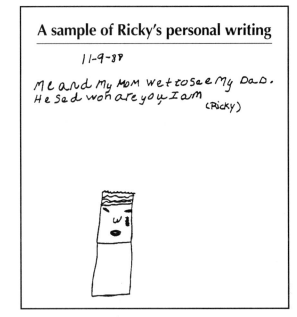

A sample of Ricky's personal writing

11-9-88

Me and My MoM wet to see My DaD. He Sed woh are you I am (Ricky)

plaining that she would like to know more about "rmkberncar," but she didn't know what it was. Reggie's October 21 response engaged Reggie with writing his longest piece to date:

> DEar Carol/I want a RemotcuntkCar/in I will Try to save you a pEES of CakE/in I will go to atlantu/fou my Birthday/in me in my frnd is going to atlantu/in we or go out to Eat/Love [Reggie]."

Reggie used friends, the birthday chart in the room, and even asked the teacher to read his letter (they added *ing* to *go*). The genuine need to communicate provided the impetus not only for extended engagement, but for engaging on a more conventional level than previously required.

Time

Even when kids have compelling reasons to read and write, they probably will not unless they have dependable, structured time to do so (Graves, 1983; Hansen, 1987). We have become adamant about the importance of this dependable time, *especially* for the students we worried about. It is often the children who need the most time engaged in real reading and writing who are allotted the least (Allington, 1983). In fact, designated time was often not enough, as we saw with Lee's engagement with the read-along tapes; we provided even more time when we saw from observation that certain students needed more. Students also found ways to increase engaged time. Shannon's writing was so important to her that her mother reported, "She writes all the time" at home. Reggie often became so engaged with writing that he continued writing during sharing—his right hand encoding, his left hand in the air to ask the author a question or request the next turn.

Time was also a major issue for Jeremiah. Jeremiah was rarely observed actually writing during writing workshop. He "created" first— book covers, puppet characters, and props; he also interacted extensively with other writers (usually not very productively). About the time others were ready for sharing, Jeremiah seemed to start writing. Betty and Barbara made different decisions about Jeremiah. In first grade, Betty allowed him to continue writing, through sharing and other parts of the day. Barbara, in second grade, tried structuring his time for him, placing him in a group of writers at a table where she provided extra support and supervision. Both strategies, extending time and restructuring time, produced more writing. We still worry and wonder if and when Jeremiah will begin managing his own time.

Supported Risk Taking

For some students, interaction with books and creating texts is a successful, rewarding experience from the beginning. This was not true of many of the students we studied. Simply creating a literate environment was not enough; supporting them in their risk taking was essential. As we looked back over our data, two things became clear: one, the fact that we were actively studying these children led us to important decisions of how and when to support them; and two, this active, intentional support seems to be crucial for increasing the success of students we worry about.

Reggie said he could not read until Barbara introduced him to the easiest Story Box Books (1980), and he experienced almost immediate success. Every day for two months he piled his desk with these little orange books and religiously read through each one. On November 15, Barbara suggested he choose a new book, talking about all the interesting choices on the shelves. "I can't read any other stories," he responded with a frown. Barbara helped him find *Thank You, Nicky* (Ziefert, 1988), a story she thought he would enjoy. They sat on the floor together, taking turns reading, until Reggie saw that he could indeed read this book. It was a turning point in his book selections.

Both Barbara and Betty have given paperback books to children on occasion, for example when they visited students in their homes or when the children were asked if their writing folders could be kept at the end of the year. We are well aware that many of the children we teach do not have their own books, but we were not prepared for what an impact actually owning a book would have. *The Doorbell Rang* (Hutchins, 1986) became the only book Shannon read with confidence all year. She viewed herself as a writer, but not as a reader; this struggle is evident in another of her "black and white" pieces, in which she tells friends who are trying to get her to read, "I just do NOT like Books...Then Brenda and Delia said Read a book now so I read a book but I skipped some paiges." With *The Doorbell Rang*, Shannon was able to read at home, as she had been writing at home. When we interviewed her in June, she told us she was learning to "read new words and read *The Doorbell Rang*...because ms. Shockley gave me the book and I read to my sister while she was in bed."

There are many accounts in our data of such "little" decisions as helping a child read a new book, suggesting that a withdrawn child read with a partner, helping a child move beyond copying a text to modifying the story, and other decisions that supported risk taking. There also were several "big" decisions. Perhaps the most radical was Betty's decision, supported by other concerned members of the Fowler Drive staff, to graduate Shannon from first to third grade rather than from first to second grade at the end of the year. Shannon had repeated both kindergarten and first grade. She had outgrown her peer group both physically and emotionally. She needed a better chance to beat the drop-out odds. With continuing support from Betty and active personal and academic support from her third-grade teacher, she made the transition.

Community

As mentioned earlier in the article, when we analyzed engagment with literacy, decisions we made that seemed to increase effective membership in the literate community were based on our beliefs that children need real reasons for reading and writing, children need to be responsible for their own learning, children need support for their risk taking, and children need to feel that they belong in a literate community. We viewed the first and third beliefs a little differently than in the earlier section, and came to understand the importance of the second and fourth.

Real Reasons

Although sharing books and writing with one's friends—being a member of the literate community—seemed to be the primary impetus for reading and writing in the lower grades (Michalove, 1990), being a member of the social community seemed more compelling for the fifth graders. Even though an official forum for writing and sharing was established, private writing seemed to be more important, as evidenced by the frequency and intensity of this activity. Marsha took this social community seriously, and helped the adolescents in her class with such important issues as fights among girlfriends, nascent gang involvement, boy-girl relationships, and "mean" substitute teachers. These issues occasionally surfaced in sanctioned writings, but they more often appeared in underground note writing. Marsha also wrote notes at times to inquire about her students' problems. Writing was an important part of operating in this social community, just as it is in adult social communities, where we write invitations, notices of events, love letters, and pleas for forgiveness.

Responsibility

Being a part of a whole language classroom means taking responsibility for your own learning (Atwell, 1987; Hansen, 1987). Having real choices to make leads to real responsibility, not just learning to do what one is told (Shockley & Allen, 1990). Choices that affected literacy development the most seemed to be the choice of reading and writing partners or groups. Reggie initially picked his good friend Lee as a reading partner, but there was little they could do to help each other. After a few weeks, he began reading with Melissa and Damron, both very capable readers. He read with them so often during the year that Barbara concluded they had actually been the ones to teach him to read—because read he did by the end of the year. Lee learned to write initially by copying what his friends (including Reggie) wrote; eventually, he became a genuine collaborator, first in the oral composing of a story, and by third grade in the physical writing.

By the end of the first year, we were beginning to see that choice was important not only to literacy learning but to development in an area that puts many students at risk: behavior. Dr. L had a group of friends he often read and wrote with, but he did not hesitate to remove himself from this group when they began wasting time or pushed the edge of acceptable behavior. Membership in an active community of learners made use of Reggie's primary skill: social interaction, a skill that had often relegated him to isolation in classrooms that were not structured for his constant verbal involvement. And for Joseph, making his own choices and taking charge of his literacy development allowed him to remain the "boss" without serving, as he did initially, as the classroom bully.

Supported Risk Taking

Supporting risk taking led not only to increased engagement, but to new and beneficial roles within the community. Children became teachers as well as learners, collaborators as well as friends. They supported one another as risk takers. These were roles some of the children had to learn. When Barbara had Jeremiah work in a reading group and a writing group, his usual pouting and squabbling diminished greatly. As one of the more competent readers and writers in these two groups, he began to be viewed as a helpful resource rather than a nuisance by the other kids. After two months of this support, he began functioning more productively as he once again chose his own places and partners for reading and writing.

Over and over, in every classroom, the children encouraged, taught, challenged, and supported one another. At the beginning of second grade, Ricky was quite withdrawn. During the first two months of school he never chose to read or write with anyone else. One day in November, two friends literally forced him to read with them. They had chosen a book neither could read, but they knew he could. It was the beginning of a total transformation of Ricky's role in the classroom, from isolate to collaborator.

Belonging

"Bonding" with the school has been identified as a critical condition for school success (Berrueta-Clement, Schwienhart, Barnett, Epstein, & Weikart, 1984; Finn, 1989). As the routines and expectations for interaction in these classrooms became internalized, children developed their roles as teachers, learners, and collaborators in their literate communities. We feel that our inclusion of all children, from the very first day, in reading and writing workshops increased the successes of students who already had experienced a great deal of failure. We worked on schedules with special education teachers to make sure students who received academic and behavior services could participate in workshops.

Everyone started and remained on equal ground with other members of the community. They chose from the same books, struggled with the same general concerns, and their contributions were valued during sharing in the same ways. At the end of September, Reggie and Lee shared "LL Cool J—LL Cool Z—LL Cool W" through several alphabet variations. The class was polite, although several cut their eyes at Barbara as if to ask, "What is this?" During questions, Nathan asked, "What does it mean?" Reggie confidently responded that it was about Lee; "He is LL Cool Z." There were no more questions. The boys grinned and chose the next author.

Profile of a Reader and Writer: Joseph, King of the Universe

Joseph's development over the past two years is a story of both engagement and community. Initially, he appeared unengaged with nearly every organized literacy event and alienated from other members of the community. In September 1988, Betty worried that Joseph did not even seem interested during her frequent read-aloud times. However, by October he was engaged with both a book and a friend. He finished "reading" a book to Cameron and said, "You want me to read this again? You can look that way and still listen." Whole books had penetrated his cultivated demeanor of indifference. He could be immediately successful in emergent readings of storybooks even though he had repeatedly failed other school literacy activities.

When he did eventually work in the basal, it was with one-to-one support from Betty. On January 30, 1988, she decided to make Joseph her reading buddy during the morning reading time with their fifth-grade partners; Betty was getting nervous about the opening of "testing season." They were both surprised when he read the first preprimer (*Bells*) in one day. When he finished *Bells*, he announced, "My mama, she be real proud when she know I can read. I be in *Drums* tomorrow when I come to school? I didn't practice it, I just read it!" Joseph had his own literacy agenda; his yardstick for school success was advancement in the basal series. It was not that he thought the basal was how kids learned to read; he told a kindergartner with a book one day, "Yeah, you keep going over it like that and you'll learn to read. That's how you learn to read." But the basal was school criterion of literacy, and he was delighted with this recognized marker of success. (See Appendix for samples of Joseph's oral reading progress in second grade.)

Joseph showed this same ownership of his own learning when he basically took himself out of special education. He began quietly refusing to go to his resource room where he received services for mental retardation and behavioral disorders. According to his resource room teacher, he correctly determined that he really did not fit in her classroom anymore. She and Betty worked out a twice-a-week schedule with Joseph that seemed to satisfy him. He chose his community of learners.

Perhaps the most important change brought about by Joseph's engagement with literacy and his membership in literate communities in first and second grade was his shift in roles. Joseph entered the classroom a bully, a tough guy who would not look at others, and would not even listen (we thought) to a story. By second grade, Joseph often directed events during reading time: he chose the book, where everyone would sit to read, and who should read first. His interest in controlling events had found an acceptable, even desirable, forum. Although most of the time he is an active, engaged learner who thanks others politely when they remind him to show the pictures, Joseph is still tough. After an intense and frustrating week of standardized testing, on March 13, 1989 Joseph shouted, "I'll kill him—shoot the brains out of that boy!" when a peer "messed" with him. But the "hoodlum" incidents became less frequent and less physical. There were only two in the first 7 months of second grade. As he becomes literate, Joseph increases his leadership options. He no longer has to rely solely on his tough guy image, because kings have even more respect than bullies.

Oh yes—he has also been "cured" of mental retardation, according to the most recent assessment. So has Lee.

So did whole language change a bully into a king, a failure into success, an isolate into a leader, a retardate into a successful learner? Are Betty and Barbara miracle workers? We have fairly convincing data in our case study (Shockley, 1990) that elements of time, choice, supported risk taking, belonging, and whole language experiences for real purposes have made a tremendous difference in Joseph's school life. We do not know what difference it will make in his real life, the one in a family that has moved four times this year, the one with numerous siblings and cousins in constant trouble with the schools and the law, the one the tooth fairy never visited. But we must exclaim along with his good friend Cory, "He got smart fast!"

Authors' Note

This research was partially funded by grants from International Reading Association's Elva Knight Research Foundation, the Spencer Foundation Small Grants Program, and The University of Georgia Research Foundation.

REFERENCES

Allen, J. (1989). Introduction. In J. Allen & J. Mason (Eds.), *Risk makers, risk takers, risk breakers: Reducing the risks for young literacy learners* (pp. 1–16). Portsmouth, NH: Heinemann.

Allen, J., & Carr, E. (1989). Collaborative learning among kindergarten writers: James learns how to learn at school. In J. Allen & J. Mason (Eds.), *Risk makers, risk takers, risk breakers: Reducing the risks for young literacy learners* (pp. 30–47). Portsmouth, NH: Heinemann.

Allen, J., Combs, J., Hendricks, M., Nash, P., & Wilson, W. (1988). Studying change: Teachers who become researchers. *Language Arts*, 65(4), 379–387.

Allington, R. (1983). The reading instruction provided readers of differing ability. *The Elementary School Journal*, 83, 255–265.

Allington, R., Boxer, N., Broikou, K., Gaskins, R., King, S., McGill-Franzen, A., & Stuetzel, H. (1987). *Strategic instructional issues in remedial reading*. Symposium presented at the National Reading Conference, St. Petersburg, FL.

Atwell, N. (1987). *In the middle: Writing, reading, and learning with adolescents*. Portsmouth, NH: Heinemann.

Avery, C. (1987). Traci: A learning-disabled child in a writing-process classroom. In G.L. Bissex & R.H. Bullock (Eds.), *Seeing for ourselves: Case-study research by teachers of writing*. Portsmouth, NH: Heinemann.

Berrueta-Clement, J., Schwienhart, L., Barnett, W., Epstein, A., & Weikart, D. (1984). *Changed lives: The effects of the Perry preschool program on youths through age 19*. Ypsilanti, MI: High/Scope.

Bissex, G. (1980). *GNYS AT WRK: A child learns to read and write*. Cambridge, MA: Harvard University Press.

Butler, A., & Turbill, J. (1984). *Towards a reading-writing classroom*. Portsmouth, NH: Heinemann.

Calkins, L. (1983). *Lessons from a child*. Portsmouth, NH: Heinemann.

Children's Defense Fund. (1987). *A children's defense budget: FY 1988. An analysis of our nation's investment in children*. Washington, DC: Author.

Committee for Economic Development. (1987). *Children in need: Investment strategies for the educationally disadvantaged*. A statement by the research and policy committee. New York: Author.

Edelsky, C., Draper, K., & Smith, K. (1983). Hookin' 'em in at the start of school in a "whole language" classroom. *Anthropology and Education Quarterly*, 14(4), 257–281.

Finn, J. (1989). Withdrawing from school. *Review of Educational Research*, 59(2), 117–142.

Gibney, S.G. (1989). An ethnographic case study of a school-based staff development process. (Doctoral dissertation, The University of Georgia, 1988). *Dissertation Abstracts International*, 50(3), (Order No. DA8910417).

Graves, D. (1983). *Writing: Teachers and children at work*. Portsmouth, NH: Heinemann.

Graves, D. (1990). *Discovering your own literacy*. Portsmouth, NH: Heinemann.

Hansen, J. (1987). *When writers read*. Portsmouth, NH: Heinemann.

Hansen, J. (1989). Anna evaluates herself. In J. Allen & J. Mason (Eds.), *Risk makers, risk takers, risk breakers: Reducing the risks for young literacy learners* (pp. 19–29). Portsmouth, NH: Heinemann.

Heath, S. (1985). Being literate in America: A sociohistorical perspective. In J. Niles & R. Lalik (Eds.), *Issues in literacy: A research perspective* (pp. 1–18). Rochester, NY: National Reading Conference.

Holdaway, D. (1979). *The foundations of literacy*. Portsmouth, NH: Heinemann.

Holmes, C.T., & Matthews, K.M. (1984). The effects of nonpromotion on elementary and junior high school pupils: A meta-analysis. *Review of Educational Research, 54(2)*, 225–236.

Martinez, M., Cheyney, M., McBroom, C., Hemmeter, A., & Teale, W. (1989). No risk kindergarten literacy environments for at risk children. In J. Allen & J. Mason (Eds.), *Risk makers, risk takers, risk breakers: Reducing the risks for young literacy learners* (pp. 93–124). Portsmouth, NH: Heinemann.

Michalove, B. (1990). Engagement and community in a second grade classroom. In M.J.M. Brown (Ed.), *Qualitative research in education: Processes, applications, and ethics in qualitative research*. Athens, GA: University of Georgia Press.

Mitchell, B. (1989). Emergent literacy and the transformation of schools, families, and communities: A policy agenda. In J. Allen & J. Mason (Eds.), *Risk makers, risk takers, risk breakers: Reducing the risks for young literacy learners* (pp. 295–313). Portsmouth, NH: Heinemann.

Ogbu, J., & Matute-Bianchi, M. (1986). Understanding sociocultural factors: Knowledge, identity, and school adjustment. In California State Department of Education, *Beyond Language* (pp. 73–141). Los Angeles, CA: Evaluation, Dissemination, and Assessment Center.

Paley, V. (1981). *Wally's stories*. Cambridge, MA: Harvard University Press.

Shepard, L., & Smith, M. (1988). Flunking kindergarten: Escalating curriculum leaves many behind. *American Educator*, 34–38.

Shockley, B. (1990). Sing a song of Joseph. In M.J.M. Brown (Ed.), *Qualitative research in education: Processes, applications, and ethics in qualitative research*. Athens, GA: University of Georgia Press.

Shockley, B., & Allen, J. (1990). A classroom story: Texts and contexts for literacy connections. In T. Shanahan (Ed.), *Reading and writing together: New perspectives for the classroom*. Norwood, MA: Christopher-Gordon.

Smith, F. (1988). *Joining the literacy club*. Portsmouth, NH: Heinemann.

Sulzby, E. (1985). Children's emergent reading of favorite storybooks. *Reading Research Quarterly, 20(4)*, 458–481.

West, M. (1990). Social uses for literacy: Fifth grade is another world. In M.J.M. Brown (Ed.), *Qualitative research in education: Processes, applications, and ethics in qualitative research*. Athens, GA: University of Georgia Press.

CHILDREN'S LITERATURE REFERENCES

Ahlberg, A. (1981). *Funnybones*. New York: Greenwillow.

Bells. (1986). Boston, MA: Houghton Mifflin.

Byars, B. (1977). *The pinballs*. New York: Scholastic.

Drums (1986). Boston, MA: Houghton Mifflin.

Hutchins, P. (1986). *The doorbell rang*. New York: Greenwillow.

Martin, B. (1970). *King of the mountain*. New York: Holt, Rinehart & Winston.

McMurtry, L. (1985). *Lonesome Dove*. New York: Pocket.

Story box books: Level 1. (1980). San Diego, CA: Wright Group.

Ziefert, H. (1988). *Thank you, Nicky*. New York: Penguin.

Appendix

Joseph: Four oral reading samples

During the second year of the study when Joseph was in Barbara's second grade, JoBeth taped the children reading to her four times during the year. She asked each child to "Read a book you've been reading lately, one you really like." She provided a copy of the Houghton Mifflin basal *Discoveries*, the designated end-of-second-grade book, and asked each child to read the first page of the play "The Princess and the Prime Minister." We used both texts as checkpoints for the children as well as for us to see their growth as readers. The children always discussed the stories with JoBeth, providing insights into their understanding; however, only the information on decoding is provided.

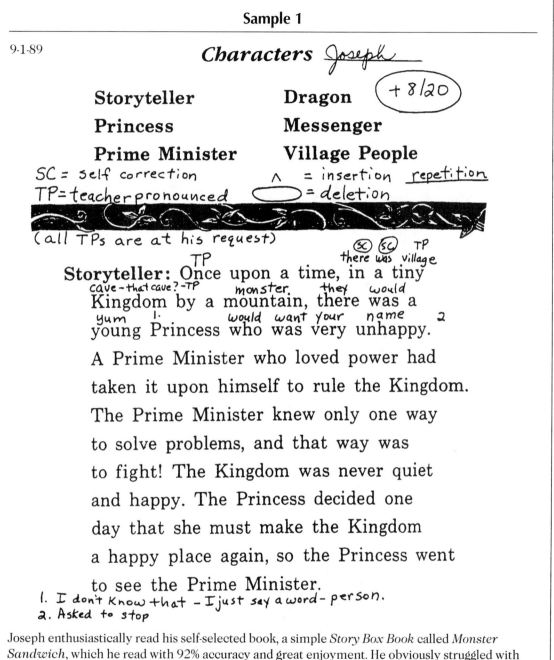

Sample 1

9-1-89

Characters Joseph

Storyteller   **Dragon**   (+ 8/20)

Princess   **Messenger**

Prime Minister   **Village People**

SC = self correction   ∧ = insertion   repetition

TP = teacher pronounced   ⬭ = deletion

(all TPs are at his request)

　　　　　　　　　　　　　　　　　　ⓈⒸ ⓈⒸ TP
　　　　　　　　　　　　　　　　　there was village
　　　　　　　TP
Storyteller: Once upon a time, in a tiny
cave–that cave?–TP　　monster.　they　would
Kingdom by a mountain, there was a
yum　　I.　　would want your　name　2
young **Princess** who was very unhappy.

A Prime Minister who loved power had

taken it upon himself to rule the Kingdom.

The Prime Minister knew only one way

to solve problems, and that way was

to fight! The Kingdom was never quiet

and happy. The Princess decided one

day that she must make the Kingdom

a happy place again, so the Princess went

to see the Prime Minister.

I. I don't know that – I just say a word – person.
2. Asked to stop

Joseph enthusiastically read his self-selected book, a simple *Story Box Book* called *Monster Sandwich*, which he read with 92% accuracy and great enjoyment. He obviously struggled with the play, and asked to stop after three lines so he could listen to himself reading *Monster Sandwich* on the tape.

From *Discoveries*, Level H of Houghton Mifflin Reading. Copyright © 1986 by Houghton Mifflin Company. "The Princess and the Prime Minister" was adapted from "The Princess and the Prime Minister and the Giant" by Helen Kromberg Olson in *The Princess Book*, originally published by Rand McNally.

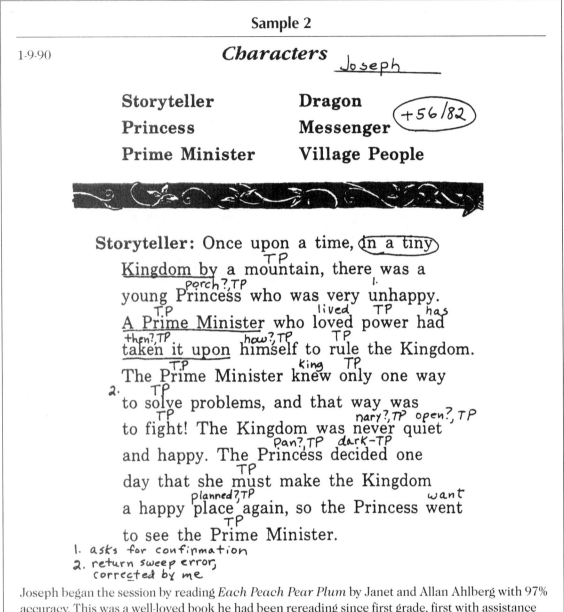

Sample 2

1·9·90

Characters   Joseph

Storyteller   **Dragon**

Princess   **Messenger**   (+56/82)

Prime Minister   **Village People**

Storyteller: Once upon a time, (in a tiny)

Kingdom by a mountain, there was a

young Princess who was very unhappy.

A Prime Minister who loved power had

taken it upon himself to rule the Kingdom.

The Prime Minister knew only one way

to solve problems, and that way was

to fight! The Kingdom was never quiet

and happy. The Princess decided one

day that she must make the Kingdom

a happy place again, so the Princess went

to see the Prime Minister.

1. asks for confirmation
2. return sweep error, corrected by me

Joseph began the session by reading *Each Peach Pear Plum* by Janet and Allan Ahlberg with 97% accuracy. This was a well-loved book he had been rereading since first grade, first with assistance and now independently. Before he began reading the play passage, he asked JoBeth to read the introduction on the previous page, as she had done in September. She complied. Joseph worked hard to read the entire passage, asking JoBeth to pronounce 18 words. Most miscue were real words that did not make much sense, but started with the same first letter as the text.

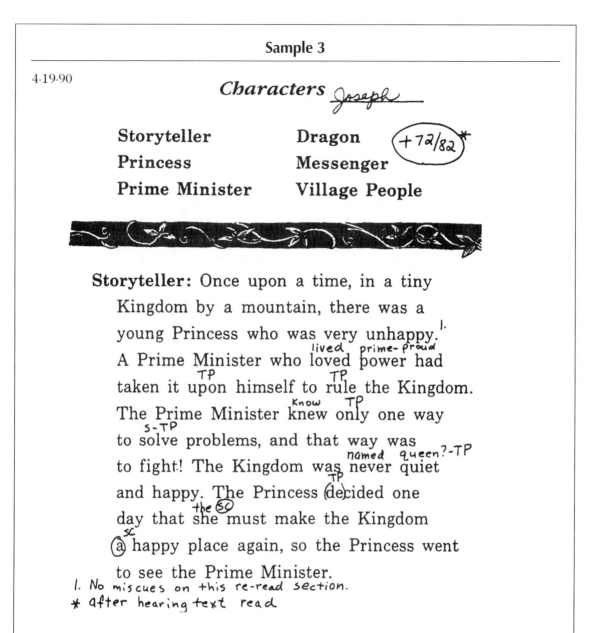

4-19-90

Characters Joseph

Storyteller   Dragon   (+72/82) *

Princess   Messenger

Prime Minister   Village People

Storyteller: Once upon a time, in a tiny
Kingdom by a mountain, there was a
young Princess who was very unhappy. 1.
A Prime Minister who loved [lived] [prime- proud] power had
taken it [TP] upon himself to rule [TP] the Kingdom.
The Prime Minister knew [Know] only [TP] one way
to [S-TP] solve problems, and that way was
to fight! The Kingdom was never quiet [named queen?-TP]
and happy. The Princess decided [TP] one
day that she [the] [SC] must make the Kingdom
a [SC] happy place again, so the Princess went
to see the Prime Minister.

1. No miscues on this re-read section.
* after hearing text read

Joseph began reading the passage after reading *Mrs. Wishy Washy* with 97% accuracy. He struggled with *mountain*, saying, "mote · motel? · motan · what is it?"; with *Minister*, saying "most—mostly—mountain"; and with *upon*, saying "up—upin—open." Note the increased sophistication of his miscues, as he processes through the whole word now, not just the first letter. In the middle of the second sentence, he suddenly asked JoBeth to read the passage to him, and then he would read it. This was a very familiar technique Joseph used in the classroom, where he often selected books Barbara had read aloud, and almost always had his buddy read the first page in a buddy-reading situation. He then read as recorded. Joseph asked JoBeth for nine words during his combined two attempts.

Sample 4

6-8-90

Characters Joseph

Storyteller   **Dragon** $\left(+69/82\right)$

Princess   **Messenger**

Prime Minister **Village People**

Storyteller: Once upon a time, [+there] [SC] in a tiny

Kingdom by a mountain [motel-huh-uh —TP], there was a

young Princess who was very unhappy [ugly].

A Prime Minister [pretty] who loved [lived] power [potter?, TP] had

taken it upon himself to rule the Kingdom.

1. The Prime Minister knew [know] only [along] one way

to solve [sello-? TP] problems, and that way was

to fight! The Kingdom was never quiet [quite]

and happy [hap-?]. The Princess [TP] decided one

day that she must make the Kingdom

a happy place again, so the Princess went

to see the Prime Minister.

1. return sweep error,
corrected by me

Joseph read a long version of *The Three Little Pigs* from a book of familiar stories with 98% accuracy and eight self corrections. He seemed eager to read the passage, telling JoBeth that he had been a villager when his class performed the play last month. This time, he asked JoBeth for only four words. He is not reading "independently" in this text yet, but he has made huge gains and he knows it. This time he asked to listen to the tape recording of *both* the texts he read.

Language, Literature, and At-Risk Children

Nancy Roser, James V. Hoffman, Cynthia Farest

No one questions that nurturing a child in a home that values literacy exerts a powerful effect on that child's literacy development. The research evidence is rapidly accumulating related to such literacy events as storytime in the home with young children and its bearing on the children's emergence as students who can read and write (Taylor & Dorsey-Gaines, 1988; Teale & Sulzby, 1985). Disturbing in this awareness is that children from economically disadvantaged homes enter school with fewer exposures to the tools of literacy and more at risk relative to their literacy acquisition. While most educators would agree that we must intensify our efforts to help parents and other caregivers provide more literacy experiences during the preschool years, there is less agreement as to what kind of school curriculum we should offer these at-risk learners.

It is our belief that all children, whether at risk or enriched, deserve to be immersed in the same kind of supportive environment at school that has served literacy growth in homes. In this article, we describe our efforts to infuse quality literature and related instructional strategies into a traditional reading and language arts program serving primarily limited English speaking students from economically disadvantaged home environments.

The Challenge

The project was initiated in response to a challenge from the Texas Education Agency to address the needs of at-risk children in Texas through innovative programming. In collaboration with the Brownsville Independent School District, we developed a proposal to answer the Agency's call. We titled our program Language to Literacy (LtL) because we believe that literacy skills develop in much the same way as oral language, and that both language and literacy are mutually enhancing, natural partners for all children. We argued that the children in Texas's southernmost, largely Hispanic school district, Brownsville, needed particular emphasis on a literate environment in their schools, one in which good books are shared and talked about, in which a wealth of response to literature is invited, and in which writing plays a major role and serves student purposes.

Implementing a Language to Literacy Program

The Participants

Brownsville, Texas, on the border between Texas and Mexico, is located in one of the poorest counties in the United States. Of

Brownsville's 90,000 residents, over 80% are Hispanic. Our plan called for working within kindergarten, first-, and second-grade classrooms in 6 of the district's 26 elementary schools. Participating schools were selected based on low test scores on the state's mandated test of basic skills. Over the 18 months of the project, we worked with 78 teachers and approximately 2,500 children.

As might be expected in communities where growth is rapid and new school buildings are opened continually, school libraries were not extensive. In addition, classroom collections of trade books were almost nonexistent. Through preliminary questionnaires, teachers indicated their interest and willingness to use trade books, but showed little familiarity with titles or the potential role of children's literature in literacy learning. They also indicated that although reading aloud to children was something they enjoyed, they could not always luxuriate in it, faced with pressing (and increasing) demands on their instructional time.

Getting Literature Into Classrooms

The first and most important step in our plan was to get children's literature into the classrooms. We used grant monies to buy about 1,000 children's books (about 750 different titles). We selected the literature based on recommendations by experts in children's literature, appearances of the titles on recommended lists for children (including other states' listings), and the books' current availability in print.

We then organized these books into literature units which are plans for sharing books that have some element in common (for example, a similar topic, theme, author or illustrator, or genre). The unit's organization establishes the set for children's discoveries of connections among pieces of literature (see Cullinan, 1989; Moss, 1984). For example, a unit titled "You're My Friend" focuses on books in which friendship between two characters is key.

Our objectives for sharing literature with children through a unit approach were these: offering exposure to a variety of children's books; contributing to a rich literary environment; motivating responsive reading; encouraging voluntary reading; expanding reading interests; helping children grow in language, reading, writing, and thinking; and helping children to discover their own connections with literature.

The project staff originally developed approximately 70 units. Each unit included 10 children's books, providing teachers with a read-aloud story each day for a 2-week period. We hoped the unit organization would encourage children's comparative study of the book selections and foster their discovery of "significant relationships, recurring patterns, and distinguishing characteristics" that linked the books within the units (Moss, 1984, p. 5).

We also developed a teaching guide to accompany each set of books. The guides included a unit focus, suggestions for kicking off the unit, suggestions for response activities for each book, and ideas for wrapping up the unit. The teaching guides were essentially sketches of teaching plans for sharing literature in the classroom; they offered support for teachers' efforts to help children comprehend, produce, and enjoy written language. A major thrust of the guides was their encouragement of response to the literature through opportunities for discussion and comparison of books, and through writing, art, and drama.

All 10 books and their unit guide were slipped into a tote bag that also had room for poetry on charts, audiotapes, posters from book publishers, and an occasional story videotape. The books were to travel from room to room and school to school in these totes, rotating every 2 weeks. As the bags traveled, teachers filled them with their own suggestions, posters, patterns, teaching tips, and paraphernalia they had used to implement the unit and were now offering to others.

Sharing Books With Children

The second part of the plan was to work together with teachers to discern effective ways to introduce and share books with children. During a 2-day inservice in which teachers were released from their regular classroom duties, we worked to develop a rationale for taking time for reading aloud to children in terms of its importance to literacy acquisition.

In addition, we worked to identify effective literature sharing techniques, and to identify ways to set up a physical space for the units in the classroom—a classroom library or trade-book center. This physical space was to serve both as an area to display the unit books and to allow for their free reading, as well as a space for other trade books, charts, and posters that invited children to read independently.

Sample literature units also were introduced in detail during the inservice, and the teachers took part in unit activities suggested in the guides. For example, they munched bread and jam with Frances as they discussed *Bread and Jam for Frances* (Hoban, 1964) from the "Books to Chew" unit.

Recording the Language of Response

Initial inservice training also introduced teachers to the uses of Language Charts as a means for collecting children's thoughts and feelings in response to books. The Language Chart, which served as an important part of each unit, was the designated space for gathering the daily language of listeners and readers. The charts themselves were simply a variation on the webs and comparison charts used effectively by others (see, for example, Cullinan, 1989, Norton, 1982). Language Charts were constructed from butcher paper, and often ruled into a lattice or matrix with headings that helped to focus the children on the linkages among books in the unit—and enabled comparisons and connections to be displayed.

Each book in a unit was to be entered onto a Language Chart for discussion and comparison. For example, in the theme unit titled "Big and Small," children were led by the columns of the chart to focus on the notion that sometimes authors include in the same story both characters that are very large and those that are very small, and that sometimes the characters even change sizes. After sharing several books that contain characters of various sizes, children discover that, regardless of size, characters can be quite satisfied with themselves.

As another example, the Language Chart for the "Being Different Is Being Special" unit encouraged children to focus on the major characters' traits and how these traits made them special. Headings on the Language Chart read: "Title," "Who Was Different?" and "What Made the Difference Special?" Each day after a book was read and discussed, teachers both followed and led a conversation about the book; at the close of the conversation, children decided what should be recorded on the Language Chart. Language Charts often were returned to and reread at the beginning of story time as review of the unit and preview for the next book.

In no instance was the chart's design intended to limit the range of talk that went on before, during, and after storytime; rather, it was intended to focus the discussion after it had ranged freely, and to nurture personal meanings and responses, as well as group-constructed meanings. Initially, the Language Charts' designs and column headings were under the direction of the teachers, but the goal was to relinquish to children the initiation of the search for meaning and connections so they could begin to discover for themselves how tales are bound (especially narratives), and how books help to answer questions (especially expository text). Language was recorded in either English or Spanish, depending upon the language user.

Encouraging Writing

The writing component of the Language to Literacy project was introduced after the book sharing was firmly established. In initial classroom "walk throughs," we could find little evidence of children's writing displayed on walls or in hallways, lying out on desks or tables, or tucked into writing folders. All of us in the project hoped to install more opportunities to write into each classroom. Inservice involved a 2-day workshop in which teachers explored the successive approximations of children's growth in written language that parallels growth in oral language. At all times, we focused on the writer's strengths, what he or she knew about the conventions of writing, as well as on trying to understand what each writer was attempting.

Although we recognized that writing serves many legitimate purposes for children other than as a follow-up to reading, we initially took advantage of children's increasing willingness to talk about books as a starting point for encouraging them to write on their own. Through drawing and writing, there seemed an especially natural transition for those children who had much more to say about stories than could be recorded on the Language Chart. Children were eager to have their words recorded, so the teachers simply encouraged them to begin to write the thoughts they wanted to share.

When these notions about writing became entrenched and teachers and children were comfortable, other reasons for writing emerged. The children maintained journals, responded to classmates' writing, selected pieces for polishing and publishing, and saw their products displayed in public ways.

Developing Reading Fluency

Two direct methods were offered for developing children's reading fluency—the use of Big Books in kindergarten and the use of a recitation method with their basal readers for first and second graders. Both of these efforts began during the third semester of the project—when those teachers who felt successful with sharing literature and with writing could volunteer for an additional component of the program.

Our Big Books were simple stories, made predictable by the repetition of a sound pattern, a refrain, a strong rhythm, a cumulative story line, or a familiar structure (see, for example, Bridge, Winograd, & Haley, 1983; Rhodes, 1981). They were used to encourage children to join in or read along, and to help them develop insights about printed language. With enlarged texts, children could experience the story much as they would in a one-to-one read-aloud event. Inservice was devoted to developing a rationale for the use of Big Books with beginning readers, as well as examining the strategies involved in sharing these books with children. Teachers read, shared, and made Big Books—discovering their recurring features.

Because the Big Books were "homemade" enlargements, children were encouraged to produce their own illustrations for the books. Their drawings were attached with clips or double-sided tape so that they could be removed when the Big Book was exchanged among teachers. Small-book versions also were available for rereadings by individuals and small groups. Books were rotated each week within the kindergarten classrooms at each participating school and then among the schools.

The recitation component of the project focused on helping low-achieving children to read their basal readers with fluency and accuracy in either Spanish or English. The recitation lesson framework was based on research conducted in first- and second-grade classrooms (Hoffman, 1987) and drew upon research in comprehension instruction, particularly the use of story grammars, as well as research in the development of fluency through oral reading using modeling and repeated reading techniques.

During recitation, children listened to the story as it was modeled by the teacher; responded to the story in the same kinds of ways they were responding during storytime; reconstructed the story using a simple mapping procedure; rehearsed (practiced) the story given teacher support; and finally "recited" the story—performing a section of the story by rereading it orally, fluently, and expressively for the group.

Program Effects

We used a variety of data collection techniques to both monitor implementation and evaluate the effects of participation for both teachers and students. Several different types of data were collected for the purpose of gauging the effects of the program on the participants' understandings, attitudes, and behaviors. We examined changes in teachers' story sharing strategies that occurred over the course of the project and found significant effects for program participation (Hoffman, Roser, & Farest, 1988).

We analyzed the teachers' own reports of their learning as well as their reports of students' learning associated with participation in the project and were able to document effects from varying participants' perspectives

(Roser, Hoffman, Farest, Isaacs, & Battle, 1989). We examined the effect of the fluency component on students' reading and found patterns of significant effects for participation (Hoffman, Isaacs, Roser, & Farest, 1989).

Finally, we examined data related to the performance of students in the program on traditional measures of academic achievement. Six schools were identified in the Brownsville Independent School District as comparison schools. The analysis focused on a comparison of student achievement on the reading and language arts areas of the California Test of Basic Skills (CTBS) at the second-grade level.

The CTBS is administered districtwide every spring to all students in the second through twelfth grades. Since no pretest data were available for the students participating in the project, a cohort analysis was conducted that involved a comparison of the second-grade students who had participated in the LtL program with students who had come through the school the previous year without LtL. The Table presents the relevant data with scores reported in percentiles.

The change in percentile scores from 1987 to 1988 in the area of language arts for the comparison schools was 6.3 and was 3.0 in the area of reading. The change in percentile scores from 1987 to 1988 in the area of language arts for the LtL schools was 10.5 and was 14.0 in the area of reading. It is important to reiterate that this is a comparison of two different cohorts of students; consequently, there are factors other than the LtL program that might be accounting for these large differences. Nevertheless, these data are encouraging for the effects of the program after 1½ years.

Of the six schools, five made statistically significant growth in their scores on the state-mandated test of basic skills (TEAMS). Of the five area schools cited as among the most improved in the state, three were participants in

CTBS achievement scores for second-grade students in LtL and comparison schools for a 2-year period

Schools	Reading 1987	Reading 1988	Language arts 1987	Language arts 1988
Comparison				
A	36	40	43	57
B	51	56	56	59
C	52	55	60	73
D	51	54	47	65
E	40	38	58	38
F	39	42	40	52
Mean	44.5	47.5	51.0	57.3
LtL project				
G	17	26	17	33
H	26	43	33	47
I	47	66	47	74
J	34	53	41	64
K	45	45	44	42
L	25	27	26	29
Mean	27.0	37.5	29.0	43.0

CTBS = California Test of Basic Skills
Note: All scores are reported in percentiles.

the LtL program. Again, we recognize the contribution of many factors other than LtL to these gains, including the presence of a supportive administration, cooperative teachers, the presence of experts in bilingual education, and the potential for regression to account for some movement.

Conclusions

It is difficult to be totally dispassionate in the presentation of results. Anyone who has had the pleasure of sharing bright and shiny new books with children and teachers who have had fewer books than they deserve can appreciate that all data cannot be recorded entirely objectively. As one teacher asked when we delivered the book totes: "Did you say you were from the University of Texas or from heaven?"

Our results indicate that a literature-based program can be implemented successfully in schools that serve at-risk students. Further, there is every indication that these students respond to such a program in the same positive ways as any student would—with enthusiasm for books, with willingness to share ideas, and with growth in language and literacy.

REFERENCES
Bridge, C.A., Winograd, P., & Haley, D. (1983). Using predictable books vs. preprimers to teach

beginning sight words. *The Reading Teacher, 36*, 884–891.

Cullinan, B.E. (1989). *Literature and the child* (2nd ed.). San Diego, CA: Harcourt Brace Jovanovich.

Hoffman, J.V. (1987). Rethinking the role of oral reading in basal instruction. *The Elementary School Journal, 87*, 367–374.

Hoffman, J.V., Roser, N.L., & Farest, C. (1988). Literature-sharing strategies in classrooms serving students from economically disadvantaged and language different home environments. In J.E. Readence & R.S. Baldwin (Eds.), *Dialogues in literacy research.* (Thirty-seventh Yearbook of the National Reading Conference, pp. 331–338). Rochester, NY: National Reading Conference.

Hoffman, J.V., Isaacs, M.E., Roser, N.L., & Farest, C. (1989). *Developing reading fluency and story comprehension using a recitation framework.* Paper presented at the annual meeting of the National Reading Conference, Austin, TX.

Moss, J.F. (1984). *Focus units in literature: A handbook for elementary school teachers.* Urbana, IL: National Council of Teachers of English.

Norton, D.E. (1982). Using a webbing process to develop children's literature units. *Language Arts, 59*, 348–355.

Rhodes, L.K. (1981). I can read! Predictable books as resources for reading and writing instruction. *The Reading Teacher, 36*, 511–518.

Roser, N.L., Hoffman, J.V., Farest, C., Isaacs, M.E., & Battle, J. (1989). *Teachers' developing insights about the use of children's literature for language and literacy growth.* Paper presented at the annual meeting of the National Reading Conference, Austin, Texas.

Taylor, D., & Dorsey-Gaines, C. (1988). *Growing up literate: Learning from inner-city families.* Portsmouth, NH: Heinemann.

Teale, W., & Sulzby, E. (Eds.). (1985). *Emergent literacy: Writing and reading.* Norwood, NJ: Ablex.

CHILDREN'S LITERATURE REFERENCE

Hoban, R. (1964). *Bread and jam for Frances.* New York: Harper.

SECTION IV

Fostering Reading for Meaning

Making sense of what one reads is the only real reason for reading. No one would long persist in reading random strings of words. But reading accurately and even fluently is no guarantee that understanding or appreciation will follow automatically. In this section each article offers useful ideas on how we might support the development of comprehension. The articles provide information and strategies for fostering comprehension in both narrative and informational texts. In addition, several of the articles provide useful strategies for monitoring understanding or for identifying the sources of difficulties in gaining meaning from text.

Helping children who find learning to read difficult develop thoughtful reading habits and strategies must be an early and primary focus. A necessary first step is to help many of these children understand how literate people talk about books and stories. Our efforts must move beyond the traditional assign and check model of answering comprehension questions that has too long dominated in our classrooms. Understanding is much more than remembering details from the text, and fostering strategies that enhance understanding requires an intervention different from the most common approaches used in the past.

Modeling Mental Processes Helps Poor Readers Become Strategic Readers

Gerald G. Duffy, Laura R. Roehler, Beth Ann Herrmann

odeling, a physical demonstration of how to do a task, is what a teacher does to show novice readers how to do something they do not know how to do. It is a frequently recommended instructional technique (Good, 1983; Rosenshine, 1986; Rosenshine & Stevens, 1984). However, emphasis on the strategic and metacognitive aspects of reading (Paris, Lipson, & Wixson, 1983; Pressley et al., 1985) highlights the need for modeling not only the physically observable aspects of reading but also the invisible mental processes that are at the core of reading. This "mental modeling" has not been well described, especially from the perspective of its use with poor readers.

The Role of Modeling in Intentional Learning

Students are active interpreters of instructional encounters and they make inferences about the meaning of instructional information (Winne & Marx, 1982). Consequently, instructional information must be presented in ways that minimize student misinterpretation of the teacher's intentions.

Modeling accomplishes this goal by providing explicit information, thereby reducing instructional ambiguity. Decreasing uncertainty is particularly important for poor readers because their background knowledge about what reading is and how it works is sparse and, in the absence of explicit instructional information, they often draw erroneous conclusions about lesson objectives. In short, modeling minimizes the guesswork in learning how reading works.

In its usual form, modeling focuses on physical demonstration of task *performance*. This kind of modeling is typified by practices such as Uninterrupted Sustained Silent Reading (USSR) in which, during designated times in the school day, both the teacher and students engage in recreational reading. In doing so, the teacher physically models the performance of the reading act and, by laughing out loud while reading or otherwise demonstrating appreciation and enjoyment, models the aesthetic outcomes associated with reading. Students do not have to infer the joy of reading because the teacher provides explicit evidence of its existence.

162

Mental Modeling

USSR type modeling is appropriate for making explicit the act of reading and the joy associated with it. However, it does not make explicit the invisible cognitive activity that is the basis for strategic reading. This mental processing remains invisible during such modeling.

To model cognitive activity, teachers must make their reasoning visible to the novice. We call this kind of modeling "mental modeling." It is based on research of mental rehearsals (Bandura, 1986), and on "think alouds" (Whimbey, 1985), as well as on comprehension instruction research (Duffy et al., 1987; Herrmann, 1986).

To provide mental modeling, teachers must focus on two things. First, they must focus on transferring metacognitive control from themselves to the students; second, they must model mental processes, not procedural steps.

Metacognitive Control

Metacognitive control, in which the *student* consciously directs the reasoning process, is a particularly important aspect of strategic reading. When students are conscious of the reasoning involved, they can access and apply similar reasoning in future reading situations. However, comprehension instruction does not always provide students with enough information about the reasoning for them to assume metacognitive control.

For instance, reading teachers may routinely ask inferential questions and check the accuracy of student answers. However, if they do not also explain the mental processes used to answer such questions, their students cannot assume metacognitive control because they are left relatively uninformed about the thinking expert readers do when answering such questions. Consequently, they are unable to direct their own inferential reasoning

when independently reading their own text in the future.

Similarly, teaching comprehension by asking students questions before, during, and after the reading of a selection helps students comprehend that particular selection but does not necessarily result in metacognitive control of the *process* of comprehending text generally.

To illustrate, when asking comprehension questions before the reading, the teacher decides what prior knowledge needs to be activated and asks students to answer questions which will cause them to activate that knowledge, but the teacher controls the process of deciding what prior knowledge to access and the student merely responds to the teacher's request. During the reading the teacher decides what meaning must be monitored and asks the students to answer questions that will focus them on that meaning, but the teacher makes the crucial decision about what to monitor and the student merely responds to the teacher's cue. After the reading the teacher decides what meaning needs to be clarified and summarized and asks the students questions that focus them on these clarifications and summaries, but again students merely follow the teacher's lead.

In short, the teacher—not the student—directs the reasoning in activating knowledge before reading, in monitoring meaning during reading, and in focusing meaning after reading. Students must infer what the teacher's reasoning is. Poor readers seldom make this inference, or else they make it poorly and end up with misconceptions.

Mental modeling, in contrast, makes explicit the reasoning expert readers employ as they comprehend. To illustrate, an example of a lesson on activating background knowledge is presented. The teacher promotes metacognitive control by making visible to students her invisible mental processing so the students have an example of appropriate reasoning they can use as a basis for activating background knowledge themselves.

Teacher: Before you start to read a story, you should get your background knowledge ready so you can use it when you read. Thinking about what you already know will help you understand when you start reading. Watch me think out loud and I'll show you how to get your background knowledge ready. The title of this story is *Things in My House*. Let's see, this title is about things in a house, that's easy enough. I have background knowledge about things in a house. In my house, I have a couch, bed, desk, and a hamster. Let's see if thinking about those things helps me understand this story as I read.

[Teachers reads.] "It was dark in the house when Alex came inside. The storm had knocked down some wires and the lights were not working. Slowly he tried to make his way to the kitchen where the matches were kept. Suddenly, Alex felt pain. He ran into something very big and heavy and it hurt. He started to feel around and discovered that he had run into the couch."

[Teacher stops reading and closes his or her eyes.] I'm picturing that in my mind. I can see Alex walking around my living room and tripping over my couch.

[Teacher addresses the children.] You couldn't see my thoughts, but I was thinking about that while I was reading, and then thinking about it again after I read helped me understand what was happening to Alex. Now, let's see if you can do that.

In contrast, note that the teacher in the following lesson on activating background knowledge points out cues such as pictures and words but does not explain how she reasoned with background knowledge about these pictures and words to understand the text. Because only the teacher knows how she did what she did, the teacher retains metacognitive control.

Teacher: I'm going to first read the title. The title is *Sign Language Fun* and the author is Linda Bove. I'll look at the pictures. There are pictures of Sesame Street characters but there are also pictures of a lady doing sign language...and there are some words that kind of tell about the book such as what the publishers are like. I predict that this book is going to be about how to do sign language. OK, now you try it.

We have rewritten the preceding lesson excerpt to illustrate how the teacher, by making visible the invisible thinking processes she used, could provide students with more information and help them gain metacognitive control of the process of activating background knowledge. The revised lesson excerpt follows:

Teacher: Watch me think out loud while I try to predict what this story is going to be about. The title is *Sign Language Fun*.

[Teacher is looking at the pictures.] Here is a picture of Sesame Street characters and a picture of a lady doing sign language. And the title says it is going to be about sign language. I know something about Sesame Street characters from my past experience. I've seen them do some pretty fantastic things. And the people on Sesame Street teach things to the puppets. Since the lady is doing sign language, maybe she is going to teach the Sesame Street characters how to do sign language. I'm going to guess that in this story the lady is going to teach them how to use sign language.

Failure to make reasoning processes explicit leaves poor readers in doubt about how expert readers make sense of text. Mental modeling minimizes such doubts by including illustrations of appropriate reasoning that students can use to construct their own schemata for how to make sense of text.

Modeling Mental Processes Versus Modeling Procedural Steps

Mental modeling makes visible invisible mental processes. This is in sharp contrast to modeling of procedures, which consists of telling students directions or steps to follow in completing a specific task.

For instance, when assigning seatwork during reading period, teachers often demonstrate procedural steps to follow by saying something like "OK, first you look at the picture on the left side—like this—and then you look over here to see what letter it goes with—like this—and then you draw a line from the picture to the letter it goes with—like this." The focus is steps to follow, not the thinking one does to complete the steps.

This kind of modeling is also seen in skill teaching when teachers emphasize accurate completion of isolated worksheet tasks. For instance, a teacher teaching prefixes and suffixes may model a list of steps to be followed rigidly, saying something like "OK, the first thing you do is look for the root word and circle it—like this—then you draw a line between the root word and the prefix—like this." The focus is a finite set of physically observable steps to be followed in a rigid manner.

Mental processes associated with strategic reading, however, cannot be reduced to a finite set of steps. Because each individual processes information differently and because each text is structured differently, expert readers make adaptations in every processing situation. That is, what an expert reader does when encountering an unknown affixed word in one text situation may differ from what is done when an unknown affixed word is met in another textual situation. Although good readers often infer the need for such flexibility, poor readers often remain unaware of the need for adaptability or of the distinction between strategic reasoning and rule following unless they are provided with mental modeling.

To illustrate the difference between modeling mental processes and modeling steps, note that the teacher in the following lesson excerpt, while being explicit, also conveys a flexibility about the reasoning she does when using context clues.

Teacher: I want to show you what I look at when I come across a word I don't know the meaning of. I'll talk out loud to show you how I figure it out.

[Teacher reads.] "The cocoa steamed fragrantly." Hmm, I've heard that word *fragrantly* before, but I don't really know what it means here. I know one of the words right before it though—*steamed*. I watched a pot of boiling water once and there was steam coming from it. That water was hot, so this must have something to do with the cocoa being hot. OK, the pan of hot cocoa is steaming on the stove. That means steam coming up and out, but that still doesn't explain what *fragrantly* means. Let me think again about the hot cocoa on the stove and try to use what I already know about cocoa as a clue. Hot cocoa bubbles, steams, and...smells!

Hot cocoa smells good. "The cocoa steamed fragrantly." That means it smelled good!

[Teacher addresses the students.] Thinking about what I already know about hot cocoa helped me figure out what that word meant.

In contrast, note the following example from another teacher's context lesson. This teacher, like the one in the previous example, is very explicit. However, she is explicit about procedural steps, not about the reasoning used.

Teacher: The first thing you do is try to guess from your own experience what the word is. Do you know what experience means? If you can predict what the word is, then fit the word into the sentence to see if it makes sense.

Second, if you can't guess, ask yourself this: Is the word defined in the passage? Look before and after the word. If it is, then see if the word makes sense.

Third, ask yourself this: Is there a synonym for the word before or after the word? Do you know what a synonym is? It's when the words have the same meaning, like *big* and *large*.

Fourth, ask yourself if you can guess what the word is by the general mood or feeling of the passage. Using these steps will help you predict what the word might mean and it's faster than going to a dictionary.

The first teacher conveyed a sense of flexibility in using context clues and background knowledge to figure out the meaning of an unknown word, but this teacher tells the students to follow a set of steps. She does not communicate to students the flexibility essential to strategic reading.

Relation Between Modeling and Lesson Interaction

Although mental modeling is important, it is only one aspect of an effective instructional sequence. To be successful, modeling must be interspersed with opportunities for student expression.

Students come to instruction with their own ideas about how reading works. As they listen to the teacher's mental modeling, they mediate what is heard, combining what the teacher says with their already existing schema for how reading works and restructuring that schema to make sense out of the instructional information. Although mental modeling moves students closer to an understanding of how to think like a reader, there is no guarantee that students' restructured understandings will be precisely the understanding the teacher intends.

To find out what students' understandings are, the teacher must ask students to express their understandings and then, on the basis of what students say, the teacher must provide additional information that will gradually move students toward the intended outcome. This instructional stage has been described as the "gradual release of responsibility" (Pearson, 1985). It calls for teacher action which has been described as "alternative representations" (Wilson & Shulman, in press) and as "responsive elaboration" (Duffy & Roehler, 1987).

In both descriptions, the teacher monitors students' evolving understandings of the intended learning and responds to these understandings with appropriate elaborations. The teacher's spontaneously generated statements, cues, prompts, analogies, metaphors, and other forms of assistance help students refine their understanding of what the teacher's mental modeling was designed to illustrate. Consequently, to be effective, mental modeling must be implemented in tandem with fluid teacher-student dialogues to ensure that students do not misinterpret the modeling and end up with misconceptions.

Conclusion

Mental modeling is difficult. To accomplish it, teachers must:

- present the strategy in the context of connected text (not in an artificial context, such as a workbook page);

- describe mental maneuvers illustrative of what one does when doing the reasoning so students have enough information to assume metacognitive control of the mental processing;

- provide examples and nonexamples that communicate that flexibility of thinking (rather than mimicry of thinking) is sought; and

- intersperse modeling with student opportunities for expression so that the students' reasoning when reading can be observed and the teachers can provide them with elaborative instructional information as needed.

In conclusion, helping poor readers become strategic readers demands modeling of mental processes. This type of modeling is an instructional component that works with poor readers.

REFERENCES

Bandura, A. (1986). *Social foundations of thought and action.* Englewood Cliffs, NJ: Prentice Hall.

Duffy, G., & Roehler, L. (1987). Improving reading through the use of responsive elaboration. *The Reading Teacher, 40,* 514–521.

Duffy, G., Roehler, L., Sivan, E., Rackliffe, G., Book, C., Meloth, M., Vavrus, L., Wesselman, R., Putnam, J., & Bassiri, D. (1987). The effects of explaining the reasoning associated with using reading strategies. *Reading Research Quarterly, 22,* 347–367.

Good, T. (1983). Research on classroom teaching. In L. Shulman & G. Sykes, (Eds.), *Handbook of teaching and policy.* New York: Longman.

Herrmann, B.A. (1986). *Strategic problem solving of mathematic story problems: A descriptive study of the effects and characteristics of direct teacher explanation.* Paper presented at the annual meeting of the American Educational Research Association annual conference, San Francisco, CA.

Paris, S., Lipson, M., & Wixson, K. (1983). Becoming a strategic reader. *Contemporary Educational Psychology, 8*(1), 293–316.

Pearson, P.D. (1985). Changing the face of reading comprehension instruction. *The Reading Teacher, 38,* 724–738.

Pressley, M., Forest-Pressley, D., Elliott-Faust, D., & Miller, G. (1985). Children's use of cognitive strategies, how to teach strategies and what to do if they can't be taught. In M. Pressley & C. Brainard (Eds.), *Cognitive learning and memory in children.* New York: Springer Verlag.

Rosenshine, B. (1986). Synthesizing research on explicit teaching. *Educational Leadership, 43,* 60–69.

Rosenshine, B., & Stevens, R. (1984). Classroom instruction in reading. In P.D. Pearson, M. Kamil, P. Mosenthal, & R. Barr (Eds.), *Handbook of reading research: Volume 1.* New York: Longman.

Wilson, S., & Shulman, L. (in press). 150 different ways of knowing: Representations of knowledge in teaching. In J. Calderhead (Ed.), *Exploring teacher thinking.* Eastbourne, England: Holt, Rinehart, & Winston.

Winne, P., & Marx, R. (1982). Students' and teachers' views of thinking processes for classroom learning. *The Elementary School Journal, 82,* 493–518.

Whimbey, A. (1985). Reading, writing, reasoning linked in testing and training. *Journal of Reading, 29,* 118–123.

Two Approaches for Helping Poor Readers Become More Strategic

Beth Ann Herrmann

Since the late 1970s our understanding of the reading process has changed dramatically. Reading is no longer thought of as the "mindless" application of isolated skills. Instead, recent research shows us that reading is a strategic, meaning-getting process requiring awareness and control of complex reasoning processes.

Some readers learn how to be more strategic than others, but researchers are not quite sure why. Somehow expert readers discover reasoning processes associated with strategic reading and with little assistance, learn how to apply these processes to construct meaning and to study and learn from text. Poor readers, on the other hand, need explicit instruction on how to be strategic when reading.

Not surprisingly, various methods for teaching poor readers how to think like expert readers have gained in popularity. This article describes and compares two effective approaches. Direct explanation emphasizes helping poor readers understand how the reading process works. Reciprocal teaching emphasizes helping students understand how to study and learn from text strategically.

Direct Explanation

Direct explanation lessons help students understand how the reading process works (Duffy et al., 1987). The teacher's primary role is to teach students how to monitor their comprehension and how to fix a comprehension breakdown. Success depends largely on how effective the teacher is with two important aspects of direct explanation.

First, the teacher models specific reasoning processes used by good readers to construct meaning from text. This kind of modeling differs greatly from modeling of procedures, which consists of telling students directions or steps to follow when completing a specific task. Mental modeling, in contrast, makes visible to students invisible reasoning processes expert readers employ as they make sense of text (Duffy, Roehler, & Herrmann, 1988).

Second, as the lesson progresses, the teacher monitors and shapes students' evolving understandings of reasoning processes by asking them to explain how they made sense of the text and, on the basis of what they say, providing additional explanation to help them reason like experts. The teacher's response consists of spontaneous statements, cues, prompts, analogies, metaphors, or other forms of assistance which help students refine their understanding of what the teacher's mental modeling was designed to illustrate (Duffy & Roehler, 1987).

Planning Direct Explanation

The following eight-step decision-making process is followed when planning a direct explanation lesson:

1. Decide which reasoning process to teach, why it is important, and when the students will need to use it.

2. Decide how the reasoning process works. For example, when good readers use context clues, they think about what they already know about the topic while at the same time examining the context for syntactic or meaning relations that might give clues to what an unknown word is and predicting what the word might be.

3. Collect several text examples and nonexamples that can be used when explaining and modeling the reasoning process.

4. Assess the textbook prescription for a description of the reasoning process, its usefulness, and how to use it. Disregard text prescriptions that do not help explain the reasoning process.

5. Decide what to say when introducing the lesson, including a statement of the reasoning process that will be taught, why it is important, and when it should be used.

6. Decide what to say and do while modeling when and how to use the reasoning process.

7. Assess the text for opportunities to use the reasoning process. Disregard passages that do not include such opportunities.

8. Anticipate the kinds of problems the students may have learning when and how to use the reasoning process. Decide how to explain or model the reasoning process again if

necessary, and select passages that may be used to clarify misunderstandings.

Direct Explanation Lesson

The following eight-step is used when conducting a direct explanation lesson:

1. Activate the students' prior knowledge of the selection topic by discussing the title and pictures and asking them to share experiences relative to the topic. Then, state what reasoning process will be taught, why it is important, and when it will be used. Use difficult text parts to demonstrate the usefulness of the reasoning process, as illustrated in the following lesson excerpt:

Teacher: Today we're going to read a story about a birthday party. How many of you have been to a birthday party? [Students respond.] Look at this picture of the boy in our story. His name's Russ. What is he doing in this picture? [Students respond.] That's right, he's blowing out the candles on his cake. Let's read the title of our story together. [Reading] "The Birthday Surprise." Good. Now there's something I want you to know about this story. There are some hard words in it that might give you some trouble. Here's one right here. [Shows students.] Before we read the story, I'm going to teach you how to figure out hard words like this so that when you come to them in the story, you'll be able to figure them out yourselves.

2. Think out loud to model when the reasoning process should be used.

Teacher: Okay. I'm going to pretend I don't know a hard word in this story. Watch what happens. [Teacher reads and pretends to have trouble with a hard word.] Hmmm. I don't know that word; let me skip it and keep going. Maybe I won't need to know it. [Teacher continues reading, pretends to be confused.] Oh, now I'm really in trouble. Not knowing that word back there is getting me confused. [Addressing the students] I want you to understand that right now is when I need to stop and go back and figure out what that word is, because I've stopped understanding the story.

3. Think out loud to model how to use the reasoning process to repair the comprehension breakdown.

Teacher: Okay. I'm in trouble now because of this hard word. Watch what I do to figure out what it is. Let me think. I know something about birthday parties. My son just had one, but when he tried to blow out his candles, they didn't go out, because we tricked him with special candles. Let me read this part again and think about that. [Reading] "But Russ's candles didn't go out because they were /p/, pony-phony." The candles were phony! That makes sense now.

4. Check how the students interpreted the modeling information by asking them to tell or show when and how to use the reasoning process. If they understand, provide supportive feedback and move to the next phase of the lesson. If, however, the students do not understand, provide ongoing cues, prompts, analogies, metaphors, or other forms of elaboration that help the students refine their understanding of the reasoning process.

Teacher: Now, I want to give you all a chance to show me what I did when I got confused. Sherene, let's start with you.

Can you show me how to figure out this hard word in this sentence?

Student: Well, I'd go back and read the sentence again.

Teacher: That's good. And let's do something more. Do you remember what I was thinking about when I reread my sentence?

Student: How to sound out the word?

Teacher: That sometimes helps but there's something else to try. Watch me again. [Teacher rereads and again reasons aloud about the context of the hard word.]

5. Share the title and the pictures again and ask the students to predict what the selection will be about. Jot down a few predictions (including any of your own) on the chalkboard. Remind the students that when they come to difficult words, they are to try to figure them out by using the reasoning process.

Teacher: Now we're going to read the story about Russ's birthday party. I want you to look again at the title and some of the pictures. [Shows title and pictures.] What do you think this story will be about? [Students respond; teacher writes a few predictions on chalkboard.] That's good thinking. Now remember, there are hard words in this story and when you come to one, I want you to try to figure it out like I showed you.

As the students read, provide individual assistance to those who have difficulty using the reasoning process to figure out unknown words.

6. Discuss predictions made earlier as well as individual use of the reasoning process.

Teacher: Let's look again at the guesses we made about what would happen in the story. Marsha, you said you thought Russ would get a bike for his birthday. Did you find out anything about that when you read? [Students respond; teacher continues a discussion on each prediction, erasing those that are not confirmed.] Glen, I noticed you were figuring out a hard word. Can you show us which word was giving you trouble and what you did to figure it out?

7. Close the lesson by summarizing the content of the selection and when and how to use the reasoning process.

Teacher: All right. Let's think about what we learned today. First, we learned that Russ got faked out by some phony candles, didn't we? We also learned he didn't get everything he was expecting, and he got some things that he wasn't expecting. You also learned how to figure out hard words by thinking about what you already know. Doing that will help you with other things you read, too, so I want you to try it this afternoon when we read our social studies chapter.

8. Provide opportunities for the students to practice using the reasoning process.

Reciprocal Teaching

Reciprocal teaching helps students understand how to study and learn from text (Brown & Palincsar, 1989; Palincsar & Brown, 1984.) The teacher's primary role is to show students how expert readers use four comprehension fostering and monitoring activities—generating questions, summarizing, predicting, and clarifying. Success largely depends on how effective the teacher is with two important aspects of reciprocal teaching.

First, the teacher performs each of the four activities while leading a dialogue about a section of text. After observing the teacher, each student assumes the teacher's role. The teacher monitors each performance to help the students understand the meaning of the text, evaluate the author's message, remember the content, and apply new knowledge.

Second, if a student has difficulty with any of the activities, the teacher modifies the task. For example, if a student has difficulty generating a question about the text, the teacher adjusts the expectation and focuses on something the student has learned from the text. The teacher then takes the idea the student has proposed and prompts a question using that information. If the prompt is insufficient, the teacher models a question and asks the student to try another question, but provides less support. Note how the teacher adjusts the task demand in the following lesson excerpt:

Teacher: Let's try for another question. Let me read a part of this again. [Teacher reads second paragraph again.]

Student: I never heard that before.

Teacher: Can you think of a question? [Pause.]

Student: I know. They can see themselves.

Teacher: Hmmm. You could use a question about that sentence, couldn't you? Start the question with "how."

Student: How can the...

Teacher: aquanauts...

Student: see themselves in the mirror?

Teacher: Okay. That's close. You answered your question. What's the mirror?

Student: The water.

Teacher: So you might ask "How could the aquanauts see themselves?" or "What was the water like?" Let's go on now.

Planning Reciprocal Teaching

Planning for a reciprocal teaching lesson has two phases. First, become familiar with the text selection by following this five-step procedure:

1. Identify which text segments will be used to demonstrate the four comprehension activities.

2. Identify salient questions in the selection and generate additional questions about the material.

3. Generate possible predictions about each text segment.

4. Underline summarizing sentences and generate possible summaries for each text segment.

5. Circle difficult vocabulary or concepts.

Second, make two diagnostic decisions about the students who will participate:

1. Decide what activities the students already use when reading and what is needed to help them learn from the text.

2. Evaluate the students' abilities to generate text questions, summarize, predict, and clarify, and decide what kind of support they will need to participate in and eventually lead each of these activities.

Reciprocal Teaching Lesson

Reciprocal teaching lessons follow a six-step procedure:

1. Read the text title and have the students tell what they expect or would like to learn from the selection. Summarize the group's predictions and, if appropriate, add a few of your own. Note how the lesson begins in the following lesson excerpt.

Teacher: What's the title of our new passage?

Student: "The Miracle of Butterflies."

Teacher: Right. What's the miracle of butterflies? In your own words, what would you predict this is going to be about?

Student: How butterflies fly?

Teacher: Oh, that's a good prediction!

Student: What they do.

Student: What season they come out, like summer.

Teacher: Okay. Those are some excellent predictions. Let's begin.

2. Read a small portion of the text aloud, paragraph by paragraph.

3. Ask a question about the content. Invite the group to answer the question. Invite individuals to share additional questions generated while they read the selection.

Teacher: My question is: What have the people of Butterfly City, USA done to protect the butterflies?

Student: They made a law making it illegal.

Teacher: To do what?

Student: To kill butterflies.

Teacher: Exactly. Does anyone else have a question?

4. Summarize what has been read by identifying the gist of the segment and explain how you arrived at this summary. Invite the group to comment on the summary. Note how the teacher summarized in the following lesson excerpt.

Teacher: My summary is that this is about the migration of monarch butterflies. I thought of that summary because the authors introduced the story with a good topic sentence. That was a good clue. Do you have anything that should be added to my summary?

5. Lead a discussion to clarify any words or ideas that are unclear or confusing.

Teacher: Let me ask you something here. Is there an unclear meaning in this paragraph?

Student: Yes. Where it says "scrawls in wavy light."

Teacher: Now, does the sun ever write a message in the sky?

Student: No.

Teacher: No. What is the author doing here?

Student: Making up the whole thing in his mind.

Teacher: All right. It doesn't really happen but the author is using this expression to say that the sun sends us a message and that it can be used as an energy source. But certainly you will never look at the sky and see a message written by the sun.

6. Signal preparation to move on to the next portion of the selection by eliciting pre-

---

Comparing direct explanation to reciprocal teaching

Similarities

Both require face-to-face teacher-student interaction.
Both may be used with stories or expository prose.
Both involve students in making predictions about text.
Both take place during regular reading instruction.

Differences

Goals:

Direct explanation teaches the reasoning processes used by strategic readers. (Lessons show students how to make sense out of text.)	Reciprocal teaching deals with how to study and learn from text. (Lessons focus on questioning, summarizing, predicting, and clarifying while processing content.)

Role of modeling:

In direct explanation, the teacher uses modeling to make visible the invisible reasoning processes. (Thoughts about mental processes are verbalized.)	In reciprocal teaching, the teacher models procedures expert readers follow to study and learn from text. (Mental processes are not verbalized.)

Teacher responses:

In direct explanation, when students misunderstand reasoning processes, the teacher re-explains, remodels, and clarifies by eliciting student feedback and providing more elaboration.	In reciprocal teaching, when students have difficulty generating questions, summarizing, predicting, or clarifying, the teacher lowers the demands of the task.

dictions regarding upcoming content. Select a student to be the next "teacher."

The Two Approaches

Direct explanation and reciprocal teaching are similar in some respects yet they differ critically, too—in their goals, in the role that modeling plays, and in the way the teacher responds to student misunderstanding. These similarities and differences are displayed in the Figure.

Although the two methods are used to achieve different outcomes, both are necessary for teaching poor readers how to become more strategic. The key to incorporating both approaches into basal reader lessons is to gradually adjust your regular instructional routine. Use direct explanation at the beginning of the lesson to show students how to construct meaning from the story. Use reciprocal teaching later to show students how to understand the author's message.

Teaching poor readers how to think like expert readers is a difficult task. You must be patient. Adjusting your instructional routine will take time. Begin with small changes and wait until you adapt to them before making additional adjustments. Over time, your students will adapt too, and they will begin to think more strategically about their reading.

REFERENCES

Brown, A., & Palincsar, A. (1989). Guided, cooperative learning and individual knowledge acquisition. In L. Resnick (Ed.), *Knowing, learning, and instruction: Essays in honor of Robert Glaser* (pp. 393–451). Hillsdale, NJ: Erlbaum.

Duffy, G., & Roehler, L. (1987). Improving reading instruction through the use of responsive elaboration. *The Reading Teacher, 40*, 514–521.

Duffy, G., Roehler, L., & Herrmann, B.A. (1988). Modeling mental processes helps poor readers become strategic readers. *The Reading Teacher, 41*, 762–767.

Duffy, G., Roehler, L., Sivan, E., Rackliffe, G., Book, C., Meloth, M., Vavrus, L., Wesselman, R., Putnam, J., & Bassiri, D. (1987). The effects of explaining reasoning associated with using reading strategies. *Reading Research Quarterly, 22*(3), 347–367.

Palincsar, A., & Brown, A. (1984). Reciprocal teaching of comprehension-fostering and comprehension-monitoring activities. *Cognition and Instruction, 1*, 117–175.

Interactive Storybook Reading for At-Risk Learners

Janell P. Klesius, Priscilla L. Griffith

major concern of educators is that literacy acquisition is not inclusive, that for many children, learning to read is a frustrating task. Juel's (1988) discouraging finding that first-grade children who performed at the bottom of the class remained in that position through 4 years of schooling provides empirical evidence of the failure many children experience. Snow (1983) suggested that home literacy is a determining variable in the acquisition of school literacy; early readers typically come from homes in which storybook reading is a frequent event (Clark, 1984; Durkin, 1974/1975). The term *lapreading* has been coined to describe home reading experiences because they occur in close contact with a caring adult. Lapreading experiences prepare children to take advantage of formal reading instruction and acquaint children with the kinds of social behaviors expected in school. Figure 1 lists the benefits of lapreading experiences for children.

Conversely, children who have not experienced lapreading at home may begin kindergarten limited in oral language development, literacy development, world knowledge, and attentive behavior. Unfortunately, these children often are thrust into a literacy curriculum in kindergarten that is more appropriate for children who have experienced numerous hours of lapreading. The curriculum mismatch may prove detrimental for many children because it places them at risk of not learning to read and to write. (In this article at-risk learners are defined as those children who begin school with limited lapreading experiences.)

Interactive storybook reading is a school reading experience that closely parallels the home lapreading experience. The term *interactive storybook reading* was introduced in a study comparing kindergarten students' verbal interactions in groups of varying sizes (Morrow & Smith, 1990). Like lapreading, interactive storybook reading has a flexible routine (Snow, 1983) that varies according to the age and the ability level of the children. Interactive storybook reading and the shared book experience (Holdaway, 1979), with which most teachers are familiar, are contrasted in Figure 2. We suggest that interactive storybook reading experiences in kindergarten classrooms can be used to build the language and literacy understandings and the basic world knowledge that are essential for the successful acquisition of reading and writing ability.

In this article, we will (a) identify the characteristics of lapreading in parent-child dyads; (b) describe our implementation of interactive storybook reading routines with kindergarten children, including the components of lapreading that emerged; and (c) explain what we learned about the use of interactive story-book reading in kindergarten classrooms.

Lapreading in Parent-Child Dyads

Lapreading is a social activity. While reading, the parent comments about the story, and the child spontaneously comments, asks questions, or shares experiences (Cochran-Smith, 1986; Flood, 1977; Morrow, 1988; Ninio & Bruner, 1978; Roser & Martinez, 1985). The story readings resemble conversations, and although they consist of text reading, the reading is "continuously broken apart by, and intertwined with, talk" (Cochran-Smith, 1986, p. 38).

Figure 1
The benefits of family storybook reading experiences

---

1. Helps children build a storehouse of information about the world outside of family and everyday life (Cochran-Smith, 1986; Strickland & Taylor, 1989; Taylor & Strickland, 1986).

2. Helps children develop a sense of how stories are constructed (Cochran-Smith, 1986; Strickland & Taylor, 1989; Taylor & Strickland, 1986).

3. Provides children with the meanings of words that may not be a part of their everyday speech (Holdaway, 1979; Strickland & Taylor, 1989; Taylor & Strickland, 1986).

4. Provides children with an opportunity to hear a variety of language patterns that are not usually a part of their everyday speech (Taylor & Strickland, 1986).

5. Engages children in language play that is centered on the sounds of language (Griffith & Olson, 1992; Taylor & Strickland, 1986).

6. Fosters the ability to listen (Taylor & Strickland, 1986).

7. Allows children to practice oral turn-taking (Cochran-Smith, 1986; Strickland & Taylor, 1989).

8. Helps children become aware of literacy conventions (Cochran-Smith, 1986; Holdaway, 1979; Strickland & Taylor, 1989).

9. Teaches children that books are for reading, not for manipulating (Snow & Ninio, 1986).

10. Makes children aware that in book reading, the topic of conversation is controlled by the book being read (Snow & Ninio, 1986).

11. Teaches children that language is symbolic, that the words and pictures in the book are not things but representations of things (Holdaway, 1979; Snow & Ninio, 1986).

12. Helps children understand that book events occur outside real time (Snow & Ninio, 1986).

13. Teaches children to distinguish between contextualized firsthand experiences and decontextualized representations of experiences in books (Heath, 1983).

14. Helps children become aware of the difference in the sound of the contextualized language of oral conversations and the decontextualized language written in books (Cochran-Smith, 1986; Heath, 1983).

15. Teaches the social behavior that accompanies reading instruction in school (Heath, 1983).

16. Allows children to observe and practice the comprehension strategies of expert readers (Mason, Peterman, & Kerr, 1989; Snow & Ninio, 1986; Strickland & Taylor, 1989).

Figure 2
Characteristics of interactive storybook reading and shared book experience

Interactive storybook reading experience	Shared book experience
• Informal	• Formal
• Small group of children	• Large group of children
• Conversational	• Teacher reading and questioning
• Balance of teacher- and student-initiated events	• Teacher-guided instruction
• Nonpredictable sequence	• Predictable sequence
• Strong oral language emphasis	• Strong literacy emphasis
• Small book used	• Big book used
• Emphasis on negotiating meaning	• Emphasis on print concepts and word identification

The specific characteristics of lapreading vary as children's language, literacy, and attentiveness develop. With children 10 to 18 months old, lapreading routines consist primarily of labeling. During the routine, both parent and child look at and talk about single pictures, and a key element for advancing children's oral language and literacy skill is this interaction between the adult and the child (Flood, 1977; Heath, 1983; Ninio, 1983; Teale, 1983). Like conversation, the dialogue has a turn-taking structure. A common sequence of elements in a lapreading routine includes (a) an attentional vocative (e.g., "Look."), (b) a query (e.g., "What's that?"), (c) a label (e.g., "It's a _____."), and (d) feedback (e.g., "Yes."). Initially, the parent completes most of the elements, but as the child becomes familiar with the format, he or she frequently initiates the sequence (Ninio & Bruner, 1978).

Parents' responses and pacing show a high degree of sensitivity to children's understanding of concepts and vocabulary. Parents provide labels for pictures only when they feel children do not know the word. Otherwise, they generally attempt to elicit recognition of the label (Ninio, 1983). Parents correct wrong labels given by a child, but their corrections do not diminish the child's subsequent labeling of the picture. In fact, the label reappeared in 87.5% of the cases and was correct 85% of the time (Ninio & Bruner, 1978).

As children mature, and stories with more complex illustrations are used, lapreading interactions progress beyond the one-word and simple labeling stage (Snow & Goldfield, 1983). At this stage, labeling is continued for vocabulary development but is used less frequently. Text reading continues to be interspersed with discussion about the pictures and story content; however, these more complex discussions involve temporal sequencing, motives, consequences, and cause and effect (Snow & Goldfield, 1983).

Scaffolding, steps taken by the adult to facilitate the child's comprehension of the story, is conspicuously present in lapreading sessions. Semantic contingency statements such as expansions that focus on content, extensions that add new information, questions that clarify, and answers to the child's questions were noted during observations of parent-child interactions (Dore, as cited in Snow, 1983). During storybook reading sessions with children in preschool settings, teachers provided metanarratives of the story, another type of scaffolding, by adding information beyond that available in the text in order to inform the children about how to read and to interpret the story (Prince, as cited in Cochran-Smith, 1986).

Implementing Interactive Storybook Reading With At-Risk Kindergarten Children

Story read-alouds and shared book experiences play an important role in the curriculum for all children. However, we believe at-risk children also need interactive storybook reading experiences because the conversational nature of the routine provides the greatest match with the lapreading experiences they may lack.

We conducted a study of interactive storybook reading with 10 kindergarten children. The participants, two groups of five each, were identified by the classroom teacher as children whose language and literacy development fell below that of the other students. These children were the least attentive when stories were read to the whole class, and their interactions with print indicated limited understanding of the alphabetic nature of written English and other concepts about print. Additionally, the teacher commented on the constricted range of their oral responses in book-related as well as other academic situations. In general, the teacher believed these children engaged in fewer self-initiated activities with books than did the other children in the class.

We implemented the interactive storybook reading routines with a group size of five so that all children would have adequate opportunities to participate. We knew that this group size, if effective, would be feasible for classroom settings. We each took turns directing the interactive storybook reading routines, reading two books during each session: a new story and a previously read book selected by the children for rereading. While one of us guided the interactive storyreading, the other recorded adult and child behaviors. Each routine lasted 15 to 20 minutes, depending on the length of the story and the children's interest and attention.

Adult and child behaviors varied depending on the children's familiarity with the vocabulary and information in the story. The dialogue in Table 1, noted during the reading of *The Pig in the Pond* (Waddell, 1992), is an example of the interactions that occurred. The children included four boys (Rick, Randy, Mitch, and Stan) and one girl (Tonya). Immediately following each entry are parentheses containing our classification of the observed behavior.

The elements listed in Table 1 are typical of all the interactive storybook reading routines. As we expected, many of the components of lapreading in parent-child dyads emerged during these interactive storybook reading routines. The classification of adult and child behaviors shows the conversational nature of the routine, in which the adult reader served more as a co-responder and informer than as a director. These storybook reading sessions were interactive in that the adult and children drew attention to information in the illustrations, predicted what would happen next, and shared related experiences.

Lapreading Components Emerged

We observed several types of adult and child behaviors during the interactive storybook reading routines completed over a 3-week period. The elements for each routine

Table 1
Interactive storybook reading example

Reader behaviors	Child behaviors
1. Showed front of *The Pig in the Pond*.	
	2. Rick predicted the story would be titled "Splash, Pig, Splash." (self-initiated prediction)
3. Praised for prediction. Explained how he got idea from previous story, *Hatch, Egg, Hatch*. (extend student response)	
4. What is a pond? (extend vocabulary)	
	5. Tonya: Mom said ducks live in a pond. (question response)
	6. Stan: Whales live in a pond. (question response)
7. Explanation about where whales live. (clarify)	
8. Asked students to predict what the pig would do. (scaffold strategies)	
	9. Stan: Pig will get in the pond. (prediction)
	10. Rick: Neligan is looking for the pig. (attention to information in illustration)
	11. Stan: The pig will follow the farmer in the cart. (prediction)
12. Praised student for prediction. (praise) Related it to following like a dog. (extend student response)	
13. Is the pig cool? (develop story structure, i.e, that the pig is hot is the problem in the story)	
	14. Tonya: Pig is hot. (question response)
	15. Students kept predicting the pig would jump in. (self-initiated prediction)
16. Pointed out sweat on pig's brow. (metanarrate)	
17. Why is the pig's foot up by his head? (metanarrate)	
	18. Stan: To help see. (question response)
	19. Tonya: Once I fell in... relates story. (self-initiated personal experience)
	20. Tonya: He could drown. (self-initiated prediction)
21. Did the pig fall in or jump in? (extend vocabulary; metanarrate)	

(continued)

Table 1
Interactive storybook reading example (continued)

Reader behaviors	Child behaviors
	22. Mitch: Jumped in. (question response)
	23. Stan: They are honking. (attention to information in illustration)
	24. Randy: The leg is broke. Points to animal's leg (attention to information in illustration)
25. We still have words to read. (metanarrate)	
26. Pointed out animals and let students name. (draw attention to illustrations)	
	27. Rick: That's a goat. (labeling)
	28. Mitch: That's a dalmatian. (labeling)
29. What are they doing? (draw attention to illustrations)	
	30. Stan: Running. (question response)
	31. Randy: Looking. (question response)
32. What might they be saying if they could talk? (scaffold strategies—prediction)	
33. Read and paused for students to give animal sounds. (scaffold strategies—prediction through cloze)	
	34. Students give animal sounds. (response)
	35. Students laugh. (reaction to text)
36. What happened next? (scaffold strategies—prediction)	
	37. Students actively examine illustration for what is splashed out of pond. Point out fish, frogs. (attention to information in illustrations)
	38. Randy: All the animals going to get in the pond. (self-initiated prediction)
39. Pointed out that all the O's in the word make it say "splooooosh." (point out text feature)	

varied, and more child-initiated comments and questions occurred after the children became aware of our receptiveness to their participation. The second-language learners were particularly reluctant to participate for the first week of the study.

Questioning

Questioning emerged as an important component during the interactive storybook reading routines. Although questioning served several purposes, it was used prudently so as not to place the adult in a director's role, diminishing the conversational nature of the interaction. Metacognitive process questions were used to help the children get in touch with their own abilities to construct meaning (for example, "Why do you think the title might be *Hatch, Egg, Hatch?*"). On occasion, a question was used to draw a child into the conversation about the book (for example, "Tonya, what do you see in the picture?").

Because there was a mismatch between the vocabulary and world knowledge of these at-risk learners and the concepts in the stories, labeling (regularly prompted by "What is that?") was an element borrowed from lapreading. As the children became more comfortable, they also asked "What's that?" questions (for example, "What's a spinning wheel?"), which frequently resulted in group discussions. Meanings were expanded through explanation, demonstration (for example, how one snores), and sharing of related personal experiences. Question responses enabled assessment of the children's knowledge about the topic. For example, "What do pigs eat?" elicited a response of "pizza," an indication of a limited knowledge about animal diets. Fortunately, in this case, the adult affirmed that a pig would probably eat pizza because pigs will eat most foods people eat; thus, the reference to someone who eats everything as a pig. However, the adult reader described a preferred pig diet of corn and peanuts and recalled an illustration in a previously read story to add visual support to the explanation.

Prediction questions proved excellent for generating conversation and for modeling how a reader uses information from past experiences to make inferences about a new story. The storyreader drew attention to how details in pictures could provide additional information about the story. Children began to comment about the illustrations. For example, during the initial reading of *Silly Sally* (Wood, 1992), in which Sally walks into town upside down and backwards, children made predictions based on the illustrations: "She could bust her head." "Her dress will go down." "That one is going to knock them over."

After the first few stories, the necessity for posing prediction questions as part of the story introduction diminished because prediction had become part of the children's routine for looking at a book. They began to make predictions about new stories based on their experiences with other books. For example, because the mouse sank the boat in *Who Sank the Boat?* (Allen, 1982), the children predicted that the bed would collapse when the mouse got on it in *The Napping House* (Wood, 1984).

Scaffolding

A second component that emerged during the interactive routines involved the reader subtly expanding ideas during the storybook reading, and giving explanations to clarify or extend information provided in the text. Sometimes the reader shared a related personal experience or gave meanings for words. The reader also pointed out details in the illustrations that added to the enjoyment of the story (for example, Entries 16 and 17 in Table 1) and provided important clues to understanding vocabulary or story content (for example, Entries 4 and 7 in Table 1).

Direct instruction about print was not the primary objective of the interactive storybook reading routines. We did, however, connect the print to the story by comments such as "We still have words to read" (Entry 25 in Table 1) or "Let me read what the words say." The children's growing awareness of the relation between print and illustrations was demonstrated when one child asked where was the picture that went with the part of the story just read. Occasionally children became impatient with the discussion and directed the reader to "Read it" or "Read what it says."

We supported the children's efforts to answer questions by making sure our questions matched the children's ability levels, pointing out illustration details before a question was posed, giving choices for answers to questions, and discussing important details before predictions were elicited.

Lapreading Ambiance

A third component of the interactive storybook reading sessions was the establishment of a lapreading ambiance. Both the adults and the children contributed to the ambiance, the adults by responding positively to the children's self-initiated comments. Comments were praised, but not as a regular part of the routine. Praise was used as a way to establish warmth in the group, although with caution, so as not to isolate the reader as a director. Entry 12 of Table 1 contains an example of the judicious use of praise combined with a comment that extended a child's response. In this example, the reader helped the group understand the thought process one child had used to make a prediction about the pig's behavior.

During these interactive reading sessions the children wanted to establish a physical closeness with the reader. The usual setting for the reading sessions was a traditional circle of chairs in the foyer outside the kindergarten classroom. However, the children gradually moved their chairs closer and closer to the reader. At times they knelt directly in front of the reader. At other times individual children stood next to the reader with a hand resting on his or her shoulder. The children delighted in being able to touch the pictures in the book while simultaneously commenting on illustrations. During the reading of *Alphabetics* (MacDonald, 1986), Juan was compelled to

trace the outlines of the pictures, and we were reminded of Daniel B., one of Sulzby's (1985) emergent storybook readers, who "pointed to the items in the pictures as he gave their names or comments about them" (p. 465).

Children's Talk

According to Morrow (1988), repeated story readings give children the opportunities to deal with text on a variety of levels. Other researchers have reported that after subsequent readings of the same text, children's comments and questions increase (Martinez & Roser, 1985), and they discuss more aspects of the text and in greater depth (Snow, 1983; Snow & Goldfield, 1983).

We found that as the experience of storybook reading became more familiar to the children, they began to internalize the interaction that was occurring. They also replicated many teacher behaviors, such as when they used details of the illustrations to retell parts of the story.

To illustrate, during the second reading of *Who Sank the Boat?* (Allen, 1982), one child used an illustration to explain how the cumulative weight of all the animals resulted in the small mouse sinking the boat. Similarly, after a second reading of *Silly Sally* (Wood, 1992), children examined an early, double-page illustration in the book that contains partial images of all the characters Sally meets on her way to town. They enjoyed being able to recognize the characters and to tell the part each played in the story.

Over time the children built a store of knowledge about writing conventions that they connected to the texts they heard. For example, we read *Hatch, Egg, Hatch* (Roddie, 1991), a pop-up story that had particular appeal because the children had watched eggs hatch in their classroom. When shown the cover illustration of *The Pig in the Pond* (Waddell, 1992) picturing a pig next to a pond, Rick spontaneously predicted the title as "Splash, Pig, Splash," demonstrating his understanding of how to construct a title for a story (note this at Entry 2 in Table 1).

As Table 1 demonstrates, not all children were talkative participants, and the amount of individual involvement varied day to day. Sometimes children who were extremely attentive were not active participants in the conversation about the story. Children were given an opportunity to share personal experiences; however, lengthy sharing by one child often led to impatience among the others.

Interest in Books

An expected benefit of the interactive storybook readings was the children's heightened interest in books. The classroom teacher reported that the children were more attentive during the large-group story read-alouds. They began to look at books during free time and engaged in more book reenactments. One of the children had been spending his daily allowance on candy at the corner store, but after becoming involved in the interactive storybook reading sessions, he saved his money for the school's book fair.

What Did We Learn?

Our purpose was primarily to determine whether the interactive storybook routine could be implemented effectively in a kindergarten classroom. We also wanted to identify the knowledge and skills teachers would need to support children during these storybook reading events.

We questioned whether a group size of five was too large for adequate turn-taking and individual participation. Absenteeism often reduced the group to less than the five originally identified. Smaller group size afforded each child a greater opportunity to participate but resulted in a narrower range of comments from which children could react and learn. Morrow and Smith (1990) reported higher comprehension scores among children who participated in storybook reading in a group size of three than among children who participated in storybook reading in either a one-to-one or a large-group setting. Furthermore, most children indicated they preferred the small-group setting. In this study, two students, one in each group, were not consistently able to engage in the give-and-take of turns in the routine. We concluded that optimal group size should not exceed five and that it might be less, depending upon the turn-taking ability of the children in the group and the willingness of shy children to initiate conversation among more talkative individuals.

A literacy-rich classroom contains many opportunities for reading, including both shared and independent reading experiences (Fields & Spangler, 1995). Independent reading time is ideal for implementing interactive storybook reading. During independent reading time children have the opportunity to read alone or to share a book with a partner or with a small group. Children can be invited to enjoy a book with the teacher or the classroom aide. Also, because of the informal nature of interactive storybook reading, it easily can be carried out with volunteers or noninstructional school staff. In fact, in describing our implementation of interactive storybook reading we have purposefully used the word "adult" in reference to the reader to emphasize the flexibility of that role.

Our experiences with interactive storybook reading have resulted in the identification of a set of adult behaviors that will enhance the process. These behaviors, which are listed in Table 2, also are indicated in the parentheses following the reader behaviors recorded in Table 1. These behaviors are dependent on cues from the children, on the reader's own sensitivity to the children's existing knowledge about the topic, and on the children's ongoing comprehension of the story. The reader always serves as a co-responder and informer, and questioning is primarily for the purpose of drawing the children's attention to information they need for comprehension. Storybook reading expands children's knowledge about text structure, book language, writing conventions, and the social behavior that accompanies reading.

Conclusion

The children show their enthusiasm by pushing their chairs closer to the reader, touching the illustrations, and drawing attention to information. They may comment: "Ooh! People can see her panties" (*Silly Sally*, Wood, 1992); make predictions: "The jeep will roll down the hill" (*Sheep in a Jeep*, Shaw, 1986); or volunteer information: "A train is

heavy like an elephant" (*The Right Number of Elephants*, Sheppard, 1990). They may share fictitious experiences that reflect their world: "I had a pig. Somebody knocked me down and stole it" (*If I Had a Pig*, Inkpen, 1992) or real experiences: "I had a brown dog. It had babies." They also may provide descriptions of the illustrations: "Look, it looks like popcorn. Looks like popcorn with butter" (*Silly Sally*, Wood, 1992).

However, as comprehension of a story is being negotiated cooperatively during interactive storybook reading routines, children are learning how to use knowledge of the world along with textual information to understand the story (Cochran-Smith, 1986; Strickland & Morrow, 1989). Acquiring knowledge of structure, features, and subtle variations of different stories within a given genre requires wide exposure to literature and discussions that both encourage students' inquiries and support their elaborations. Equally as important, world knowledge, a key ingredient for successful higher level comprehension (Anderson & Pearson, 1984), is acquired through interactions that transpire during the conversation that centers around a story.

Perhaps the most significant benefit of interactive storybook reading is that children discover that books are a source of enchantment and wonder (Holdaway, 1979; Snow & Ninio, 1986). Trusted adults are seen as role models who engage in and enjoy reading experiences (Hiebert, 1981), and the social aspect of interactive storybook reading heightens the pleasure derived from the experience (Morrow & Smith, 1990; Strickland & Morrow, 1989).

Table 2
Adult behaviors during interactive storybook reading

Clarify information

Demonstrate

Develop story structure

Draw attention to illustrations

Extend student responses

Extend vocabulary

Inform

Metanarrate (text and/or pictures)

Praise

Point out text features

Scaffold strategies of a reader

REFERENCES

Anderson, R.C., & Pearson, P.D. (1984). A schema-theoretic view of basic processes in reading comprehension. In P.D. Pearson (Ed.), *Handbook of reading research: Volume 1* (pp. 255–291). New York: Longman.

Clark, M.M. (1984). Literacy at home and at school: Insights from a study of young fluent readers. In H. Goelman, A.A. Oberg, & F. Smith (Eds.), *Awakening to literacy* (pp. 122–130). London: Heinemann.

Cochran-Smith, M. (1986). Reading to children: A model for understanding texts. In E. Schieffelin & B.B. Gilmore (Eds.), *The acquisition of literacy: Ethnographic perspectives* (pp. 35–54). Norwood, NJ: Ablex.

Durkin, D. (1974/1975). A six-year study of children who learned to read in school at the age of four. *Reading Research Quarterly, 10,* 9–61.

Fields, M.V., & Spangler, K L. (1995). *Let's begin reading right.* Englewood Cliffs, NJ: Merrill.

Flood, J.E. (1977). Parental styles in reading episodes with young children. *The Reading Teacher, 30,* 864–867.

Griffith, P.L., & Olson, M. (1992). Phonemic awareness helps beginning readers break the code. *The Reading Teacher, 45,* 516–523.

Heath, S.B. (1983). *Ways with words: Language, life and work in communities and classrooms.* Cambridge, England: Cambridge University Press.

Hiebert, E.H. (1981). Developmental patterns and interrelationships of children's print awareness. *Reading Research Quarterly, 16,* 236–260.

Holdaway, D. (1979). *Foundations of literacy.* Portsmouth, NH: Heinemann.

Juel, C. (1988). Learning to read and write: A longitudinal study of 54 children from first through fourth grades. *Journal of Educational Psychology, 80,* 437–447.

Martinez, M., & Roser, N. (1985). Read it again: The value of repeated readings during storytime. *The Reading Teacher, 38,* 782–786.

Mason, J.M., Peterman, C.L., & Kerr, B.M. (1989). Reading to kindergarten children. In D.S. Strickland & L.M. Morrow (Eds.), *Emerging literacy: Young children learn to read and write* (pp. 52–62). Newark, DE: International Reading Association.

Morrow, L.M. (1988). Young children's responses to one-to-one story readings in school settings. *Reading Research Quarterly, 23,* 89–107.

Morrow, L.M., & Smith, J.K. (1990). The effects of group setting on interactive storybook reading. *Reading Research Quarterly, 25,* 213–231.

Ninio, A. (1983). Joint book reading as a multiple vocabulary acquisition device. *Developmental Psychology, 19,* 445–451.

Ninio, A., & Bruner, J. (1978). The achievement and antecedents of labeling. *Journal of Child Language, 5,* 1–15.

Roser, N., & Martinez, M. (1985). Roles adults play in preschoolers' response to literature. *Language Arts, 62,* 485–490.

Snow, C.E. (1983). Literacy and language: Relationships during the preschool years. *Harvard Educational Review, 53,* 165–189.

Snow, C.E., & Goldfield, B.A. (1983). Turn the page please: Situation-specific language acquisition. *Journal of Child Language, 10,* 551–569.

Snow, C.E., & Ninio, A. (1986). The contracts of literacy: What children learn from learning to read books. In W. Teale & E. Sulzby (Eds.), *Emergent literacy: Writing and reading* (pp. 116–138). Norwood, NJ: Ablex.

Strickland, D.S., & Morrow, L.M. (1989). Interactive experiences with storybook reading. *The Reading Teacher, 42,* 322–323.

Strickland, D.S., & Taylor, D. (1989). Family storybook reading: Implications for children, families, and curriculum. In D.S. Strickland & L.M. Morrow (Eds.), *Emerging literacy: Young children learn to read and write* (pp. 27–34). Newark, DE: International Reading Association.

Sulzby, E. (1985). Children's emergent reading of favorite storybooks: A development study. *Reading Research Quarterly, 20,* 458–480.

Taylor, D., & Strickland, D.S. (1986). *Family storybook reading.* Portsmouth, NH: Heinemann.

Teale, W.H. (1983). Parents reading to their children: What we know and need to know. *Language Arts, 58,* 902–911.

CHILDREN'S LITERATURE REFERENCES

Allen, P. (1982). *Who sank the boat?* New York: Trumpet.

Inkpen, M. (1992). *If I had a pig.* New York: Dell.

MacDonald, S. (1986). *Alphabetics.* New York: Bradbury.

Roddie, S. (1991). *Hatch, egg, hatch*. New York: Little, Brown.

Shaw, N. (1986). *Sheep in a jeep*. New York: Trumpet.

Sheppard, J. (1990). *The right number of elephants*. New York: Scholastic.

Waddell, M. (1992). *The pig in the pond*. Cambridge, MA: Candlewick.

Wood, A. (1984). *The napping house*. San Diego, CA: Harcourt Brace Jovanovich.

Wood, A. (1992). *Silly Sally*. New York: Harcourt Brace Jovanovich.

Using Think Alouds to Enhance Children's Comprehension Monitoring Abilities

James F. Baumann, Leah A. Jones, Nancy Seifert-Kessell

In a 1992 study (Baumann, Seifert-Kessell, & Jones, 1992), we asked fourth-grade students to read an excerpt from Laura Ingalls Wilder's *On the Banks of Plum Creek*, in which Laura, playing in the fast-running waters of Plum Creek, rolls off a footbridge and nearly drowns. As the students read aloud the story, we stopped them intermittently and asked, "Can you tell me what you were doing or thinking about as you read this part of the story?" Consider the following sets of responses by two different groups of children. First, Ann, Kim, Sam, and Tom responded to our question, in part, as follows:

Ann: I was asking questions, and I asked questions like "Why did she go to the creek when her mother told her not to?" And "Why did Laura take her shoes and socks off when she knew the creek was going to be rocky and muddy on the bottom?"

Kim: I was asking myself, "Is this making sense?" and I was asking if like do I think what would happen next without reading the next page—just reading that [the present] page. [Researcher:

Can you tell me a bit more about this?] She'll probably go down there again and play when the water's down and when it's not so high and when it's not so like roaring and stuff.

Sam: I retold what I read the first time to [page] 193 as I was reading the last part of the story to see if it would make sense.

Tom: I was thinking that like when she wanted to get deeper and deeper in the water, then the water would probably try and take her off or something. And I really didn't know—in the beginning I didn't think I'd be right in what I thought...because it talked about so many other things. Then when I got further on in the story, then it started to make sense.

The students who made these responses had participated in a group in which they had learned how to think aloud as they read stories. The intent behind the think-aloud lessons was to help students develop the ability to monitor their reading comprehension and employ strategies to guide or facilitate understanding. And indeed these children demonstrated various comprehension monitoring and fix-up strategies such as self questioning (Ann), asking if the story made sense (Kim), using retelling as a meaning-construction technique (Sam), or offering hypotheses and reading on to verify or modify them (Tom).

In contrast, consider how Kate, Lynn, and Ron responded to our question, "Can you tell me what you were doing or thinking about as you read this part of the story?":

Kate: Nothing. [Researcher: Nothing? What kind of ideas did you have as you read?] That her mom was very nice and understood that it could have killed her. [Researcher: Any other ideas you had?] She was nice. [Researcher: Anything else?] No.

Lynn: Oh, trying to stop at every period and trying to pause at the commas. [Researcher: Is there anything else you were trying to do as you read?] I was trying to read loud instead of talking real soft and you couldn't hear me. [Researcher: What else? Anything else you did or thought about as you were reading this section?] Not really.

Ron: I kept saying "blank." [Researcher: Can you tell me more about that? Why did you keep saying "blank?" (No student response) What do you do to help you understand what you read?] Look at the pictures. [Researcher: Can you think of anything else you do besides look at the pictures?] Ask a friend. [What kinds of things would you ask a friend?] If he could pronounce a word.

Kate, Lynn, and Ron had not received instruction in thinking aloud but instead read stories according to a conventional directed reading activity format. Rather than focusing on comprehension processes as did Ann, Kim, Sam, and Tom, these students emphasized lit-

eral comprehension (Kate), accurate oral reading (Lynn), or word identification strategies (Ron).

This article describes the think-aloud instructional program we developed to help students acquire the ability to monitor their reading comprehension and to employ various strategies to deal with comprehension breakdowns. First, we provide some background information about comprehension monitoring and the think-aloud procedure. Second, we describe the instructional program and present a sample lesson from it. Third, we present suggestions for how teachers might adapt, modify, or extend think alouds in a classroom reading program or in content-area instruction.

Comprehension Monitoring and Think Alouds

Most definitions of comprehension monitoring during reading specify two kinds of metacognitive, or reflective, knowledge a reader must possess: (1) the awareness of whether or not comprehension is occurring, and (2) the conscious application of one or more strategies to correct comprehension difficulties (Baker & Brown, 1984; Garner, 1987; Paris, Lipson, & Wixson, 1983; Wagoner, 1983). Stated more simply, comprehension monitoring "concerns the student's ability both to evaluate his or her ongoing comprehension processes while reading through a text, and to take some sort of remedial action when these processes bog down" (Collins & Smith, 1982, p. 174).

Several research studies indicate that comprehension monitoring abilities discriminate successful readers from less successful ones (for example August, Flavell, & Clift, 1984; Brown, Armbruster, & Baker, 1986; Paris & Myers, 1981). Specifically, children who are able to reflect on whether or not comprehension is occurring and employ, as necessary, strategies such as self-questioning, predicting and verifying, retelling, rereading, or withholding judgment and reading on to clarify meaning are likely to understand, interact with, and retain information contained in written texts (see Paris, Wasik, & Turner, 1991).

Think alouds require a reader to stop periodically, reflect on how a text is being processed and understood, and relate orally what reading strategies are being employed. In other words, think alouds involve the overt, verbal expression of the normally covert mental processes readers engage in when constructing meaning from texts (see Afflerbach & Johnston, 1986; Ericsson & Simon, 1980, 1984; Garner, 1987).

Several writers have proposed teaching students to think aloud while reading as a means to enhance comprehension monitoring abilities (Alvermann, 1984; Davey, 1983; Nist & Kirby, 1986). The rationale has been that the process of thinking aloud during reading represents a form of comprehension monitoring itself, and further, think alouds present an appropriate means to access and use various strategies for enhancing understanding.

We conducted a study (Baumann et al., 1992) to determine if thinking aloud is an effective technique for helping students learn to monitor their comprehension. In this study, we taught one group of fourth-grade students a variety of comprehension monitoring and fix-up strategies through the think-aloud technique, and they applied the strategies when reading realistic fiction stories. Students in comparison groups read the same stories according to either the Directed Reading-Thinking Activity (Stauffer, 1976), which involved heavy emphasis on predicting and verifying, or the directed reading activity (Tierney, Readence, & Dishner, 1990), which involved introducing new vocabulary, activating or providing background knowledge, and guiding the students' reading of the selection through questioning.

Results from a series of quantitative assessments and in-depth, individual student interviews led us to the conclusion that, while the Directed Reading-Thinking Activity demonstrated some positive impact on students' comprehension monitoring, the think-aloud instruction was highly effective in helping students acquire a broad range of strategies to enhance their understanding of text and to deal with comprehension difficulties. For example, during the interview at the end of the instructional program, we asked Tom, a think-aloud group student, what he did before reading *On the Banks of Plum Creek*. Tom reported that he looked at the title, author name, and pictures and then drew from prior knowledge and experience:

> I think it [the story] will probably be a really good one because I've read a whole bunch of books by Laura Ingalls Wilder, and it's probably about somebody that's out in the woods or something that's caught in a storm or something.

Further evidence of the success of the think-aloud instruction was provided during the interview when we asked students, "What do you do to help you understand what you read?" Think-aloud group children responded by reporting that they used various comprehension monitoring and fix-up strategies, such as the following:

Kim: When I read I think, "Is this making sense?" I might...ask questions about the story and reread or retell the story.... I was asking myself, "Is this making sense?" and I was asking if like do I think what would happen next without reading the next page.

Tom: Oh, I either close the book and recite things or sometimes...I ask questions and try to remember everything in the story.

Ann: I ask all the time "Is this making sense?" And like this week, I checked out a book and I looked at the title and I didn't really understand it. But once I got reading it, it made sense.

Instruction in Think Alouds

The instruction we provided the think-aloud group in our study involved a variety of strategies that included asking questions, drawing on prior knowledge, assessing comprehension by asking "Is this making sense?", predicting and verifying, inferring unstated ideas, retelling, and rereading and reading on to clarify meaning. We used think alouds to model for the students how to use these strategies, and we had the children use think alouds to apply the strategies as they read the stories. It is important to point out, however, that we viewed think alouds as a vehicle for helping students to acquire control over these abilities. In other words, think alouds were a means to an end—improved comprehension monitoring ability—not the end itself.

An Instructional Heuristic

To create interest and to demonstrate thinking aloud, we created the fictional figure Clark Canine–Super Reporter (CC/SR), a play on the Superman character (see Figure). CC/SR, who appeared throughout the 10 think-aloud group lessons, was presented as a special kind of reporter who interviewed writers. The students were taught to view the role of a reporter (one who interviews people) as being analogous to the role of a reader (one who interviews writers). Students were asked to think of themselves as Pup Reporters, novice writer-interviewers led by CC/SR.

CC/SR was displayed as a 3-foot-tall cutout who held a notebook that presented the "think-aloud rules." Accompanying CC/SR

was a large chart that illustrated similarities between reporters and readers (see Table). Progressively across the 10 lessons, CC/SR introduced pairs of items on cards that were affixed to the chart under the "Reporters" and "Readers" headings. For example, cards containing statements that reporters and readers are alike in that they both conduct interviews by asking questions of writers or people were taped to the chart during Lesson 1.

Ten Lessons

The think-aloud comprehension monitoring and fix-up strategies were introduced, taught, practiced, applied, and reviewed across the 10 lessons. Each lesson comprised three phases: Phase 1, an introduction that consisted of an overview and verbal explanation of the strategy; Phase 2, a teacher modeling segment in which we demonstrated the use of the strategy; and Phase 3, a guided application and independent practice period in which students tried the strategy on their own with decreasing teacher assistance.

To organize the lessons, we used the Baumann and Schmitt (1986) comprehension instructional format, which accounts for different types of metacognitive knowledge. Specifically, students were informed *what* the strategy is through description, definition, or example; it was shared with students *why* the strategy is important and how its acquisition would make students better readers; students were taught *how* the strategy functions through the sequence of verbal explanation, teachers modeling, guided practice, and independent practice; and discussions occurred regarding *when* a strategy should and should not be used and how a reader might evaluate strategy use. Synopses of the contents of the 10 lessons follow.

Lesson 1: Self-questioning After introducing CC/SR, we explained that just as reporters interview people by asking them questions, good readers likewise ask questions of writers. We modeled this using the beginning of a story and had the students share their self-questions while reading the remainder of the story. Though think alouds would not be introduced formally until Lesson 3, we modeled thinking out loud and had students employ it informally as they shared their questions.

Clark Canine–Super Reporter

Think aloud group instructional chart

How reporters and readers are alike
Reporters...   •   Readers...

Lesson 1: Self-questioning
Interview people by • Interview writers
asking them   by asking them
questions.   questions.

Lesson 2: Sources of information
Get information • Get information
from the person   from the writer
they interview and and from what
from what they   they already
already know.   know.

Lessons 3 and 4: Thinking aloud
Think aloud and ask, • Think aloud and
"Is this interview   ask, "Is this story
making sense?"   making sense?"

Lesson 5: Predicting and verifying
Predict what people • Predict what a
will say and listen   writer will say and
to check those   read to check
predictions.   those predictions.

Lesson 6: Unstated information
Add information • Add information
that the person   that the writer
leaves out.   leaves out.

Lesson 7: Retelling
Retell in their own • Retell in their own
words what the   words what the
person said.   writer wrote.

Lesson 8: Rereading and reading on
Ask the person to • Reread or read on
say things again or   when they get
continue listening   confused.
when they get
confused.

Lesson 2: Sources of information As an extension of Lesson 1, students were taught a modified form of Raphael's (1982) question-answer relation strategy. Specifically, students were taught that information can come from ideas "in the story" (that is, textually explicit and textually implicit information) and that information can come from ideas a reader may already possess "on my own" (that is, a reader's prior knowledge).

Lesson 3: Think-aloud introduction This lesson formally introduced students to thinking aloud as they read. It is described in detail in the following sample lesson.

Lesson 4: Think-aloud review and extension This was a cumulative review of the first three lessons.

Lesson 5: Predicting, reading, and verifying Students were taught to use a predict-read-verify strategy (Baumann, 1991) as a means to guide comprehension and to deal with comprehension difficulties. They expressed their predictions and their evaluations of them through think alouds.

Lesson 6: Understanding unstated information As an extension of Lesson 2, "Sources of Information," students were taught to infer unstated information in a story according to a simplified version of the inference categories recommended by Johnson and Johnson (1986). Think alouds were used to verbalize what a writer omitted, drawing from story and experience clues.

Lesson 7: Retelling a story In this lesson, it was explained that a good strategy for helping a reader to understand a story, especially when a reader becomes confused, is to retell or say in one's own words what was read. Initially, small text segments (short paragraphs) were used in instruction and application; gradually, longer text segments (one or more pages of the story) were used. The lesson concluded with practice retelling the entire story.

Lesson 8: Rereading and reading on This lesson was linked to Lesson 3 by reminding students to stop periodically while reading and to ask themselves "Is this story making sense?" When students responded negatively to this question, it was suggested that they could either reread a section to clarify meaning or employ a read-on-and-withhold-judgment strategy as a way to deal with confusion.

Lessons 9 and 10: Think aloud/Comprehension monitoring application The final two lessons consisted of review instruction and guided practice of the contents of Lessons 1–8. Specifically, the teacher reviewed the seven items on the "How Reporters and Readers Are Alike" instructional chart and then provided guided and independent practice in the use of these strategies as they read each story.

A Sample Lesson

To provide an example of the think-aloud instruction, we describe in detail Lesson 3, "Think-Aloud Introduction: Is the Story Making Sense?" For this lesson, like all lessons for all groups, the "researcher-teacher" (the first author in this particular lesson) worked from a detailed lesson plan that outlined the structure and content for the lesson. The following is a reconstruction of Lesson 3 from that plan (see the Appendix in Baumann et al., 1992, for the plan for Lesson 3).

Phase 1 The teacher began Phase 1 by using the "How Reporters and Readers Are Alike" chart to briefly review what was taught in Lessons 1 and 2 about self-questioning and sources of information in comprehension. Next the teacher informed the students that in this lesson they would learn how to improve their understanding of a story by saying out loud what goes on in their minds as they read—that is, by thinking aloud while reading. The teacher explained that the students would learn to do this by stopping occasionally as they read and asking themselves, "Is this making sense?"

The teacher continued by explaining that thinking aloud is saying what is going on in one's mind as he or she tries to understand a story or solve a problem. The teacher referred to the think-aloud "rules," as displayed on CC/SR's notebook, also writing them on the chalkboard:

> To help me read and understand:
>
> 1. Say out loud what is going on in my mind as I read.
> 2. Ask myself, "Is this making sense?"

He then asked the students if they ever thought aloud while doing a school task, for example, when doing a hard math problem or reading difficult directions. Students shared their think-aloud experiences in a brief discussion that ensued.

Phase 2 The teacher demonstrated thinking aloud by writing the following verbal and mathematical analogies on the board and thinking aloud as he solved them:

> dog : bark ⟶ cat : ??? [oink, meow, puppy, feline]
> 2 : 4 ⟶ 5 : ??? [5, 10, 2, 8]

Teacher: Let's see. *Dog* is to *bark* [pointing] as *cat* is to what? What fits here? Well, dogs bark and cats meow, so *meow* must go where the question marks are.

During the analogy-solving process, the teacher modeled asking "Is this making sense?" He then asked for volunteers to think aloud while solving the following analogies:

> puddle : lake ⟶ hill : ??? [valley, ocean, mountain, bump]
> 20 : 10 ⟶ 50 : ??? [25, 150, 30, 100]

Student: OK, 20 goes with 10, so what goes with 50? Maybe it's 150. Is that right? Twenty is two times 10. Is 50 two times 150? No, that can't be right. The second number must be smaller. Maybe it's 25. Yes, 50 is two times 25 just like 20 is two times 10.

The teacher then explained that thinking aloud also can be done during reading, and he affixed the Lesson 3 cards to the "How Reporters and Readers Are Alike" chart (see Table). Referring to the "rules" on the board, he informed the students that it is important while reading to think aloud and to ask oneself "Is this making sense?" He explained that asking this question forces a reader to check to see if a story is being understood.

Next the teacher modeled thinking aloud while reading text from the story "Food's on the Table." In this story, a family of children are invited to their aunt's new apartment for supper but mistakenly enter a different family's apartment where no one is home. The children see a table set for dinner and eat the food that they believe their aunt set out for them.

Text: [Teacher reads story title and introductory note.]
        Food's on the Table
        Sydney Taylor
        Until a door is open, you don't know what's on the other side. Ella, her sisters, and her brother opened a door to a new apartment.

Teacher: I guess this story has something to do with eating and several children who go to an apartment. I wonder exactly where they're going and what this has to do with food? This isn't making a whole lot of sense yet; I guess I'll read on.

Text: [Teacher reads from beginning of actual story text.] Ella glanced at the slip of paper in her hand. "We want 725—it must be the next block."

Teacher: Maybe this takes place in a city, since Ella said "next block." I know apartments are in cities and they have numbers. I bet the slip of paper must tell where the apartment is. Maybe they are looking for apartment number 725. Is this making sense so far? I think so, but it's a little early to really decide. I'll read on, get more information, and find out.

Text: The girls—Ella, Henny, Sarah, Charlotte, and Gertie—and little Charlie were going to their aunt's new apartment for supper. Their mother would meet them later.

Teacher: Well, I see how the apartment and food go together, since all the kids are going to their aunt's for supper. It sure is a big family—let's see, five girls and one boy. Is this making sense? It seems to, but I still have some questions, like will they find the apartment and what will they eat for supper? I'll read more.

Text: "Now," Ella said, "let's see. There is 721–723. Here it is–725. It's a nice-looking building."

Teacher: Whoops! I guess I was wrong about the 725. I don't think that's the apartment number. Instead I bet it's the address for the building, its street number. Also, my guess about this being in a city seems to be correct. Is this making sense? Yes, but I have some questions. I wonder what the kids will do next? Will they try to find their aunt's apartment? And what does this story have to do with food on the table?

The teacher modeled thinking aloud in this fashion for the first few pages of the story, referring to the rules on the board. He also applied Lesson 2, which dealt with sources of information when reading.

Phase 3 The teacher began to turn responsibility over to the students for thinking aloud. For example, after reading that Ella and her sisters and brother enter the empty apartment and see a table full of food:

Teacher: Anyone want to try reading and thinking aloud for us? [Student 1 offers an affirmative response.] Great; go ahead with the next paragraph.

Text: [Student 1 reads.] "Look, Ella," Sarah pointed. "There's a note on the table." She picked it up and read aloud: "I had to go shopping. I'll be a little late. Don't wait for me. Go ahead and eat."

Student 1: I guess the kids' aunt wrote the note. I guess the kids can go ahead and eat the supper.

Teacher: Is this making sense?

Student 1: Uh, huh.

Teacher: Any ideas about what might happen next?

Student 1: The kids will eat the supper, and they probably will get in trouble with their mother for not waiting.

Student 2: I think they will wait for their aunt to get home.

Teacher: Anyone else want to try reading and thinking aloud? [To Student 2] All right, give it a try.

Text: [Student 2 reads.] "Well, that's that," remarked Henny. "Let's eat."
"Oh, I don't think that would be very nice," Ella said. "Let's wait a little while."

"We could finish setting the table," suggested Sarah. "Lena must have been in an awful hurry. There are no plates, and just three settings of silver."

Student 2: I think I'm right. They are going to wait for their aunt because Ella said they should wait for a while. I bet Ella is the oldest of them, the tall girl with the blue checked blouse on page 13.

Teacher: Is this making sense to you?

Student 2: Yes, I think so, but I think something tricky is going to happen.

Teacher: Could you tell us more?

Student 2: The part about there being only three sets of forks and knives. That mixes me up. The kids' aunt wouldn't set out only three of everything. There's a whole bunch of kids coming for supper. I wonder if the kids aren't all mixed up and in the wrong place or something.

After several students had a chance to think aloud like this in a group setting, the teacher asked the children to work in pairs. The pairs were asked to read the rest of the story on their own, alternately reading short text sections. After reading a section, one student tried to think aloud, and the other student asked "Is this making sense?" Then the second student read and thought aloud. The teacher walked around the room, listening to pairs of students, offering encouragement, and providing guidance and suggestions as appropriate.

Following is an exchange between one pair of students. At this point in the story, Ella and her sisters and brother, being unable to restrain themselves from eating any longer, have just consumed most of the food set out on what they believed to be their Aunt Lena's table.

Text: [Student 3 reads.] Someone was at the door. It opened, and a short, stout woman came in. Her arms were piled high with shopping bags. "Hello," she said, looking around.

Student 4: Is this part of the story making sense?

Student 3: Yes, I think so. I bet the lady is the kids' aunt because the note said that she went shopping and now she came home. I think I'll read more.

Text: [Student 3 continues reading.] The girls all turned and looked at the newcomer. "My aunt hasn't gotten back yet," Ella offered.

The woman looked puzzled. She gave a quick glance at the door. "You're expecting your aunt?"

"Yes," Henny replied. "Don't go away. She should be here any minute. Here, let me help you with the packages."

"Thank you, but..."

Student 4: Are things making sense now?

Student 3: I'm not sure; I think I'm getting mixed up. If this person is Aunt Lena, Ella wouldn't say what she did. And Aunt Lena would probably be excited and say hello, but she didn't. The book said "The woman looked puzzled." Why would Aunt Lena look puzzled? I'm getting the feeling that something's wrong—somebody's made a mistake.

Student 4: Yeah; I bet the kids got mixed up or something. Let's read more and find out. It's my turn.

Text: [Student 4 reads aloud.] Her packages were set safely on a chair. The woman folded her arms and looked at the children. "Now tell me, who are you?"

"We are the nieces and this is the nephew, Charlie," Ella told her.

The woman smiled and gave a nod. "That's nice. I'm pleased to meet you." Her eyes fell on the table. A look of dismay passed over her face. "Oh, my goodness! I see you ate up the whole supper!"

Student 3: Think out loud now. Is this making sense?

Student 4: Yeah; I think it is. See, the kids got mixed up and ended up in the wrong place. This isn't their aunt's apartment; it's somebody else's. And this lady—she isn't their aunt at all.

Student 3: But that doesn't make sense. Why would there be a note on the table saying to go ahead and eat supper? Maybe their aunt just doesn't recognize them.

Student 4: [Excited, continues reading.] "Were you invited, too?" Ella asked.

"Who's invited? The supper was for my husband and my son."

"Goodness gracious!" Henny cried. "How many people were supposed to eat here tonight?"

"My dear child, you don't understand. The supper was just for the three of us—my husband, my son, and me. After all this is my apartment."

Student 4: See, I was right. The kids ended up in the wrong place. Wow! I bet they feel bad, and I bet this lady's going to be mad at them. What a mistake they made. I bet they're going to get in big trouble now.

After the pairs of children finished reading and thinking aloud to the end of the story, the teacher concluded Lesson 3 by reconvening the class and asking students to share how their think alouds proceeded. The teacher suggested that the students try using thinking aloud whenever they became confused while reading books for enjoyment. He also suggested that thinking aloud might help students study for a test, for example, when studying from a science or social studies book. At the end of the lesson, the teacher informed the students that the lesson the next day would consist of a review and more practice thinking aloud while reading.

Adaptations, Modifications, and Extensions

Though our research involved an ambitious, intensive program of instruction in thinking aloud that supplemented the regular reading instruction in the classrooms in which we worked, we can envision it being modified or adapted in various ways in other elementary classrooms. For instance, we could encourage teachers to emphasize the social construction (Vygotsky, 1978, 1986) of think alouds by their students. During Phase 3 of most lessons, children worked in pairs or small groups to apply the various comprehension monitoring strategies, as was demonstrated in the preceding sample lesson. In reflecting on our research, we believe that this component was very powerful in helping the students to internalize the process of thinking aloud. In fact, we now believe that we should have provided even more opportunities for students to collaborate while thinking aloud. Thus, we encourage teachers who choose to use think alouds as a comprehension-fostering technique to provide students ample opportunities for sharing, discussing, and creating think alouds collaboratively.

The process of children's social construction of meaning could be extended even further by inviting the children to make decisions about what comprehension strategies might be useful while thinking aloud. Teachers might turn over responsibility to groups of students for deciding how thinking aloud might aid their comprehension as a complement to or substitute for the kinds of lessons we created. For example, rather than identifying specific think-aloud strategies as we did in our lessons, a teacher might model thinking aloud generically and then have students themselves come up with specific types of think alouds (for example guessing what will happen next, figuring out what the setting is, suggesting character motives). With more opportunities for decision making, children are likely to assume ownership of and responsibility for their comprehension. Thus, inviting students to participate both in the planning of think-aloud lessons as well as in their implementation would be beneficial.

As we learned, think alouds can be an effective tool for helping students acquire a range of comprehension monitoring techniques such as evaluating understanding, predicting and verifying, and self-questioning. Think alouds also can be useful for helping students acquire various high-utility comprehension strategies such as making inferences, understanding characterization, and constructing main ideas.

Think alouds can be implemented in various instructional contexts. For example, teachers who employ literature-based reading programs could readily and naturally integrate think alouds into book discussion times or minilessons. If a teacher wished to focus on characterization, for instance, he or she could model the process of thinking aloud while reading from a book that a group of students in the class chose to read. Through think alouds, the teacher would demonstrate the intricacies and subtleties of inferring and responding to story characters. The students could then employ think alouds as they read on and further probed the profiles of characters in the book.

Teachers who use basal reading programs could easily integrate thinking aloud in the existing strategy lessons. For a basal strategy lesson on prediction, a teacher could use think alouds to model the prediction process for the students. Then, much as in the preceding sample lesson from our study, he or she could move to guided practice by having the students try thinking aloud in a group setting using a selection from the basal anthology. Finally, to promote ownership of the strategy, pairs of students could practice thinking aloud to predict and verify events as they read on in the story from the basal anthology.

Thinking aloud also can be used to promote understanding of informational trade books or content-area textbooks. For example, if a teacher wished to integrate instruction in identifying textually important ideas with a reading from a social studies book, he or she could use think alouds to model the identification of stated and unstated main ideas. The teacher could describe a strategy for identifying main ideas (for example, Baumann, 1986) and then model its application for the students through think alouds. Students could likewise think aloud as they try to construct main ideas while reading other sections from the social studies book. Students might even try thinking aloud while drafting or revising written compositions related to the social studies content materials they are reading.

In conclusion, we found from our research that using think alouds works well for helping students develop an ability to monitor their reading comprehension and to employ fix-up strategies when they detect comprehension difficulties. We also recommend that students participate in the social construction of think alouds, either as part of lessons like those we taught or within lessons for which students have assumed responsibility for creating and directing. Further, we believe that thinking aloud is an appropriate approach for helping students acquire a variety of broadly based comprehension strategies. We observed that students in the think-aloud group in our study participated enthusiastically, they enjoyed thinking aloud, and they clearly felt empowered by their increasing ability to manage their cognitive processing during reading. Thus, we believe that think alouds provide teachers an effective, useful, and flexible technique for helping students acquire control over their comprehension processing of written texts.

Authors' Note

The preparation of this article was supported in part by the National Reading Research Center of the Universities of Georgia and Maryland under the Educational Research and Development Center Program (PR/AWARD NO. 117A20007) as administered by the Office of Educational Research and Improvement, U.S. Department of Education. The findings and opinions expressed here do not necessarily reflect the position or policies of the National Reading Research Center, the Office of Educational Research and Improvement, or the U.S. Department of Education.

REFERENCES

Afflerbach, P.P., & Johnston, P.H. (1986). What do expert readers do when the main idea is not explicit? In J.F. Baumann (Ed.), *Teaching main idea comprehension* (pp. 49–72). Newark, DE: International Reading Association.

Alvermann, D.E. (1984). Second graders' strategic reading preferences while reading basal stories. *Journal of Educational Research, 77,* 184–189.

August, D.L., Flavell, J.H., & Clift, R. (1984). Comparison of comprehension monitoring of skilled and less skilled readers. *Reading Research Quarterly, 20,* 39–53.

Baker, L., & Brown, A.L. (1984). Cognitive monitoring in reading. In J. Flood (Ed.), *Understanding reading comprehension* (pp. 21–44). Newark, DE: International Reading Association.

Baumann, J.F. (1986). The direct instruction of main idea comprehension ability. In J.F. Baumann (Ed.), *Teaching main idea comprehension* (pp. 133–178). Newark, DE: International Reading Association.

Baumann, J.F. (1991). Teaching comprehension strategies. In B.L. Hayes (Ed.), *Effective strategies for teaching reading* (pp. 61–83). Needham Heights, MA: Allyn & Bacon.

Baumann, J.F., & Schmitt, M.C. (1986). The what, why, how, and when of comprehension instruction. *The Reading Teacher, 39,* 640–646.

Baumann, J.F., Seifert-Kessell, N., & Jones, L.A. (1992). Effect of think-aloud instruction on elementary students' comprehension monitoring abilities. *Journal of Reading Behavior, 24,* 143–172.

Brown, A.L., Armbruster, B.B., & Baker, L. (1986). The role of metacognition in reading and studying. In J. Orasanu (Ed.), *Reading comprehension: From research to practice* (pp. 49–75). Hillsdale, NJ: Erlbaum.

Collins, A., & Smith, E.E. (1982). Teaching the process of reading comprehension. In D.K. Detterman & R.J. Sternberg (Eds.), *How and how much can intelligence be increased?* (pp. 173–185). Norwood, NJ: Ablex.

Davey, B. (1983). Think aloud—Modeling the cognitive processes of reading comprehension. *Journal of Reading, 27,* 44–47.

Ericsson, K., & Simon, H.J. (1980). Verbal reports as data. *Psychological Review, 87,* 215–251.

Ericsson, K., & Simon, H. (1984). *Protocol analysis: Verbal reports as data.* Cambridge, MA: MIT Press.

Garner, R. (1987). *Metacognition and reading comprehension.* Norwood, NJ: Ablex.

Johnson, D.D., & Johnson, B.V. (1986). Highlighting vocabulary in inferential comprehension instruction. *Journal of Reading, 29,* 622–625.

Nist, S.L., & Kirby, K. (1986). Teaching comprehension and study strategies through modeling and thinking aloud. *Reading Research and Instruction, 25,* 256–264.

Paris, S.G., & Myers, M. (1981). Comprehension monitoring, memory, and study strategies of good and poor readers. *Journal of Reading Behavior, 13*, 5–22.

Paris, S.G., Lipson, M.Y., & Wixson, K.D. (1983). Becoming a strategic reader. *Contemporary Educational Psychology, 8*, 293–316.

Paris, S.G., Wasik, B.A., & Turner, J.C. (1991). The development of strategic readers. In R. Barr, M.L. Kamil, P. Mosenthal, & P.D. Pearson (Eds.), *Handbook of reading research: Volume 2* (pp. 609–640). White Plains, NY: Longman.

Raphael, T. (1982). Question-answering strategies for children. *The Reading Teacher, 36*, 186–191.

Stauffer, R.G. (1976). *Teaching reading as a thinking process.* New York: Harper & Row.

Tierney, R.J., Readence, J.D., & Dishner, E.K. (1990). *Reading strategies and practices* (3rd ed.). Boston, MA: Allyn & Bacon.

Vygotsky, L.S. (1978). *Mind in society: The development of higher psychological processes.* Cambridge, MA: Harvard University Press.

Vygotsky, L.S. (1986). *Thought and language.* (A. Kozalin, Trans.) Cambridge, MA: MIT Press. (Original work published 1934)

Wagoner, S.A. (1983). Comprehension monitoring: What it is and what we know about it. *Reading Research Quarterly, 18*, 328–346.

Activating Background Knowledge: Strategies for Beginning and Poor Readers

Janet Clarke Richards, Joan P. Gipe

ccessing background knowledge helps readers to remember important ideas and to anticipate the internal organization of different types of reading material. Readers who connect what they read to what they already know are more likely to make appropriate inferences for ideas that are not stated explicitly.

As reading teachers, we suggest implementing activities that provide young or poor readers with the prerequisite background knowledge for interpreting a passage. But even when such readers possess necessary background knowledge, they often fail to access or activate this information spontaneously. Two strategies which we have developed and found useful for these students are Yes/No...Why? and It Reminds Me Of.... Both strategies can be used with all types of reading materials, including basal readers, children's literature, poetry, content-area text, and language-experience stories. Teachers also use the strategies with nonreaders by reading the text aloud and having students respond orally.

Yes/No...Why?

To introduce the strategy, the teacher explains *yes* and *no* statements: a *yes* statement reflects an idea in a paragraph that a reader knows about, appreciates, or understands; a *no* statement reflects an idea in a paragraph that a reader dislikes, disputes, or does not comprehend. The reader must then supply a reason (a *why*), for each *yes* or *no*. The teacher displays a familiar text, such as the nursery rhyme "Jack and Jill," on an overhead projector or a chart, and says, "Today we're going to learn a new strategy that will help us use the ideas already in our heads to understand what we are reading. Good readers always use what is in their heads to help them understand what they read."

Then the teacher reads the material aloud while students follow along. Next, the teacher might say, "As I read this paragraph it made me think of something I really liked. This will be my *yes*, but I also have to tell *why* I liked that idea. My *yes* is that I liked the idea that Jack and Jill climbed a hill because when I was a little girl there were a lot of hills where I lived, and I used to climb them. Is there something in this passage that you like or understand very well?" At this point one or two students may volunteer something they particularly liked or understood about the passage. The teacher accepts their responses and makes sure students give a *why* for their *yes* responses.

Teacher modeling of a *yes* response is then followed by teacher modeling of a *no* response: "As I read this paragraph it made me think of something I disliked. My *no* is that I don't like the idea of Jack and Jill falling down the hill because it makes me worry that they might hurt themselves." After one or two modeling sessions of approximately 10 minutes each, most students catch on easily and enjoy using the strategy.

When students silently read new material, they are directed to pause at the end of each paragraph. Students then share their *yeses*, *noes*, and *whys* with one another or, after reading each paragraph, individually record their responses to share later with the teacher or other students (see Figure 1).

Because of differences in background knowledge and experiences, it is possible for one student's *yes* to be another student's *no*. When this occurs, it is important to explain how individual students' background knowledge has influenced *yes* and *no* responses. The fact that there are no right answers for this strategy fosters active participation and feelings of success.

Note how partners reading the first paragraph of a teacher-created fable responded:

> A Dog and a Cow
>
> Once upon a time a dog and a cow were playing together in a forest. "I am bigger than you," said the cow. "Therefore, I shall choose the next game we play." "Yes," replied the dog. "You are bigger than I. But I am smarter than you. Therefore, I get to choose the next game."

First partner: My *yes* is that I like the idea of a dog and a cow playing together. I'd rather play football than do my homework.

Second partner: My *yes* is that I know how big cows are because my grandfather has a farm, and he has a lot of cows.

Figure 1
Example of Yes/No…Why? chart for recording individual responses

Student's name ___Joey_____

Paragraph #, page #	My "Yes" and "Why?"	My "No" and "Why?"
1, 5	I like the idea of a dog and a cow playing because I like to play a lot.	I don't know what forest is. I never saw it before.

First partner:	My *no* is that I don't know this word spelled f-o-r-e-s-t. I can't figure it out.
Teacher:	(To first partner.) I'm glad you realize that you didn't know that word. It is a hard word to figure out in that sentence because there aren't many clues to help you. The word is *forest*. Have you ever heard the word *forest*? Another word for *forest* is *woods*. The story "Goldilocks and the Three Bears" takes place in the woods or forest. We'll get some books about forests from the library today.
Second partner:	My *no* is that I don't believe dogs and cows play together. I know my grandfather's dog would never play with his cows. He chases cows and snaps at them.
Teacher:	(To second partner.) You're right! I had forgotten that some dogs are working dogs. Some dogs work by herding cows and sheep. Other dogs help hunters or guard buildings. We might want to find out more about working dogs later. OK?

It Reminds Me Of...

This strategy is a variation on the format of Yes/No...Why? After each paragraph is read, students connect information in the paragraph to information from their own background experiences. As with Yes/No...Why?, students share their responses with one another or, after reading each paragraph, individually record their responses to share later (see Figure 2). An example using the dog and cow passage with a small group follows:

Teacher modeling:	This paragraph mentions cows. Cows remind me of my grandfather's cows. He has cows on his farm.
First student:	This paragraph has a dog. The dog in this paragraph reminds me of my own dog, Lucky. He likes to play too.
Second student:	In this paragraph the dog and cow are talking about who is bigger and who is smarter. That reminds me of my brother. He's always saying he's bigger and smarter than I am so I have to do what he says.
Third student:	This paragraph starts "Once upon a time." That reminds me of another story I know about a boy who climbs a beanstalk and meets a giant.
Teacher:	(To the group.) No one has mentioned forests. Has anyone ever been in a forest or read about a forest?

After sufficient teacher modeling and guided practice, students using the strategies can work in small groups, with partners, or individually to record their responses, which are later shared with the whole group. The teacher circulates around the room to encourage students and to work with individuals or small groups in need of extra help.

As these strategies become familiar, teachers can participate in ways that help expand students' interaction with the text. The teacher can lead students to think about unfamiliar concepts in material rather than simply identifying unknown sight vocabulary words as *noes*. Such scaffolded instruction in strategic reading encourages students to think about texts in more sophisticated ways.

Figure 2
Example of It Reminds Me Of... chart for recording individual responses

Student's name _Sammie_

Paragraph #, page #	It Reminds Me Of...
1, 5	The forest reminds me of Goldilocks and the Three Bears. The bears lived in the woods and woods are like forests.

Introducing Response Logs to Poor Readers

Pat Sudduth

I decided to use literature response logs with my third-grade remedial students to increase thinking and comprehension during reading. I provided blank logs and explained how to use them—basically to respond in writing or drawing to our stories, chapters, or text passages. What better way to check students' comprehension while allowing them freedom of expression and independence in learning?

However, I soon became frustrated when I saw the students did not understand how to use the log. Therefore, I would like to share a process I found necessary to develop the independent use of literature response logs. My goal is to make the implementation of this valuable strategy more pleasant and rewarding for teachers as well as students.

1. *At first, have students in the group read the same book.* By having all of the students read the same book, you can become an active participant and model for them. Read the book with the students either silently or using a variety of oral strategies.

2. *Verbalize thoughts and engage students in discussion.* By stopping and thinking aloud during reading, you model how to use background knowledge while reading. Students will begin to see how to do this and become more active readers.

3. *Write group entries in the logs.* Using the chalkboard or chart paper, start with a response guide statement, such as: "I was surprised when ____," or "Since ____ and ____ has happened I predict ____ will happen next" or "This story reminds me of the time I ____." Write the students' responses as they dictate. Then have them copy the entry into their logs. This models the log format. Once again, you are a participant, probing for thoughts by using open ended questioning, writing your own thoughts, and recording student responses. This activity also engages students in more discussion.

4. *As students become familiar with the routine, work for their independence.* First, eliminate modeling the writing but continue group discussions to generate ideas. Continue group entries but allow each student to put the ideas into his or her own words. Next, brainstorm a list of log topics the students can keep in the front of their logs to refer to if they are having difficulty with ideas for entries. Use a kitchen timer to structure the time spent between reading and log entry. This will set a daily routine for independent reading and writing (20 minutes for reading, 10 minutes for writing).

5. *Allow time regularly for students to share their log entries.* Further understand-

ing of texts may come through the sharing of ideas or facts obtained during reading. Read and write 3 or 4 days a week and share 1 to 2 days a week. Group interaction is needed for activating thinking.

Poor readers require more direct instruction in strategies that teach text interaction and take them beyond graphophonics. When using literature logs, allow for teacher participation, model the use of the log, and provide time for sharing and discussion. This gradual introduction to response logs allows the students time for growth and development in log use until they are ready to use logs meaningfully and independently.

Section V

Improving Accuracy and Fluency

Although understanding is the goal, children also must develop effective and efficient strategies for reading unfamiliar words when they encounter them in texts. Although many traditional interventions have focused on decoding skills, too few were developed using principles from available research. For instance, recent research has pointed to the importance of children's early development of phonemic segmentation strategies. When such development does not occur, and 10 to 15 percent of children routinely have difficulty in this area, reading acquisition is slowed enormously. But targeting such specific needs was unlikely before the recent research and the development of strategies for monitoring children's phonemic development. Instead, many children having difficulty were simply given traditional phonics instruction—which, unsurprisingly, was typically ineffective.

Each article in this section offers information on fostering reading accuracy and fluency. Note, however, that none of the articles recommends traditional skills and drill, memorizing abstract rules, or heavy reliance on worksheet activities. Effective decoding and fluency instruction is critical and many readers having difficulty need high-quality and explicit decoding strategy instruction. Other readers will have adequate decoding facility but still read slowly, without phrasing, intonation, or emphasis; they pronounce all the words right but still struggle to read. Fostering fluency is often neglected in interventions, but fluency is important and it can be developed.

Saying the "P" Word: Nine Guidelines for Exemplary Phonics Instruction

Steven A. Stahl

Phonics, like beauty, is in the eye of the beholder. Many people believe that "phonics" implies stacks of worksheets, with bored children mindlessly filling in the blanks. For some people, "phonics" implies children barking at print, often in unison, meaningless strings of letter sounds to be blended into words. There also are people for whom "phonics" implies lists of skills that must be mastered, each with its own criterion-referenced test, which must be passed or the teacher is "in for it." Some people think "phonics" somehow contrasts with "meaning," implying that concentrating on phonics means that one must ignore the meaning of the text. For others, "phonics" is the solution to the reading problem, and if we just teach children the sounds of the letters, all else will fall into place (see Flesch, 1955 and Republican Party National Steering Committee, 1990).

Because "phonics" can be so many things, some people treat it as a dirty word, others as the salvation of reading. It is neither. With these strong feelings, though, extreme views have been allowed to predominate, forcing out any middle position that allows for the importance of systematic attention to decoding in the context of a program stressing comprehension and interpretation of quality literature and expository text. Yet the truth is that some attention to the relations between spelling patterns and their pronunciations is characteristic of all types of reading programs, including whole language. As Newman and Church (1990) explain:

> No one can read without taking into account the graphophonemic cues of written language. As readers all of us use information about the way words are written to help us make sense of what we're reading.... Whole language teachers do teach phonics but not as something separate from actual reading and writing.... Readers use graphophonic cues; whole language teachers help students orchestrate their use for reading and writing (pp. 20–21).

"Phonics" merely refers to various approaches designed to teach children about the orthographic code of the language and the relations of spelling patterns to sound patterns. These approaches can range from direct instruction approaches through instruction that is embedded in the reading of literature. There is no requirement that phonics instruction use worksheets, that it involve having children bark at print, that it be taught as a set of discrete skills mastered in isolation, or that it preclude paying attention to the meaning of texts.

In this article, I want to discuss some principles about what effective phonics instruction should contain and describe some successful programs that meet these criteria.

Why Teach Phonics at All?

The reading field has been racked by vociferous debates about the importance of teaching phonics, when it is to be taught, and how it is to be taught. The interested reader can get a flavor of this debate by reviewing such sources as Adams (1990), Chall (1983a, 1989), and Carbo (1988). To rehash these arguments here would not be useful.

The fact is that all students, regardless of the type of instruction they receive, learn about letter-sound correspondences as part of learning to read. There are a number of models of children's initial word learning showing similar stages of development (for example, Chall, 1983b; Frith, 1985; Lomax & McGee, 1987; McCormick & Mason, 1986). Frith, for example, suggests that children go through three stages as they learn about words. The first stage is *logographic* in which words are learned as whole units, sometimes embedded in a logo, such as stop sign. This is followed by an *alphabetic* stage, in which use children use individual letters and sounds to identify words. The last stage is *orthographic* in which children begin to see patterns in words, and use these patterns to identify words without sounding them out. One can see children go through these stages and begin to see words orthographically by the end of the first grade. Following the orthographic stage children grow in their ability to recognize words automatically, without having to think consciously about word structure or spelling patterns.

These stages in the development of word recognition take place while children are learning about how print functions (what a written "word" is, directionality, or punctuation), that it can signify meanings, about the nature of stories, and all of the other learnings that go on in emergent literacy (see Teale, 1987). Learning about words goes hand in hand with other learnings about reading and writing.

All children appear to go through these stages on their way to becoming successful readers. Some will learn to decode on their own, without any instruction. Others will need some degree of instruction, ranging from some pointing out of common spelling patterns to intense and systematic instruction to help them through the alphabetic and orthographic stages. This article will outline some components of what exemplary instruction might look like. These components could be found in classrooms based on shared reading of literature, as in a whole language philosophy, or in classrooms in which the basal reader is used as the core text.

Exemplary Phonics Instruction...

1. Builds on a Child's Rich Concepts About How Print Functions

The major source of the debates on phonics is whether one should go from part to whole (begin by teaching letters and sounds and blend those into words) or from whole to part (begin with words and analyze those into letters). Actually, there should be no debate. Letter-sound instruction makes no sense to a child who does not have an overall conception of what reading is about, how print functions, and what stories are, so this instruction must build on a child's concept of the whole process of reading.

A good analogy is baseball. For a person learning to play baseball, batting practice is an important part of learning how to play the game. However, imagine a person who has never seen a baseball game. Making that person do nothing but batting practice may lead to the misconception that baseball is about standing at the plate and repeatedly swinging at the ball. That person would miss the purpose of baseball and would think it a boring way to spend an afternoon.

Adams (1990) points out that children from homes that are successful in preparing children for literacy have a rich idea of what "reading" is before they get to school. They are read to, play with letters on the refrigerator door, and discuss print with their parents. Other children may have had only minimal or no exposure to print prior to school. The differences may add up to 1,000 hours or more of exposure to print.

For the child who has had that 1,000 hours or more of print exposure, phonics instruction is grounded in his or her experiences with words. Such a child may not need extensive phonics instruction. Because good phonics instruction should help make sense of patterns noticed within words, just mentioning the patterns might suffice with these children. However, for the child with little or no exposure, phonics instruction would be an abstract and artificial task until the child has additional meaningful encounters with print.

To develop this base of experience with reading, one might begin reading in kindergarten with activities such as sharing books with children, writing down their dictated stories, and engaging them in authentic reading and writing tasks. Predictable books work especially well for beginning word recognition (Bridge, Winograd, & Haley, 1983). Stahl and Miller (1989) found that whole language programs appeared to work effectively in kindergarten. Their effectiveness, however, diminished in first grade, where more structured, code-emphasis approaches seemed to produce better results. In short, children ben-efited from the experiences with reading that a whole language program gives early on, but, once they had that exposure, they benefited from more systematic study.

2. Builds on a Foundation of Phonemic Awareness

Phonemic awareness is not phonics. Phonemic awareness is awareness of sounds in *spoken* words; phonics is the relation between letters and sounds in *written* words. Phonemic awareness is an important precursor to success in reading. One study (Juel, 1988) found that children who were in the bottom fourth of their group in phonemic awareness in first grade remained in the bottom fourth of their class in reading four years later.

An example is Heather, a child I saw in our clinic. As part of an overall reading assessment, I gave Heather a task involving removing a phoneme from a spoken word. For example, I had Heather say *meat* and then repeat it without saying the /m/ sound (*eat*). When Heather said *chicken* after some hesitation, I was taken aback. When I had her say *coat* without the /k/ sound, she said *jacket*. Looking over the tasks we did together, it appeared that she reviewed words only in terms of their meaning. For her, a little less than *meat* was *chicken*, a little less than *coat* was *jacket*.

For most communication, focusing on meaning is necessary. But for learning to read, especially learning about sound-symbol relations, it is desirable to view words in terms of the sounds they contain. Only by understanding that spoken words contain phonemes can one learn the relations between letters and sounds. The alternative is learning each word as a logograph, as in Chinese. This is possible, up to a certain limit, but does not use the alphabetic nature of our language to its best advantage.

Heather was a bright child but she was having specific difficulties learning to decode.

Other children like Heather, or children with more complex difficulties, are going to have similar problems. We worked for a short period of time on teaching her to reflect on sounds in spoken words, and, with about 6 weeks of instruction, she took off and became an excellent reader. The moral is that phonemic awareness is easily taught, but absence of it leads to reading difficulties.

3. Is Clear and Direct

Good teachers explain what they mean very clearly. Yet, some phonics instruction seems to be excessively ambiguous. Some of this ambiguity comes from trying to solve the problem of pronouncing single phonemes. One cannot pronounce the sounds represented by many of the consonants in isolation. For example, the sound made by *b* cannot be spoken by itself, without adding a vowel (such as /buh/).

To avoid having the teacher add the vowel to the consonant sound, however, some basals have come up with some terribly circuitous routes. For example, a phonics lesson from a current basal program begins with a teacher presenting a picture of a key word, such as *bear*, pronouncing the key word and two or three words with a shared phonic element (such as *boat*, *ball*, and *bed*). The teacher is to point out that the sound at the beginning of each word is spelled with a *b*. The teacher then might say some other words and ask if they, too, have the same sound. Next, written words are introduced and may be read by the whole class or by individuals. After this brief lesson, students might complete two worksheets, which both involve circling pictures of items that start with *b* and one that includes copying upper- and lowercase *b*'s.

In this lesson, (a) nowhere is the teacher supposed to attempt to say what sound the *b* is supposed to represent and (b) nowhere is the teacher directed to tell the children that these relations have anything to do with reading words in text. For a child with little phonemic awareness, the instructions, which require that the child segment the initial phoneme from a word, would be very confusing. Children such as Heather view the word *bear* not as a combination of sounds or letters, but as identical to its meaning. For that child, the question of what *bear* begins with does not make any sense, because it is seen as a whole meaning unit, not a series of sounds that has a beginning and an end.

Some of this confusion could be alleviated if the teacher dealt with written words. A more direct approach is to show the word *bear*, in the context of a story or in isolation, and pointing out that it begins with the letter *b*, and the letter *b* makes the /b/ sound. This approach goes right to the basic concept, that a letter in a word represents a particular phoneme, involving fewer extraneous concepts. Going the other direction, showing the letter *b* and then showing words such as *bear* that begin with that letter, also would be clear. Each of these should be followed by having children practice reading words that contain the letter *b*, rather than looking at pictures. Children learn to read by reading words, in stories or in lists. This can be done in small groups or with pairs of children reading with each other independently. Circling pictures, coloring, cutting, and pasting wastes a lot of time.

4. Is Integrated Into a Total Reading Program

Phonics instruction, no matter how useful it is, should never dominate reading instruction. I know of no research to guide us in deciding how much time should be spent on decoding instruction, but my rule of thumb is that at least half of the time devoted to reading (and probably more) should be spent reading connected text—stories, poems, plays, and trade books. No more than 25% of the time (and possibly less) should be spent on phonics instruction and practice.

Unfortunately, I have seen too many schools in which one day the members of the reading group do the green pages (the skills instruction), the next day they read the story, and the third day they do the blue pages. The result is that, on most days, children are not reading text. Certainly, in these classes, children are going to view "reading" as filling out workbook pages, since this is what they do most of the time. Instead, they should read some text daily, preferably a complete story, with phonics instruction integrated into the text reading.

In many basals, the patterns taught in the phonics lessons appear infrequently in the text, leading students to believe that phonics is somehow unrelated to the task of reading (Adams, 1990). What is taught should be directly usable in children's reading. Juel and Roper/Schneider (1985) found that children were better able to use their phonics knowledge, for both decoding and comprehension, when the texts they read contained a higher percentage of words that conformed to the patterns they were taught. It is best to teach elements that can be used with stories the children are going to read. Teachers using a basal might rearrange the phonics lessons so that a more appropriate element is taught with each story.

Teachers using trade books might choose elements from the books they plan to use, and either preteach them or integrate the instruction into the lesson. A good procedure for doing this is described by Trachtenburg (1990). She suggests beginning by reading a quality children's story (such as *Angus and the Cat*), providing instruction in a high-utility phonic element appearing in that story (short *a* in this case), and using that element to help read another book (such as *The Cat in the Hat* or *Who*

Took the Farmer's Hat?). Trachtenburg (1990) provides a list of trade books that contain high percentages of common phonic elements.

Reading Recovery is another example of how phonics instruction can be integrated into a total reading program. Reading Recovery lessons differ depending on the child's needs, but a typical lesson begins with the rereading of a familiar book, followed by the taking of a "running record" on a book introduced the previous session (see Pinnell, Fried, & Estice, 1990, for details). The phonics instruction occurs in the middle of the lesson and could involve directed work in phonemic awareness, letter-sound correspondences using children's spelling or magnetic letters, or even lists of words. The teacher chooses a pattern with which the child had difficulty. The "phonics" instruction is a relatively small component of the total Reading Recovery program, but it is an important one.

5. Focuses on Reading Words, Not Learning Rules

When competent adults read, they do not refer to a set of rules that they store in their heads. Instead, as Adams (1990) points out, they recognize new words by comparing them or spelling patterns within them to words they already know. When an unknown word such as *minatory* is encountered, it is not read by figuring out whether the first syllable is open or closed. Instead most people that I have asked usually say the first syllable says /min/ as in *minute* or *miniature*, comparing it to a pattern in a word they already know how to pronounce. Effective decoders see words not in terms of phonics rules, but in terms of patterns of letters that are used to aid in identification.

Effective phonics instruction helps children do this, by first drawing their attention to the order of letters in words, forcing them to examine common patterns in English through sounding out words, and showing similarities among words. As an interim step, rules can be useful in helping children see patterns. Some rules, such as the silent *e* rule, point out common patterns in English. However, rules are not useful enough to be taught as absolutes. Clymer (1963) found that only 45% of the commonly taught phonics rules worked as much as 75% of the time.

A good guideline might be that rules be pointed out, as a way of highlighting a particular spelling pattern, but children should not be asked to memorize or recite them. And, when rules are pointed out, they should be discussed as tentative, with exceptions given at the same time as conforming patterns. Finally, only rules with reasonable utility should be used. Teaching children that *ough* has six sounds is a waste of everyone's time.

6. May Include Onsets and Rimes

An alternative to teaching rules is using onsets and rimes. Treiman (1985) has found that breaking down syllables into onsets (or the part of the syllable before the vowel) and rimes (the part from the vowel onward) is useful to describe how we process syllables in oral language. Teaching onsets and rimes may be useful in written language as well.

Adams (1990) points out that letter-sound correspondences are more stable when one looks at rimes than when letters are looked at in isolation. For example, *ea* taken alone is thought of as irregular. However, it is very regular in all rimes, except *-ead* (bead vs. bread), *-eaf* (sheaf vs. deaf), and *-ear* (hear vs. bear). However, the rime *-ean*, for example, nearly always has the long *e* sound. Of the 286 phonograms that appear in primary grade texts, 95% of them were pronounced the same in every word in which they appeared (Adams, 1990).

In addition, nearly 500 words can be derived from the following 37 rimes:

-ack	-ain	-ake	-ale	-all	-ame
-an	-ank	-ap	-ash	-at	-ate
-aw	-ay	-eat	-ell	-est	-ice
-ick	-ide	-ight	-ill	-in	-ine
-ing	-ink	-ip	-ir	-ock	-oke
-op	-or	-ore	-uck	-ug	-ump
-unk					

Rime-based instruction is used in a number of successful reading programs. In one such program, children are taught to compare an unknown word to already known words and to use context to confirm their predictions (Gaskins et al., 1988). For example, when encountering *wheat* in a sentence, such as *The little red hen gathered the wheat*, a student might be taught to compare it to *meat* and say "If m-e-a-t is *meat* then this is *wheat*." The student would then cross-check the pronunciation by seeing if *wheat* made sense in the sentence. This approach is comprehension oriented in that students are focused on the comprehension of sentences and stories, but it does teach decoding effectively (see also Cunningham, 1991).

7. May Include Invented Spelling Practice

It has been suggested that when children work out their invented spellings, they are learning phonic principles, but learning them "naturally." For this reason, many whole language advocates suggest that practice in writing with invented spelling might be a good substitute for direct phonics instruction. Practice with invented spelling does improve children's awareness of phonemes, which, as discussed earlier, is an important precursor to learning to decode.

However, there is very little research on the effects of invented spelling. That research is positive, but I know of only one study that directly addresses the question. Clarke (1989) found that children who were encouraged to invent spelling and given additional time for writing journals were significantly better at decoding and comprehension than children in a traditional spelling program. However, the classes she studied used a synthetic phonics program as their core reading program. These results may not transfer to a whole language program or even to a more eclectic basal program. An evaluation of the Writing-to-Read program, a computer-based program incorporating writing, found that it had little effect on children's reading abilities (Slavin, 1991). Yet we need not wait for the research to evaluate the use of invented spelling. Writing stories and journal entries using invented spelling does not seem to hurt reading or spelling abilities, and it may help them; it certainly improves children's writing.

8. Develops Independent Word Recognition Strategies, Focusing Attention on the Internal Structure of Words

The object of phonics instruction is to get children to notice orthographic patterns in words and to use those patterns to recognize words. Effective strategies, whether they involve having a child sound out a word letter by letter, find a word that shares the same rime as an unknown word, or spell out the word through invented or practiced spelling, all force the child to look closely at patterns in words. It is through the learning of these patterns that children learn to recognize words efficiently.

Good phonics instruction should help children through the stages described earlier as quickly as possible. Beginning with bookhandling experiences, storybook reading and Big Books, and other features of a whole language kindergarten support children at the logographic stage. Frith (1985) suggests that writing and spelling may aid in the development of al-

phabetic knowledge. This can be built upon with some direct instruction of letters and sounds, and showing students how to use that knowledge to unlock words in text. Sounding out words also forces children to examine the internal structure of words, as does rime-based instruction. These can help children make the transition to the orthographic stage. In the next stage, the child develops automatic word recognition skills, or the ability to recognize words without conscious attention.

9. Develops Automatic Word Recognition Skills So That Students Can Devote Their Attention to Comprehension, Not Words

The purpose of phonics instruction is *not* that children learn to sound out words. The purpose is that they learn to recognize words, quickly and automatically, so that they can turn their attention to comprehension of the text. If children are devoting too much energy to sounding out words, they will not be able to direct enough of their attention to comprehension (Samuels, 1988).

We know that children develop automatic word recognition skills through practicing reading words. We know that reading words in context does improve children's recognition of words, an improvement that transfers to improved comprehension. There is some question about whether reading words in isolation necessarily results in improved comprehension. Fleisher, Jenkins, and Pany (1979–1980) found that increasing word recognition speed in isolation did not result in improved comprehension; Blanchard (1981) found that it did. Either way, there is ample evidence that practice reading words in text, either repeated readings of the same text (Samuels, 1988) or just reading of connected text in general (Taylor & Nosbush, 1983), improves children's comprehension.

Good phonics instruction is also over relatively quickly. Anderson, Hiebert, Wilkinson, and Scott (1985) recommend that phonics instruction be completed by the end of the second grade. However, stretching out phonics instruction too long, or spending time on teaching the arcane aspects of phonics—the schwa, the silent *k*, assigning accent to polysyllabic words—is at best a waste of time. Once a child begins to use orthographic patterns in recognizing words and recognizes words at an easy, fluent pace, it is time to move away from phonics instruction and to spend even more time reading and writing text.

The "Politics" of Phonics

Given that all children do need to learn about the relations between spelling patterns and pronunciations on route to becoming a successful reader, why all the fuss about phonics?

Part of the reason is that there is confusion about what phonics instruction is. A teacher pointing out the "short *a*" words during the reading of a Big Book in a whole language classroom is doing something different from a teacher telling her class that the short sound of the letter *a* is /a/ and having them blend in unison 12 words that contain that sound, yet both might be effective phonics instruction. The differences are not only in practice but in philosophy.

In discussions on this issue, the philosophical differences seem to predominate. These exaggerated differences often find people arguing that phonics proponents oppose the use of literature and writing in the primary grades, which is clearly false, or that whole language supporters oppose any sort of direct teaching, also clearly false. The truth is that there are commonalities to be found in effective practices of widely differing philosophies, some of which are reflected in the nine guidelines discussed here.

In this article, I have proposed some characteristics of exemplary phonics instruction. Such instruction is very different from what I see in many classrooms. But because phonics is often taught badly is no reason to stop attempting to teach it well. Quality phonics instruction should be a part of a reading program, integrated and relevant to the reading and writing of actual texts, and based on and building on children's experiences with texts. Such phonics instruction can and should be built into all beginning reading programs.

REFERENCES

Adams, M.J. (1990). *Beginning to read: Thinking and learning about print*. Cambridge, MA: MIT Press.

Anderson, R.C., Hiebert, E.F., Wilkinson, I.A.G., & Scott, J. (1985). *Becoming a nation of readers*. Champaign, IL: National Academy of Education and Center for the Study of Reading.

Blanchard, J.S. (1981). A comprehension strategy for disabled readers in the middle school. *Journal of Reading, 24*, 331–336.

Bridge, C.A., Winograd, P.N., & Haley, D. (1983). Using predictable materials vs. preprimers to teach beginning sight words. *The Reading Teacher, 36*, 884–891.

Carbo, M. (1988). Debunking the great phonics myth. *Phi Delta Kappan, 70*, 226–240.

Chall, J.S. (1983a). *Learning to read: The great debate* (Rev. ed.). New York: McGraw-Hill.

Chall, J.S. (1983b). *Stages of reading development*. New York: McGraw-Hill.

Chall, J.S. (1989). Learning to read: The great debate twenty years later. A response to "Debunking the great phonics myth." *Phi Delta Kappan, 71*, 521–538.

Clarke, L.K. (1989). Encouraging invented spelling in first graders' writing: Effects on learning to spell and read. *Research in the Teaching of English, 22*, 281–309.

Clymer, T. (1963). The utility of phonic generalization in the primary grades. *The Reading Teacher, 16*, 252–258.

Cunningham, P.M. (1991). *Phonics they use.* New York: HarperCollins.

Fleisher, L.S., Jenkins, J.R., & Pany, D. (1979–1980). Effects on poor readers' comprehension of training in rapid decoding. *Reading Research Quarterly, 15,* 30–48.

Flesch, R. (1955). *Why Johnny can't read.* New York: Harper & Row.

Frith. U. (1985). Beneath the surface of developmental dyslexia. In K.E. Patterson, K.C. Marshall, & M. Coltheart (Eds.), *Surface dyslexia: Neuropsychological and cognitive studies of phonological reading.* Hillsdale, NJ: Erlbaum.

Gaskins, I.W., Downer, M.A., Anderson, R.C., Cunningham, P.M., Gaskins, R.W., Schommer, M., & The Teachers of Benchmark School (1988). A metacognitive approach to phonics: Using what you know to decode what you don't know. *Remedial and Special Education, 9,* 36–41.

Juel, C. (1988). Learning to read and write: A longitudinal study of fifty-four children from first through fourth grade. *Journal of Educational Psychology, 80,* 437–447.

Juel, C., & Roper/Schneider, D. (1985). The influence of basal readers on first grade reading. *Reading Research Quarterly, 20,* 134–152.

Lomax, R.G., & McGee, L.M. (1987). Young children's concepts about print and reading: Toward a model of reading acquisition. *Reading Research Quarterly, 22,* 237–256.

McCormick, C.E., & Mason, J.M. (1986). Intervention procedures for increasing preschool children's interest in and knowledge about reading. In W.H. Teale & E. Sulzby (Eds.), *Emergent literacy: Writing and reading* (pp. 90–115). Norwood, NJ: Ablex.

Newman, J.M., & Church, S.M. (1990). Commentary: Myths of whole language. *The Reading Teacher, 44,* 20–27.

Pinnell, G.S., Fried, M.D., & Estice, R.M. (1990). Reading Recovery: Learning how to make a difference. *The Reading Teacher, 43,* 282–295.

Republican Party National Steering Committee. (1990). *Position paper on teaching children to read.* Washington, DC: Author.

Samuels, S.J. (1988). Decoding and automaticity: Helping poor readers become automatic at word recognition. *The Reading Teacher, 41,* 756–760.

Slavin, R.E. (1991). Reading effects of IBM's "Writing to Read" program: A review of evaluations. *Educational Evaluation and Policy Analysis, 13,* 1–11.

Stahl, S.A., & Miller, P.D. (1989). Whole language and language experience approaches for beginning reading: A quantitative research synthesis. *Review of Educational Research, 59,* 87–116.

Taylor, B.M., & Nosbush, L. (1983). Oral reading for meaning: A technique for improving word identification skills. *The Reading Teacher, 37,* 234–237.

Teale, W.H. (1987). Emergent literacy: Reading and writing development in early childhood. In J.E. Readence & R.S. Baldwin (Eds.), *Research in literacy: Merging perspectives.* (Thirty-sixth Yearbook of the National Reading Conference, pp. 45–74). Rochester, NY: National Reading Conference.

Trachtenburg, P. (1990). Using children's literature to enhance phonics instruction. *The Reading Teacher, 43,* 648–653.

Treiman, R. (1985). Onsets and rimes as units of spoken syllables: Evidence from children. *Journal of Experimental Child Psychology, 39,* 161–181.

Read-Aloud Books for Developing Phonemic Awareness: An Annotated Bibliography

Hallie Kay Yopp

The relation between phonemic awareness and learning to read is extremely important (Stanovich, 1994). In fact, research suggests that phonemic awareness may be the "most important core and causal factor separating normal and disabled readers" (Adams, 1990, p. 305). A critical question, then, is how do children become phonemically aware? Studies reveal that the ability to segment and otherwise manipulate sounds in speech can be taught explicitly to children and that those children who receive training in phonemic awareness perform at higher levels on subsequent reading and spelling achievement tests than their control group counterparts (Ball & Blachman, 1988; Bradley & Bryant, 1983; Cunningham, 1990; Lundberg, Frost, & Peterson, 1988).

Phonemic awareness also may be facilitated in a less direct, but perhaps more natural and spontaneous way, by providing children with language-rich environments in which attention is often turned to language itself by means of word play in stories, songs, and games. Classroom teachers are in the ideal position to capitalize on what Geller's (1982a, 1982b, 1983) observations reveal as children's natural propensity to experiment with sounds in their language. Geller recommends that teachers observe children's play with speech sounds and design activities that stimulate this play, arguing that word play enables children to explore and experiment with systems of sound separate from their meanings, which has positive implications for literacy learning. Other researchers also have encouraged teachers to provide their young students with activities, such as word games, rhymes, riddles, and songs, that are linguistically stimulating (Adams, 1990; Mattingly, 1984; Yopp, 1992).

Probably the most accessible, practical, and useful vehicles to enhance students' sensitivity to the phonological basis of their language are children's books that deal playfully with speech sounds through rhyme, alliteration, assonance, or other phoneme manipulation (Griffith & Olson, 1992). The purpose of this article is to provide teachers with an annotated bibliography of children's literature that draws attention to language sounds and so may be useful in facilitating the acquisition of phonemic awareness.

Criteria for Selection

The following three criteria were used for inclusion of books in this bibliography:

1. Play with language is explicit and is a critical, dominant feature of the books so that children are encouraged to shift their focus from the message of the text to the language that is used to communicate the message. Only books that make very obvious use of rhyme, alliteration, assonance, phoneme substitution, or segmentation are included.

2. The books are appropriate for young children. Neither the vocabulary nor the story lines are too advanced for most kindergarten or first-grade students. For example, although Kellogg's (1987) *Aster Aardvark's Alphabet Adventures* makes clever use of alliteration, the vocabulary and content are rather sophisticated: "Entering an elite eating establishment escorted by an enormously eminent elephant...." Thus, the book is inappropriate for this list.

3. The books lend themselves easily to further language play. Their patterns are explicit, their structures readily accessible, and their content simple enough that the stories can be extended.

How To Use These Books

Read and reread the story   Read the story aloud several times simply for the pure joy of reading and sharing.

Comment on the language use   After several readings, teachers may encourage students to comment on the story. Teachers may ask "Did you enjoy the book? Was it fun? What was fun about it?" and let the children discover for themselves that the word play added tremendous entertainment to the story. Or teachers may laugh at several points in a rereading and say "That was funny! Did you notice how those words rhyme?" or "Did you notice how the character got all mixed up in what he was saying?" and gently guide children's attention to the word play.

Encourage predictions   Most of these stories are very predictable. Teachers should encourage their students to predict sounds, words, or phrases and then ask the students how they arrived at their predictions. Generally, the answer will address the author's use of language: "He's making the words rhyme!" "She's starting everything with the same sound!"

Examine language use   Depending on the children, teachers may wish to examine more closely the language use in a story. Teachers may explicitly point out and analyze phonemic features. With younger children (perhaps ages 3 to 5), simply commenting on the language is likely most appropriate: "Those words start alike! That's silly that the author did that! Listen: *kitten, cape, coat*." With older children (perhaps ages 4 to 7), closer examinations may be fruitful: "What sound do you hear at the beginning of all those words? Yes—the /k/ sound. Isn't it interesting how the author uses so many words with the /k/ sound? What are some other words that begin with that sound?"

Create additional verses or make another version of the story   Children can change the story yet maintain the language pattern to develop their own versions of the story. My 3½ year-old son enjoyed listening to *"I Can't," Said the Ant* (Cameron, 1961) and after the first reading began reciting chunks of the story retaining the dialogue but changing the speaker. For instance, instead of the author's "'Don't break her!' said the shaker," Peter prefers to say "'Don't break her,' said the baker." He is quite amused by his changes in the story and insists that we read it his way.

After reading *Zoophabets* (Tallon, 1979) each child may wish to make his or her own Zoophabets book by drawing pictures of nonsense animals and dictating words to the teacher; or each student could be responsible for a particular letter sound and make a single page of the alphabet book to be included in a class compilation.

After reading *More Bugs in Boxes* (Carter, 1990), children can make their own "open the flap" book with drawings of interesting bugs hidden away under each flap. Each bug represents a particular sound. The child who chooses /s/ may decide to draw six laughing bugs who are looking off to the side and dictate, "six silly bugs looking sideways." Or instead of making a book, children actually may construct boxes, make three dimensional bugs, and have fun naming them: "carrot-eating, colorful cucumber bugs!"

A Final Note

The children with whom I have read these books responded quickly to both the form of the language and the content of the text. The books stimulated experimentation with sounds, and children readily, enthusiastically, and often spontaneously innovated on the patterns provided.

Of course, this type of book should not be read to the exclusion of other works of children's literature. Books of this nature should, however, be included in the classroom repertoire of reading experiences, because they can serve as a means to help young children attend to and play with the phonemes in their language.

Annotated Bibliography

Brown, M.W. (1993). *Four fur feet*. New York: Doubleday.

In this simple book, the reader is drawn to the /f/ sound as the phrase "four fur feet" is repeated in every sentence as a furry animal walks around the world. The same pattern is used throughout the story as we see four fur feet walk along the river, and into the country. The book must be turned around as the animal makes its way around the world.

Buller, J., & Schade, S. (1988). *I love you, good night*. New York: Simon and Schuster.

A mother and child tell how much they love each other. When the child says she loves her mother as much as "blueberry pancakes," the mother responds that she loves her child as much as "milkshakes." The child says she loves the mother as much as "frogs love flies," to which the mother responds she loves her child as much as "pigs love pies." The two go back and forth in this manner until "good night" is said. The rhyme invites the listener to participate and continue the story.

Cameron, P. (1961). *"I can't," said the ant*. New York: Coward-McCann.

Household items discuss the fall of a teapot from the counter in a kitchen and how to put it back. In a series of brief contributions to the conversation, each item says something that rhymes with its own name. "'Don't break her,' said the shaker" and "'I can't bear it,' said the carrot."

Carle, E. (1974). *All about Arthur (an absolutely absurd ape)*. New York: Franklin Watts.

Arthur, an accordion-playing ape who lives in Atlanta, feels lonely and travels from Baltimore to Yonkers making friends. In each city he makes a friend whose name matches the initial sound of the city, from a banjo-playing bear in Baltimore to a young yak in Yonkers.

Carter, D. (1990). *More bugs in boxes*. New York: Simon and Schuster.

This pop-up book presents a series of questions and answers about make-believe bugs who are found inside a variety of boxes. Both the questions and answers make use of alliteration: "What kind of bug is in the rosy red rectangle box? A bright blue big-mouth bug." Following a similar pattern is the author's *Jingle bugs* (1992, Simon and Schuster), which has a Christmas theme and makes use of rhyme: "Who's in the chimney, warm and snug? Ho, ho, ho! It's Santa Bug!"

de Regniers, B., Moore, E., White, M., & Carr, J. (1988). *Sing a song of popcorn.* New York: Scholastic.

A number of poems in this book draw attention to rhyme and encourage children to experiment with it. Also included are poems that play with sounds within words. In "Galoshes" the author describes the slippery slush "as it slooshes and sloshes and splishes and sploshes" around a child's galoshes. In "Eletelephony" sounds are mixed up and substituted for one another: "Once there was an elephant, Who tried to use the telephant...."

Deming, A.G. (1994). *Who is tapping at my window?* New York: Penguin.

A young girl hears a tapping at her window and asks, "Who is there?" The farm animals each respond, "It's not I," and she discovers that it is the rain. The book is predictable in that each pair of responding animals rhymes: The loon responds, followed by the raccoon. The dog's response is followed by the frog's.

Ehlert, L. (1989). *Eating the alphabet: Fruits and vegetables from A to Z.* San Diego, CA: Harcourt Brace Jovanovich.

Fruits and vegetables are offered in print and pictures for each letter of the alphabet in this book. For example, the following items are displayed for *B*: a blueberry, a Brussels sprout, a bean, a beet, a broccoli, and a banana.

Emberley, B. (1992). *One wide river to cross.* Boston, MA: Little, Brown.

This Caldecott Honor Book is an adaptation of the traditional African American spiritual about Noah's ark. Through the use of rhyme, the author describes the animals gathering on board one by one (while "Japhelth played the big bass drum"), two by two ("The alligator lost his shoe"), and so on up to ten, when the rains begin.

Fortunata. (1968). *Catch a little fox.* New York: Scholastic.

A group of children talk about going hunting, identifying animals they will catch and where they will keep each one. A frog will be put in a log, a cat will be put in a hat, and so forth. The story concludes with the animals in turn capturing the children, putting them in a ring and listening to them sing. All are then released. The music is included in this book. A different version of this story that includes a brontosaurus (who is put in a chorus) and armadillo (who is put in a pillow) is J. Langstaff's (1974) *Oh, a-hunting we will go*, published by Atheneum, New York.

Galdone, P. (1968). *Henny Penny.* New York: Scholastic.

A hen becomes alarmed when an acorn hits her on the head. She believes the sky is falling, and on her way to inform the king she meets several animals who join her until they are all eaten by Foxy Loxy. This classic story is included here because of the amusing rhyming names of the animals. Another release of this story is S. Kellogg's *Chicken Little* (1985), published by Mulberry Books, New York.

Geraghty, P. (1992). *Stop that noise!* New York: Crown.

A mouse is annoyed with the many sounds of the forest and implores the cicada to stop its "zee-zee-zee-zee," the frog to stop its "woopoo," until it hears far more disturbing sounds—the "Brrrm" and "Crrrrrr

RACKA-DACKA-RACKA-SHOONG" of a bulldozer felling trees. The presentation of animal and machine sounds makes this book useful in drawing attention to the sounds in our language.

Gordon, J. (1991). *Six sleepy sheep*. New York: Puffin Books.

Six sheep try to fall asleep by slurping celery soup, telling spooky stories, singing songs, and sipping simmered milk. The use of the /s/ sound, prevalent throughout, amuses listeners as they anticipate the sheep's antics.

Hague, K. (1984). *Alphabears*. New York: Henry Holt.

In this beautifully illustrated book, 26 teddy bears introduce the alphabet and make use of alliteration. Teddy bear John loves jam and jelly. Quimbly is a quilted bear, and Pam likes popcorn and pink lemonade.

Hawkins, C., & Hawkins, J. (1986). *Tog the dog*. New York: G.P. Putnam's Sons.

This book tells the story of Tog the dog who likes to jog, gets lost in the fog, and falls into a bog. With the exception of the final page, where the letters *og* appear in large type, the pages in the book are not full width. As the reader turns the narrower pages throughout the text a new letter appears and lines up with the *og* so that when Tog falls into the bog, for example, a large letter *b* lines up with *og* to make the word *bog*. This is a great book for both developing phonemic awareness and pointing out a spelling pattern. Also by these authors are *Jen the hen* (1985), *Mig the pig* (1984), and *Pat the cat* (1993), all published by G.P. Putnam's sons.

Hymes, L., & Hymes, J. (1964). *Oodles of noodles*. New York: Young Scott Books.

Several of the poems in this collection make use of nonsense words in order to complete a rhyme. In "Oodles of Noodles," the speaker requests oodles of noodles because they are favorite foodles. In "Spinach," the authors list a series of words, including *spin*, *span*, *spun*, and *spoony*, each beginning with the /sp/ sound until they finally end with the word *spinach*. Many of the poems point out spelling patterns that will be entertaining to an older audience.

Krauss, R. (1985). *I can fly*. New York: Golden Press.

In this simple book, a child imitates the actions of a variety of animals. "A cow can moo. I can too." "I can squirm like a worm." The rhyming element combined with the charm of the child's imaginative play makes the story engaging. On the final page, nonsense words that rhyme are used, encouraging listeners to experiment with sounds themselves: "Gubble gubble gubble I'm a mubble in a pubble."

Kuskin, K. (1990). *Roar and more*. New York: HarperTrophy.

This book includes many poems and pictures that portray the sounds that animals make. Both the use of rhyme and presentation of animal sounds ("Ssnnaaaarrll" for the tiger, "Hsssssss" for the snake) draw children's attention to sounds. An earlier edition of this book won the 1979 NCTE Award for Excellence in Poetry for Children.

Lewison, W. (1992). *Buzz said the bee*. New York: Scholastic.

A series of animals sit on top of one another in this story. Before each animal climbs on top of the next, it does something that rhymes with the animal it approaches. For instance, the hen dances a jig before sitting on the pig. The pig takes a bow before sitting on the cow.

Martin, B. (1974). *Sounds of a powwow*. New York: Holt, Rinehart, & Winston.

Included in this volume is the song "K-K-K-Katy" in which the first consonant of several words is isolated and repeated.

Marzollo, J. (1989). *The teddy bear book*. New York: Dial.

Poems about teddy bears adapted from songs, jump rope rhymes, ball-bouncing chants, cheers, and story poems are presented. Use of rhyme is considerable, from the well known, "Teddy bear, teddy bear, turn around, Teddy bear, teddy bear, touch the ground" to the less familiar, "Did you ever, ever, ever in your teddy bear life see a teddy bear dance with his wife?" and the response, "No I never, never, never...." Play with sounds is obvious in the poem "Teddy Boo and Teddy Bear" where the author says, "Icabocker, icabocker, icabocker, boo! Icabocker, soda cracker, phooey on you!"

Obligado, L, (1983). *Faint frogs feeling feverish and other terrifically tantalizing tongue twisters*. New York: Viking.

For each letter of the alphabet, one or more alliterative tongue twister is presented, accompanied by humorous illustrations. *S* has smiling snakes sipping strawberry sodas, a shy spider spinning, and a swordfish sawing. *T* presents two toucans tying ties, turtles tasting tea, and tigers trying trousers.

Ochs, C.P. (1991). *Moose on the loose*. Minneapolis, MN: Carolrhoda Books.

A moose escapes from the zoo in the town of Zown and at the same time a chartreuse caboose disappears. The zookeeper runs throughout the town asking citizens if they have seen a "moose on the loose in a chartreuse caboose." No one has seen the moose but each has seen a different animal. Included among the many citizens is Ms. Cook who saw a pig wearing a wig, Mr. Wu who saw a weasel paint at an easel, and Mrs. Case who saw a skunk filling a trunk. Each joins in the search.

Otto, C. (1991). *Dinosaur chase*. New York: HarperTrophy.

A mother dinosaur reads her young one a story about dinosaurs in which "dinosaur crawl, dinosaur creep, tiptoe dinosaur, dinosaur seek." Both alliteration and rhyme are present in this simple, colorful book.

Parry, C. (1991). *Zoomerang-a-boomerang: Poems to make your belly laugh*. New York: Puffin Books.

Nearly all of the poems in this collection play with language, particularly through the use of predictable and humorous rhyme patterns. In "Oh my, no more pie," the meat's too red, so the writer has some bread. When the bread is too brown, the writer goes to town, and so forth. In "What they said," each of 12 animals says something that rhymes with its name. For instance, a pup says, "Let's wake up," and a lark says, "It's still dark."

Patz, N. (1983). *Moses supposes his toeses are roses*. San Diego, CA: Harcourt Brace Jovanovich.

Seven rhymes are presented here, each of which plays on language to engage the listener. Rhyme is predictable in "Sweetie Maguire" when she shouts "Fire! Fire!" and Mrs. O'Hair says, "Where? Where?" Alliteration makes "Betty Botter" a tongue twister: "But a bit of better butter—that will make my batter better!" Assonance adds humor to "The tooter" when the tooter tries to tutor two tooters to toot!

Pomerantz, C. (1993). *If I had a paka*. New York: Mulberry.

Eleven languages are represented among the 12 poems included in this volume. The author manipulates words as in "You take the blueberry, I'll take the dewberry. You don't want the blueberry, OK take the bayberry...." Many berries are mentioned, including the "chuckleberry." Phonemes are highlighted when languages other than English are introduced. The Vietnamese translation of the following draws attention to rhyme and repetition: I like fish, Toy tik ka; I like chicken, Toy tik ga; I like duck, Toy tik veet; I like meat, Toy tik teet.

Prelutsky, J. (1982). *The baby Uggs are hatching.* New York: Mulberry.

Twelve poems describe unusual creatures such as the sneepies, the smasheroo, and the numpy-numpy-numpity. Although some of the vocabulary is advanced (the Quossible has an irascible temper), most of the poems will be enjoyed by young children who will delight in the humorous use of words and sounds. For instance, "The Sneezysnoozer sneezes in a dozen sneezy sizes, it sneezes little breezes and it sneezes big surprises."

Prelutsky, J. (1989). *Poems of A. Nonny Mouse.* New York: Alfred A. Knopf.

A. Nonny Mouse finally gets credit for all her works that were previously attributed to "Anonymous" in this humorous selection of poems that is appropriate for all ages. Of particular interest for developing phonemic awareness are poems such as "How much wood would a woodchuck chuck" and "Betty Botter bought some butter."

Provenson, A., & Provenson, M. (1977). *Old Mother Hubbard.* New York: Random House.

In this traditional rhyme, Old Mother Hubbard runs errand after errand for her dog. When she comes back from buying him a wig, she finds him dancing a jig. When she returns from buying him shoes, she finds him reading the news.

Raffi. (1987). *Down by the bay.* New York: Crown.

Two young children try to outdo each other in making up rhymes with questions like, "Did you ever see a goose kissing a moose?" and "Did you ever see a bear combing his hair?" Music is included.

Raffi. (1989). *Tingalayo.* New York: Crown.

Here the reader meets a man who calls for his donkey, Tingalayo, and describes its antics through the use of rhyme and rhythm. Phrases such as "Me donkey dance, me donkey sing, me donkey wearin' a diamond ring" will make children laugh, and they will easily contribute additional verses to this song which is also a story.

Sendak, M. (1990). *Alligators all around: An alphabet.* New York: HarperTrophy.

Sendak introduces the reader to the alphabet with the help of alligators who have headaches (for H) and keep kangaroos (for K).

Shaw, N. (1989). *Sheep on a ship.* Boston, MA: Houghton Mifflin.

Sheep sailing on a ship run into trouble when facing a sudden storm. This entertaining story makes use of rhyme (waves lap and sails flap), alliteration (sheep on a ship), and assonance ("It rains and hails and shakes the sails").

Showers, P. (1991). *The listening walk.* New York: HarperTrophy.

A little girl and her father go for a walk with their dog, and the listener is treated to the variety of sounds they hear while walking. These include "thhhhh...," the steady whisper sound of some sprinklers, and "whithh whithh," the sound of other sprinklers that turn around and around. Some phonemes are elongated as in "eeeeeeyowwwoooo...," the sound of a jet overhead. Some phonemes are substituted as in "bik bok bik bok," the sounds of high heels on the pavement.

Silverstein, S. (1964). *A giraffe and a half.* New York: HarperCollins.

Using cumulative and rhyming patterns, Silverstein builds the story of a giraffe who has a rose on his nose, a bee on his knee, some glue on his shoe, and so on until he undoes the story by reversing the events.

Staines, B. (1989). *All God's critters got a place in the choir*. New York: Penguin.

This lively book make use of rhyme to tell of the places that numerous animals (an ox and a fox, a grizzly bear, a possum and a porcupine, bullfrogs) have in the world's choir. "Some sing low, some sing higher, some sing out loud on the telephone wire."

Seuss, Dr. (1963). *Dr. Seuss's ABC*. New York: Random House.

Each letter of the alphabet is presented along with an amusing sentence in which nearly all of the words begin with the targeted letter. "Many mumbling mice are making midnight music in the moonlight...mighty nice."

Seuss, Dr. (1965). *Fox in socks*. New York. Random House.

Before beginning this book, the reader is warned to take the book slowly because the fox will try to get the reader's tongue in trouble. Language play is the obvious focus of this book. Assonance patterns occur throughout, and the listener is exposed to vowel sound changes when beetles battle, ducks like lakes, and ticks and clocks get mixed up with the chicks and tocks.

Seuss, Dr. (1974). *There's a wocket in my pocket*. New York: Random House.

A child talks about the creatures he has found around the house. These include a "nooth grush on my tooth brush" and a "zamp in the lamp." The initial sounds of common household objects are substituted with other sounds to make the nonsense creatures in this wonderful example of play with language.

Tallon, R. (1979). *Zoophabets*. New York: Scholastic.

Letter by letter the author names fictional animals and, in list form, tells where each lives and what each eats. All, of course, begin with the targeted letter. "Runk," for example, lives in "rain barrels" and eats "raindrops, rusty rainbows, ripped rubbers, raincoats, rhubarb."

Van Allsburg, C. *The Z was zapped*. Boston, MA: Houghton Mifflin.

A series of mishaps befall the letters of the alphabet. *A* is crushed by an avalanche, *B* is badly bitten, *C* is cut to ribbons, and so forth. Other alphabet books using alliteration include G. Base's *Animalia* (1987), published by Harry N. Abrams, K. Greenaway's (1993) *A apple pie*, published by Derrydale, and J. Patience's (1993) *An amazing alphabet*, published by Random House.

Winthrop, E. (1986). *Shoes*. New York: HarperTrophy.

This rhyming book surveys familiar and some not-so-familiar types of shoes. The book begins, "There are shoes to buckle, shoes to tie, shoes too low, and shoes too high." Later we discover, "Shoes for fishing, shoes for wishing, rubber shoes for muddy squishing." The rhythm and rhyme invite participation and creative contributions.

Zemach, M. (1976). *Hush, little baby*. New York: E.P. Dutton.

In this lullaby, parents attempt to console a crying baby by promising a number of outrageous things including a mockingbird, a diamond ring, a billy goat, and a cart and bull. The verse is set to rhyme, for example, "If that cart and bull turn over, Poppa's gonna buy you a dog named Rover," and children can easily innovate on the rhyme and contribute to the list of items being promised.

REFERENCES

Adams, M.J. (1990). *Beginning to read: Thinking and learning about print*. Cambridge, MA: Massachusetts Institute of Technology Press.

Ball, E., & Blachman, B. (1988). Phoneme segmentation training: Effect on reading readiness. *Annals of Dyslexia, 38*, 208–225.

Bradley, L., & Bryant, P. (1983). Categorizing sounds and learning to read—A causal connection. *Nature, 301*, 419–421.

Cunningham, A.E. (1990). Explicit versus implicit instruction in phonemic awareness. *Journal of Experimental Child Psychology, 50*, 429–444.

Geller, L.G. (1982a). Grasp of meaning in children: Theory into practice. *Language Arts, 59*, 571–579.

Geller, L.G. (1982b). Linguistic consciousness-raising: Child's play. *Language Arts, 59*, 120–125.

Geller, L.G. (1983). Children's rhymes and literacy learning: Making connections. *Language Arts, 60*, 184–193.

Griffith, P.L., & Olson, M.W. (1992). Phonemic awareness helps beginning readers break the code. *The Reading Teacher, 45*, 516–523.

Lundberg, I., Frost, J., & Peterson, O. (1988). Effects of an extensive program for stimulating phonological awareness in preschool children. *Reading Research Quarterly, 23*, 263–284.

Mattingly, I. (1984). Reading, linguistic awareness, and language acquisition. In J. Downing & R. Valtin (Eds.), *Language awareness and learning to read* (pp. 9–25). New York: Springer-Verlag.

Stanovich, K.E. (1994). Romance and reality. *The Reading Teacher, 47*, 280–291.

Yopp, H.K. (1992). Developing phonemic awareness in young children. *The Reading Teacher, 45*, 696–703.

Making Words: Enhancing the Invented Spelling-Decoding Connection

Patricia M. Cunningham, James W. Cunningham

ince the pioneering work of Read (1971, 1975) and Beers and Henderson (1977), young children's invented spellings (incorrect attempts to spell words while writing) have been recognized as powerful indicators of their developing phonemic awareness and knowledge of sound-letter relations (Adams, 1990; Henderson, 1990). In recent years, a number of studies have documented a strong general relation between spelling ability and the ability to identify words in reading. Zutell and Rasinski (1989) discovered that the spelling variables are highly related to children's oral reading accuracy rate and phrasing. Similarly, Gill (1989) determined that the spelling and word recognition abilities of first, second, and third graders are closely related processes. Hall (1991) demonstrated that second-grade students' ability to spell words correctly is a near-perfect predictor that they will also be able to read those words.

Research suggests that invented spelling and decoding are mirror-like processes that make use of the same store of phonological knowledge. Morris and Perney (1984), Mann, Tobin, and Wilson (1987), and Ferroli and Shanahan (1987) found children's developmental spelling in kindergarten or beginning first grade to be a strong predictor of reading achievement at the end of first grade. In complementary fashion, Nelson (1990) discovered that early phonics instruction accelerates students' development of correct short vowel spelling.

In addition to providing a window on the growth of children's phonetic knowledge, invented spelling during writing is increasingly seen as possessing reading instructional value as well (Clay, 1991; Cunningham, 1991a). Having young students engage in invented spelling during writing not only helps them become better spellers but also facilitates their development of decoding ability in reading (Adams, 1990; Chomsky, 1971; Richgels, 1987). Clarke (1988) compared the effectiveness of invented spelling versus an emphasis on correct spelling in first-grade classrooms. The children who had invented spellings were superior to the others on measures of word decoding at the end of the year. In general, as children improve in the phonetic sophistication of their invented spellings, their later success in learning to read words becomes much more likely (Mann et al., 1987; Morris & Perney, 1984).

More and more children in kindergarten and first grade are being encouraged to engage in writing with invented spelling, in part at least to help develop their decoding ability in reading. Although many children will benefit from this practice, some authorities (Adams, 1990; Clay, 1991) have expressed the concern that at-risk readers and writers will not learn enough from writing with invented spelling because of its indirect nature and because these students often lack phonemic awareness and knowledge of letter-sound and sound-letter relations. This concern has led some researchers to guide students' invented spelling in the early stages to help them achieve phonemic abilities they might not otherwise develop.

In Reading Recovery, for example, part of each lesson is dedicated to guided invented-spelling activities. Reading Recovery teachers use Elkonin boxes, word building with a subset of magnetic letters, and story writing with listening for the sounds in words to guide invented spelling (Clay, 1985). Such guidance provides a "slicing" of the invented spelling task. Because the number of phonemes is limited and the task of attending to them is made more explicit, a guided invented spelling task is more likely to help children develop phonemic awareness than is unguided invented spelling.

The attempt to apply some of the principles of Reading Recovery to a group setting, as well as the desire to enhance the benefits of writing with invented spelling, has led us to the development of a group-guided invented-spelling instructional strategy that we call Making Words. Our strategy, however, should *not* be used *instead* of writing with invented spelling; rather, Making Words should be used *along with* regular writing activities to increase the likelihood that children will develop decoding ability. Writing with invented spelling should be a regular part of every basic reading program.

Making Words is currently being used by a number of first- and second-grade teachers who are doing it daily along with daily writing with invented spelling. Although Making Words has only been investigated as one component of multimethod, multilevel reading instruction, initial results of this combination are very encouraging (Cunningham, 1991b; Cunningham, Hall, & Defee, 1991).

How to Plan and Teach Making Words Lessons

Making Words is an activity in which children are individually given some letters that they use to make words. During the 15-minute activity, children make 12–15 words, beginning with two-letter words and continuing with three-, four-, five-letter and longer words until the final word is made. The final word (a six-, seven-, or eight-letter word) always includes all the letters they have that day, and children are usually eager to figure out what word can be made from all the letters. Making Words is an active, hands-on manipulative activity in which children discover sound-letter relations and learn how to look for patterns in words. They also learn that changing just one letter or even the sequence of the letters changes the whole word.

Planning a Making Words Lesson

To plan a Making Words lesson, begin with the word you want to end with (*spider* in the following lesson). Write the word you want to end with on an index card and then consider what other words you could have the children make with some of the same letters. There are always more words possible than can be made in a 15-minute lesson. Select the words and the order in which they are to be made so that children begin to see that when you change or add a letter, the word changes in a predictable way. At the end of each lesson, draw children's attention to certain spelling patterns and use these words to help them think about how they might spell words needed in their own writing. Table 1 presents a detailed set of steps to be taken when planning a Making Words lesson.

Teaching a Making Words lesson

Following is an example of a Making Words lesson done in one first-grade classroom. Table 2 presents a summary of the steps involved in teaching a Making Words lesson.

For this particular lesson, each child had four consonant letters (*d, p, r, s*) and two vowel letters (*i, e*). In a pocket chart at the front of the room, the teacher had placed large cards with the same six letters. Her cards, like the small letter cards used by individual children, had the uppercase letter on one side and

the lowercase letter on the other side. The consonant letters were written in black, and the vowel letters were written in red.

The teacher began by making sure that each child had all the letters needed. "What two vowel letters will we use to make words today?" she asked. The children held up their red *i* and *e* and responded appropriately. "Why are vowels important?" she asked. "Because every word has to have at least one," responded the children in chorus.

The teacher then wrote the numeral 2 on the board and said, "The two-letter word I want you to make today is *Ed*. I have a cousin whose name is Ed." She watched as the children quickly put the letters *E* and *d* in their holders and was glad to see most children proudly displaying the uppercase *E*. The children knew that she usually put at least one name in every Making Word lesson, and they

---

Table 1
Steps in planning a Making Words lesson

1. Decide what the final word in the lesson will be. In choosing this word, consider its number of vowels, child interest, curriculum tie-ins you can make, and letter-sound patterns you can draw children's attention to through the word sorting at the end.

2. Make a list of shorter words that can be made from the letters of the final word.

3. From all the words you listed, pick 12–15 words that include: (a) words that you can sort for the pattern(s) you want to emphasize; (b) little words and big words so that the lesson is a multilevel lesson; (c) words that can be made with the same letters in different places (e.g., *barn, bran*) so children are reminded that when spelling words, the order of the letters is crucial; (d) a proper name or two to remind them where we use capital letters; and (e) words that most of the students have in their listening vocabularies.

4. Write all the words on index cards and order them from shortest to longest.

5. Once you have the two-letter, three-letter, etc., words together, order them further so that you can emphasize letter patterns and how changing the position of the letters or changing or adding just one letter results in a different word.

6. Store the cards in an envelope. Write on the envelope the words in order and the patterns you will sort for at the end.

Table 2
Steps in teaching a Making Words lesson

1. Place the large letter cards in a pocket chart or along the chalk ledge.

2. Have designated children give one letter to each child. (Let the passer keep the reclosable bag containing that letter and have the same child collect that letter when the lesson is over.)

3. Hold up and name the letters on the large letter cards, and have the children hold up their matching small letter cards.

4. Write the numeral 2 (or 3, if there are no two-letter words in this lesson) on the board. Tell them to take two letters and make the first word. Use the word in a sentence after you say it.

5. Have a child who has the first word made correctly make the same word with the large letter cards. Encourage anyone who did not make the word correctly at first to fix the word when they see it made correctly.

6. Continue having them make words, erasing and changing the number on the board to indicate the number of letters needed. Use the words in simple sentences to make sure the children understand their meanings. Remember to cue them as to whether they are just changing one letter, changing letters around, or taking all their letters out to make a word from scratch. Cue them when the word you want them to make is a proper name, and send a child who has started that name with a capital letter to make the word with the big letters.

7. Before telling them the last word, ask "Has anyone figured out what word we can make with all our letters?" If so, congratulate them and have one of them make it with the big letters. If not, say something like, "I love it when I can stump you. Use all your letters and make _____."

8. Once all the words have been made, take the index cards on which you have written the words, and place them one at a time (in the same order children made them) along the chalk ledge or in the pocket chart. Have children say and spell the words with you as you do this. Use these words for sorting and pointing out patterns. Pick a word and point out a particular spelling pattern, and ask children to find the others with that same pattern. Line these words up so that the pattern is visible.

9. To get maximum transfer to reading and writing, have the children use the patterns they have sorted to spell a few new words that you say.

Note: Some teachers have chosen to do steps 1–7 on one day and steps 8 and 9 on the following day.

were showing that they knew names should have a capital letter at the beginning. Then the teacher sent a child who had correctly made *Ed* at his seat to the pocket chart to make *Ed* with the big letters. She congratulated the child for starting it with a capital letter. The teacher then put an index card with the word *Ed* written on it along the chalk ledge.

Next the teacher erased the 2 and wrote a 3 on the board. "Add just one letter to *Ed* to make the three-letter word *red*," she instructed, noticing that some (but not all) of the children turned the *E* card over to display the lowercase *e* while making *red*. She chose a child to make *red* with the big pocket chart letters. When he turned the *E* over in the pocket chart, she asked him why he had done that, and he explained, "You can't have a capital letter in the middle of a word!" The lesson continued with all children making words with their individual letter cards, with selected children going to the pocket chart to make the word, and with the teacher putting a card with that word along the chalk ledge.

Later the teacher asked the children to make another three-letter word, *pie.* While making *pie,* many children quickly put the *p* with the *i* in their holders, but they noticed that they only had two letters. You could see them looking at their remaining letters and trying to decide if they should add the *d, s, r,* or *e* to spell *pie.* Most of the children made the right choice. When *pie* was made at the pocket chart, the teacher reminded the children that sometimes it takes two vowel letters to spell a word even though you may hear only one of the vowels.

The teacher erased the 3, wrote a 4 on the board, and asked the children to add just one letter to pie to make *pies.* Next they changed one letter to make *dies.* At this point the teacher said, "Now, don't take any letters away and don't add any, but just change your letters around and like magic you can change your *dies* to *side.*" She watched as the children thought about which letters to move in order to perform this magic trick. After making *side,* they changed it to *ride,* then to *ripe,* and then to *rise.*

The teacher erased the 4 and wrote a 5, and the children used five of their letters to make the words *pride* and *drips.* As a child was making *drips* at the pocket chart, many of the other children were manipulating all their letters trying to come up with another word. They did so because they knew that each lesson ended with a word that used all their letters, and they always liked to figure it out before the teacher said it. Today, however, the children were stumped. The teacher told them

to take all six letters and make a bug that they were going to read about in science—*spider.*

To conclude the lesson and draw the children's attention to letter patterns, the teacher asked the children to look at the words in the pocket chart: *Ed, red, rid, sip, pie, pies, dies, side, ride, ripe, rise, pride, drips, spider.* She picked up *Ed* and asked, "Who can come up here and hand me a word that rhymes with *Ed?*" A child handed her the word *red.* She then had someone find the two words that rhymed with *side—ride* and *pride.* The children spelled the rhyming words aloud in unison and decided that these words all had the same spelling pattern and that they rhymed. The teacher reminded the children that words having the same spelling pattern usually rhyme and that knowing this helps many good readers and writers read and spell words. The teacher then asked, "What if I wanted to spell *fed?* What words that you have made today rhyme with *fed?*" The children decided that *fed* rhymes with *Ed* and *red* and probably would be spelled *f-e-d.* They also decided that *slide* rhymes with *side, ride,* and *pride* and would probably be spelled *s-l-i-d-e.*

Next the teacher had the children find the three words that ended in *s: pies, dies,* and *drips.* She reminded them that an *s* is often added to a word when you mean more than one, like the word *pies.* She also stated that sometimes an *s* is added to a word when it is used in a sentence like *The water faucet drips.* She then pointed to the words *sip, ride,* and *spider* and asked them, if they were writing, how they would spell *sips, rides,* and *spiders.*

A Beginning Making Words Lesson

For the first Making Words lesson, we give the children only one vowel letter, but a different one for each lesson. The vowel letter is always written in red, and the children know they have to use it for every word. Here is a sample first lesson. The children have the vowel letter *i* and the consonant letters *g*, *n*, *p*, *r*, and *s*. Here is a possible set of steps or directives to students to follow in this first lesson:

• Take two letters and make *in*.

• Add a letter to make the three-letter word *pin*.

• Change just one letter, and turn your *pin* into a *pig*.

• Now change just one letter, and your *pig* can become a *rig*—sometimes we call a big truck a rig.

• Let's make one more three-letter word, *rip*.

• Now, let's make a four-letter word. Add a letter to *rip* and you will have *rips*.

• Change just one letter and you can change your *rips* to *nips*—sometimes a very young puppy nips at your feet.

• Now, and this is a real trick, do not add any letters and do not take any away. Just change where some of the letters are and you can change *nips* to *spin*.

• Believe it or not, you can make another word with these same four letters. Move your letters around and change *spin* to *snip*.

• There is one more word that you can make with these same four letters. Move your letters around one more time and change *snip* to *pins*—he found two safety pins.

• Let's make two more four-letter words. Use four letters to make *sing*.

• Now, change just one letter, and change *sing* to *ring*.

• Now, we will make a five-letter word. Add a letter to change *ring* to *rings*.

• Has anyone figured out what word we can make with all six letters?

• Take all six of your letters and make *spring*.

When the children have made *spring*, we draw their attention to the words they made and help them sort for a variety of patterns: *in*, *pin*, *pig*, *rig*, *rip*, *rips*, *nips*, *spin*, *snip*, *pins*, *sing*, *ring*, *rings*, *spring*. First, we might have them bring the four words that they made with the same four letters—*nips*, *spin*, *snip*, and *pins*. The children pronounce the words and listen for where they hear each of the letters. Many children are amazed to learn that more than one word can be made with the same letters and that you can make a different word simply by putting the same letters in different places.

Next, we might have them find the words that have more than one letter before the vowel, *spin*, *snip*, and *spring*, and help them to hear how these beginning letters are blended together. We could ask them to think how they would begin to spell *snake*. Would it begin like *spin*, like *snip*, or like *spring*? They could also determine that *spout* begins like *spin* and that *spray* begins like *spring*.

Two-Vowel Making Words Lessons

In the preceding beginning lessons culminating in the spelling of *spring*, the emphasis is on how words change as different letters are added and on helping children begin to understand the importance of where in the words letters occur. It becomes easier to construct Making Words lessons when using two vowels as in the prior lesson in which spider was spelled. Here is another sample lesson with two vowels.

Letters: a e b d n e r
Words to make: be bed bad ban Ben bean bead
 read dear Brad bran brand
 Brenda

In this lesson, you might want children to notice how the word changes when the vowel is an *a* by itself, an *e* by itself, and the *ea* together. You would end the lesson by sorting the words into these categories and then talking about the letter patterns. Depending on how far along children are in their understanding of letter patterns, you may want to include the word *bread* and then point out that sometimes the *ead* pattern has the sound you hear at the end of *bead* and sometimes it has the sound at the end of *bread*. In Making Words lessons, the teacher decides which words to have them make and in which order so that children are led to discover the most common spelling patterns and their predictable variations.

Young children will need much practice with the various vowel combinations in order to be able to use them effectively to spell words in their writing. Many teachers teach several lessons in a row that end in different words but that emphasize the same vowel combinations. Here are two more lessons used to help children work with *e*, *a*, and *ea*:

> Letters: a e d g n r s
> Words to make: an Dan den Ned red read dear near Dean grade garden gardens
>
> Letters: a e c d n l
> Words to make: Al ad Ed Ned led lad land lend lean lead deal clean candle

Once children understand that there are five vowels, plan a lesson that has the letter *y* in it. Make the *y* letter card in green or some color other than the red and black used for the others. Children notice immediately that the *y* is a different color, and you can explain that *y* is sometimes a vowel and sometimes a consonant. Following is a lesson that introduces *y* as both vowel and consonant. After making the words, the children sorted them according to whether *y* was a consonant letter or a vowel let-

ter and noticed that when *y* is a vowel letter it can represent the sounds in *try* and *country*.

> Letters: o u y c n r t
> Words to make: you toy try cry your Troy corn corny court count county country

Additional sets of letters and words to spell can be found in the Appendix to this article.

Making Big Words Lessons

Most of the lessons just described would be used with first- or second-grade students. We also have done Making Words lessons with intermediate-grade children and with older remedial readers. We call these lessons Making Big Words. For Making Big Words lessons, we print the letters on strips of paper (vowels followed by consonants in alphabetical order, so as not to give away the big word) and duplicate these. The children cut their strips into letters and manipulate these to make words. Many big words contain the letters to make hundreds of other words. We pick and choose which words we want them to make and the order in which we want them to make them so as to maximize the possibilities for the children to see patterns.

Just as in Making Words, we end each Making Big Words lesson by sorting the words for a variety of patterns. Sometimes this sorting takes place in another lesson on the day after the words have been made. Because there are so many words that can be made with these letters, we give the children 2 minutes at the beginning of each Making Big Words lesson to manipulate the letters and see what words they can come up with. After this "free play," we direct them to make certain words in a certain order so that they will see how words change in predictable ways as you change and add letters. Here is a sample Making Big Words lesson.

Letters: e e i i o l n s t v
Words to make: vest vent sent event novel inlet
           invite invest vision violin violet
           violent novelist novelties televi-
           sion
Sort for: sion vio in ent

Why Making Words Works

The classrooms in which Making Words and writing with invented spelling are being used side by side are having encouraging results on the decoding abilities of the students without traditional phonics instruction (Cunningham, 1991b; Cunningham et al., 1991). Making Words is apparently a multilevel activity for children. Those who lack phonemic awareness seem to develop that awareness through participation in the lessons. Because the students listen intently for the sounds in words in order to make them and then try to remember or select the letters that can represent those sounds, Making Words has similarities to the most effective training in phonemic awareness (Ball & Blachman, 1991; Ehri & Wilce, 1987). Those children who have phonemic awareness learn letter-sound correspondences a few at a time, and they learn other strategies and insights about decoding and spelling phonetically regular words.

If you ask the children what they think of Making Words, they will probably answer, "It's fun!" From the moment that they get their letters, they begin moving them around and making whatever words they can. They are particularly eager to figure out the word that can be made with all the letters. Once the children begin making the words the teacher asks them to make, the activity is fast paced and keeps the children involved. They also enjoy the sorting. Finding words that rhyme, words that begin alike, words that can all be changed into other words just by moving around the letters, and other patterns is like solving a riddle or a puzzle. After children have been making words and sorting for several weeks, they begin telling the teacher in what patterns the words should be sorted.

Making Words is a powerful activity because within one instructional format there are endless possibilities for discovering how our alphabetic system works. It is a quick, every-pupil-response, manipulative activity with which children get actively involved. By beginning every Making Words activity with some short easy words and ending with a big word that uses all the letters, the lessons provide practice for the slowest learners and challenge for all.

References

Adams, M.J. (1990). *Beginning to read: Thinking and learning about print.* Cambridge, MA: MIT Press.

Ball, E.W., & Blachman, B.A. (1991). Does phoneme awareness training in kindergarten make a difference in early word recognition and developmental spelling? *Reading Research Quarterly, 26,* 49–66.

Beers, J.W., & Henderson, E.H. (1977). A study of developing orthographic concepts among first graders. *Research in the Teaching of English, 11,* 133–148.

Chomsky, C. (1971). Write first, read later. *Childhood Education, 47,* 296–299.

Clarke, L.K. (1988). Invented versus traditional spelling in first graders' writings: Effects on learning to spell and read. *Research in the Teaching of English, 22,* 281–309.

Clay, M.M. (1985). *The early detection of reading difficulties* (3rd ed.). Portsmouth, NH: Heinemann.

Clay, M.M. (1991). *Becoming literate: The construction of inner control.* Portsmouth, NH: Heinemann.

Cunningham, P.M. (1991a). *Phonics they use: Words for reading and writing.* New York: HarperCollins.

Cunningham, P.M. (1991b). Research directions: Multimethod, multilevel literacy instruction in first grade. *Language Arts, 68,* 578–584.

Cunningham, P.M., Hall, D.P., & Defee, M. (1991). Nonability grouped, multilevel instruction: A year in a first-grade classroom. *The Reading Teacher, 44,* 566–571.

Ehri, L.C., & Wilce, L.S. (1987). Does learning to spell help beginners learn to read words? *Reading Research Quarterly, 22,* 47–65.

Ferroli, L., & Shanahan, T. (1987). Kindergarten spelling: Explaining its relationship to first-grade reading. In J.E. Readence & R.S. Baldwin (Eds.), *Research in literacy: Merging perspectives.* (Thirty-sixth Yearbook of the National Reading Conference, pp. 93–99). Rochester, NY: National Reading Conference.

Gill, J.T., Jr. (1989). The relationship between word recognition and spelling in the primary grades. *Reading Psychology, 10,* 117–136.

Hall, D.P. (1991). *Investigating the relationship between word knowledge and cognitive ability.* Unpublished doctoral dissertation, University of North Carolina at Greensboro.

Henderson, E.H. (1990). *Teaching spelling* (2nd ed.). Boston, MA: Houghton Mifflin.

Mann, V.A., Tobin, P., & Wilson, R. (1987). Measuring phonological awareness through the invented spellings of kindergarten children. *Merrill-Palmer Quarterly, 33,* 365–391.

Morris, D., & Perney, J. (1984). Developmental spelling as a predictor of first-grade reading achievement. *The Elementary School Journal, 84,* 440–457.

Nelson, L. (1990). The influence of phonics instruction on spelling progress. In J. Zutell & S. McCormick (Eds.), *Literacy theory and research: Analyses from multiple paradigms.* (Thirty-ninth Yearbook of the National Reading Conference, pp. 241–247). Chicago, IL: National Reading Conference.

Read, C. (1971). Pre-school children's knowledge of English phonology. *Harvard Educational Review, 41,* 1–34.

Read, C. (1975). *Children's categorization of speech sounds in English.* Urbana, IL: National Council of Teachers of English.

Richgels, D.J. (1987). Experimental reading with invented spelling (ERIS): A preschool and kindergarten method. *The Reading Teacher, 40,* 522–529.

Zutell, J., & Rasinski, T. (1989). Reading and spelling connections in third and fifth grade students. *Reading Psychology, 10,* 137–155.

Appendix: Sample Making Words Lessons

These lessons go from very simple (5–6 letters with only one vowel) to moderate (6–8 letters with 2 vowels) to complex (at least 9 letters, unlimited vowels). List the letters with all the vowel letters first then all the consonant letters in alphabetical order so as not to give any clues to the big word that will end the lesson. Words separated by a / indicate places in the lesson where the same letters can be rearranged to form a different word.

Lessons using only one vowel:

Letter cards:	u k n r s t
Words to make:	us nut rut run sun sunk runs ruts/rust tusk stun stunk trunk trunks
Sort for:	rhymes s pairs (run runs; rut ruts; trunk trunks)
Letter cards:	o p r s s t
Words to make:	or top/pot rot port stop/spot sort sorts stops/spots sport sports
Sort for:	or o s pairs
Letter cards:	e d n p s s
Words to make:	Ed Ned/end/den pen pens dens/send sped spend spends
Sort for:	rhymes names s pairs
Letter cards:	a h l p s s
Words to make:	Al pal/lap Sal sap has/ash sash lash pass pals/laps/slap slaps slash splash
Sort for:	rhymes names s pairs
Letter cards:	a c c h r s t
Words to make:	art/tar car cat cart cars/scar star scat cash rash trash crash chart scratch
Sort for:	a ar rhymes
Letter cards:	i c k r s t
Words to make:	is it kit sit sir stir sick Rick tick skit skirt stick trick tricks
Sort for:	i ir sk rhymes

Lessons with two vowels, 6–8 letters:

Letter cards:	e u d h n r t
Words to make:	red Ted Ned/den/end her hut herd turn hunt hurt under hunted turned thunder
Sort for:	u ur e er ed pairs
Letter cards:	e u l r s t t
Words to make:	us use/Sue let set true rule test rest rust trust result turtle turtles
Sort for:	e u ue rhymes
Letter cards:	a e c h p r t
Words to make:	at art car cat hat chat cart heat heap cheap cheat/teach peach preach chapter
Sort for:	c h ch a ar rhymes
Letter cards:	a o c r r s t t
Words to make:	at rat rot cot cat/act coat cast cost coast toast roast actor carrot carrots tractors
Sort for:	a o oa rhymes act actor
Letter cards:	a e l n p s t
Words to make:	pat pet pen pan pal pale/peal pets/pest pane plan plane plant plate/pleat planets
Sort for:	a e ea a-e p pl rhymes

(continued)

Letter cards:	a u y d h r s t
Words to make:	say day dry try shy stay tray rust dust duty dusty rusty stray sturdy Thursday
Sort for:	ay y-try rusty tr st
Letter cards:	a u b b h s t t
Words to make:	us bus/sub tub/but bat/tab hut hat that bath stab tubs/stub bathtubs
Sort for:	a u th rhymes
Letter cards:	e i d f n r s
Words to make:	Ed red rid end fin fine fire ride side send dine diner rides fires friends
Sort for:	e i i-e s pairs rhymes
Letter cards:	a e h n p r t
Words to make:	an at hat pat pan pen pet net ate/eat heat neat path parent panther
Sort for:	a e ea rhymes
Letter cards:	e i k n s t t
Words to make:	it in ink kit sit net/ten tin tint tent skit skin/sink stink kittens
Sort for:	i e sk rhymes
Letter cards:	a e g m n s t
Words to make:	man men met mat Nat net/ten tan mean/mane mate/meat neat stem steam magnets
Sort for:	a e ea a-e rhymes
Letter cards:	e e n p r s t
Words to make:	see ten teen tree step/pest rest rent sent steep stern enter serpent/present
Sort for:	e ee er rhymes
Letter cards:	a e g n r s t
Words to make:	ant age sag rag rage star stag stage great/grate grant agent range strange
Sort for:	st gr g-rag rage rhymes

Lessons for big words

Letters on strips:	a a a e i b c h l l p t
Words to make:	itch able cable table batch patch pitch petal label chapel capital capable alphabet alphabetical
Sort for:	el le al itch atch
Letters on strips:	a a e e u h k q r s t
Words to make:	use heat rake take shake quake quart earth reuse square quaker retake reheat/heater karate request earthquake
Sort for:	qu re ake-take rake quake shake retake earthquakes
Letters on strips:	a e e i o g n n r t
Words to make:	got gene genie giant tiger great/grate orange nation ration ignore enrage entire engine ignorant nitrogen tangerine generation
Sort for:	en tion g g (got gene)
Letters on strips:	e i u m n n r s s t t
Words to make:	sun set tie use rest rise trust untie unrest misuse sunset sunrise sunnier sunniest mistrust instruments
Sort for:	un mis er est sun sunnier sunniest sunset sunrise
Letters on strips:	e o o y c c l m r s t

(continued)

Appendix: Sample Making Words Lessons (continued)

Words to make:	room cost sore/rose rosy loot lose loser motor storm roomy cycle cycler stormy sorely costly looter motorcycles
Sort for:	ly y(rose rosy; room roomy) er
Letters on strips:	a e e e u m p r r t t
Words to make:	treat trump temper tamper repeat mature mutter trumpet pretreat repeater tamperer mutterer trumpeter premature temperature
Sort for:	pre ture er
Letters on strips:	e e o o c d k p r w
Words to make:	row cow pow owe owed word work wood cook coop cord cork droop power powder cowpoke woodpecker
Sort for:	oo(wood coop) ow(cow owe) or(work cork)

Procedures for Word Learning: Making Discoveries About Words

Irene W. Gaskins, Linnea C. Ehri, Cheryl Cress, Colleen O'Hara, Katharine Donnelly

Many first graders appear to make discoveries about words and learn to read without explicit instruction. Being read to, reading and rereading favorite books, inventing spellings, and composing text seem sufficient to get them on the road to becoming readers. However, other equally bright first graders, with similar backgrounds, experience this same rich literacy environment but do not learn to read. These are the students we teach—children who have failed in their initial attempts to learn to read.

Our students have not made discoveries about how our written language works, in some cases despite systematic phonics instruction. They are students who have devised strategies for learning words that are not very reliable or efficient. Some of our students may attempt to remember words based on their shapes or salient visual features. Others may rely on a few symbol-sound associations, often for the first and last letters of words. A few laboriously sound out syllables but are unable to blend the sounds together to produce recognizable words. Still others memorize text or rely on context clues to guess at the identities of words. In contrast, good readers read familiar words accurately and rapidly. They remember spelling patterns shared by known words and use this knowledge in decoding unknown words.

Several years ago we began to deal with the word-reading difficulties of our students by adding the Benchmark Word Identification (BWI) program (Gaskins et al., 1988; Gaskins, Gaskins, & Gaskins, 1991, 1992; Gaskins, Gaskins, Anderson, & Schommer, 1995) to our literature-based reading and writing program. In the BWI program, students are taught to read a set of key words that are high-frequency words in English and have common spelling patterns. The key words are listed on a word wall in the classroom for all to view. Students are taught that when they come to a word they do not know, they should apply the strategy of using key words to read the unknown word. We implemented this program in our school and were delighted with the results. Each year our students completed the year reading better than our students had before we began using BWI. Despite our success, however, teachers commented that some of our former BWI students (approximately 15% in 1993–1994) continued to be slow readers and tended to spell phonetically, though not necessarily accurately.

Collaborative Program Evaluation

In the fall of 1994 we decided to reevaluate our approach to word learning to see how well it matched the strengths and needs of our 13 at-risk students in the first-grade class. Eight of these students were virtual nonreaders and were repeating first grade. Five were entering first graders identified as at risk for failure in first grade. To evaluate our program, we observed in the classroom, watched videotapes of BWI lessons, and organized a study group to review the research literature about word learning. Our group was composed of the principal, reading supervisor, and two first-grade teachers. We planned to use the information gained from our observation and study to determine how instruction might be supplemented to reach our struggling readers. This investigative process led to new ways of thinking about beginning readers and their word learning and to hypotheses about what might be missing from our instruction. This article details our evaluation of the match between our students and the first-grade BWI program, our rationale for extending the program, and the kinds of extensions we introduced.

Beginning on the first day of school and continuing throughout the school year, the reading supervisor observed daily in the first-grade classroom, and the principal either observed or watched videotapes of the BWI lessons. Lessons were audiotaped to capture the dialogues used for explicit instruction, and the principal and supervisor kept running notes of their observations. The principal's notes, written in an interactive journal, were circulated each day to members of the study group who added comments based on their observations. These notes became a record of our reflections and collaboration. When one of us had a suggestion for change, that person often would teach the word identification portion of the literacy lesson block for a few days to try the new approach while other members of the study group critiqued the lessons. Thoughtful reflection was crucial to the process; thus, the videotaped lessons were critiqued daily by at least one member of the study group to examine and evaluate the changes we were making. Informal meetings also occurred daily as we fine-tuned instruction based on our observations. In addition, the study group met weekly for $1\frac{1}{2}$ hours after school to discuss possible instructional applications derived from the reading of chapters in *Reading Acquisition* (Gough, Ehri, & Treiman, 1992) and *Learning to Read: Basic Research and Its Implications* (Rieben & Perfetti, 1991). References in these texts led us to journals and other texts, as well as to discussions with several of the authors, in search of answers to our questions about word learning. Daylong retreats to develop and revise lesson plans also were built into the school year.

Our observations during the early months of the school year revealed a common weakness among our beginning readers. These beginners seemed unable to segment spoken words into their smallest sounds. They could, however, divide words into onset (the initial consonant sound or sounds) and rime (the vowel and what follows); for example, they could divide *stop* into *st* and *op*, but they could not break *stop* into four sounds. They had little awareness of letter-sound relations except in the initial positions of words. Many seemed to approach learning to read by treating each word as a new character to be memorized by any visual cue that distinguished it from the other words they knew.

Not all of our students' word identification errors, however, could be attributed solely to lack of knowledge about how language works. Some students' errors appeared to result from an impulsive style combined with anxiety about their difficulties in learning to read.

These students responded too quickly to words without looking carefully at all the letters. Despite our emphasis on using known words to decode unknown words, students tended to use other strategies when reading words in context, such as guessing the pronunciation of a word based on context alone, on context plus initial letter, or on pictures. Calling to mind one of the key words they had been taught seemed extremely difficult for most of the students.

To illustrate, one of our younger students, Adam, was able to apply what he knew about individual letter-sound matches for initial consonants and long vowels. However, after sounding out a word accurately, he often could not blend it to construct a word he recognized, perhaps because he had difficulty holding all the sounds in memory. He also gamely attempted to use the analogy approach but rarely could think of a key word with the same spelling pattern as the unknown word. As a result, he had to resort to searching the word wall for the key word. On one occasion, when he was reading with his teacher and had scanned the word wall in search of a key word, Adam said, "Tell you what, if you tell me the key word, I'll tell you the new word." When given the key word, he had no difficulty decoding the unknown word because he knew how to divide key words into onsets and rimes and how to sound out the onsets of new words. Holding in mind and blending only two sounds was much easier than dealing with many smaller sounds. Adam's major problem was calling to mind key words, as it was for most of the other students.

All 13 students enjoyed the word identification lessons and could use the key words on the word wall and on worksheets to decode unknown words. Within the first 8 weeks of school, applying the concept of onset and rime seemed natural to them. Decoding a word such as *bumper* was a cinch, when the key words *jump* and *her* were in front of them. What was not a cinch was decoding words when the key words were not visible. Our dilemma was how to move the key words that were introduced each week into each student's memory so that the words could be accessed automatically without looking at the wall. Dictating stories using key words and the daily BWI activities using these words to decode, spell, and play word games did not seem to provide the foundation these students needed to retain the key words in memory in a way that made them independent decoders. Something was missing. We turned to the research literature seeking what that might be.

Four Ways to Read Words

As we read and discussed theory and research about word learning, we gained a clearer view of the various ways that beginners read words: by sight, letter-sound decoding, analogy, and contextual guessing (Ehri, 1991, 1994). To read words by sight, readers retrieve information about the words stored in memory from previous experiences reading the words. Decoding involves sounding out the letters and blending them into sounds. Analogizing consists of accessing in memory information about familiar sight words to read unknown words; for example, reading *fellow* by recognizing how it is similar to the known word *yellow*. Contextual guessing involves using meaning-based cues in preceding text or in pictures to predict what a word might be. Whereas sight word reading is the principal way that familiar words are read, the other ways are used to read unfamiliar words that have not been stored as sight words in memory.

We had observed our students using each of these approaches to read words; however, the form of word reading receiving primary instructional attention in our program was analogizing. In the BWI program nonreaders learn as sight words a core set of words with high-frequency spelling patterns (for example, -et, -ot, -in, -and, -up). These words become the known words that are used to decode unknown words. Yet, in observing unsuccessful readers attempt to use the analogy strategy, we realized that something was missing in their processing. Although we had taught them to read the sight words they needed to analogize to new words, they seemed not to recognize the resemblance between the words they knew and similar patterns in unknown words. They did not call to mind an analogous known word to decode an unknown word. For example, upon seeing a new word such as *fellow*, they did not recognize its similarity to *yellow* even though they knew *yellow* as a sight word. We suspected it was because these students did not look carefully at the letters that composed each word but rather remembered whatever characteristics were most salient in the words they were learning.

Memory for Sight Words

We realized that we needed to find out more about how sight words are retained in memory. Research and theory (for example, Ehri, 1992) suggested that the most effective way to remember how to read sight words is not the way suggested by conventional wisdom, which is to memorize shapes or other strictly visual features of words. Rather the most effective way involves bonding the letters to the word's pronunciation held in memory so that sight of the word immediately activates its spoken form and meaning. Letter-sound correspondences are the tools that the mind uses to form the bond. However, the process of sight word reading is different from that of using letters and sounds to decode unknown words. In sight word reading, the words are read from memory, not from decoding and blending operations, because the words are familiar. As a result, the act of reading them is carried on by memory processes, not by decoding processes.

According to Ehri's (1992) work, the most effective way for beginning readers to store sight words in memory is to fully analyze the sounds in the spoken word and to match those sounds to the letters in the printed form of words. To do this, readers must know how to segment pronunciations of words into their smallest sounds, and they must know which letters typically symbolize those sounds.

Figure 1 illustrates a few fully analyzed connections that skilled beginning readers are thought to form between sounds detected in the pronunciation of words and the letters in their spellings. These readers segment words into their smallest sounds, compare the sounds to the letters they see, and determine which letter or letters match each sound. To accomplish this analysis, pronunciations as well as spellings must be segmented into the units that create the best match.

For example, in learning *can* as a sight word, the child segments *can* into its individual sounds—/c/, /a/, /n/—and matches the three sounds to the three letters in *can*. In learning *will*, the child segments three sounds /w/, /i/, /l/ and matches them to four letters. Thus, the child discovers that *w* and *i* each represent one sound, while it takes two *l*s to represent the final sound.

Similarly, in *look, snail, smash,* and *phone* it takes two letters (such as, *oo, ai, sh, ph*) to represent one of the sounds in each word. Words that students practice reading several times in this way are thought to be retained in memory as sight words. In Figure 3, we have depicted how letters in spellings match with sounds in the pronunciations of 93 BWI key words taught during 28 weeks of first-grade instruction.

In summary, Ehri's theory suggested that if we wanted students to remember and use

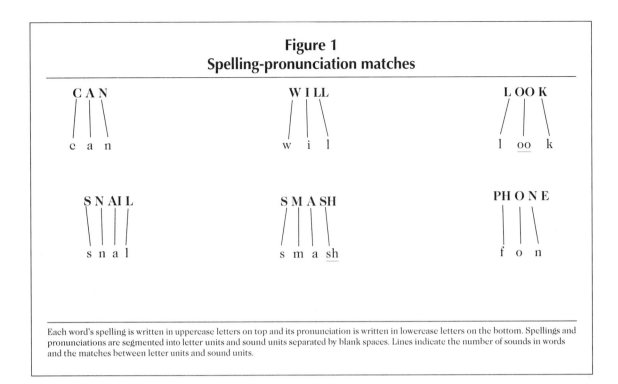

Figure 1
Spelling-pronunciation matches

CAN → can

WILL → wil

LOOK → look (oo)

SNAIL → snal

SMASH → smash (sh)

PHONE → fon

Each word's spelling is written in uppercase letters on top and its pronunciation is written in lowercase letters on the bottom. Spellings and pronunciations are segmented into letter units and sound units separated by blank spaces. Lines indicate the number of sounds in words and the matches between letter units and sound units.

key words to decode analogous words, students would need to fully analyze the spellings of the key words by matching the sounds they heard to the letters they saw. Results of various studies performed by Ehri, as well as her theoretical papers (for example, 1992, 1994), persuaded us that this view of sight word learning might be correct.

Two months into the school year we reflected on whether the first graders in our BWI program had the requisite skills to be taught this type of sight word reading. Our students had learned some of the components: letter shapes and names, sounds for consonants, and how to segment and spell initial sounds in words. Their use of invented spellings in their writing probably enabled them to segment other sounds in words as well. However, we suspected that they were not able to recognize how all the letters in spellings of words symbolized sounds in pronunciations. We had not

taught phonemic segmentation (the decomposition of spoken words into their component sounds), and from other research we realized that phonemic segmentation is difficult for students to pick up on their own, particularly students experiencing reading difficulties (Juel, Griffith, & Gough, 1986; Liberman, Shankweiler, Fischer, & Carter, 1974; Stanovich, 1986). In addition, we had not taught vowel letter-sound correspondences as separate units but only as parts of letter patterns (phonograms) appearing in BWI key words.

Nevertheless, we had observed our students learning to read the sight words they practiced on word cards each day. They could also read many of the BWI key words by sight. What they did not do easily or automatically was call up the key words from memory when they looked at new words that shared letter patterns with the key words. How might this difficulty be reconciled with Ehri's view of sight word memory? Were students learning sight words in the way described by Ehri or in some other way? Further inspection of the literature provided clarification.

Phases of Sight Word Learning

We realized that beginners can learn to read words by sight long before they are capable of performing the mature form of sight word reading. We found it helpful to consider the full course of sight word learning and how instruction might promote development through the four phases based on Ehri's (1991, 1994, 1995) work.

Children appear to move through four phases of sight word learning. During the *prealphabetic phase* before children's letter knowledge has developed, they read sight words by remembering distinctive visual cues in or around the word, referred to as visual-cue reading. For example, they might read *yellow* by remembering the two tall posts in the middle, as illustrated in Figure 2. This is how preschoolers read environmental print, by remembering visual features of logos rather than letters in the print itself.

The *partial alphabetic phase* becomes possible when children acquire some knowledge of letters and their names or sounds. They remember how to read specific words by

---

Figure 2
Phases of sight word learning

Prealphabetic phase
(Remembering a distinctive, purely *visual* cue)
Example: tall posts

ye**ll**ow

Partial alphabetic phase
(Remembering limited matches between salient letter sounds)
Example: matches between *K* and *N* only

KitteN
↓   ↓
k it n

Full alphabetic phase
(Remembering matches between *all* letters and sounds)
Example: 4 letter units matched to 4 sound units

C L O CK
↓ ↓ ↓ ↓
k l o k

Consolidated alphabetic phase
(Remembering matches between multiletter units and syllabic units)
Example: matching onset and rime units

CR ATE
↓   ↓
kr   at

noticing how a few letters correspond to salient sounds in the word's pronunciation, referred to as phonetic-cue reading. For example, they might read *kitten* by detecting and remembering the presence of initial *k* for the sound /k/ and *n* for the final sound /n/ but fail to remember other letters in the word (see Figure 2). One problem confronting phonetic-cue readers is that they misread words sharing the same partial cues; for example, misreading *kitchen* as *kitten*. They also have difficulty decoding unfamiliar words because they lack sufficient knowledge about the alphabetic system, particularly vowels.

It is not until the third *full alphabetic phase* that students completely analyze the spellings of words by matching all the letters to sounds in pronunciations. As shown in Figure 2, they are able to segment the spelling of *clock* into four letter units that match the four sounds detected in the pronunciation. This enables students to remember the full forms of sight words in memory, which is necessary for recognizing that the spellings of unfamiliar words are analogous to those of known sight words. Full alphabetic readers know enough about the alphabetic system to decode unknown words.

As students practice reading and remembering many words with similar spelling patterns, these patterns become consolidated into multiletter units consisting of blends of letter-sound matches. For example, the following commonly occurring patterns may be among the first to become consolidated: -ed, -ing, -ate. During the fourth, *consolidated alphabetic phase*, students use these larger units to remember how to read sight words. For example, they might remember how to read *crate* by segmenting into two units, *cr* and *ate*, and linking these to onset and rime units in the pronunciation (see Figure 2). Knowing consolidated units makes it easier to read and remember multisyllabic words as sight words, for it enables readers to deal with chunks of letters rather than each individual letter.

We realized that the phase theory of sight word learning offered one explanation why our students might be having problems using key words to read unfamiliar words: They had not progressed beyond the two initial phases in their sight word learning. Although they could read words by sight, they were using visual cues or partial letter-sound cues and hence did not know the written forms of key words well enough to recognize when they resembled unknown words. To enable students to analogize, we needed to help them advance to the full alphabetic phase in their sight word learning. Once they developed the habit of processing all the letters and their related sounds in printed words, they could store the key words in memory as fully analyzed sight words and access them to read unfamiliar words sharing the same letters.

With practice students would achieve the goal of word learning—the ability to read words rapidly and automatically (Ehri & Wilce, 1983; Gough & Hillinger, 1980). When words are known automatically, they can be read without effort or attention. As soon as the reader's eyes focus on a word known automatically, his or her brain processes the word's pronunciation and meaning without any effort directed at decoding the word. A key determinant of automaticity is the quality of the word's representation in memory (Perfetti, 1991), as discussed above. Automaticity is fostered by the intervention of a teacher who provides explicit instruction in the use of externalized dialogue to control learning (Lovett et al., 1994), teaches students to fully analyze words (Stanovich, 1991), and provides daily opportunities for students to read connected text containing words with high-frequency phonograms or spelling patterns (Ehri, 1992). Students need plenty of practice reading words in order for words to be stored in memory as fully connected sight words that can be read automatically.

Insights for Instruction

Our teaching experiences over the years had convinced us that children who had difficulty learning to read did not figure out on their own what the teacher left unsaid about the word-learning process. Now Ehri's (1991) theory of sight word learning gave us insight into what we had left unsaid. If we wanted students to have fully represented words in memory, we needed to provide them with a model of how to analyze and talk about the words they were learning, as well as to provide teacher-mediated opportunities for them to stretch and hear sounds in words and to talk about letter-sound matches. We also needed to convince students of the value of being reflective and analytic. And, finally, we needed to provide many occasions for students to process key words and analogous new words as they read connected text.

Students were enthusiastic about our initial attempts at modeling "word detective" techniques for analyzing new words. In fact, when the teacher began to think aloud about new words, students eagerly chimed in and shared their observations. For example, in mid-October Drew read the word *hop* as *skip*, then looked at the teacher for confirmation. The teacher said:

> The word you are wondering about is a word that we haven't read before. We also haven't learned the spelling pattern for that word. Let's be word detectives and see what clues we can use to solve the mystery of how to pronounce the new word. Hmmmm. The word begins like a word I know—*house*. I also notice that it has one vowel—an *o*—in the middle just like our key word *not*. I wonder if it will have the same sound for *o* as we hear in *not*?

At this point Drew jumped in and said, "I said it was *skip*. It couldn't be *skip* because the word

begins like *house*. *House* is a long word, so the word can't be *house*." Another student pointed out that the new word ended with *p*, and that he heard an *s* at the end of *house*. The teacher said she thought she would try the *o* sound from the key word not "just to see what will happen." "/H/, /o/, /t/," the teacher said as she stretched out the sounds. Immediately, one of the students said, "I don't think so—the word ends with *p*." "Great detective work!" the teacher replied. "So what is the word?" The students pronounced the word, then shared what they had learned from their detective work. Gavin said, "It looks like whenever *o* is between two consonants it will have the sound I hear in *not*." Drew said, "We have to look at all the letters in a word instead of just guessing from the sense of the sentence."

We were sure that Perfetti (1991) was right in his belief that the more reflective and analytic a child is about words and spelling patterns, the more rapidly he or she progresses in learning to read. We suspected that the acquisition of fully represented words in memory might be the missing ingredient in our instructional program. Thus, word detective activities became the foundation of our first-grade word-learning program.

The Addition of Word-Learning Procedures to BWI

Clearly, the way we introduced key words in the original BWI program had to change. For students to use key words to decode unknown words, the words needed to be bonded in memory in a fully analyzed form. Incorrect or partial representations of the key words would interfere with students' ability to access them for decoding by analogy. Our goal was to extend the BWI program to teach these processes. We thought that the following elements would be critical ingredients:

1. Helping teachers and students understand what it means to analyze words fully.

2. Selecting a core group of words that represent common sound-letter properties in English and that illustrate the various ways to analyze words fully.

3. Designing a set of explicit procedures that could be taught to students and that would enable them to analyze words fully.

We selected 93 of the 120 key words from the BWI program for students to analyze during the school year (see Figure 3). These words were picked to meet several criteria. They contained phonograms (spelling patterns) that were frequent in English (Fry, Fountoukidis, & Polk, 1985; Wylie & Durrell, 1970) and occurred often in the trade books our students would be reading. The words contained the full variety of initial consonants, digraphs, and blends that beginning readers would encounter in their books. For example, *truck* was chosen to represent the *-uck* phonogram and the *tr* blend. We planned to teach three or four key words per week.

We adopted explicit teaching as our model of instruction to provide teachers with a systematic framework. The word analysis procedures taught to students included the following: stretching out the pronunciations of words to analyze constituent sounds in the words, analyzing the visual forms of words, talking about matches between sounds and letters (and grouping letters into chunks where necessary), noting similarities to sounds and letters in other words already learned, and remembering how to spell the words. Students were given several activities to provide practice in these procedures.

Word-Learning Procedures in Action

The revised program had several key ingredients: clarifying the goals and rationale for students, teaching and modeling how to analyze words and how to talk about segmenting sounds and matching them to letters, guiding students' practice to develop metacognitive awareness and control over their own word learning, helping students apply word-learning procedures in reading connected text, and reviewing what students have learned about our language to enhance their enthusiasm for exploring letter-sound matches in unfamiliar words in order to discover new relations.

Clarifying Goals and Rationale

We believe that learners need to understand the goals and rationale of the instruction they receive and that these understandings will provide the motivation and foundation for students to manage their own learning. This belief is congruent with researchers' assertions that children need to acquire metacognitive control over word-learning processes (Gaskins et al., 1988; Lovett et al., 1994). So we decided to share with students what we had learned from our literature search about the phases of word learning and the need for fully analyzing words. We gave real-life examples of visual-cue reading, phonetic-cue reading, and contextual guessing that we had witnessed in the classroom, examples with which our students readily identified.

The example of visual-cue reading that we shared was the way students had learned the key word *cat*. Initially *cat* was written on a word wall card shaped like a cat's head. Students consistently read it correctly on the word wall but had difficulty thinking of the key word for the *-at* pattern. We suspected, and students confirmed, that they were using the cat's head as the cue for learning *cat* and had not paid much attention to letters in the spelling.

Other examples we shared were attempts to recall or decode words based on identical initial consonants. Students would misread

Figure 3
Spelling-pronunciation matches for BWI key words

Listed below are the matches between spellings and pronunciations for the key words that are taught in Word Detectives: Benchmark Extended Word Identification Program for Beginning Readers. The words are listed in the order they are introduced, from Week 1 to Week 28 in Phase II of the program. Each word's spelling is written in uppercase letters first, and its pronunciation is written in lowercase letters beneath. Spellings and pronunciations are segmented into letter units and sound units separated by blank spaces with vertical lines to indicate matches. The number of letter-sound matches within each word is written after the pronunciation (bottom line). In addition to lowercase letters, a few special symbols are used to designate sounds. Long vowels saying their own letter names are topped by a horizontal bar; short vowels are unmarked. Other vowels are indicated by two letters underlined to represent one sound. Schwa vowels are represented by the letter U. The purpose of the pronunciation symbols is to clarify how we segment words into sounds and the identities of the sounds. These symbols are not taught to students. Readers should note that this analysis assumes a dialect that may not characterize all readers.

In the course of encountering key words and analyzing constituent letter units and sound units to achieve an optimal match, some complexities arise. These are addressed by structuring lessons and reading materials in such a way that student word detectives will discover the following:

1. Some letters combine to match up to a single sound, among them the following doubled consonants and vowels: ng, ck, ch, th, sh, ph, wh, wr, kn, oa, ou, ow, oi, oy, aw, ai, ay, ea, ew, ie, igh, augh, ti, ci, gu.

2. A few words have silent letters that do not match any sound within a specific word, although they may match sounds in other words: *l* in *talk*, *l* in *could*, final silent *e*; these letters are marked with an asterisk below.

3. Final *e* is very often a silent letter that occurs when the preceding vowel says its own name.

4. Vowel letters preceding *r* match up to a separate vowel sound that is barely heard; for example, *e* in *her*.

5. In some words such as *little*, the final letters *l* and *e* match up to sounds /u/ and /l/ but the letters reverse the order of the sounds.

6. *X* may match up to two sounds /ks/, as in *tax*.

Complexities 4 and 5 are taught in this way to conform to the general principle that every chunk or syllable in a word has to have both a vowel sound and a vowel spelling.

Week 1	I N	A N D	U P
	i n 2	a n d 3	u p 2
Week 2	K I NG	L ONG	J U M P
	k i ng 3	l o ng 3	j u m p 4
Week 3	L E T	P I G	D AY
	l e t 3	p i g 3	d ā 2
Week 4	T R U CK	B L A CK	N O T
	t r u k 4	b l a k 4	n o t 3

(continued)

Figure 3
Spelling-pronunciation matches for BWI key words (continued)

Week 5

CAT → k a t 3 IT → i t 2 GO → g ō 2 LOOK → l o͟o k 3

Week 6

RED → r e d 3 FUN → f u n 3 HE → h ē 2

Week 7

NAME* → n ā m 3 SWIM → s w i m 4 MY → m ī 2 MAP → m a p 3

Week 8

CAR → k a͟u r 3 VINE* → v ī n 3 SEE → s ē 2 CAN → k a n 3

Week 9

TENT → t e n t 4 ROUND → r o͟u n d 4 SKATE* → s k ā t 4 TEN → t e n 3

Week 10

OLD → ō l d 3 FROG → f r o g 4 RIGHT → r ī t 3

Week 11

SLIDE* → s l ī d 4 STOP → s t o p 4 TELL → t e l 3 HER → h u r 3

Week 12

AN → a n 2 SMASH → s m a s͟h 4 BRAVE* → b r ā v 4

Week 13

COW → k o͟u 2 SLEEP → s l ē p 4 SCOUT → s k o͟u t 4

Week 14

FOR → f o r 3 ALL → a͟u l 2 SAW → s a͟u 2

Week 15

HAD → h a d 3 KICK → k i k 3 SNAIL → s n ā l 4 GLOW → g l ō 3

(continued)

Figure 3
Spelling-pronunciation matches for BWI key words (continued)

Week 16

BOAT → b ō t

THINK → th i ng k 4

NEST → n e s t 4

Week 17

TREAT → t r ē t 4

MAKE* → m ā k 3

THANK → th a ng k 4

Week 18

MICE* → m ī s 3

LITTLE → l i t u l 5

MORE* → m o r 3

Week 19

SHIP → sh i p 3

CLOCK → k l o k 4

WASH → w au sh 3

STATION → s t ā sh u n 6

Week 20

SKUNK → s k u ng k 5

WHALE* → w ā l 3

BOY → b oi 2

BABY → b ā b ē 4

Week 21

SQUIRT → s k w u r t 6

SCHOOL → s k oo l 4

COUL*D → k ōō d 3

Week 22

CAUGHT → k au t 3

COIN → k oi n 3

TAL*K → t au k 3

Week 23

PAGE* → p ā j 3

FLEW → f l oo 3

FLU → f l oo 3

Week 24

USE* → ū s 2 / ū z 2

BUG → b u g 3

RAIN → r ā n 3

Week 25

PAL → p a l 3

FUR → f u r 3

PLACE* → p l ā s 4

(continued)

ship as *sleep* and read *bam* as *bong*, *beep*, or even *baseball*. We also shared that some students seemed to ignore all letter clues and rely completely on meaning, reading *path* as *road* and *sea* as *ocean*. Students recognized their own word-reading habits in these examples and were eager to share additional instances.

We also pointed out that not all of these word identification errors could be attributed solely to students' lack of knowledge about how to analyze words fully. Some students' errors appeared to result from an impulsive style—instances where students responded too quickly to words without looking carefully at all the letters. From our discussion of the phases of word learning, we hoped that students would understand the need to analyze words fully and realize the value of being reflective and analytic about the words they were learning.

We shared that becoming full alphabetic readers was necessary if they were to become good readers. Much to our delight, the class was fascinated to learn about the phases of word learning, and they accepted with enthusiasm our challenge that they become

thoughtful and analytic word detectives. As we reflected on the success of this metacognitive lesson, we realized the importance of giving students a rationale for the laborious, and what might seem monotonous, process of stretching words and matching the sounds they heard with the letters they saw. To our surprise, they did not regard the process as monotonous. They loved the grown-up rationale, and they loved the excitement of discovering clues about words even more.

As part of each lesson, teachers explained and provided examples that illuminated why one of the goals of word identification lessons is to have students analyze every single letter and sound in the key words. For example, one teacher explained, "We fully analyze words, because, if we get into our heads every single letter for a word matched to every single sound, we will be able to get the word back out when we want to read it or write it again." Practical examples were shared to clarify the importance of fully analyzing words. For example, during one lesson the teacher placed on the chalkboard two signs that one might find in a store undergoing minor renovations.

Stop was written on one sign; *step* was written on the other. The teacher asked her first graders why people might have a problem if they impulsively guessed what these signs said based on letters that "popped out at them." She pondered aloud whether it might be better to study and remember all the letters in words so that no mistakes were made. This example underscored the importance of fully knowing the spellings of words.

Teaching and Modeling How To Self-Talk

The sequence of instruction has been fine-tuned based on students' reactions. For example, in the early months of the program, the teacher placed the word to be learned on the chalkboard, pronounced the word, and asked students how many letters they saw. This was followed by stretching the sounds in the word and analyzing the number of sounds. We discovered that seeing the word prior to analyzing the sounds seemed to make it harder for students to determine the number of sounds. For example, in a word with a greater number of letters than sounds, such as *right*, students would claim to hear too many sounds. We decided to alter the procedure by not allowing students to view the word until after they had analyzed the sounds.

This revised procedure worked much better. The teacher pronounces the word, students analyze the sounds, then the word is placed on the chalkboard. Hearing a word without seeing it makes it easier for students to detect and correctly identify the number of sounds. The teacher explains and models how to analyze words fully in this way:

> First we stretch out the word so that we can hear all the sounds in the word. As we stretch out each sound, we hold up a finger to count the number of sounds. Next, we look at the word and count the letters. Do we have the same number of letters

as sounds, or will it take more than one letter to represent some of the sounds? Next, we figure out what letters go with what sounds.

> Listen as I analyze *stop*: /s/, /t/, /o/, /p/. I hear four sounds. I see four letters. That means each letter will probably have a sound. The *o* has a different sound than I hear in *go*. In *go* the *o* doesn't come in the middle like it does in *stop*. The *o* in *stop* has the same sound as in *not*, and the *o* is in the middle of two consonants as it is in *stop*. The spelling pattern is *-op*. Some words that rhyme with *stop* are....

Providing Guided Practice

The word detective activities for learning new words varied on different days but always required students to stretch sounds in words, to analyze and talk to themselves about letter-sound matches, and to summarize the clues they discovered about sounds and letters. On the day that the word *tell* was introduced, the teacher pronounced it (the word was not in view), then the class chorally stretched the sounds in the word, with the teacher's voice ringing above the other voices to model this process. As they stretched the word, students were asked to hold up a finger for each sound they heard.

Next, *tell* was placed on the chalkboard written on a rectangular piece of colored paper. Students were instructed to count the number of letters they saw and be prepared to make a statement using the form: "I hear _____ sounds and I see _____ letters because...." Thus, Ivan stated, "I hear three sounds and I see four letters because the two *l*s make one *l* sound."

The teacher asked the students what the spelling pattern was in *tell* and asked them to share words that rhymed with *tell*. These words were written on the chalkboard. Students commented that all of the words that rhymed with *tell* had the same letter for the vowel sound. However, a few of the words, such as *gel*, were not spelled exactly the same way.

Next, the teacher asked the students to stretch the word quietly to themselves and, as they did, to write the letter for the first sound they heard. Students shared the letter they wrote, then continued to stretch *tell* in preparation for writing the letter that matched the second sound. While the students were still pondering what to write, the teacher modeled what she was thinking as she decided how to represent the second sound in *tell*.

> Hmmmm. I'm unsure what letter goes with that sound. Maybe I can find a word on the word wall that has the same sound. I'm pretty sure that the next letter is a vowel and that the vowel is between two consonants. Maybe if I look at the word wall words with a vowel between two consonants, I can figure out what vowel to write. /C/-/a/-/t/—no, that isn't it. /F/-/u/-/n/—that doesn't sound right either. /L/-/e/-/t/. Hmmmmm.

After the students had written a letter, she asked them to explain their reasoning for the letter they chose. The children did not know any rules about words, and none were encouraged. Thus, terms such as short and long were not part of the discussion. The emphasis was on talking about words in child-centered language that would help students remember the mapping of sounds to letters. The position of vowels in relation to consonants was the focus of much of their talk. The students were asked once again to stretch *tell* and write the last sound that they heard. A discussion followed about the fact that it took two *ls* to represent the last sound in *tell*.

Finally, the teacher asked whether anyone could summarize what the class had learned about the word *tell*. She suggested that this summary should include the number of sounds and the number of letters as well as anything special they had noticed about how our language works. Gavin replied, "*Tell* has four letters, but only three sounds. The reason *tell* only has three sounds is that two *ls* next to each other make one *l* sound."

Instruction includes self-assessment activities. Students check on themselves to see if they have really gotten the week's key words into their heads. They talk to themselves about each key word by following the six steps on the Talk-To-Yourself Chart (see Figure 4). Next, the key word is covered and students listen to each sound, then write the corresponding letter or letters on a card. Once again, the teacher models stretching and talking to herself about the words as the students reflect on each word.

**Figure 4
Talk-to-yourself chart**

1. The word is _____.
2. Stretch the word.
   I hear _____ sounds.
3. I see _____ letters because _____.
   (Students reconcile the number of letters they see with the number of sounds they hear.)
4. The spelling pattern is _____.
5. This is what I know about the vowel: _____.
6. Another word on the word wall with the same vowel sound is _____.

On another day, a partner-sharing component is added. Students self-assess as mentioned earlier, then they are instructed to find another key word on the word wall "that has something the same about the sounds and letters as the word you wrote on your card." Students share with partners what they have learned by following the statements on the Partner-Sharing Chart shown in Figure 5. The teacher circulates to monitor and provide support when needed.

Once students have analyzed key words, they practice changing one letter in the words to create new words. To clarify how to do this, the teacher might say the following:

> My word is *fun*. My new word is *fin*. I made this word because I know the word wall word *pig*. *Pig* is like *fin* because the only vowel in the word is between two consonants, so the vowel in *pig* and *fin* probably makes the same sound.

Using the statements for making words shown in Figure 6, students share their newly discovered words with their partners and discuss what they know about sounds and letters that explain the changes they made.

Students also spell the key words. At first they practice with the assistance of Elkonin boxes (Elkonin, 1973). Students place in each individual box all the letters needed to represent one sound. For example, three boxes would be used to spell *dog*. Three boxes would also be used to spell *right*, with letters *igh* placed in the middle box. Later in the week, the words are spelled from memory without the use of boxes.

Applying Word-Learning Procedures

Each day students apply what they have learned about words by reading texts that contain words with familiar spelling patterns. The text they read is either a predictable rhyme

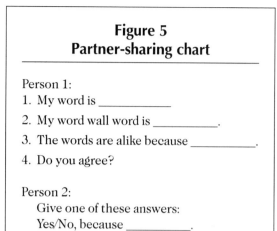

**Figure 5
Partner-sharing chart**

Person 1:
1. My word is _____
2. My word wall word is _____.
3. The words are alike because _____.
4. Do you agree?

Person 2:
   Give one of these answers:
   Yes/No, because _____.

Switch roles.

**Figure 6
Making words chart**

Person 1:
1. My word is _____.
2. My new word is _____.
3. I made this word because I know _____.
4. Do you agree?

Person 2:
   Give one of these answers:
   Yes/No, because _____.

Switch roles.
If you finish early, pick other word wall words and make them into new words.

written by one of the researchers or an easy-reading trade book. These texts are first read to students as they point and follow, then they are echo and choral read. Finally, students read all or parts of the text on their own. In addition, the predictable rhyme for the week is sent home in each child's homework folder with instructions for parents to read the predictable rhyme with their child.

Reviewing Features of Our Language

At the conclusion of each day's lesson, students share what they have learned about their language. Also they tell their parents what they have learned, and parents write notes in their child's What-I-Know-About-My-Language journal recording these discoveries. We have been surprised by the insights that students have discovered on their own.

For example, early in February after reading *Frog Ball*, the following discussion took place when the teacher asked what students had noticed that day about how our language works:

Jeff: *Old*, *stroll*, and *ball* are all alike. (Teacher writes the words on the chalkboard.)

Teacher: How are they alike?

Jeff: The vowels are all followed by *l* and say their own name.

Teacher: Class, let's all stretch out the three words on the board. What vowel sound do you hear in *old*? In *stroll*? in *ball*?
           (All the students stretch the sounds in each word. Jeff gets very excited and raises his hand.)

Jeff: The *os* say their name, and the *a* has a different sound than in *cat*. Maybe the *l* changes the vowel's sound.

Teacher: Jeff, that's an interesting theory. Let's be on the lookout for words with an *l* following the vowel and see if your theory is correct.
           (Matt raises his hand.)

Matt: You remember last week when I told you that the vowel in *child* doesn't do what it's supposed to? Well, in *child* there is an *l* after the vowel.

Teacher: You are saying that *child* is additional evidence that Jeff's theory may be correct. Let's continue to notice words in which a vowel is followed by an *l* to see if Jeff's theory is correct.

This example suggests that students are successful word detectives. Use of such self-teaching strategies should put students in control of their own word learning, help them learn how the alphabetic system is structured, and facilitate their acquisition of a fully analyzed sight vocabulary. Although our observations of students' progress during the year convinced us that our beginning readers made greater gains in their ability to decode and spell than students had in previous years, we plan to document the effectiveness of this program by following these readers as they develop and by comparing them to students in previous years.

To obtain preliminary data regarding the success of the program, we administered to our class of 1994–1995 first graders reading and spelling tests that had been administered to the previous year's first graders. The Wide Range Achievement Test (WRAT) word-reading and spelling tests were given at the beginning and end of each year. There were 13 students in each comparison group. Statistical tests showed that the 1994–1995 first-grade class made significantly greater gains in reading than the previous year's class. Mean performances in the spring were 63 words read correctly by our first graders in the enhanced BWI program versus 57 words read by the previous year's first graders. Also mean spelling performances favored the 1994–1995 class, but the difference fell short of statistical significance. We will be interested to see whether differences grow larger as students' reading and spelling skills continue to develop in subsequent years.

Concluding Thoughts

First graders who are at risk for failure in learning to read do not discover what teachers leave unsaid about the complexities of word learning. As a result it is important to teach them procedures for learning words. Our adoption of the original BWI program was a first step in teaching students how to decode words as one simple process—identifying and applying spelling patterns. Students were taught to use known spelling patterns to decode unknown words. The simplicity of the process gave most of our at-risk students the boost they needed to overcome decoding problems they had suffered in the past, such as trying to memorize rules or synthesize isolated sounds into words. For students who were able to master the key words, BWI effectively launched them as readers. Some students, however, were not successful in learning key words well enough to be able to retrieve them automatically for use in decoding other words. Something was holding these students back from becoming mature word learners. Something seemed to be missing in our program.

Students needed explicit instruction in how to learn the key words so that they would remember their spelling patterns well enough to analogize. Our review of the word-learning literature made us aware of the phases of word learning. We realized that word-learning efficiency could be improved by teaching students procedures for learning words in a fully analyzed way, rather than expecting students to figure out the spelling system on their own. We decided that it was important to put students in control of their own learning by guiding their discovery and induction processes as

they analyzed words and explored regularities of the spelling system. Phonics rules were not taught, but rather students generated and verbalized their discoveries about regularities in language. Teachers paid special attention to helping students develop metacognitive knowledge about their learning processes. Our observations of students analyzing words on their own have convinced us that motivation for self-directed learning is high when students understand the whats, whys, whens, and hows of our instruction.

The addition of word-learning procedures to the Benchmark Word Identification program is monitored daily. Decisions about how to modify the program to improve its effectiveness are based on students' reactions to the activities. The program is still evolving. However, as we observe these students in the second year of the program, we believe that they are reading and spelling with greater proficiency and enthusiasm than our students did in previous years. They like being word detectives and, even more, they are excited about the fact that they can read.

References

Ehri, L.C. (1991). Development of the ability to read words. In R. Barr, M. Kamil, P. Mosenthal, & P.D. Pearson (Eds.), *Handbook of reading research: Volume II* (pp. 383–417). White Plains, NY: Longman.

Ehri, L.C. (1992). Reconceptualizing the development of sight word reading and its relation to recoding. In P. Gough, L. Ehri, & R. Treiman (Eds.), *Reading acquisition* (pp. 107–143). Hillsdale, NJ: Erlbaum.

Ehri, L.C. (1994). Development of the ability to read words: Update. In R.B. Ruddell, M.R. Ruddell, & H. Singer (Eds.), *Theoretical models and processes of reading* (4th ed., pp. 323–358). Newark, DE: International Reading Association.

Ehri, L.C. (1995). Phases of development in reading words. *Journal of Research in Reading, 18*, 116–125.

Ehri, L.C., & Wilce, L.S. (1983). Development of word identification speed in skilled and less skilled beginning readers. *Journal of Educational Psychology, 75*, 3–18.

Elkonin, D.B. (1973). U.S.S.R. In J. Downing (Ed.), *Comparative reading* (pp. 551–579). New York: Macmillan.

Fry, E.B., Fountoukidis, D.L., & Polk, J.K. (1985). *The new reading teacher's book of lists.* Englewood Cliffs, NJ: Prentice Hall.

Gaskins, I., Downer, M., Anderson, R., Cunningham, P., Gaskins, R., Schommer, M., & the Teachers of Benchmark School. (1988). A metacognitive approach to phonics: Using what you know to decode what you don't know. *Remedial and Special Education, 9*, 36–41.

Gaskins, R.W., Gaskins, I.W., Anderson, R.C., & Schommer, M. (1995). The reciprocal relation between research and development: An example involving a decoding strand for poor readers. *Journal of Reading Behavior, 27*, 337–377.

Gaskins, R.W., Gaskins, J.C., & Gaskins, I.W. (1991). A decoding program for poor readers—and the rest of the class, too! *Language Arts, 68*, 213–225.

Gaskins, R.W., Gaskins, J.C., & Gaskins, I.W. (1992). Using what you know to figure out what you don't know: An analogy approach to decoding. *Reading and Writing Quarterly, 8*, 197–221.

Gough, P.B., Ehri, L.C., & Treiman, R. (Eds.). (1992). *Reading acquisition.* Hillsdale, NJ: Erlbaum.

Gough, P.B., & Hillinger, M.L. (1980). Learning to read: An unnatural act. *Bulletin of the Orton Society, 30*, 180–196.

Juel, C., Griffith, P., & Gough, P. (1986). Acquisition of literacy: A longitudinal study of children in first and second grade. *Journal of Educational Psychology, 78*, 243–255.

Liberman, I., Shankweiler, D., Fischer, F., & Carter, B. (1974). Reading and the awareness of linguistic segments. *Journal of Experimental Child Psychology, 18*, 201–212.

Lovett, M.W., Borden, S.L., DeLuca, T., Lacerenza, L., Benson, N.J., & Brackstone, D. (1994). Treating the core deficits of developmental dyslexia: Evidence of transfer of learning after phonologically- and strategy-based reading training programs. *Developmental Psychology, 30*, 805–822.

Perfetti, C.A. (1991). Representations and awareness in the acquisition of reading competence. In L. Rieben & C.A. Perfetti (Eds.), *Learning to read: Basic research and its implications* (pp. 33–44). Hillsdale, NJ: Erlbaum.

Rieben, L., & Perfetti, C.A. (Eds.). (1991). *Learning to read: Basic research and its implications.* Hillsdale, NJ: Erlbaum.

Stanovich, K.E. (1986). Matthew effects in reading: Some consequences of individual differences in the acquisition of literacy. *Reading Research Quarterly, 21*, 360–407.

Stanovich, K.E. (1991). Changing models of reading and reading acquisition. In L. Rieben & C.A. Perfetti (Eds.), *Learning to read: Basic research and its implications* (pp. 19–31). Hillsdale, NJ: Erlbaum.

Wylie, R., & Durrell, D. (1970). Teaching vowels through phonograms. *Elementary English, 47*, 787–791.

Fluency for Everyone: Incorporating Fluency Instruction in the Classroom

Timothy V. Rasinski

lthough there is no universal agreement about what constitutes reading fluency, most authorities would agree that it refers to the smooth and natural oral production of written text.

Harris and Hodges (1981), for example, define fluency as expressing oneself "smoothly, easily, and readily," having "freedom from word identification problems," and dealing with "words, and larger language units" with quickness (p. 120). Thus, at a minimum one might expect the fluent reader to read orally with accuracy, quickness, and expression.

Achieving fluency is recognized as an important aspect of proficient reading, but it remains a neglected goal of reading instruction (Allington, 1983). Most basal reading programs give little recognition to fluency as an important goal, and few reading textbooks for prospective teachers provide an in-depth treatment of the topic.

Reading fluency often becomes a salient issue only when students demonstrate significant deficiencies. These students often are referred to corrective or remedial classes where they finally receive special instruction in the development of fluent reading.

How can classroom teachers teach fluency to their students? Several methods have been proven successful. These include repeated readings (Dowhower, 1987; Herman, 1985; Samuels, 1979), reading while listening or echo reading (Carbo, 1978; Chomsky, 1976; Gamby, 1983; Laffey & Kelly, 1981; Schneeberg, 1977; Van Der Leij, 1981), the neurological impress method (Heckelman, 1969), and reading in phrases (Allington, 1983; Amble & Kelly, 1970; Gregory, 1986).

One potential problem with these fluency training methods is that they were, in general, originally intended for use in corrective reading situations involving an instructor working with one, two, or a very small group of students. Despite many positive aspects of these methods, the focus of their application is overly narrow.

Teachers who wish to make fluency instruction an integral part of the regular reading curriculum may be at a loss in attempting to use corrective fluency methods in a way that is appropriate for the more normal reader.

Fortunately, the methods shown to be effective in helping less fluent readers suggest a set of principles that teachers may find helpful. In the remainder of this article those principles will be identified and discussed.

Proven Methods

Repetition

Achieving fluency requires practice with one text until a criterion level is achieved. Although the principle of repetition is often translated into repeated exposures to target words in isolation, research has shown that repetition is most effective when students meet the target words in a variety of texts or through repeated exposures to one text.

Although repetitions of texts may seem to be a dull activity, there are several ways to make it interesting and appealing. For example, young children love to hear their favorite stories read to them repeatedly (Beaver, 1982) and students enjoy working in pairs on repeated reading tasks (Koskinen & Blum, 1986).

Rasinski (1988) suggests several ways to use natural classroom events to encourage repeated readings. Activities such as putting on plays and having older students read short books to primary students require that students practice the text they will have to perform later on.

Modeling

Young students and other less fluent readers may not always know what fluent reading should be like. Poor readers, for example, usually are assigned to reading groups in which the predominant model of reading is other disfluent readers. It seems clear that students need frequent opportunities to see and hear fluent reading.

Because the most fluent reader in the classroom is the teacher, the teacher should be the primary model. The easiest and most stimulating way to do this is to read good children's literature to the class. Daily periods should be set aside for teachers (and other fluent readers) to read aloud.

Direct Instruction and Feedback

Research into metacognition in reading is demonstrating that it may be important for readers to be aware of what happens when they read and why they have reading problems. This awareness may be particularly helpful in the development of fluency.

Prior to reading aloud, the teacher could remind the class to listen to the expression in his or her voice during the reading, the speed at which the text is read, or when stops or pauses occur. A short discussion of these factors after the reading or before students' own oral reading could heighten students' sensitivity to their own reading.

Similarly, providing feedback to students after they read orally can facilitate growth in fluent reading. Koskinen and Blum (1986), for example, propose a model of instruction in which students are trained to provide feedback to each other. The reader benefits from a formative critique of his or her reading and the student critic benefits from a heightened metacognitive sense of what it means to be a fluent reader.

Support During Reading

The notion of scaffolding or support while performing is critical to the development of fluency, especially in the beginning stages or with students having difficulty. Support is achieved through the student hearing a fluent rendition of a passage while simultaneously reading the same text. Several types of support are available.

Choral reading is perhaps the most common form of support reading and is highly appropriate for the regular classroom. Here students read a selected passage in unison. The teacher needs to ensure that several fluent readers are part of the group or that his or her own voice leads the way in choral reading.

The neurological impress method (Heckelman, 1969) was designed as a remedial technique for use one on one. The teacher begins by reading slightly ahead of and louder than the student, and later, as the students gains in fluency, softly shadows the student's reading of the passage. Although labor intensive, the technique can be adapted for regular classroom use with aides, volunteers, or fluent classmates.

The use of tape-recorded passages is another way to provide support during reading. Carbo (1978) reported students making good progress in reading while simultaneously listening to passages on tape. This format is especially appealing as it allows students to work on their fluency independently. They may need to be reminded to concentrate on reading the passage, not simply listen passively to it.

Text Unit

Fluency involves reading texts in multi-word chunks or phrases. Word by word reading, even if it is accurate and fast, is not fluent reading. Timely reminders should drive the point home.

Research has shown (for example, Weiss, 1983) that marking phrase boundaries in student texts with a penciled slash or vertical line may aid fluency. Occasionally reading short texts such as poems, famous speeches, or popular songs marked in this way may help students develop and maintain a mature sense of phrasing.

Easy Materials

Fluency is best promoted when students are provided with materials that they find relatively easy in terms of word recognition, so that they can move beyond decoding to issues of phrasing, expression, and comprehensibility of production. These materials help students develop a sense of power and confidence.

Teachers, then, need to stock their classroom libraries with books that represent a variety of difficulty levels and interests. For their independent reading, students can be directed to those materials that they will not find frustrating.

Combining Principles

These principles offer some building blocks and guidelines for developing reading instruction and activities that promote the development of fluency. Rather than think of them in isolation, teachers can design lessons and activities that combine two or more of these principles.

In her study of disfluent third graders, Carol Chomsky (1976) combined the principles of repetition and support. She had students listen to and read a tape-recorded text until they could read it with fluency. Then they received instruction in various components of the text.

In a similar vein Koskinen and Blum's (1986) instructional model for fluency combines repetition and direct instruction. Students read a text three times and receive formative feedback (direct instruction in fluency) from their peers. In both the Chomsky and Koskinen and Blum models, students made substantial improvements in fluency.

Hoffman (1987) and Aulls (1982) offer even more complex models of fluency instruction that combine elements of modeling, repetition, support, and direct instruction.

Teachers Empowered

The point is not that teachers should blindly endorse any of the models identified and described here. Rather, relying on the principles of fluency instruction, informed and creative teachers can design instructional activities that meet the unique needs of their classrooms. They can incorporate one or more principles into the stories that students encounter in their daily lessons or pleasure reading, and depending on students' progress can employ principles more or less strenuously.

Fluency is an issue that needs to be taken seriously in the reading classroom. The principles outlined here, while neither prescription nor panacea, offer teachers several tools for making their reading instruction reflect their own professional judgment.

Through the use of principles such as these, prepackaged and "teacher proof" reading programs that foster deskilling and promote a perception of teachers as incompetent can be turned back in favor of alternative and effective teacher-designed instruction.

REFERENCES

Allington, R.L. (1983). Fluency: The neglected reading goal. *The Reading Teacher, 36,* 556–561.

Amble, B.R., & Kelly, F.J. (1970). Phrase reading development training with fourth grade students: An experimental and comparative study. *Journal of Reading Behavior, 2*(1), 85–96.

Aulls, M.W. (1982). *Developing readers in today's elementary school.* Boston, MA: Allyn & Bacon.

Beaver, J.M. (1982). Say it! Over and over. *Language Arts, 59,* 143–148.

Carbo, M. (1978). Teaching reading with talking books. *The Reading Teacher, 32,* 267–273.

Chomsky, C. (1976). After decoding: What? *Language Arts, 53,* 288–296.

Dowhower, S.L. (1987). Effects of repeated reading on second-grade transitional readers' fluency and comprehension. *Reading Research Quarterly, 22*(4), 389–406,

Gamby, G. (1983). Talking books and taped books. *The Reading Teacher, 36,* 366–369.

Gregory, J.F. (1986). Phrasing in the speech and reading of the hearing impaired. *Journal of Communication Disorders, 19*(4), 289–297.

Harris, T.L., & Hodges, R.E. (Eds.). (1981). *A dictionary of reading.* Newark, DE: International Reading Association.

Heckelman, R.G. (1969). A neurological impress method of reading instruction. *Academic Therapy, 4,* 277–282.

Herman, P.A. (1985). The effect of repeated readings on reading rate, speech pauses, and word recognition accuracy. *Reading Research Quarterly, 20,* 553–564.

Hoffman, J.V. (1987). Rethinking the role of oral reading in basal instruction. *The Elementary School Journal, 87*(3), 367–373.

Koskinen, P., & Blum, I. (1986). Paired repeated reading: A classroom strategy for developing fluent reading. *The Reading Teacher, 40,* 70–75.

Laffey, J.L., & Kelly, D. (1981). Repeated reading of taped literature: Does it make a difference? In G. McNinch (Ed.), *Comprehension: Process and change.* (First Yearbook of the American Reading Forum). Hattiesburg, MS: University of Southern Mississippi Press.

Rasinski, T.V. (1988). Making repeated readings a functional part of classroom reading instruction. *Reading Horizons, 28,* 250–254.

Samuels, S.J. (1979). The method of repeated readings. *The Reading Teacher, 32,* 403–408.

Schneeberg, H. (1977). Listening while reading: A four year study. *The Reading Teacher, 30,* 629–635.

Van Der Leij, A. (1981). Remediation of reading-disabled children by presenting text simultaneously to eye and ear. *Bulletin of the Orton Society, 31,* 229–243.

Weiss, D.S. (1983). The effects of text segmentation on children's reading comprehension. *Discourse Processes, 6*(1), 77–89.

SECTION VI

Improving Family and Community Collaboration

Schools work better when they support families and when communities support them. Unfortunately, too much of the educational discourse about families and communities is narrow and negative—focusing on perceived family limitations. More recently, however, articles have appeared offering a clearer view of family strengths and of the untapped possibilities that might be pursued. In this section, each article offers a vision of what collaborative activity can accomplish. The topics range from large scale community efforts to ideas that could be implemented by individual teachers with little or no added support.

Early Literacy at Home: Children's Experiences and Parents' Perspectives

Jamie L. Metsala, Editor

Linda Baker, Susan Sonnenschein, Robert Serpell, Deborah Scher, Sylvia Fernandez-Fein, Kimberly Munsterman, Susan Hill, Victoria Goddard-Truitt, Evangeline Danseco, Authors

lthough public schooling is designed to be equally effective for all children, in practice some sociocultural groups have consistently fared better in the system than others. Many factors probably contribute to these differences in achievement, including children's literacy-related home experiences (Sonnenschein, Brody, & Munsterman, 1996; Thompson, Mixon, & Serpell, 1996). Early research on the effects of home environment on literacy focused on family status characteristics, such as socioeconomic level and parent education level. Later research focused on characteristics of the home environment, identifying a common core of characteristics associated with positive reading outcomes (for example, Morrow, 1989). These include, for example, readily available children's books, frequent reading to and with children, special space and opportunities for reading, positive parental attitudes and models of reading, frequent visits to libraries, and many parent-child conversations.

These studies are informative, but we do not yet have a detailed understanding of how children's everyday activities contribute to literacy development. Moreover, we do not know how factors such as the beliefs and values of adults in the children's environment and the processes of adult-child interaction afford opportunities for literacy learning.

Understanding the literacy environments of children from diverse socioeconomic and cultural groups could help teachers in their goal of being responsive to children's differing needs. In this column we highlight our research on these diverse home experiences and parental perspectives. Our information is based on findings from our ongoing longitudinal study, the Early Childhood Project (Baker, Sonnenschein, Serpell, Fernandez-Fein, & Scher, 1994).

Methods of the Study

Participants are families with children who were enrolled in prekindergarten in Baltimore, Maryland, USA, public elementary schools in 1992–1993. The schools serve four neighborhoods populated mainly by (1) low-income African American families, (2) low-income European American families, (3) a mix of low-income African American and European American families, and (4) a mix of middle-income African American and European American families.

The information about children's everyday home experiences was collected by asking parents to keep a diary of their children's activities during a 1-week period and then questioning them about their children's participation in specific activities likely to foster literacy development. We learned about parents' perspectives on literacy through their comments in the diaries, their responses to interview questions about the goals they had for their children, and their beliefs about the purposes of reading and the processes of learning to read. Children's emergent literacy competencies were also assessed. We administered a variety of tasks tapping knowledge about print, phonological awareness, and narrative competence. (Details about methods and findings are available in Baker, Serpell, & Sonnenschein, 1995; Baker et al., 1994; Serpell et al., in press; Sonnenschein, Baker, & Serpell, 1995.)

Major Findings

Families in all sociocultural groups reported frequent opportunities for their children to engage in activities related to several aspects of literacy: orientation toward print (for example, storybook reading); phonological awareness (such as in singing); knowledge of the world (for example, television viewing); and narrative competence (such as during mealtime conversation). The parents' diaries enriched our understandings of the children's home experiences, as reflected in this excerpt from a diary written by a low-income European American mother:

She start saying her ABC twice. then she asked her father for a quarter to buy wrestling cards she asked her sister to take her to the store to get them Her sister and brother take her to the store at 1:20. She comes back and said its too windy it will blow me away. I tell her no it won't it never blowed me away when I was little like you. she said mom you were never little like me your my mom so how can you be little like me. then she starts counting on the calender. then she play with her ABC maginets on the regirator singing ABC's...she sing Hot Cross buns she plays mario with her brother listen to radio 92 Q with her sister and try to sing along. I call her father to help me with Angle in the Ged [General Equivalency Diploma] book and she comes in to show us her right Ankel and left we told her we're talking about Angle not Ankel they may sound alike but difference.

This entry illustrates specific opportunities for learning about print (playing with ABC magnets, counting on the calendar), developing phonological awareness (singing songs, discussing the similarity of sounds in the words angle and ankle), acquiring knowledge of the world (going to the store), and developing narrative competence (conversing with her mother about various events, including those that occurred when her mother was not present).

The information parents provided us suggested that their interactions with their children were guided by one or more of the following perspectives on literacy: Literacy is a source of entertainment; literacy is a set of skills to be deliberately cultivated; and literacy is an integral ingredient of everyday life. Analysis of the diaries showed that middle-income families tended to report that their children engaged in more activities consistent with the view that literacy is a source of entertainment, such as joint storybook reading or independent interaction with print, than did low-income families. For example, one middle-income mother wrote that her child went to his room and got some books, which he and his younger sister "pretended to read to each other."

Low-income families described fewer print-related activities overall, and when they did describe literacy activities these were designed for the cultivation of literacy skills, such as using flashcards and reciting the alphabet. One low-income mother wrote that she was "teaching her [daughter] how to spell and to identify the letters in her name using paper and pencils and flashcards." Despite these trends, many of the low-income families also emphasized the entertainment value of literacy and the cultivation of intrinsic motivation. For example, one low-income mother said she reads to her child every night before bed and tries to make it exciting: "Why make reading boring? It stops a person from liking it."

These differing perspectives were reflected in parents' responses to a question about the most effective mode of intervention for promoting early literacy, with some parents emphasizing provision of enjoyable opportunities for reading and others focusing on skills training. One parent said the most effective way to help her child learn to read was by "enforcing how fun and pleasurable reading is, not approaching it as a chore." Another parent said by "being there and letting him read to you, making sure enough books which he can read are around the house, more or less being there and if he needs help, help him." Reflecting the contrasting skills perspective, one low-income mother said, "When I sits here and read with her, I points to the word as I read along with her so she'll know how to identify the word that I am reading." Similarly, another mother said, "helping learn the sounds of the letters; you have to learn the phonics before you can read."

Parents' perspectives on literacy are related not only to the experiences they make available to their children in the home but also to children's independent performance on tasks designed to assess emergent literacy. Children growing up in homes where there was a greater emphasis on literacy as a source of entertainment performed better on our measures of knowledge about print (for example, identification of letters, concepts about print, and functions of print materials) and story understanding than children growing up in homes where there was a relatively greater emphasis on skills.

Conclusions and Implications

The home literacy environments of European American and African American families did not differ in the data we have analyzed to date as strongly as those of middle-income and low-income families. Many middle-income parents seem to prefer to provide their children with opportunities for constructing their own understandings of literacy by making literacy materials readily available for independent use. Many low-income parents, in contrast, place relatively more emphasis on structured activities and on ostensible component skills in literacy. Thus, middle-income families tend to adopt a more playful approach in preparing their children for literacy than low-income families.

Should this finding be a concern to teachers? We concur with Goldenberg, Reese, and Gallimore (1992) who argue that it may be more effective and adaptive to encourage home involvement that is consistent with parents' existing beliefs than to try to change parents' views. After all, skills such as letter-sound correspondence knowledge do contribute to reading achievement. That the children in our study did not appear to benefit from a skills perspective may indicate that parents did not translate their beliefs into effective instruction. Teachers may increase the connection between home and school through sharing with parents what skills their children are mastering and how classroom literacy-based activities are fostering these skills. Relating classroom literature-based activities to the basic components of reading, which low-income parents already deem important, may help parents embrace both a skills and an entertainment perspective of literacy.

It would be a mistake to assume that the home experiences of all children within a sociocultural group are comparable; we found a great deal of variability in the opportunities available to children for learning about literacy. Therefore, we believe that children will benefit from teachers and parents who are willing to learn and incorporate practices from each setting into an integrated literacy environment for children. Teachers may learn more about the home environments of their students through some of the methods and tools that we used to address this question (Sonnenschein, Baker, & Serpell, 1995). For example, our ecological inventory was designed to reveal the nature of everyday resources and opportunities available to children outside of the school.

Through gathering information with semi-structured interviews, teachers may be better able to involve parents in children's literacy in ways that are commensurate with parents' resources, literacy abilities, and beliefs. For example, teachers may become aware that willing parents are not able to engage in school-assigned home literacy activities due to lack of knowledge about available library resources or due to language and literacy barriers. Such barriers to home-school relations can be overcome only if teachers and parents form positive partnerships through both awareness and proactive steps. Appropriate steps will vary for differing home situations but might include varying home assignments to align with resources and parental strengths and beliefs, sending appropriate materials home when they are otherwise not available, and putting parents in contact with literacy support groups when language or literacy barriers require a parent-focused intervention (Morrow, 1989).

Finally, just as we wish parents to model literacy engagement for children in the home, teachers may serve as models of literacy instruction for parents. By inviting parents into the classroom, teachers have an opportunity to model characteristics of motivating literacy environments, such as letting children exercise choice in their literacy activities and interact socially through print materials, giving children responsibility for their literacy learning, and helping children experience success (see Morrow, 1989).

Understanding home experiences and parents' perspectives on literacy are important prerequisites to building connections between home and school, especially when the cultures of home and school are dissimilar (Baker et al., 1996; Thompson et al., 1996). We hope that our exploration of the home literacy experiences of children from diverse sociocultural backgrounds will provide clues to enable teachers to design activities that are consistent with these experiences and involve parents more fully in their children's education.

REFERENCES

Baker, L., Allen, J.B., Shockley, B., Pellegrini, A.D., Galda, L., & Stahl, S. (1996). Connecting school and home: Constructing partnerships to foster reading development. In L. Baker, P. Afflerbach, & D. Reinking (Eds.), *Developing engaged readers in school and home communities* (pp. 21–41). Mahwah, NJ: Erlbaum.

Baker, L., Serpell, R., & Sonnenschein, S. (1995). Opportunities for literacy learning in the homes of urban preschoolers. In L.M. Morrow (Ed.), *Family literacy connections in schools and communities* (pp. 236–252). Newark, DE: International Reading Association.

Baker, L., Sonnenschein, S., Serpell, R., Fernandez-Fein, S., & Scher, D. (1994). *Contexts of emergent literacy: Everyday home experiences of urban pre-kindergarten children* (Research

Rep. No. 24). Athens, GA: Universities of Georgia and Maryland, National Reading Research Center.

Goldenberg, C., Reese, L., & Gallimore, R. (1992). Effects of literacy materials from school on Latino children's home experiences and early reading achievement. *American Journal of Education, 100,* 497–536.

Morrow, L.M. (1989). *Literacy development in the early years.* Englewood Cliffs, NJ: Prentice-Hall.

Serpell, R., Sonnenschein, S., Baker, L., Hill, S., Goddard-Truitt, V., & Danseco, E. (in press). *Socialization goals and beliefs among parents of children on the threshold of schooling* (Research Rep.). Athens, GA: Universities of Georgia and Maryland, National Reading Research Center.

Sonnenschein, S., Baker, L., & Serpell, R. (1995). *Documenting the child's everyday home experience: The Ecological Inventory as a resource for teachers* (Instructional Resource No. 11). Athens, GA: Universities of Georgia and Maryland, National Reading Research Center.

Sonnenschein, S., Baker, L., Serpell, R., Scher, D., Fernandez-Fein, S., & Munsterman, K. (1996). *Strands of emergent literacy and their antecedents in the home: Urban preschoolers' early literacy development* (Research Rep.). Athens, GA: Universities of Georgia and Maryland, National Reading Research Center.

Sonnenschein, S., Brody, G., & Munsterman, K. (1996). The influence of family beliefs and practices on children's early reading development. In L. Baker, P. Afflerbach, & D. Reinking (Eds.), *Developing engaged readers in school and home communities* (pp. 3–20). Mahwah, NJ: Erlbaum.

Thompson, R., Mixon, G., & Serpell, R. (1996). Engaging minority students in reading: Focus on the urban learner. In L. Baker, P. Afflerbach, & D. Reinking (Eds.), *Developing engaged readers in school and home communities* (pp. 43–63). Mahwah, NJ: Erlbaum.

Connecting School and Home Literacy Experiences Through Cross-Age Reading

Barbara J. Fox, Maripat Wright

y little sister likes Dr. Seuss, so maybe I'll read this book," Michelle told a 9-year-old classmate. Turning the pages of *Ten Apples Up on Top!* (LeSieg, 1961), Phillip said to a 10-year-old in his class, "This book looks good. It would be funny to a little kid." As Keiba looked at *In the Tall, Tall Grass* (Fleming, 1991), she remarked to an 11-year-old friend, "This is great! My little brother loves animal stories."

Michelle, Phillip, and Keiba do not normally pay close attention to storybooks for younger children. These learners thought carefully about storybooks because they took books home to read to children as part of a cross-age reading program called Storymates, which connected school and home literacy experiences through storybook reading. Activities in school included practice reading storybooks with a teammate, exploring the narrative structure of stories, and writing retellings of familiar storybooks. Children then read these same storybooks to younger brothers, sisters, cousins, and neighborhood friends at home.

This article describes the 9-week Storymates program, provides examples of the sto-rybooks that learners enjoyed, and explains the results and reactions to this cross-age program. The program was developed as a direct link between home and school literacy designed to provide meaningful experiences with easy books to 9-, 10-, and 11-year-old children who had difficulty reading books written at their grade level. Participants included 288 students across 12 classrooms from a school located in a rural, southeastern U.S. community where farming and unskilled manufacturing are the major sources of employment. The median household income in this community is well below the poverty level, nearly one third of the parents did not have a high school diploma or the equivalent, and kindergarten children were at high to moderate risk of school failure. Reading material was scarce in many homes, and some children grew up in families where daily life did not include listening to storybooks read aloud.

Many of these 9-, 10-, and 11-year-olds could not read and comprehend library books written for their grade level. On a standardized test, the mean percentile for Total Reading (a composite of comprehension and vocabulary subtests) was 23 for 9-year-olds, 32 for 10-year-olds, and 34 for 11-year-olds (Gates-MacGinitie

Reading Tests, 1989). The school librarian observed that many of the students seemed uninterested in the books and activities provided by the library program and were reluctant to check out books. When they wrote their recollections of familiar storybooks, these children left out important information.

The retelling in Figure 1 was written by an 11-year-old who had read *Dirty Dave* (Hilton, 1987), a story about a family of bushwhackers who change their lifestyle from being outlaws to making and marketing clothes. This retelling was characteristic of those written by the other students in that it lacked most of the major structural elements of a narrative story.

Narrative stories like *Dirty Dave* include structural elements such as the setting, characters, a problem, attempts to solve the problem, and a solution. An understanding of these elements helps children make sense of the stories they read (Armbruster, Anderson, & Ostertag, 1989; Spiegel & Fitzgerald, 1986). Familiarity with these elements allows children also to identify information, make predictions, organize thinking, and write about the stories (Fitzgerald, 1989). Because the older children frequently did not include many of these elements in their retellings, it was important for them to explore the structure of narrative stories. Books written for the children's grade level were not particularly suited for exploring story structure because they were too difficult for many learners. However, these children could successfully read books written for younger children.

Storybooks for young children have several advantages. They contain less text than books written for older children, which makes them less daunting. Storybooks also have illustrations that intentionally describe and extend the text, thus providing meaning cues to readers. In addition, many books for young children use predictable language patterns, which give readers opportunities to anticipate repetitious words, sentences, and ideas. Finally, storybooks usually recount simple, uncomplicated stories, the structure of which is more transparent than in books with complex plot lines. This makes storybooks for young children a good source for gaining insight into structural elements.

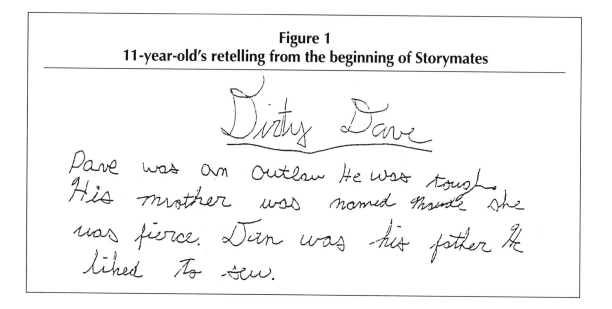

Figure 1
11-year-old's retelling from the beginning of Storymates

Dirty Dave

Dave was an outlaw He was tough
His mother was named Maude she
was fierce. Dan was his father He
liked to sew.

Exploring Story Structure in the Classroom

Each week for 9 weeks, 12 teachers (4 in each grade) read one storybook aloud to their class to provide a model of good read-aloud behaviors and to create a common experience with literature that formed the basis for exploring story structure. An important characteristic of the storybooks read aloud is that they had themes that appealed both to young children and to older ones. Examples include *The Tenth Good Thing About Barney* (Viorst, 1971), a thoughtful treatment of the death of a pet; *Tacky and the Penguins* (Lester, 1988), a humorous look at the value of being different from the crowd; and *Wilfrid Gordon McDonald Partridge* (Fox, 1985), an exploration of aging in today's society. Other examples of the books that teachers read aloud are listed in the Children's Literature References at the end of this article.

Each week older children were challenged to analyze the structural elements of the storybooks that teachers read aloud by making graphic representations such as recipes (Irwin & Baker, 1989), maps (Johns, VanLeirsburg, & Davis, 1994), frames (Armbruster et al., 1989; Fowler, 1982) and webs (Freeman & Reynolds, 1980). Other activities challenged learners to work with teammates to rewrite story endings, identify cause and effect, make predictions, find transition words, summarize events, make inferences, draw conclusions, and compare and contrast characters or events.

Reading Storybooks in School and at Home

Reading takes place in social settings, whether in classrooms, in the library, at home, or in the supermarket. A number of factors affect comprehension in social contexts, including the reasons for reading, knowledge of the subject, characteristics of the text, and interactions with others (Goodman, 1985). One type of social context involves students reading storybooks to their classmates, which is particularly helpful when the same storybooks are read more than once. This procedure, called repeated reading, was an important feature of the Storymates program because it exposed children in a holistic way to an author's vocabulary, sentence structure, and message. Repeated reading improves vocabulary, fluency, and comprehension (Dowhower, 1989) and is particularly beneficial for poor readers whose rate and word recognition accuracy improve with multiple readings (Herman, 1985).

Twice each week during the Storymates program, teams of two learners followed the paired repeated reading procedure (Koskinen & Blum, 1986) to practice reading the storybooks they would later take home to be read to young children. One teammate read a storybook aloud while the other teammate listened, rated reading fluency, and wrote one or more good things about the way the story was read; the reader also rated his or her own reading performance. In addition, the listener wrote questions that the reader answered after the second reading. Listeners were encouraged to frame questions that asked about the structure of stories, which gave both listeners and readers extra opportunities to think about story elements. After the same storybook was read at least twice by the first reader, teammates exchanged roles so that each had a turn reading and listening.

After a storybook had been read twice, children wrote a retelling of the story. Though retelling is often done orally, Emory (1989) has shown that written retellings are just as productive and rich as oral retellings. Traditional children's stories are the best type of text for retelling because they are more likely to be familiar to learners, to be predictable, and to have stylistic features that learners recognize (Brown & Cambourne, 1990). Research shows that learners' knowledge of story structure is increased when they retell the stories they read (Koskinen, Gambrell, & Kapinus, 1993). Retelling helps children develop greater insight into how to use the structure of stories to organize their thinking and helps them recall more information (Koskinen, Gambrell, Kapinus, & Heathington, 1988).

Another type of social context is cross-age reading in which older children read to younger children. Leland and Fitzpatrick (1994) reported that cross-age reading had a positive effect on learners. They found that sixth graders who read to kindergartners became more interested in reading and writing. In the Storymates program, 9-, 10-, and 11-year-olds read two storybooks a week at home to younger brothers, sisters, cousins, or neighborhood friends. These books were chosen from boxes of 50 books that were rotated weekly among the 12 classrooms.

The storybooks that students read at home were judged by their teachers to be well written, well illustrated, and appropriate for children ages 1 to 7 years. Because some of the books were easy picture books and others contained more challenging text, the older children could choose books written at a level they could read independently and with confidence.

Comparisons of Retellings From the Beginning to the End of Storymates

Figure 2 shows a retelling of *The Witch Next Door* (Bridwell, 1986) that was written at the end of the 9-week Storymates program by the same 11-year-old who wrote the retelling of *Dirty Dave* in Figure 1.

According to Brown and Cambourne (1990), when children have internalized in-formation and concepts, their retellings reflect the structure and stylistic forms of the book they have read. One way to find out if learners incorporate structural elements in their retellings is to score retellings with a procedure like the one developed by Koskinen et al. (1993). Retellings were scored with a modification of this procedure in which scores from 0 (no evidence) to 3 (strong evidence) were given for (a) awareness of story structure, (b) major plot episodes, (c) use of stylistic devices, and (d) coherence (see Figure 3). A total of 30 points was possible.

Twenty children from each age group were selected randomly, and their written retellings from the beginning and end of Storymates were scored. Because some children were absent when the last retelling was written, 50 wrote both retellings: 19 of the 9-year-olds, 16 of the 10-year-olds, and 15 of the 11-year-olds. Three teachers from a different school scored the children's writing. The interrater reliability was .957 for the first retellings scored and .896 for the second. Table 1 shows the mean retelling scores for each age group. A repeated measures analysis of variance was used to test for differences in retelling scores across the three grades and from the first to the last retelling. No significant differences were found for the main effect of age or for the interaction of age and time of retelling (beginning to end). However, a significant difference was found for the time of the retelling, $F(2, 47) = 49.08$, $p < .001$. These data may be interpreted to mean that the experiences learners had in the Storymates program helped them write better renditions of the stories they read.

Reactions of Teachers, Students, and Parents

At the beginning of the Storymates program, the school librarian reported the 9-, 10-,

Figure 2
11-year-old's retelling from the end of Storymates

The witch Next Door

There was a little girl and a little boy. They look next door and the little boy said that is a witch. But he was not shore. So they decided to see if it was a witch and they hid behide a tree. She got on he brum and went to the drug store She come out with alot of stuff. They said we are going to find out, So they found out, She is a witch but she is a nice witch. She is nice to alot of people. Their was two people that could not stand witches so they went over their and told her she has to move, we don't want witches in our neighborhood. The witch got made and the little boy and girl never seen her this mad.

The witch put a spell on them she could not see them and the were a prince and a princess. Of course they forgot about asking our witch to leave. The little girl asked if she would conge us in a prine and a princess please. The hoped on the brum and flyed around happly ever after.

and 11-year-olds "walked right past the shelves with books for young children." However, in contrast to this observation, during the program learners sought, checked out, and read storybooks. Teachers reported that the box of 50 storybooks was a focal point in the classroom and that many learners spent their spare time reading storybooks. Some students read all 50 books each week. As one teacher put it, "Most [children] were eager to read and share. It's [Storymates] a great self-esteem builder." When it was time to exchange boxes at the end of the week, learners were not always ready to let the books go. For example, one Friday, a 9-year-old boy was overheard saying to his teacher, "Do we have to move our box? I want to read *The Seven Chinese Brothers* (Mahy, 1990) again."

The comment of an 11-year-old girl illustrates the advantage of repeated reading with a teammate in the classroom. After a halting first reading of *Cloudy with a Chance of Meatballs* (Barrett, 1978) and a fluent second reading, she said to her teammate, "I didn't think I could

---

Figure 3
Retelling scoring criteria

Score each item according to the following:
0 = No evidence
1 = Meager evidence
2 = Fair evidence
3 = Strong evidence

Awareness of story structure
   1. Setting includes time and place   _____
   2. Identification of central characters   _____

Major plot episodes
   3. Statement of problem   _____
   4. Statement of plan to solve the problem _____
   5. Statement of problem resolution   _____

Use of stylistic devices
   6. Formal beginning of story   _____
   7. Formal conclusion   _____

Coherence
   8. Logical story sequence   _____
   9. Correct sequence of events   _____
  10. Use of transition terms   _____

Total   _____

Adapted from Koskinen et al., 1993.

Table 1
Retelling scores from the beginning and end of Storymates

| Age | Retelling 1 | | Retelling 2 | |
	Mean	Standard deviation	Mean	Standard deviation
9-year-olds	10.91	6.05	18.80	5.40
10-year-olds	13.77	8.37	22.00	4.93
11-year-olds	15.55	7.80	21.64	4.90

Table 2
Parent questionnaire and responses

| Questions | Responses | | | |
| | Positive | | Negative | |
	n	Percent	n	Percent
Have you seen your child reading at home?	177	98	3	2
Is your child reading more at home than at the beginning of the program?	166	92	14	8
Did your child enjoy reading to younger children?	169	93	11	7
Did younger children enjoy being read to?	169	93	11	7

read that well!" The success this group had reading storybooks helped them perceive themselves as competent readers. Teachers observed that learners were more willing to participate in class: volunteering information, making comments, or doing projects.

By the end of the 9-week program, younger brothers, sisters, cousins, and neighborhood children had listened to at least 18 different storybooks that were selected for them by each of the older children. In order to gauge parents' reactions to the home reading, a questionnaire was sent to the parents of all 288 learners. Parents were asked to circle yes or no to four questions and were invited to write personal comments if they wished to do so. One hundred eighty questionnaires were returned to school, for a return rate of 62% (see results in Table 2).

Parents' comments suggested that they perceived positive changes in their children. One parent observed, "The older children are working better with the younger kids." Another parent wrote, "[Child's name] grades have improved. She reads twice as much. Her 5-year-old cousin enjoys her reading to her." The parent of a 10-year-old wrote, "I think this program has made a lot of difference in my whole household as far as reading. I find my 5- and 6-year-olds trying to read to my 3-year-old, trying to do like their fifth-grade brother." One parent of a 9-year-old commented, "I think this is a good project. It helps younger children learn to listen when they are being read to."

In this era of fast-paced television programs and action-packed video games, it is important to strengthen the connections between literacy experiences in school and at home. Storymates helped foster this connection in which school literacy experiences flowed naturally into children's daily lives at home, and, in turn, home activities were meaningful, useful, and integral to literacy experiences in school. One parent of an 11-year-old wrote on the questionnaire, "Thank [you] for doing that program. I hope you will have it again." This view was echoed by teachers, one of whom declared, "We need to extend the [Storymates] program to the entire school year."

Authors' Note

Storymates was funded by a grant from the Metropolitan Life Foundation.

REFERENCES

Armbruster, B.B., Anderson, T.H., & Ostertag, J. (1989). Teaching text structure to improve reading and writing. *The Reading Teacher, 43,* 130–137.

Brown, H., & Cambourne, B. (1990). *Read and retell.* Portsmouth, NH: Heinemann.

Dowhower, S.L. (1989). Repeated reading: Research into practice. *The Reading Teacher, 42,* 502–507.

Emory, P. (1989). The effects on reading comprehension scores using the oral retelling or written retelling strategies. *Dissertation Abstracts International, 51,* 805.

Fitzgerald, J. (1989). Research on stories: Implications for teachers. In K.D. Muth (Ed.), *Children's comprehension of text* (pp. 2–36). Newark, DE: International Reading Association.

Fowler, G.L. (1982). Developing comprehension skills in primary students through the use of story frames. *The Reading Teacher, 37,* 176–179.

Freeman, G., & Reynolds, T.V. (1980). Enriching basal reader lessons and semantic webbing. *The Reading Teacher, 33,* 677–684.

Goodman, K.S. (1985). Unity in reading. In H. Singer & R.B. Ruddell (Eds.), *Theoretical models and processes of reading* (2nd ed., pp. 470–496). Newark, DE: International Reading Association.

Herman, P.A. (1985). The effect of repeated readings on reading rate, speech pauses and word recognition accuracy. *Reading Research Quarterly, 20,* 553–565.

Irwin, J.W., & Baker, I. (1989). *Promoting active reading comprehension strategies.* Englewood Cliffs, NJ: Prentice Hall.

Johns, J.L., VanLeirsburg, P., & Davis, S.J. (1994). *Improving reading: A handbook of strategies.* Dubuque, IA: Kendall/Hunt.

Koskinen, P.S., & Blum, I.H. (1986). Paired repeated reading: A classroom strategy for developing fluent reading. *The Reading Teacher, 40,* 70–75.

Koskinen, P.S., Gambrell, L.B., & Kapinus, B.A. (1993). The use of retellings for portfolio assessment of reading comprehension. In J.F. Almasi (Ed.), *Literacy: Issues and practices* (Vol. 10, pp. 41–77). Silver Spring, MD: State of Maryland International Reading Association Yearbook.

Koskinen, P.S., Gambrell, L.B., Kapinus, B.A., & Heathington, B.S. (1988). Retelling: A strategy for enhancing students' reading comprehension. *The Reading Teacher, 41,* 892–896.

Leland, C., & Fitzpatrick, R. (1994). Cross-age interaction builds enthusiasm for reading and writing. *The Reading Teacher, 47,* 292–301.

Spiegel, D.L., & Fitzgerald, J. (1986). Improving reading comprehension through instruction about story parts. *The Reading Teacher, 39,* 676–682.

CHILDREN'S LITERATURE REFERENCES

Allard, H., & Marshall, J. (1977). *Miss Nelson is missing.* New York: Scholastic.

Barrett, J. (1978). *Cloudy with a chance of meat-balls*. New York: Scholastic.

Bridwell, N. (1986). *The witch next door*. New York: Scholastic.

DePaola, T. (1975). *Strega Nona*. New York: Simon & Shuster.

Esbensen, B.J., & Davie, H.K. (1988). *The star maiden*. Boston, MA: Little, Brown.

Fleming, D. (1991). *In the tall, tall grass*. New York: Henry Holt.

Fox, M. (1985). *Wilfrid Gordon McDonald Partridge*. Brooklyn, NY: Dane/Miller.

Hilton, N. (1987). *Dirty Dave*. New York: Orchard.

Jeschke, S. (1980). *Perfect the pig*. New York: Scholastic.

LeSieg, T. (1961). *Ten apples up on top!* New York: Random House.

Lester, H. (1988). *Tacky and the penguins*. Boston, MA: Houghton Mifflin.

Lobel, A. (1979). *A tree full of pigs*. New York: Scholastic.

Lobel, A. (1982). *Ming Lo moves the mountain*. New York: Scholastic.

Lord, J.V., & Burroway, J. (1972). *The giant jam sandwich*. Boston, MA: Houghton Mifflin.

Mahy, M. (1990). *The seven Chinese brothers*. New York: Scholastic.

Morimoto, J. (1985). *Mouse's marriage*. New York: Puffin

Thaler, M. (1989). *The teacher from the black lagoon*. New York: Scholastic.

Viorst, J. (1971). *The tenth good thing about Barney*. New York: Aladdin.

Zemach, M. (1976). *It could always be worse*. New York: Scholastic.

A Community Volunteer Tutorial That Works

Marcia Invernizzi, Connie Juel, Catherine A. Rosemary

Schools are microcosms of the social, economic, and political context in which they exist. When money is scarce and the needs are great, school divisions face some tough choices. This is a story about one school division's response to such a predicament, a story of creativity, collaboration, community commitment, and making the most of what research has to say about early intervention.

Charlottesville, Virginia, USA, is a city of contradictions. It is simultaneously the academic village of Thomas Jefferson and the hub of social services for a five-county radius. One fourth of its population lives below the poverty level; two fifths of its children live in single-parent homes. Seventeen percent of its adult population hold graduate or professional degrees, while 25% have not graduated from high school. This sociological disparity is mirrored in the bimodal distribution of reading achievement in the schools. In 1994, 60% of the fourth-grade elementary population scored below the 50th percentile and 40% scored at or above the 50th percentile on the Iowa Test of Basic Skills in reading achievement (Charlottesville City Schools, 1994).

To begin closing the gap between the high and low achievers as evidenced in fourth grade (the first year that the students are administered a standardized reading achievement test), the Charlottesville City Schools initiated an aggressive plan directed at first-grade intervention. After careful planning, the Charlottesville City Schools launched their divisionwide Reading Initiative. This comprehensive plan put literacy at the forefront of staff development for teachers and instructional assistants, varied formats for federal government-funded Title I [U.S. federally funded education program for at-risk children; formerly Chapter 1] services, and implemented student peer coaching (Weincek & O'Flahavan, 1994). Interested in the research on the effectiveness of one-on-one tutorials (Clay, 1985; Hiebert & Taylor, 1994; Slavin, Madden, & Karweit, 1989), school division personnel began exploring alternative forms of one-on-one intervention programs.

A partnership was thus formed among the Charlottesville City Schools, the McGuffey Reading Center of the University of Virginia, and the Charlottesville community. The Charlottesville Volunteer Tutorial has become an integral part of the Charlottesville City Schools' long-range Reading Initiative. The goals of the Charlottesville Volunteer Tutorial are to improve the reading and writing skills of at-risk children and to establish and maintain the community's involvement in and responsibility for the education of all children.

Program Description

The Charlottesville Volunteer Tutorial has several unique features. A volunteer recruiter solicits interested community members through the media, public meetings with community service groups, business associations, and personal contacts. Each tutor is trained by the authors in research-based methods three times a year during 2-hour training sessions. Each session incorporates video demonstration lessons of actual tutorials and a walk-through of the lesson plan. At each school, the reading coordinator provides ongoing training and support for the tutors by writing lesson plans, arranging materials for each lesson, and providing routine feedback regarding specific activities, techniques, and pacing. Each coordinator supervises 15 volunteer tutors and their respective tutees. Tutors instruct children twice weekly in 45-minute sessions.

Settings for the tutorials vary, depending on individual classroom teacher preferences. The majority of the tutorials are pull-outs occurring in separate classrooms designated as tutoring centers. Tutorials are scheduled during seatwork time or "specials" (for example, music, art, or library) to avoid conflicts with academic instruction in the classroom.

Parents, community volunteers, university students and faculty, and school personnel work together to provide tutorial services. During the 3 years of the program, we served 358 children in all six of the city's elementary schools.

The Charlottesville Volunteer Tutorial began as a local grant-sponsored program in one pilot school. The first 3 years were funded by the Charlottesville City Schools and local and national grants awarded to the McGuffey Reading Center. In 1995–1996, the school division funded salaries paid to the reading coordinators and the volunteer recruiter, as well as expenses for books and materials. Significant in-kind contributions from school personnel and University of Virginia faculty and graduate students have continued to support the program from the outset.

The Key Triad

The heart of the Charlottesville Volunteer Tutorial is a triad composed of the child, the volunteer tutor, and the reading coordinator. The coordinators, each of whom is a current or former graduate student in reading education, supervise the volunteers and provide ongoing support throughout the duration of the program. Their responsibilities include (a) assessing students individually twice a year to design an appropriate instructional program and to monitor children's progress; (b) training and providing continual support for volunteers; (c) coordinating the instructional program with the classroom teacher and Title I teacher through biweekly meetings; (d) writing individualized lesson plans to assure that the needs of each student are being met; and (e) documenting time, testing data, and anecdotal information regarding the program. Coordinators report the children's progress to parents through parent-teacher conferences and written correspondence. Coordinators work approximately 17 hours per week.

The tutors are primarily volunteers from the Charlottesville community. Females outnumber male volunteers by four to one. The majority of the community volunteers are Caucasian. The ages of the tutors are split evenly across the age brackets of 20–39, 40–59, and 60 years old and above. The staying power of our volunteers is remarkable: 96% of the volunteer tutors complete the full school year, and 52% have tutored for 2 to 3 years.

The volunteer tutors have several responsibilities. They attend formal training sessions two to three times a year to prepare them to work with their assigned child. They follow the instructional plan developed for each child by the reading coordinator, and they provide written evaluation regarding each tutorial. In addition, volunteer tutors meet informally with their reading coordinator weekly to give and receive feedback on their lessons. Regular communication is maintained through personal contacts, telephone conversations, and written exchanges.

The children are primarily first-grade students recommended for the program by their classroom teachers. Selection is determined by teacher referral and by the children's scores on an adaptation of Morris' Early Reading Screening Inventory (ERSI) (Morris, 1992). Children who score poorly on the ERSI have little or no alphabet knowledge, no concept of word, and little or no phonemic awareness. First-grade children are served first. Some second graders are included, depending on the availability of resources. On the average, 60% are male, 40% are female; 68% are African American, 30% are Caucasian, and 2% are from other ethnic groups. Seventy percent of the children qualify for free lunch.

The volunteer recruiter matches the schedules and number of volunteers needed at each elementary school with the schedules of volunteers who are available during particular times. The reading coordinators are in constant communication with the volunteer recruiter as children move between schools in the division and as other children are added to their case loads.

The Tutoring Lesson

Instruction consists of reading, writing, and phonics. Tutors follow a sequence of core activities planned by the reading coordinators in a four-part lesson plan described in a volunteer tutoring manual by Johnston, Juel, and Invernizzi (1995). The tutoring lessons include (1) rereading familiar story books, (2) word study, (3) writing, and (4) reading a new book.

The child begins each session by warming up with the rereading of familiar books. The tutor then harvests words from familiar texts for the child to identify, writes the words on cards to form a word bank, and later uses these word cards for phonics lessons. Tutors follow the word studying activity by dictating sentences from familiar texts, or allowing the children to compose their own pieces that relate to the books they have read. The tutor concludes by introducing a new book to the child. The tutor models ways to anticipate the content and wording of the book using titles and picture clues, and talks about vocabulary and key concepts, encouraging the child to state predictions and observations about the story content.

The reading coordinators assist the tutors by modeling instructional techniques, observing the tutors during sessions, and providing ongoing feedback to help tutors refine their techniques and develop effective ways to interact with their children. A closer look at the lesson plan reveals many similarities between this volunteer tutorial and other one-on-one interventions that rely on highly trained reading specialists.

Rereading Familiar Books

The value of repeated readings has been well documented by educators and researchers from a variety of theoretical orientations. Rehearsal of the same text cultivates reading fluency and other benefits of repeated practice including automaticity in word recognition (Samuels, 1979), improved comprehension (Dowhower, 1987; Rasinski, 1990), and improved prosodic reading expression (Schreiber, 1987). Children become comfortable reading in meaningful phrases rather than in a choppy, word-by-word fashion. Many educators espouse the benefits of warming up with repeated readings (Samuels, Schermer, &

Reinking, 1992). The rereading of familiar story books has become a hallmark activity associated with Reading Recovery (Pinnell, 1989). Every Charlottesville Volunteer Tutorial opens with the repeated reading of three or four familiar books followed by independent reading of the new book from the previous session. Books are retired from the warm-up routine as children become automatic in their reading. Children then move on to other books with which they are not yet fluent.

Word Study

Word study is a unique aspect of this intervention program. Word study refers to the cultivation of a concept of word in print (Morris, 1981) and the pacing of instruction in alphabet, spelling, and phonics in accordance with the developmental word knowledge of the child (Bear, Invernizzi, & Templeton, 1996; Henderson & Beers, 1980; Henderson & Templeton, 1986; Templeton & Bear, 1992). Developmental word knowledge refers to what the child knows about written words: their letter formation, sound segments within words, letter-sound correspondences, spelling patterns, and meanings. Developmental spelling theory posits that what a child knows about words is revealed in spellings, which act as windows to their word knowledge. According to developmental spelling theory, an informed analysis of children's invented spellings can guide the content and pacing of instruction in word recognition, alphabet, spelling, and phonics. Rather than a preestablished scope and sequence of phonics and spelling features to be taught, word study instruction is differentiated according to what each learner knows (Invernizzi, Abouzeid, & Gill, 1994).

Word study instruction uses a compare-and-contrast approach to word features, comparing words that start with *b*, for example, with words that start with *m*, *r*, or *s*. Instructional activities consist of sorting tasks, first with picture cards, then with word cards as words become known. These activities, known as word sorts, form the bulk of the word study component of the Charlottesville Volunteer Tutorial (Barnes, 1989; Bloodgood, 1991; Morris, 1982). Sorting usually begins with the child sorting picture cards, writing words, and sorting word bank words, all by using beginning sounds. As beginning sounds are learned, word study shifts to more complex features such as consonant blends and short vowels. Reading coordinators prepare the cards to be sorted and determine the categories for manipulation.

Writing

The writing component of the Charlottesville Volunteer Tutorial is referred to as writing for sounds. We want children to learn how to segment their speech and to match letters to those segmented sounds. At the same time, we want to encourage children to use reading as a scaffold for their initial writing attempts (McGill-Franzen, Lanford, & Killian, 1994). Tutors are encouraged to dictate sentences from familiar texts, or to have children compose their own sentence(s) about the books they have read. Whenever possible, tutors guide children in writing a transformation in which the sentence varies from the original in only two or three words. For example, "In a dark, dark house, there was a dark, dark staircase" might become "In a dark, dark basement, there was a dark, dark closet." The tutor dictates the sentence and models the segmentation process by elongating the sounds in the words for children to match the letters to the sounds they hear. Children are encouraged to do their own elongating of sounds as needed.

There is considerable evidence to suggest that the act of segmenting speech and matching letters to sounds is a rigorous exercise of phonics in and of itself (Blachman, 1992).

Indeed, some researchers have used children's spellings as an indicator of phonemic awareness (Clay, 1985; Morris, 1992). Research has shown that writing in invented spellings enhances children's memory of words, at least at the beginning stages (Ehri & Wilce, 1987). Spellings change as word knowledge grows, and word knowledge grows as exercise and instruction are paced to the child's zone of proximal development (Vygotsky, 1962).

The children in the Charlottesville Volunteer Tutorial are encouraged to use their own knowledge of letter-sound correspondences and to produce "sound spellings" even if these are incorrect. Children are, however, held accountable for those features they have been taught during the word study component of the tutorial. Errors specifically related to features examined through word study are "negotiated toward correctness" (Clay, 1988). Those features not yet taught directly are allowed to stand as invented spellings.

Introducing the New Book

A new book is introduced at the end of every tutorial. The tutor and the child first preview the book and talk about its content in think-aloud fashion (Baumann, Seifert-Kessel, & Jones, 1992). Tutors are encouraged to point out items in the pictures that correspond to the words the child will later see in print and to talk about concepts or vocabulary found in the story. After the preview and discussion, children are encouraged to read the book independently. If the child appears to flounder, the tutor supports the child with choral and echo reading during the first attempt. If such support is necessary, a second, independent reading ensues.

Program Evaluation

Program evaluation is conducted annually. The measures consist of pre- and postliteracy assessments, child and tutor surveys, and annual cost analyses. Information from these sources is analyzed at the end of each year to refine the program and to report back to the community.

Pre- and Posttesting

Pre- and posttesting is used to measure growth, to guide instructional plans, and to make programmatic changes from one year to the next. The assessment includes (a) alphabet recognition (upper and lower) and production; (b) concept of word (speech-to-print tracking) in text; (c) phonemic awareness (sound sorting and spelling); and (d) word recognition using graded word lists, the Wide Range Achievement Test (1984), and the Diagnostic Survey (Clay, 1985). In addition, children are asked to read *Little Bear* (Minarik, 1957) at the end of the school year. Because *Little Bear* is considered a prototypical milestone for first-grade reading (Invernizzi, Juel, Rosemary, & Richards, 1994), the ability to read the story with better than 90% accuracy unassisted has been adopted as a major criterion for success.

Each year pre- to posttest gain scores have shown statistically significant increases on measures of alphabet, phonemic awareness, and word recognition. Thus far, the third-year gain scores have been the strongest on all measures ($p < .001$).

The functionality of the program is seen more clearly by controlling for pretest scores and analyzing the number of sessions the children received. Because the lowest scoring children on the pretest were served first, they received more sessions than higher scoring children. Children with the lower pretest scores and higher number of sessions (>40) outperformed children with the higher pretest scores and lower number of sessions (<40). When they received more than 40 sessions, the lower scoring children on the pretest received the higher posttest scores on measures of phonemic awareness ($t = 2.98$, $p = .004$), word recognition ($t = -6.00$, $p < .001$), and contextual reading ($x^2 = 4.24$, $p < .01$).

The success of this intervention program also is based on whether the children can independently read *Little Bear* with greater than 90% accuracy in word recognition. At the end of our first year, only 50% of the children with more than 40 sessions could read *Little Bear* with greater than 90% accuracy. At the end of our second year, 72% of the children with more than 40 sessions read *Little Bear* with 90% accuracy. At the end of our third year, 86% of all children read *Little Bear* with 90% accuracy. Ninety percent of the children with more than 40 sessions and 73% with fewer than 40 sessions read *Little Bear* to criterion (see Table).

The first-year data clearly indicated a need for refinement. Therefore, in our second year, we made several improvements: (a) tutoring began earlier in the school year; (b) volunteer training procedures included more small-group, building-level seminars; and (c) lesson plans included more word study. In addition, we, the tutors, and the coordinators realized that some children needed more than 1 year of tutoring. Some tutors expressed an interest in working with the same child a second year.

As a result, we expanded our program to include second-grade children and matched returning tutors with their same children if the children needed the extra boost. Of the 143 children in the second-year cohort, 41 were second graders. Of the 122 children in the third-year cohort, 18 were second graders. Preliminary analysis of second-grade results indicated that a third of the second graders achieved a second-grade reading level as measured by an informal reading inventory.

Survey Data

Tutors and children are surveyed each year. Tutor surveys address communication routines (for example, "What kinds of communication did you have with your coordinator and how often?"); quality and frequency of coordinator feedback and guidance (for example, "How often did your reading coordinator observe your tutoring sessions?"); and fidelity to the prepared lesson plans (for example, "With regard to the lesson plan, rate the flexibility you feel you had as a tutor"). Results of these surveys are used to fine-tune the training and communication aspects of the program.

Children are surveyed one on one by their reading coordinators. They are asked about

Oral reading of *Little Bear* with greater than 90% accuracy as a function of number of sessions and program year

Year	More than 40 sessions	Fewer than 40 sessions	Chi square
1994–1995	90% ($n = 71$)	73% ($n = 16$)	4.24*
1993–1994	72% ($n = 43$)	39% ($n = 43$)	9.24**
1992–1993	50% ($n = 12$)	45% ($n = 51$)	.09

*$p < .05$.   **$p < .01$.

their favorite part of the lesson plan, areas in which they felt the most success, and whether or not they read at home. Results are used to refine the activities and to find ways to encourage reading at home.

Tutor survey return rates ranged from 62–70% of approximately 100 community volunteers per year. Findings revealed that tutors volunteered for a variety of personal reasons. Most reported a commitment to making a difference for the children of Charlottesville. This commitment was best reflected in the words of a retired coach, who said, "I was in the company of some gentlemen who were discussing the subject of youth gone bad. I simply responded by saying that if we'd all put our time where our mouths are, we could make a difference."

Ninety-six percent of the tutor respondents indicated that they enjoyed the tutoring and the unexpected benefits derived from it. Most cited the Charlottesville Volunteer Tutorial as the highlight of their volunteering experiences. In the words of a tutor, "At first I volunteered because of Mary Ann [the volunteer recruiter]. The second year I volunteered because of the progress I saw with my child, and now, I've realized it's the only *real* thing I do all week."

The appropriateness of the premade lesson plan raised questions. Some school personnel worried that not allowing the volunteers to make their own plans was too rigid, while others worried that volunteers would not adhere to the plan. However, the correlation between the degree of lesson plan flexibility the tutor reported *having* versus the degree of flexibility the tutor reported *wanting* was .60 (p < .01). In all written reports, tutors indicated their appreciation of their coordinators' plans and guidance.

On the average, 98% of the children responded to the end-of-the-year survey. The children's favorite activities included learning a

new book and journal writing. Ninety-four percent reported that they read at home; 51% reported that they read at home *every day*.

Cost Analysis

Cost effectiveness is determined by an annual accounting of reading coordinators' and volunteer recruiters' salaries and expenses for books, materials, and video training tapes. The sum total of these expenses is divided by the number of children served each year to yield a per-pupil cost. In-kind contributions from the school, community, and the university are not included in the cost analysis.

Cost analyses of the first 3 years showed an average cost per child of US$595.00. This cost was considerably less than other one-on-one interventions. Hiebert's analysis of the cost of Reading Recovery, for example, ranged from $3,000 to $3,488 per student at Grade 1 (Hiebert, 1994).

The results of the program are reported back to the community in both official and unofficial ways. We report the program results to the school board and to the community at a public meeting during the fall term. Local news reporters publish the results, and local media also feature various aspects of the program throughout the year.

Staying Power

All partners in the Charlottesville Volunteer Tutorial collaboration have sustained their commitment to helping our at-risk first-grade children by contributing their time, talents, and money. The number of children who are served by the program is climbing. In 1992–1993, the Charlottesville Volunteer Tutorial served 93 first graders in four of six elementary schools. In 1993–1994, the program expanded to serve 143 first- and second-grade children in all six elementary schools. In

1994–1995, the third year of the program, 122 children were served, bringing the total number of children served during the first 3 years to 358. Low per-pupil expenditures underscore the cost effectiveness of the program, and our research demonstrates that community volunteers can make effective tutors.

Bronfenbrenner (1985), Comer (1990), and Heath and McLaughlin (1987) have called for greater community involvement in schools and for schools to reach out to communities for supportive services. The Charlottesville Volunteer Tutorial combines the concern, expertise, and human resources inherent in every community, its schools, and its universities. The program offers one model of an affordable, alternative form of early intervention that meets the needs of a struggling city. And, according to one of our tutors, "There's a lot of love that comes from it, actually."

Authors' Note

This program was made possible in part by the Hershey Foundation of Cleveland, Ohio, USA; the Inez D. Bishop Foundation of Charlottesville, Virginia, USA; and the Charlottesville/Albemarle Community Foundation of Charlottesville, Virginia, USA.

REFERENCES

Barnes, W.G. (1989). Word sorting: The cultivation of rules for spelling in English. *Reading Psychology, 10*, 293–307.

Baumann, J.F., Seifert-Kessel, N., & Jones, L.H. (1992). Effect of think-aloud instruction on elementary students' comprehension monitoring abilities. *Journal of Reading Behavior, 24*, 143–172.

Bear, D.R., Invernizzi, M., & Templeton, S. (1996). *Words their way: Word study for phonics, vocabulary, and spelling instruction.* Englewood Cliffs, NJ: Merrill.

Blachman, B. (1992). Effects of phoneme awareness instruction on kindergarten children's invented spelling. *Journal of Reading Behavior, 24*, 233–261.

Bloodgood, J. (1991). A new approach to spelling instruction in language arts programs. *The Elementary School Journal, 92*, 203–211.

Bronfenbrenner, U. (1985). The three worlds of childhood. *Principal, 64*, 7–11.

Charlottesville City Schools. (1994). *Summary report: 1993–1994 testing program.* Charlottesville, VA: Author.

Clay, M.M. (1985). *The early detection of reading difficulties.* Auckland, NZ: Heinemann.

Clay, M.M. (1988, March). *The Reading Recovery program.* Paper presented at the 4th annual George Graham Lecture Series, Charlottesville, VA.

Comer, J.P. (1990). Home, school and academic learning. In J. Goodlad & P. Keating (Eds.), *Access to knowledge: America's agenda for our nation's schools* (pp. 23–43). New York: The College Entrance Exam Board.

Dowhower, S.L. (1987). Effects of repeated reading on second grade transitional readers' fluency and comprehension. *Reading Research Quarterly, 22*, 389–406.

Ehri, L., & Wilce, L.S. (1987). Does learning to spell help beginners learn to read words? *Reading Research Quarterly, 22*, 47–65.

Heath, S.B., & McLaughlin, M.W. (1987). A child resource policy: Moving beyond dependence on school and family. *Phi Delta Kappan, 68*, 576–580.

Henderson, E.H., & Beers, J. (1980). *Developmental and cognitive aspects of learning to spell.* Newark, DE: International Reading Association.

Henderson, E.H., & Templeton, S. (1986). A developmental perspective of formal spelling instruction through alphabet, pattern, and meaning. *The Elementary School Journal, 86*, 30–41.

Hiebert, E. (1994). Reading Recovery in the United States: What difference does it make to an age cohort? *Educational Researcher, 23*(9), 15–25.

Hiebert, E.H., & Taylor, B.M. (Eds.). (1994). *Getting reading right from the start: Effective early literacy interventions.* Boston, MA: Allyn & Bacon.

Invernizzi, M., Abouzeid, M., & Gill, T. (1994). Using students' spellings as a guide for spelling instruction that emphasizes word study. *The Elementary School Journal, 95,* 155–167.

Invernizzi, M., Juel, C., Rosemary, C., & Richards, H. (1994, November). *Building a community of readers.* Paper presented at the annual meeting of the National Reading Conference, San Diego, CA.

Johnston, F., Juel, C., & Invernizzi, M. (1995). *Guidelines for volunteer reading tutors.* Charlottesville, VA: P.S. Publishing Service.

McGill-Franzen, A., Lanford, C., & Killian, J. (1994). *Case studies of literature-based textbook use in kindergarten: Teachers' instructional practices and children's literacy and literacy development.* Unpublished manuscript, State University of New York at Albany.

Morris, D. (1981). Concept of word: A developmental phenomenon in the beginning reading and writing processes. *Language Arts, 58,* 659–668.

Morris, D. (1982). "Word sort": A categorization strategy for improving word recognition ability. *Reading Psychology, 3,* 247–257.

Morris, D. (1992). What constitutes at-risk: Screening children for first grade reading intervention. In W.A. Secord (Ed.), *Best practices in school speech-language pathology* (pp. 43–51). San Antonio, TX: Psychological Corporation.

Pinnell, G.S. (1989). Reading Recovery: Helping at-risk children learn to read. *The Elementary School Journal, 90,* 160–183.

Rasinski, T. (1990). Effects of repeated reading and listening-while-reading on reading fluency. *Journal of Educational Research, 83,* 147–150.

Samuels, S.J. (1979). The method of repeated readings. *The Reading Teacher, 32,* 403–408.

Samuels, S.J., Schermer, N., & Reinking, D. (1992). Reading fluency: Techniques for making decoding automatic. In S.J. Samuels & A.E. Farstrup (Eds.), *What research has to say about reading instruction* (pp. 124–144). Newark, DE: International Reading Association.

Schreiber, P.A. (1987). Prosody and structure in children's syntactic processing. In R. Horowitz & S.J. Samuels (Eds.), *Comprehending oral and written language* (pp. 243–270). San Diego, CA: Academic.

Slavin, R., Madden, N., & Karweit, N. (1989). Effective programs for students at risk: Conclusions for practice and policy. In R. Slavin, N. Karweit, & N. Madden (Eds.), *Effective programs for students at risk* (pp. 355–372). Boston: Allyn & Bacon.

Templeton, S., & Bear, D. (Eds.). (1992). *Development of orthographic knowledge and the foundations of literacy: A memorial festschrift for Edmund Hardcastle Henderson.* Hillsdale, NJ: Erlbaum.

Vygotsky, L.S. (1962). *Thought and language* (E. Hanfmann & G. Vakar, Trans.). Cambridge, MA: MIT Press. (Original work published in 1934)

Weincek, J., & O'Flahavan, J. (1994). From teacher-led to peer discussions about literature: Suggestions for making the shift. *Language Arts, 71,* 488–498.

CHILDREN'S LITERATURE REFERENCE

Minarik, E.H. (1957). *Little bear.* New York: HarperTrophy.

Reading Together: A Community-Supported Parent Tutoring Program

Susan B. Neuman

When he was 4 years old, Benjamin and his mother made up the game of doctor. He would pick up the phone: "Hello. Fine. You sick? And you still broke your legs?" Taking out his "prescription" pad, Benjamin would say to his mother, "He's got a feber. A bad feber." "What should we do for him?" his mother would ask. She'd look at a book, "He needs some medicine." Benjamin would reply, "Yup. Medicine. I gotta write it down." (He would "write" a prescription). On the phone again, he'd say, "You better come here fast. It's an emergency!"

For many children, the beginnings of literacy appear just like this. Through pretend play, reading, conversations, and writing, children begin to actively explore how literacy fits into their lives and the lives of adults (Neuman & Roskos, 1993b; Strickland & Morrow, 1989; Teale & Sulzby, 1989). In their playful ways, they try to make sense and acquire a broad range of knowledge and skills related to reading and writing. Along with the most important activity of being read to (Schickedanz, 1986; Snow, 1983), it is through these kinds of experiences that children begin to recognize and form letters, to

read familiar words encountered in books, and to recognize countless other places and things in their environment.

Much has been written about the influence of activities in literacy-enriched home environments on children's later success in reading (Durkin, 1966; Wells, 1985) and the potential problems for those who do not come from such circumstances (Heath, 1983; Tough, 1982). According to Stanovich (1986), a Matthew effect is thought to occur: Children who engage in playful reading and writing opportunities are likely to come to school with some basic understandings of literacy and are eager to learn more, while those who do not, may not. Further, as Juel, Griffith, and Gough (1986) reported in a longitudinal study, this gap between the "rich getting richer" and the "poor getting poorer" appears to widen in years to come.

The parent volunteer tutoring program described in this article was developed to benefit kindergarten and pre-first-grade children who come from economically distressed neighborhoods. Not designed to supplant classroom instruction, its purpose is to provide additional opportunities for children to try out and practice reading and writing in a playful context. Unlike other approaches to intervention, however, ours was designed to encourage the people in the community to help one another, empowering both parents and children to experience the confidence, joys, and power associated with literacy learning.

Program Setting

Sponsored by the AmeriCorps VISTA program (Volunteers in Service to America, a U.S. national service program that places individuals with community-based agencies) since 1992, and called "Reading Together," our program is designed on Schorr's principle (1988) of "investing in two generations at a time." Many of the families in the program live in the poorest neighborhoods in Philadelphia, Pennsylvania, USA, and are not literate in their primary language. Our goal, therefore, has been to develop a "reciprocal relationship" (Harry, 1992; Neuman, Hagedorn, Celano, & Daly, 1995) with families, based on trust and respect, that would encourage them to view the school as a vital part of their neighborhood. We knew, as Delgado-Gaitan (1990) has suggested, that not only is the family influenced by the school, but the school is influenced by the family. Successful programs are ones that see children in the context of their families and the families in the context of their surroundings (Schorr, 1988).

Our project is based in five elementary schools in Philadelphia, all of which receive federal Chapter 1 [U.S. federally funded education program for at-risk children now called Title I] funds and serve culturally diverse students. The school population at Duckery and Hunter Elementary Schools is largely African American (99.9%; 95%); John Welsh and Cramp Elementary Schools are mostly Hispanic (97%; 80%); and Williard Elementary serves a diverse population with 65% Caucasian, 18% African American, and 10% Hispanic children. Between 75% to 99% of the children in these schools receive free lunches.

Involving community leaders to engage others within the community has been a centerpiece of the project. To do so, we approached individuals who seemed to be highly respected by other families in the neighborhoods of these five elementary schools. Ruth, for example, had been active in leadership activities in the local church and had volunteered often in John Welsh school, knowing the school not only as a parent, but as a former student as well. Ana, a Hispanic parent at Cramp school, had been a lunchtime aide and a bus driver and was respected by parents and children alike.

Consequently, after conversations with people in the community, we selected 10 adults (4 African American, 4 Hispanic, 2 Caucasian; 9 women, 1 man) whom we believed might encourage others to volunteer actively in schools. Committed to working with families, these adults were designated as leaders of the Reading Together program in their respective schools. As Carmen, one of our leaders, put it,

> "I'm Puerto Rican. My people are often reluctant to volunteer in the school because of the language barrier. Many can't read or write in Spanish or English. I got involved in this program because I wanted to help parents get more self-esteem by having them work with children and motivating them. I thought I could make a difference in their lives."

The Reading Together Program

Beginning in the fall of 1992, these leaders and I met regularly to discuss early literacy development and how parents might enhance children's interests and skills in learning to read and write. Specifically, we focused on the importance of phonemic awareness activities, storybook reading, and playful opportunities for children to engage in expressive language (oral and written). Given this background, I then introduced them to the concept of a literacy prop box. Expanded from a previous intervention model (Neuman & Gallagher, 1994), the literacy prop box is a thematically based set of four basic activities, all contained in a box (see Figure).

A Chant, Jingle, or Fingerplay

Each prop box contains a chant, jingle, fingerplay, or song related to a particular theme. For example, our post office literacy box included the following chant (with hand motions):

> Lick it,
> Stamp it,
> Put it in a box,
> Hope that grandma
> Likes it lots

Chants and jingles introduce children to hearing the sounds of language in a very natural way. They can also act as a "tuning-in" (Holdaway, 1979) that provides children with the linguistic rituals that associate learning to read and write with a sense of pleasure and security. Further, as reported by Maclean, Bryant, and Bradley (1987) in their study of 3-year-olds, rhyming knowledge tends to be a strong predictor of subsequent growth in reading.

Storybooks

Each literacy prop box includes about three to five books, all related to a theme. Some of these books are narrative and others are informational, but regardless of genre, they all encourage active responses from the children. For example, *The Jolly Postman* (Ahlberg & Ahlberg, 1986), in our post office prop box, encourages children to handle letters and envelopes as adults and children read together. Other books enhance children's reading through predictable stories and repetitive phrases. Still others extend children's labeling of objects that are central to the theme, like the words *envelope* or *letter*. Such a variety of books also provides parents with many different options for reading, allowing them to select materials appropriate to their own reading levels as well.

Play Objects

Included in the literacy box is a set of theme-related play objects. For example, in our post office box we included stamps, letterhead stationery, envelopes, a blue shirt, and a mail bag. These inexpensive objects are designed to encourage children to reenact many of the scenes from the books and to generate new, creative ideas of their own. Research by Neuman and Roskos (1992, 1993a) indicates that literacy play objects have been found to assist children in conveying meaning, making the language of literacy the children's own.

Writing Books

Each literacy box includes blank writing books for children to write about the theme. In some cases, children may scribble and tell their stories; in other cases, they may attempt to write a favorite line from a storybook. Still other children may combine pictures or stickers with their writing. All writing books are eventually sent home, providing parents with evidence of their children's writing development.

These basic components in the prop boxes—chants, storybooks, play objects, and writing books—focus on receptive and expressive language and are designed to approximate many of the activities that naturally occur in literacy-rich environments (Neuman & Roskos, 1993b). Following this basic format, I encouraged each leader to create prop boxes sensitive to themes in their respective cultural community. For example, Ana created a "celebration" prop box, including piñatas and

Contents of two sample literacy prop boxes

A literacy prop box provides chants, jingles, or fingerplays; picture books; plenty of time for play; and writing materials.

Theme: Dental Clinic

Chant: From Wescott, N.B. (1988). *The lady with the alligator purse.* Boston: Little, Brown.

Call for the doctor,
Call for the nurse,
Call for the lady
With the alligator purse.

Song: "I Brush My Teeth" (sung to the tune of "Jingle Bells")

I brush my teeth, I brush my teeth,
Morning, noon, and night.
I brush them, floss them, rinse them clean,
I keep them nice and white.

Suggested books:

Brown, M. (1985). *Arthur's tooth.* Boston: Little, Brown.
Mayer, M. (1990). *Just going to the dentist.* New York: Western.
McPhail, D. (1972). *The bear's toothache.* Boston: Little, Brown.
Rey, H.A., & Rey, M. (1989). *Curious George goes to the dentist.* Boston: Houghton Mifflin.

Props:

white coat
face mask
message pad and pencils
dental posters
file folders and paper for dental charts
"Dentist is in"/"Dentist is out" signs
appointment cards

Theme: Let's Eat

Action chant: From Beaty, J. (1994). *Picture book storytelling.* Fort Worth, TX: Harcourt Brace Jovanovich.

Munch, munch
What's for lunch?
Yum, yum
Try some,   (hold out hand)
Time to bake,
Carrot cake;   (stir with hand)
Time to mash
Succotash;   (pound with hand)
Time to stop
Licking chops;   (cover mouth with hand)
LET'S EAT!   (uncover mouth and shout!)

(continued)

Contents of two sample literacy prop boxes (continued)

Suggested books:

Buchanan, J. (1988). *Nothing else but yams for supper!* Toronto: Black Moss.
Gugler, L.D. (1988). *Mashed potato mountain.* Toronto: Black Moss.
Lessac, R. (1985). *My little island.* New York: Lippincott.
Lord, J.V. (1972). *The giant jam sandwich.* Boston: Houghton Mifflin.
Ross, T. (1987). *Stone soup.* New York: Dial.

Props:

food boxes
food utensils
chefs' hats (we had three—for parent and children)
aprons
play dough
cookie cutters
small pots and pans
plastic food

---

other cultural traditions from Puerto Rico. Robert created a prop box based on food, and included play objects representing favorite African American foods. These prop boxes became the key materials used in our Reading Together program.

Program Procedures

Armed with a number of prop boxes, leaders began the ambitious task of recruiting regular parent volunteers to each school. Our goal was to have each parent work as a tutor/mentor using these prop box activities with one or two children at a time. Teachers selected children who needed help as those to be tutored. Many of these children had not shown any awareness of print concepts or had difficulty verbalizing or attending to stories read aloud.

To develop both parent and child commitment, we felt it essential to have parents work with the same one or two kindergarten or pre-first-grade children each session (not their own child), for 30 to 45 minutes twice per week. Beginning recruiting efforts were difficult. As Robert noted, "I found out my first year that a lot of parents can't read themselves and are embarrassed about it." And Yvonne found, "Some of these parents have so many family problems, they don't want to be bothered by the school."

But here is where the leaders' knowledge and familiarity within the parent community really played a key role. On their own initiative, the leaders stood outside their respective schools, chatting, coaxing parents to volunteer, and making them feel wanted and welcome in the school with coffee, tea, snacks, and neighborhood conversation. (One of our leaders even had a connection with a local bakery.) Leaders showed parents that even with rudimentary reading skills, they could successfully read simple texts to the children. With the leaders' continued efforts, senior citizens, parents of the young children, and parents in the community began to volunteer in the school. Each school reported an average of 15 to 20 volunteers coming twice a week after several months. Carmen described some of her recruiting techniques:

> First we tell them about the program and the importance of reading to children. And we lie a little bit. We tell them all they have to give us is an hour a week, but it doesn't work like that—it's really 2 hours a week. They come in and we show them the literacy prop box. We ask if they volunteered before. We go through the steps: how we would do it if we were going to work with a child. We tell them the first time is only an introduction, so when they work with the child they will be comfortable. We want them to work with this kid for a long time.

When leaders felt that parents were sufficiently familiar with the materials (at times they practiced reading the stories together before meeting the children), they began to schedule the twice-weekly tutorial sessions, coordinating both parent-tutors' and children's available time. The sessions are scheduled during children's noninstructional class time (i.e., gym, free play time). Each day a parent visits the classroom and invites one or two children at a time to either a resource room or more often an area in the hallway, where they begin working together with the prop box. Queen, a regular volunteer, said,

> I come every Tuesday and Thursday and work with the same children each time I come. It's important for the children to get a set-aside time to read and play. The kids seem to be so excited and I have to tell them, "Wait a minute." They go right to the box and are ready to work.

The parent-tutor begins the session with the chant or jingle, attempting to get the children to repeat it. Following the chant, the parent-tutor reads one of the stories to the children. In some cases, it will not be read in its entirety. Rather, the point is to encourage both the parent and the child to have fun with the book, to use it interactively in conversation and extended thinking. Sometimes this might mean that a child spends all the reading time on a page or two. For example, we watched with fascination Edward's interest in a picture of a trash truck in a story. Because trash pick-up was a source of great concern in his community, his questions about trash seemed unending.

Generally this reading lasts about 15 minutes, after which play objects relating to the books are taken out of the box. This is where the children begin to take charge, playing with the objects and recounting the events in the story, often using words they have just heard. Finally, the session ends with about 5 to 10 minutes of children writing "their way" and the parent collaborating in the process.

Most of the parents will use the same boxes with children for a month or so, hearing the same chants and stories and playing with objects repeatedly until they feel ready to move on to a new theme. In this way, one inexpensive prop box literally provides hours of literacy engagement for many parents and children.

Each week, the VISTA leaders and I meet to discuss various aspects of the program. These sessions provide an informal opportunity for me to train the leaders. Particularly in the beginning, we tended to focus on issues related to emergent literacy, like invented spelling. As the weeks went by, some of our conversations began to address specific parts of the program, such as strategies for recruiting parents. Sometimes our sessions are like workshops—making sock puppets together or sharing book titles and favorite finger plays. One of our ongoing goals, for example, has been to gather favorite chants, rhymes, and jingles from varying cultural traditions to make a booklet to share with others.

All ongoing training of the volunteers has been conducted by the leaders in their respective schools. Occasionally I visit these sessions and praise their efforts; other times,

I simply go to schools and help greet the volunteers. But my efforts primarily have been to support their leadership, ensuring the continuation of their work once the 4-year VISTA program is completed. This process, described by VISTA as institutionalization, reminds us that ultimately the success of any program lies in the hands of the families and the community in which it resides.

Evidence of Success and Lessons Learned

Following the second year of its implementation, we conducted an informal evaluation of the program. Our numbers indicated that 108 kindergarten and pre-first-grade children, all of whom were most in need of help, received parent tutoring throughout the year. Over 2,000 hours of reading to children were logged as a result of parent efforts! Further, 89 parents volunteered regularly at least 2 hours a week to read to children.

Leaders made 44 literacy prop boxes throughout the year. These literacy prop boxes were so popular that leaders invited volunteers to help construct summer take-home boxes. Ninety-nine boxes in all were made and given to children to take home as a summer reading program (see Figure for several ideas). These materials were distributed at a large celebration at Temple University in Philadelphia, honoring the VISTA leaders, parent volunteers, school community workers, and children.

Why has the program become so successful? We believe there are several powerful lessons to be learned from our experience.

At the School Level

First, from the beginning, each principal clearly welcomed the program, viewing it as highly consistent within a larger school improvement effort. One of the principals, for example, indicated:

> Welsh, at one point, was one of the lowest achieving schools in this city. We began to assess why this occurred, looked at the expectations of teachers, parents and created a 5-year school plan. Working to enhance the achievement of kids, their self-esteem, and involving parents in the process is a key goal. I see Reading Together as working in an integrated way to achieve these same goals for us.

Second, the program was also consistent with teacher goals. With children's Concepts of Print scores (Clay, 1979) in the fall of 1993 averaging 4.2 out of 24, teachers badly needed some extra help (no Chapter 1 services for kindergarten and pre-first-grade were available). Careful not to take precious time away from classroom instruction, VISTA leaders organized the program in a way that provided for consistency and support to teachers as well as children. For example, they took all responsibility for recruiting, organizing, and training volunteers, and would even step in to read with children if a parent volunteer was absent. In other words, these leaders continually attended to program details to make it work. Students' Concepts of Print scores rose to an average of 12.4 in June. Teachers very much appreciated these efforts:

> Mario Mendez is making very good progress recently. At the beginning of the year, he hardly spoke. He is now very verbal. A few weeks ago, his mother wrote a note describing his change in attitude about school. In class he has started to do his work much more carefully. I feel that the help he's getting from the parent volunteer has helped him become a better student.

Third, the leaders created an infectious enthusiasm for reading throughout the school. For example, one of our leaders, Ruby, had herself only recently learned to read. She knew well the problems associated with not being literate. She and the other VISTA leaders virtually blanketed the schools with bulletin board posters, pamphlets, and notices of meetings for parents. Pictures of the volunteer of the month, reading tips, and certificates of achievement for reading to children were displayed prominently. The leaders attended yard sales, went regularly to Goodwill Industries, and cut up old workbooks in order to provide materials and play objects for the program. In their own way, their spirit was the key to the program's success.

At the Program Level

Several aspects of the program contributed to its success. Of primary importance was the individual attention lavished on the children. Parent volunteers seemed to reach them in ways that few others had done. The parent-tutors provided a kind of "big mother" program, supporting children in ways that they may not often receive when they leave the school environment. Faye, one of the leaders, described it like this, "You can see it in the child's eyes when it's time to read. They look forward to the one-to-one nourishment—you can actually see the difference in their behavior. With that parent taking their little hand—it's tremendous." And another parent found:

> I had this little girl Casey last year. She would put her head down when she walked in the hall—didn't talk to anybody. If you asked her to write, she would say she couldn't because everyone would make fun of her. But after a couple of sessions, she'd walk down the hall, raise her head way high, write everyone stories because I let her know she was OK.

And Norma, a leader, told this story:

> This one little guy, Brian—he was a real behavior problem. I read to him myself because I didn't want to lose volunteers over him. And so one day, I went to get him, and he wasn't allowed to get out of the classroom because he was misbehaving. So, the next day, I went to see if he could come out. He was sitting there waiting, with his hands folded, not saying a word so he could come out and read with me.

Second, the program created connections. Working together twice a week, parents and children developed a bond—a relationship important to both of them. Lee Ann, a parent, described it this way, "I worked with the same four children, two times a week, all year long. I like the one-on-one because I get to see their good qualities. I take my time with them and you can see the improvement in their work."

These connections were not just one way, however. Robert, a Duckery School leader, found that a "Guess who's waiting for you?" welcome to incoming parent volunteers would often bring smiles to their faces, making them, too, feel special. In fact, when one leader, Esther, was asked why parents continued to volunteer, she responded, "It's not what we do—it's what the children do for them."

A third successful element of the program was that by "investing in two generations at a time" (Schorr, 1988), leaders could actually observe positive changes in parents. Yvonne, for example, told me that some of her parent-tutors were trying to model the prop box activities with their own young children at home. Working with the students gave parents additional confidence in their own abilities: "One of our favorite volunteers, Marge, didn't think she could do this with children because she says she's not a very good reader. But these are children's books, so she's doing really well and it's good for her self-esteem in reading as well." Another leader, Vanessa, found some parents in the program beginning to attend adult literacy programs in the school so they could read more proficiently with the children. Others, in the primarily Hispanic schools, began reading children's storybooks in English by first practicing with audiotaped versions of the book specially made by the leaders. Consequently, the program appeared to have a dual effect, enhancing the self-esteem of both parents and children.

Finally, the literacy prop boxes and the activities within them seemed to provide for an effective intervention by parent-tutors. Parents enjoyed the structure and the materials: "Everything's there for you, all the supplies so you can be ready to work." Within this structure, parents had a specific job and were not dependent on someone else's guidance. It was also clear that the task was "doable," even for those whose literacy skills were not well developed (about half of the parents did not have a high school diploma). The activities seemed naturally engaging, with many parents saying that the program was "a lot of fun." In some cases, in fact, leaders would have to remind them that it was time to return to class. One mother told us, "When I see a child hold a book in his hands and recognize that sentences are words put together—you could lose yourself in that world."

Starting Your Own Reading Together Program

Can schools create their own Reading Together program without VISTA's support or some other type of outside funding? We believe they can. In one Philadelphia school, for example, parent volunteers have begun a Reading Together project using library materials to create thematic literacy prop boxes and have used small carrels in the library for parents and children to read together. The program, staffed by parents, runs from 8:00 in the morning until 8:00 at night. In another school, the parent-teacher association has taken on a small fund-raising effort to buy new books and play objects for prop boxes. Headed by a parent volunteer responsible for all scheduling, the association has held workshops and sessions that highlight how parents can support

children's early literacy activities. Several key suggestions can contribute to the success of these programs.

• Keep the program community based. The power of the project lies in supporting parents' leadership and creative initiatives. A good starting point is to identify parents who are well connected and respected by others in the community to serve as project facilitators. Encourage them to develop their own personal strategies to get the word out to other parents. Our parents, for example, used a range of techniques: parent-teacher association meetings, brochures, bulletin board information centers, and bake sales.

• Offer training to the facilitators of the project on strategies to support children's early literacy. Parents often need explicit information focusing on the importance of precursors to formal literacy instruction such as rhyming, reading, playing, and writing, and their linkage to literacy development. Describe how various components of the program emphasize the integration of these language processes.

• Encourage the facilitators to give workshops to other parents. Such a forum enhances facilitators' ownership of the program. In our case, because many of our parents had never before assumed the role of speaking before a group, we created a short videotape with parents engaging in Reading Together with children. This provided supplementary information on the various steps of the program. In subsequent workshops, parents should begin to collect favorite books, rhymes and jingles, and play objects for use in literacy prop boxes.

• Provide a place in the school for the Reading Together program. Whether it is a room or a designated area in the library, parents need a place where they can pick up their materials and work quietly with children. Space is often at a premium in schools. At a minimum, however, try to provide a coat rack, a closet for materials, and a table for parents and children to work together. In most schools, we also have a place for coffee and refreshments and a lending library for them in order to make them feel welcome and wanted in the school.

• Informally evaluate the program to determine if it is meeting the needs of the parents and children. In one of our schools, for example, we found that some parents needed more books in Spanish; in another school, parents wanted even more structure in reading books with the children. This suggests that, over time, programs will take on their own unique features to meet the needs of the community.

Two years of implementing Reading Together have demonstrated that, despite poor economic circumstances, families in these communities continue to hold strong beliefs about the power of literacy and its importance in their lives. However, lacking confidence in their own abilities and at times overwhelmed with family problems, many parents are reluctant to become involved in schools. Few of the VISTA leaders, for example, had ever before held leadership positions in schools (or school programs). None were formally trained in any of the roles they undertook. They had no special degrees or qualifications other than commitment to their community and a shared determination to reach families "where they are." And in doing so, they continue to provide a powerful demonstration that caring community members can make a difference. Just look at their children's faces.

Author Notes

This article is dedicated to the families and children at the Cramp, Duckery, Hunter, John Welsh, and Williard Elementary Schools in North Philadelphia. I sincerely appreciate Pauline Daly's many efforts in helping make the project successful. I would like to acknowledge the help of Robert Carter, Ruth Duprey, Faye Jones, Norma Pesante, Ana Ramos, Ruby Redding, Carmen Rivera, Esther Gonzales, Yvonne Wabels, and Vanessa Wiggins, community leaders in the Reading Together program.

REFERENCES

Clay, M. (1979). *The early detection of reading difficulties*. Portsmouth, NH: Heinemann.

Delgado-Gaitan, C. (1990). *Literacy for empowerment.* New York: Falmer Press.

Durkin, D. (1966). *Children who read early*. New York: Teachers College Press.

Harry, B. (1992). *Cultural diversity, families, and the special education system*. New York: Teachers College Press.

Heath, S.B. (1983). *Ways with words: Language, life, and work in communities and classrooms*. Cambridge, UK: Cambridge University Press.

Holdaway, D. (1979). *The foundations of literacy*. Portsmouth, NH: Heinemann.

Juel, C., Griffith, P.L., & Gough, P. (1986). Acquisition of literacy: A longitudinal study of children in first and second grade. *Journal of Educational Psychology, 78*, 243–255.

Maclean, M., Bryant, P., & Bradley, L. (1987). Rhymes, nursery rhymes, and reading in early childhood. *Merrill-Palmer Quarterly, 33*, 255–281.

Neuman, S.B., & Gallagher, P. (1994). Joining together in literacy learning: Teenage mothers and children. *Reading Research Quarterly, 29*, 382–401.

Neuman, S.B., Hagedorn, T., Celano, D., & Daly, P. (1995). Toward a collaborative approach to parent involvement in early education: A study of teenage mothers in an African American community. *American Educational Research Journal, 32*(4), 801–827.

Neuman, S.B., & Roskos, K. (1992). Literacy objects as cultural tools: Effects on children's literacy behaviors in play. *Reading Research Quarterly, 27*, 202–225.

Neuman, S.B., & Roskos, K. (1993a). Access to print for children of poverty: Differential effects of adult mediation and literacy-enriched play settings on environmental and functional print tasks. *American Educational Research Journal, 30*, 95–122.

Neuman, S.B., & Roskos, K. (1993b). *Language and literacy learning in the early years: An integrated approach.* Fort Worth, TX: Harcourt Brace Jovanovich.

Schickedanz, J. (1986). *More than the ABC's: The early states of reading and writing.* Washington, DC: National Association for the Education of Young Children.

Schorr, L. (1988). *Within our reach.* New York: Doubleday.

Snow, C. (1983). Literacy and language: Relationships during the preschool years. *Harvard Educational Review, 53*, 165–189.

Stanovich, K.E. (1986). Matthew effects in reading: Some consequences of individual differences in the acquisition of literacy. *Reading Research Quarterly, 21*, 360–406.

Strickland, D., & Morrow, L.M. (Eds.). (1989). *Emerging literacy: Young children learn to read and write.* Newark, DE: International Reading Association.

Teale, W.H., & Sulzby, E. (1989). Emergent literacy: New perspectives. In D. Strickland & L.M. Morrow (Eds.), *Emerging literacy: Young children learn to read and write* (pp. 1–15). Newark, DE: International Reading Association.

Tough, J. (1982). Language, poverty, and disadvantage in school. In L. Feagans & D.C. Farran (Eds.), *The language of children reared in poverty* (pp. 3–18). New York: Academic.

Wells, G. (1985). *The meaning makers.* Portsmouth, NH: Heinemann.

CHILDREN'S LITERATURE REFERENCE

Ahlberg, J., & Ahlberg, A. (1986). *The jolly postman.* Boston: Little, Brown.

Training Parents as Reading Facilitators

Ruth Hayden

he time for the second parent-teacher interviews had come. Mrs. Wilson usually enjoyed these sessions. Two of her three children's report cards indicated that they were progressing satisfactorily. However, Jennifer's teacher, Mrs. Klein, had noted that the Grade 4 student needed to spend more time reading at home. Such a comment mirrored what had been recorded on that child's previous report card. Over the past 4 months, Mrs. Wilson had listened to Jennifer read each day at home, an activity that the child sometimes resented. But the mother had persevered, and every night after supper Jennifer read out of a book she had borrowed from school while Mrs. Wilson listened. Now it appeared that, in spite of the daily 20-minute ritual, the expected progress had not been realized. In anticipation of her interview with Mrs. Klein, Mrs. Wilson reflected upon the daily homework activity. What was she doing wrong?

Parent Listening and Parent Training Studies

Since the era of the McGuffey readers, parents have listened to their children read. The practice of sending books home with children so that parents may hear them read continues to be widespread today in elementary schools. Teachers encourage this practice most frequently for their poor readers as one avenue for improving their literacy abilities. The premise on which the child oral reading-parent listening procedure is based centers upon the assumption that with practice comes perfection. Although there is no doubt that such an assumption has merit as an approach for extending the literacy abilities of many children, a review conducted by Toomey (1993) of over 40 studies of parents' hearing their children read at home indicates this practice may not result in literacy gains, particularly for the at-risk reader, unless parents have received some training in specific procedures to assist their children during the reading sessions.

Toomey makes a distinction in his review between "parent listening studies," where parents are provided only an explanation of what they should do at home (listen), and "parent training studies" in which the adults receive instruction focused toward particular reading strategies such as modeling and corrective behaviors. The popularity of requesting that parents listen to their children read derives, in part, from the influential, 2-year Haringey study (Tizard, Schofield, & Hewison, 1982), that demonstrated "highly significant improvement by children who received extra practice at home" (p. 1). However, four other studies (Ashton, Stoney, & Hannon, 1986; Bloom, 1987; Friend, 1983; Hannon, 1989) failed to replicate the project.

With respect to the listening studies, Toomey (1993) notes that

> studies with relatively lengthy programs of parents hearing reading, without parent training procedures and dealing with school populations unselected by reading competence, have failed to demonstrate significant gains for children's reading achievements, as measured by standardized tests. On the other hand, relatively short-term programs with careful training procedures for parents of low competence readers have shown repeated and substantial gains. (p. 229)

Although Toomey sees value in the practice of parents hearing their children read, his review illustrates that low competence students may need more than a listening parent to improve their reading abilities.

When considering parent training studies, Toomey identifies three different approaches: the behavioral; the pause, prompt, praise (PPP); and paired reading. Although the nine reported studies involving the first two approaches resulted in statistically significant student reading gains, the numbers involved in each study were small. The paired reading studies, however, involved large to very large groups of students. Fifteen of the 17 paired reading investigations reported significant reading gains for comprehension, word accuracy, and attitudes about reading for less able students from low socioeconomic groups in particular.

The Paired Reading Approach

With the exception of emergent or early readers for whom the approach does not appear to be suitable, the paired reading approach allows less able readers of all ages to experience success with text under the guidance of a more able reader. As a literacy learning activity for outside regular classroom use,

it is particularly suitable as a home-reading activity between parents and children.

Keith Topping from Britain is the most noted researcher of paired reading. His investigations have consistently shown positive results for reading achievement (for example, Topping & Whiteley, 1990). The paired reading strategies are based on the theoretical framework that parents scaffold their children's literacy development by reading to them. Supported by the research that addresses the centrality of meaning in the reading process, these strategies encourage less able readers to move from supportive (reading with parent) to independent reading as parents and children share texts together over a relatively short period of time.

Although it is not possible to provide a detailed reporting of the paired reading method within this article, its central components are presented. Initially, the child selects a book or other reading material he or she would like to read with the parent. The parent and child then simultaneously read the text. The parent should synchronize his or her reading speed to that of the child, so that rather than echoing the parent's reading, the child reads the words as the adult paces his or her reading to fit the child. The child is expected to read all words correctly; if he or she does not, the parent repeats the word correctly while pointing to it and subsequently continues reading in duet with the child.

When the child feels sufficiently secure to begin reading the text independently, he or she gives the parent a nonverbal signal, which has previously been agreed upon, for this solo reading attempt. The child is praised for the independent reading effort, and quiet approval continues as he or she reads. The child continues reading alone until he or she makes an error—a word substitution, an omission, or a mispronunciation. The parent waits 4 seconds for the child to correct the mistake. If self-correction is unsuccessful, the parent points to the word while saying it, and the child repeats the word. Duet reading recommences and continues until the child indicates a desire to read solo again. In short, the reading cycle moves back and forth between duet and solo reading. Discussion about what is being read occurs at opportune points during the reading episodes. When the child selects a book that is easy to read, more independent reading will take place; if he or she chooses a more difficult text, greater frequency of duet reading will occur.

Training for parents together with their children usually takes place in a group session that lasts approximately $1^1/_2$ hours. Teachers who are very familiar with the approach can train 20 to 30 parents in a single session without much difficulty. After 2 or 3 weeks in the program, a follow-up session is held, again in groups, to ensure that the techniques of the approach are being adhered to. Parents commit to using the paired reading strategies with their child five times a week for 10 minutes a day for a period of 8 to 12 weeks.

Reflection

Why does the paired reading approach appear to be more successful than other home reading activities? When parents simply listen, the onus is placed on the child to perform as a reader even though the child knows he or she is not a good reader and may feel unable to carry out the task competently and independently. The parents' role during this reading session is one of apparent inactivity, and they often may feel they should not interrupt by correcting the child's errors or by discussing the meaning of the text. Because the adult's responsibility is just to listen, it may be possible to carry out tasks such as preparing supper or other household duties while listening to the child read aloud.

Listening does not necessitate that the dyad follow the print together. Although there is no doubt that many parents attend carefully as they hear their children read, they are often unaware of specific strategies that may assist the struggling reader. Expecting parents to simply listen to their children read may demonstrate to the child the importance of reading as a task to be completed rather than an event in which meaning is interactively and socially constructed.

Within a paired reading approach, the child and adult together take time to share text. The parent models fluent reading. The child is supported when he or she struggles with text, his or her attempts to self-monitor are rewarded, and he or she is encouraged to read independently and is verbally congratulated for doing so. The child also can risk choosing challenging texts that interest him or her. Parents see that the paired reading approach allows them to contribute in a positive way to the reading episode. From a pedagogical perspective, the parent is trained to provide assistance when it is required and to reduce that support when the child feels confident to interact with text independently.

Most parents are aware of the importance of their interest in their child's literacy learning. Parents of children who are competent readers may not need training schemes as presented in the paired reading approach. However, training may make sense for parents whose children are not succeeding as literacy learners. Home assistance when the reading task is occurring may result in the child's developing greater ability with text.

As the scenario that introduced this article demonstrated, Mrs. Wilson felt responsible for her child's lack of progress in spite of the daily listening-to-read routine. She was doing nothing wrong, but the activities were not sufficient assistance to allow for more appropriate literacy learning behaviors to develop.

Both parent and child viewed the reading episodes as exercises for oral reading rather than as occasions for mutually supportive text-meaning constructions because of the lack of direction with respect to strategic literacy behaviors; the absence of adult modeling as reader; and the inadequacy of the sessions as demonstrations of interactive, social literacy constructs.

The paired reading approach is not a panacea for dealing with all the difficulties less able readers encounter as they attempt to make sense of text. Nor is paired reading intended to replace the professional instruction provided within the school setting. Rather, it is one way for parents with minimal training to assist their children's literacy development in the home environment. As Toomey (1993) has noted, less able children's enthusiasm for, interest in, and ability with text expands under the guidance of a parent who has participated in training. As professionals, when we ask parents to hear their children read at home, it may be wise to show them how they may participate in the reading event and how to offer assistance within a framework that reaffirms reading as a meaning-making activity. In addition, the literacy learning connections for in- and out-of-school contexts are enhanced when parents know how to demonstrate and support literacy learning strategies that are similar to those practiced in the classroom.

Author Notes

Paired Reading: Positive Reading Practice is available from the International Reading Association. The 30-minute training video and accompanying manual provide a complete guide to the paired reading approach, which has also been used successfully in adult literacy and cross-age/peer tutoring settings.

REFERENCES

Ashton, C., Stoney, A., & Hannon, P. (1986). A reading at home project in a first school. *Support for Learning*, 6(1), 43–49.

Bloom, W. (1987). *Partnership with parents in reading*. Seven Oaks, Kent, UK: Hodder & Stoughton.

Friend, P. (1983). Reading and the parent: After the Haringey Project. *Reading (UKRA)*, 17(1), 7–12.

Hannon, P. (1989). How shall parental involvement in the teaching of reading be evaluated? *British Educational Research Journal*, 15(1), 33–40.

Tizard, J., Schofield, W., & Hewison, J. (1982). Collaboration between teachers and parents in assisting children's reading. *British Journal of Educational Psychology*, 52(1), 1–15.

Toomey, D. (1993). Parents hearing their children read: A review. Rethinking the lessons of the Haringey Project. *Educational Research*, 35, 223–236.

Topping, K., & Whiteley, M. (1990). Participation evaluation of parent-tutored and peer-tutored projects in reading. *Educational Research*, 32, 14–27.

Home Writing Activities: The Writing Briefcase and the Traveling Suitcase

Kimberly Miller-Rodriguez

As a first-grade teacher and an advocate of early developmental writing experiences, I try to find entertaining ideas for children to write about. One idea that sparked enthusiasm for writing in my young students is an adaptation of Rich's (1985) writing suitcase.

I found an old briefcase at a garage sale. It was basically in good condition except the handle was missing. I replaced the handle and decorated the outside with stickers and labeled it the "Writing Briefcase."

Inside the Writing Briefcase is a laminated, typewritten letter to parents that explains why writing is important for young children:

> Dear Parents,
>
>   Young children become interested in reading and writing as they enter school. When children have ready access to books, paper, markers, and similar materials, and are encouraged to use them, their literacy development blossoms. This Writing Briefcase is a great way to build your child's interest in reading and writing. Please take the time to listen to what your child has written. Have your child return his or her story and the Writing Briefcase tomorrow.
>
> Sincerely,
> Mrs. Rodriguez

I also include another laminated typewritten sheet that briefly describes the various stages of writing development. This is very important because parents might not perceive scribbles and letter-like forms as legitimate writing.

Also in the Writing Briefcase is a spiral-bound notebook titled "All About the Author." This notebook allows the child to write about his or her family, hobbies, travel, or pets, and to draw a self-portrait. The other children enjoy reading about their classmates, and parents also find the autobiographies interesting. The authors' notebook remains in the briefcase along with the laminated information sheets.

The following is a list of the items contained in the Writing Briefcase:

markers	index cards
crayons	lined paper
colored pencils	unlined paper
pencils	books in shape of animals, trains, cars, etc.
magazine pictures	transparent tape
word cards	stapler
picture dictionary	paper clips
easy-to-read books	rubber bands
	scissors

Children returning the Writing Briefcase have produced some excellent work. Because I have modeled ways to create pop-up, eight-page, and accordion books at school, children often create similar books at home.

Sharing their work is a very important time for young writers. When children read their work, they wear a star-studded visor labeled "Author." Afterward, their story is placed in the "Hall of Fame" (a bookshelf) for other children to read during free time.

Along the lines of the Writing Briefcase is another home-writing activity called the Traveling Suitcase. The Traveling Suitcase is a small overnight suitcase labeled with stickers from various countries, states, and theme parks. Inside are the same writing materials found in the Writing Briefcase; also included are items representing places the suitcase has traveled. For example, if the suitcase has been to Disneyland, I place Mickey Mouse ears, postcards, brochures, or anything that refers to Disneyland inside the suitcase. Other objects I have used include posters, costumes, dolls, hats, license plates, bumper stickers, and toy vehicles such as cars, boats, or planes.

A child takes the suitcase home, creates a story, and returns the story and suitcase the next day. He or she shares the story with the class, and then it is placed in the Hall of Fame.

The Traveling Suitcase also is used to incorporate geography into writing lessons. The different places the suitcase has traveled are located on a world map. Map pins are then placed in the areas where the suitcase has been. Sometimes children of families in the military write stories about places the suitcase has not visited. They share their stories as well as pictures, costumes, and other related memorabilia.

Both writing experiences described here can be modified to fit teacher and student needs. Introducing writing activities such as these in the primary grades fosters enthusiasm for reading and writing and provides the basis for future growth.

REFERENCE
Rich, S.J. (1985). The writing suitcase. *Young Children, 40,* 42–44.

Subject Index

Note: An "*f*" following a page number indicates that the reference may be found in a figure; a "*t*" indicates that it may be found in a table.

intervention programs, 39; independent learning, 66–67, 88; individualized instruction, 73–74, 88; large group, 71–72; paired reading, 102, 297–298; pairs, 63f–64f, 66; research and history of practices, 80–81; small groups, 14, 63f–64f, 65–66, 73, 86; whole class, 13, 62–66, 63f–64f, 74, 81–82, 85; working collaboratively to create text, 86

GUIDED PRACTICE, 251

GUIDED READING, 21–22

GUIDELINES FOR THE SPECIALIZED PREPARATION OF READING PROFESSIONALS (INTERNATIONAL READING ASSOCIATION), 98

GUTHRIE, J.T., 117

H

HAGEN, E.P., 53–54

HANSEN, J., 135, 138

HARRIS, T.L., 257

HATCH, EGG, HATCH (RODDIE), 181–182

HEAD START, 32

HIEBERT, E., 40

HILTON, N., 268, 268f, 270

HODGES, R.E., 257

HODGKINSON, H., 11–12, 16

HOFFMAN, J.V., 102

HOLDAWAY, D., 48

HOME INVOLVEMENT. *See* Family involvement; Parent involvement

HOMELESS CHILDREN, 11

HOOKS, W.H., 125

HORNSBY, D., 95

"HURRIED CHILD," 33

HUTCHINS, P., 142

I

"I HAVE A DREAM" (KING), 125

IF I HAD A PIG (INKPEN), 184

IMMERSION (WHOLE LANGUAGE), 70–71

INCENTIVES, 118

INCLUSION MODEL, 28–29

INFORMAL READING INVENTORY (IRI), 96

INKPEN, M., 184

INSTRUCTION: active involvement in reading, 102; appropriate to child development, 31–34

INSTRUCTIONAL TIME, 14–15, 39–40, 43, 137, 141–142

INTELLIGENCE, 1–2

INTERACTION BETWEEN INSTRUCTION AND DEVELOPMENT, 33–34

INTERACTIVE STORYBOOK READING, 175–186, 179t–180t, 184t; benefits of, 176f; characteristics of, 177f

INTERNATIONAL READING ASSOCIATION, 14; *Guidelines for the Specialized Preparation of Reading Professionals*, 98

INTERVENTION. *See* Early intervention programs

INTERVIEWS, 138; expert interview, 86, 87f; parents, 19–20

INVENTED SPELLING, 213, 226–233

IRA SLEEPS OVER (WABER), 103

IRI. *See* Informal Reading Inventory (IRI)

IT REMINDS ME OF..., 203f

J

JINGLES, 287

JOHNSON, L.J., 92

THE JOLLY POSTMAN (AHLBERG & AHLBERG), 287

JOURNALS, 81, 82t; response logs, 204–205; sharing related background knowledge, 85; What-I-Know-About-My Language journals, 254

JOYFUL NOISE: POEMS FOR TWO VOICES (FLEISCHMAN), 125

THE JUDGE (ZEMACH), 124

JUEL, C., 12

JUMP ROPE RHYMES, 125, 129f

K

KATZ, L., 94

KEAR, D., 126

R

Rasinski, T.V., 258
Ratty-Tatty (Cowley), 73
Read-aloud books, 217–224
Readers (engaged), 110*f*, 110–111
Reader's theatre, 125, 130*f*
Reading: cross-age, 267–273; fostering motivation, 108–119; information building, 103–104; interactive storybook, 175–186, 176*f*–177*f*, 179*t*–180*t*, 184*t*; learning from difficult text, 85–86; motivation (*See* Motivation); paired, 102, 297–298; parents as facilitators, 296–299; providing active involvement in, 102; relevancy, 140–141, 143; shared, 285–294; support, 258; text units, 259; words, 240–241. *See also* Instruction; Phonics
Reading Acquisition (Gough, Ehri, & Treiman), 239
Reading aloud, 269
Reading difficulties, 1
Reading disabilities, 19–29
Reading efficacy, 15, 35–45
Reading frequency, 3, 13–14
Reading Initiative (Charlottesville City Schools), 276
Reading Is Fundamental (RIF), 111
Reading motivation, 108–119
Reading records, 138
Reading Recovery, 28, 38–43, 212, 227
Reading specialists, 29, 91–99; *Guidelines for the Specialized Preparation of Reading Professionals* (International Reading Association), 98
Reading Together program, 286–295
Reciprocal teaching, 171–174, 173*f*
Reducing risks of literacy learning, 134–146
Reese, L., 264
Reflection (student), 88
"Reform Versus Reality" (Hodgkinson), 11–12
Reluctant readers, 107–159; at-risk children, 153–159; authors that appeal to, 127, 131*f*; books for, 122–128; intelligence and, 1–2
Remediation: coordinating with classroom instruction, 100–105; cost of, 35
Repitition, 258
Response, 70–71
Response logs, 204–205
Retellings, 268*f*, 268–270, 271*f*
Retention, 137
Rhymes, jump rope and street, 125, 129*f*
Rieben, L., 239
RIF. *See* Reading Is Fundamental
The Right Number of Elephants (Sheppard), 184
Rimes and onsets, 213
Risk taking, 137, 142–144
Robinson, S., 32
Roddie, S., 181–182
RS. *See* Running Start (RS)
Running records, 42
Running Start (RS), 111–114, 118
Rylant, C., 124

S

Santeusanio, N., 101
Scaffolding, 181–182, 258
Schafer, W., 117
Schedule (daily), 71
Schmitt, M.C., 190
Schorr, L., 286
Scottish Council for Educational Research, 49
Self-evaluation (student), 48
Sendak, M., 103
Shapp, M.C., 104
Shared book experience, 175–186; characteristics of, 177*f*
Shaw, N., 184
Sheep In a Jeep (Shaw), 184
Shepard, L., 34
Sheppard, J., 184
Shockley, B., 136

V

VEATCH, J., 93
THE VERY HUNGRY CATERPILLAR (CARLE), 72, 74
VIORST, J., 269
VIRGINIA, CHARLOTTESVILLE CITY SCHOOLS, 276–283
VISTA. *See* Volunteers in Service to America
VOCABULARY, 238–256
VOLUNTEER TUTORS, 276–283
VOLUNTEERS IN SERVICE TO AMERICA (VISTA), 286, 290–291
VYGOTSKI, L.S., 33

W

WABER, B., 66, 103
WADDELL, M., 178, 182
WANG, Y., 117
WASHBURNE, C., 33
WELLS, G., 65
WEST, M., 136
WHERE THE WILD THINGS ARE (SENDAK), 103
WHITCOMBE, B., 103
WHO SANK THE BOAT? (ALLEN), 181–182
WHOLE CLASS. *See* Groups
WHOLE LANGUAGE, 14, 68–79, 136–144; advantages of, 77–78; beliefs and assumptions, 137–138; Cambourne's conditions for successful literary acquisition, 70–71; integrated language processes, 71–76; phonics, 208–215
WIDE RANGE ACHIEVEMENT TEST (WRAT), 254
WILDER, L.I., 187, 189
WILFRID GORDON MCDONALD PARTRIDGE (FOX), 269

WINSTON-SALEM PROJECT, 37–43
THE WITCH NEXT DOOR (BRIDWELL), 270, 271*f*
WOOD, A., 181–182, 184
WORD LEARNING, 238–256
WORD RECOGNITION, 12, 214–215
WORD STUDY, 279
WRAT. *See* Wide Range Achievement Test
WRIGHT GROUP, 73
WRITE ON: A CONFERENCE APPROACH TO WRITING (PARRY & HORNSBY), 95
WRITING: activities, 74–75; books, 287–289; case study, 22; Charlottesville Volunteer Tutorial, 279; *Classroom Experiences: The Writing Process in Action* (Gordon), 95; culminating activity, 75; early intervention programs, 41–43; extension activities, 102–103; home activities, 300–301; individual creative, 74; individual directed, 74; invented spelling, 213, 226–233; language to literacy program, 156; portfolios, 42; relevancy, 140–141, 143; used for assessment, 138; *Write On: A Conference Approach to Writing* (Parry & Hornsby), 95
WRITING BRIEFCASE ACTIVITY, 300–301

Y

YES/NO...WHY?, 201*f*
YOLEN, J., 125

Z

ZEMACH, H., 124
ZIEFERT, H., 147
ZWOYER, R., 49